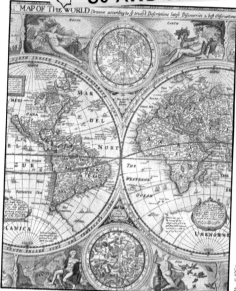

A Performer's Guide to
Renaissance Music

Performer's Guides to Early Music
Published by Schirmer Books in collaboration with Early Music America
Jeffery T. Kite-Powell, Series Editor

Published

A Performer's Guide to Renaissance Music
Jeffery T. Kite-Powell, Editor

In Preparation

A Performer's Guide to Medieval Music
Ross W. Duffin, Editor

A Performer's Guide to Seventeenth-Century Music
Stewart Carter, Editor

A Performer's Guide to the Eighteenth-Century Baroque and Galant Periods
Charles E. Brewer and Stephen E. Hefling, Editors

A Performer's Guide to the Classical and Early Romantic Periods
Kenneth Slowik, Editor

A Performer's Guide to
Renaissance Music

Edited by

JEFFERY T. KITE-POWELL

SCHIRMER BOOKS
An Imprint of Macmillan Publishing Company
NEW YORK

Maxwell Macmillan Canada
TORONTO

Maxwell Macmillan International
NEW YORK   OXFORD   SINGAPORE   SYDNEY

Schirmer Books   Maxwell Macmillan Canada, Inc.
An Imprint of Macmillan Publishing Company   1200 Eglinton Avenue East, Suite 2C
866 Third Avenue   Don Mills, Ontario M3C 3N1
New York, NY 10022

Library of Congress Catalog Card Number: 93–48544

Printed in the United States of America

Printing number
1   2   3   4   5   6   7   8   9   10

Library of Congress Cataloging-in-Publication Data

A Performer's guide to Renaissance music / edited by Jeffery T. Kite-Powell.
    p.   cm. —(Performer's guides to early music)
    Includes bibliographical references and index.
    ISBN 0–02–871231–5
    1. Performance practice (Music)—15th century.   2. Performance practice
(Music)—16th century.   I. Kite-Powell, Jeffery T.   II. Series.
ML457.P48   1994
781.4′3′09031—dc20   93–48544
                                                                  CIP
                                                                  MN

The paper used in this publication meets the minimum requirements of American
National Standard for Information Sciences-Permanence of Paper for Printed Library
Materials. ANSI Z39.48-1984. ∞™

Contents

Illustrations

Tables

Music Examples

Octave Designations
c' = middle c; c'' = one octave above middle c, etc.
c = one octave below middle c
C = two octaves below middle c
C_1 = three octaves below middle c, etc.

Contributors

Jack Ashworth is Professor of Music History and director of the Collegium Musicum at the University of Louisville. He has published on continuo realization and is active as a harpsichordist and Renaissance violinist. He has performed with the Newberry Consort, the King's Noyse, and the Folger Consort. In addition, he participates frequently as a teacher at early-music workshops.

Alexander Blachly has been active in early music as both performer and scholar. He has taught early music and directed collegia musica at Columbia University, Sarah Lawrence College, New York University, Rutgers University, and the University of Pennsylvania. He recently assumed the post of Director of Choral Music at the University of Notre Dame. Mr. Blachly founded the 13-voice *a cappella* ensemble Pomerium in 1972 to present music composed for the virtuoso chapel choirs of the Renaissance. The ensemble has earned worldwide recognition for its interpretations. In addition to record and concert reviews, Mr. Blachly has written studies of the German "dialect" of Gregorian chant, the music of the Codex Calixtinus, and Tinctoris's understanding of fifteenth-century mensuration. He is currently completing a Ph.D. dissertation on "Mensuration and Tempo in 15th-Century Music" for Columbia University.

Ingrid Brainard, musicologist and dance historian, is director of the Cambridge Court Dancers of Boston. She was a former fellow of the Bunting Institute in Cambridge, Massachusetts, and has taught music history from the Middle Ages to the Baroque at Wellesley College and Northeastern University. She is at present on the faculty of the Boston Conservatory of Music. She has published numerous articles on Renaissance and Baroque dance history and is currently preparing the expanded version of her *The Art of Courtly Dancing in the Early Renaissance* for publication.

Stewart Carter teaches music history and theory and directs the Collegium Musicum at Wake Forest University in Winston-Salem, North Carolina. He teaches sackbut annually at the Amherst Early Music Institute and co-directs the Early Brass Festival. He is editor of *Historical Performance*, executive editor of *The Historic Brass Society Journal*, and is also editor of the Seventeenth-Century volume in this series.

Phillip Crabtree teaches at the College-Conservatory of Music of the University of Cincinnati, where he is Professor of Musicology and director of the

Early Music Laboratory. Formerly on the faculty of the University of Hawaii, he was also founder/editor of the Roger Dean Publishing Company. He has published various articles and editions of early music and is co-author of *Sourcebook for Research in Music.*

David Douglass is widely recognized as the leading exponent of the Renaissance violin, and performs its virtuosic solo and ensemble repertory with the Newberry Consort, the Musicians of Swanne Alley, and Affetti Musicali. He is also the founder and director of the King's Noyse, a Renaissance violin band. He has been Artist Faculty at the Aston Magna Academy and is a frequent lecturer on early violin technique and repertory. Mr. Douglass has recorded for harmonia mundi usa, Virgin Classics, Erato, Smithsonian, and Focus Records.

Ross W. Duffin is Fynette H. Kulas Associate Professor and Chair of the Department of Music at Case Western Reserve University. A Noah Greenberg Award winner, his many research interests include fifteenth-century chansons, Franco-Flemish motets, ensemble improvisation, musical iconography, and Jacobean domestic music. He is also the editor of the Medieval volume in this series.

Frederick K. Gable has taught performance practice and directed the Collegium Musicum at the University of California, Riverside, since 1968. He received a Ph.D. from the University of Iowa with a dissertation on the polychoral motets of Hieronymus Praetorius and has published some of these works. He has recently prepared reconstructed versions of Hamburg church services from the mid-seventeenth century, which were recreated in Göteborg, Sweden, and Hamburg in 1991 and 1993.

Wendy Gillespie has played and recorded extensively with ensembles from the New York Pro Musica and Ensemble for Early Music to the Dowland Consort and Taverner Players. She is a founding member of the viol consorts Fretwork and Les Filles de Sainte-Colombe. Associate Professor at the Early Music Institute of Indiana University, she teaches performance practice, early notation, and bowed strings in addition to ensemble coaching; she also teaches at many early music workshops in the United States and Europe.

Ellen Hargis, soprano, is a member of the King's Noyse, the Cambridge Bach Ensemble, and Affetti Musicali, and has been a guest artist with many leading early and new music ensembles, including the Portland Baroque Orchestra, the City Musick, the Newberry Consort, the Kronos Quartet, Mother Mallard, Theatre of Voices, Ex Machina Baroque Opera Co., Fretwork, and the Musicians of Swanne Alley. She has served as Artist Faculty at the Aston Magna Academy, and is frequently invited to teach at workshops. Ms. Hargis has recorded for harmonia mundi usa, Virgin Classics, and Erato Records.

Ben Harms is a member of CALLIOPE Renaissance Band and the Metropolitan Opera Orchestra; he also performs with numerous other early music groups. He attended the College-Conservatory of Music of Cincinnati and Curtis Institute of Music for undergraduate studies, and the City University of New York for his M.A.; further study was conducted in Hamburg, Germany. He is the proprietor of Harms Historical Percussion.

Douglas Kirk is a postdoctoral fellow in musicology at the Université de Montréal and instructor of cornetto and historical brass instruments at McGill University. He has performed and recorded with many English and North American early music ensembles, notably the Taverner Consort, the Gabrieli Consort, the Boston Camerata, Tafelmusik, and the Boston Shawm and Sackbut Ensemble.

Jeffery Kite-Powell is Professor of Musicology at Florida State University where he is also director of the Early Music Ensembles and the Early Music Certificate Program. His current research includes work on a translation of Praetorius's *Syntagma Musicum* III. He is the series editor of this series. Dr. Kite-Powell is a frequent clinician at the Amherst Early Music Institute and at workshops around the Southeast.

Mark Lindley's books in English include *Ars ludendi, early German keyboard fingerings* (1994), *Early keyboard fingerings, a comprehensive guide* (1992, with Maria Boxall), *Mathematical models of musical scales* (1993, with Ronald Turner-Smith), and *Lutes, viols and temperaments* (1984). He served on the executive committee of the *New Grove* and is a contributor to some seventy scholarly publications in various languages; in addition, he is a member of the editorial boards of *Performance Practice Review* and the *Journal of Music Theory*.

Sarah Mead is an artist-in-residence at Brandeis University where she directs the early-music ensembles; she has also directed early-music ensembles at Tufts and Northeastern Universities. She holds degrees in music and performance practice from Yale and Stanford, and teaches and performs on the viola da gamba. She serves on the Higher Education committees of both Early Music America and the Viola da Gamba Society of America, and has been developing techniques to help student ensembles to use music analysis and communication skills to improve their performance.

Herbert W. Myers is Lecturer in Renaissance winds and curator of the instrument collection at Stanford University, from which he holds a DMA in Performance Practices of Early Music. As a member of the New York Pro Musica from 1970–73 he toured North and South America, performing on a wide range of early winds and strings. He currently performs with the Whole Noyse and Magnificat. He has published articles and reviews in *Early*

Music, Historical Performance, The American Recorder, Strings, and the *Journal of the American Musical Instrument Society.*

L. Dean Nuernberger is a Professor Emeritus at the Oberlin Conservatory of Music where he founded the Collegium Musicum and served as its director for many years. His main interest, choral music from the Spanish Renaissance, has resulted in editions of motets and Masses of Sebastián de Vivanco.

Paul O'Dette is a lutenist and researcher specializing in Renaissance and early Baroque music. He can be heard on more than fifty recordings as a soloist as well as a continuo player. Director of Early Music at the Eastman School of Music, Mr. O'Dette is also co-director of the Musicians of Swanne Alley and artistic director of the Boston Early Music Festival. He is currently writing a method book for the Renaissance lute co-authored by Patrick O'Brien.

Alejandro Planchart is a composer, conductor, and music historian who teaches at the University of California at Santa Barbara where he leads the early music ensembles. His fields of specialization as a scholar are medieval plainsong and the liturgical music of the late Middle Ages and the Renaissance. As a performer he is known for his work in fifteenth- and sixteenth-century music.

Beverly Simmons is executive director of Early Music America. Having earned a DMA in Performance Practice from Stanford University, she has spent most of her career in arts administration, specializing in early music. Her positions have included university professor, radio broadcaster, artists' representative, concert presenter, and workshop administrator. She retains a lectureship at Case Western Reserve University, where she directs the Early Music Singers.

James Tyler is Associate Professor and director of the Early Music Performance Program at the University of Southern California. He is a soloist on the lute, Baroque guitar, and early mandolin, was the founder-director of the London Early Music Group, and has recorded for Archiv, Hyperion, Nonesuch, and Philips. He has contributed articles to *Early Music,* the *New Grove,* and the *New Grove Dictionary of Musical Instruments;* further, he is the author of *The Early Guitar* (Oxford, 1980) and *A Brief Tutor for the Baroque Guitar* (Helsinki, 1984), co-author of *The Early Mandolin* (Oxford, 1989), and editor of *Gasparo Zanetti: Il Scolaro, 1645* (London, 1984).

Preface

Jeffery Kite-Powell

This book is designed to assist anyone interested in the performance of Renaissance music. The approach was to solicit articles from people who have both the practical expertise and the historical insight in the area in which they have written. Each author strived to present his or her material in a manner that would be easy to understand and put into practice, yet sufficiently scholarly to satisfy those in need of more detail or source material. Every contribution was read and critiqued by several of the contributors to this *Guide,* and most of the book was "field tested" in a somewhat smaller version produced by Early Music America in 1989. Other than the essays new to this publication, all of the remaining ones have been revised by their writers.

The actual time span to be covered by the term "Renaissance" was left up to the individual writer. Most began their discussion somewhere in the second half of the fifteenth century and continued until 1600 or even 1620 or 1630 (particularly those writing on English topics). The chapter on mixed consorts is restricted to the sixteenth century.

The thorough coverage of Renaissance instruments and their use in this volume is not intended to convey a sense of supremacy of instrumental music throughout the period, or to suggest that there was a preponderance of it, but merely to provide information for those in need. To be sure, vocal music was everpresent in fifteenth- and sixteenth-century Europe, and it is with that thought in mind that the needs of the champions of the voice and of the choral enthusiasts have been provided for in three separate chapters by leading practitioners in the field. However, the place of instruments in the Renaissance should not be underestimated; instruments, after all, were heard on a daily basis—in the streets, homes, churches, and courts, and from towers—in towns and villages throughout Europe during the sixteenth century. Then, too, discussing a large number of instruments in the detail necessary here simply requires more bulk than writing about the voice—a multifaceted but singular topic—which would be largely speculative at best. Most people who are inclined to sing in the first place begin singing at an early age, eventually working their way into high school choirs, college madrigal groups, community choruses, and church choirs. The bottom line is that most choristers have a general idea of how to make an acceptable sound come out of their mouths. A good choral conductor can improve that sound only so much, and if it should prove to be insufficient, he must ask the participant to leave. On the other hand, how many people know enough about recorders and viols or "buzzies" and "bombards" to be able to talk intelligently about them or play them, much less lead a group of players performing on them?

The ensemble that performs early music today must take pains to bring vocal and instrumental music together in performance—certainly not in every composition, perhaps not on every program, but often enough and in sufficiently convincing ways to demonstrate an awareness of the possibilities and an understanding and appreciation of the music of the period.

Duplication of effort in two or more chapters (i.e., mention of *musica ficta*, tempo, tuning, pitch, transposition, and proportions to list just a few) has intentionally not been expunged by the editor, as it was felt that the reader would benefit from the variety of approaches some of the writers have taken—even differing viewpoints—to these difficult issues. The index will help guide the reader to topics of interest.

It should be clearly stated here exactly what the book does *not* attempt to do. For one thing it does not pretend to paint a harmonious picture of a modern theory of performance practice. Just as sixteenth-century writers often disagreed with one another, I have allowed the airing of differing points of view in situations in which a particular issue is shrouded in ambiguity or uncertainty—the use of percussion in Renaissance music is a case in point (see the chapters by Harms and Tyler).

Another thing this book is not attempting to be is a catholicon for the *sole* use of the university "collegium" (a term somewhat skewed by modern usage). Granted, its foremost use may be by the director of a collegiate early-music ensemble—there is even a chapter specifically devoted to the problems relating to such an ensemble—and it was originally conceived with junior faculty members in mind, that is, those who learn a few weeks before the semester begins that they have been assigned the duty of directing the early-music ensemble. Most of the essays in this *Guide* were in fact written by directors of early-music ensembles at colleges and universities all across the country; many of them wear two hats, that is to say, when they are not teaching, they are touring with professional early-music groups or taking part in a recording session somewhere. But in spite of its strong higher education bent, the book has been greeted with approbation by community and professional early-music organizations, as well as by private individuals throughout the country.

Yet another item to add to the list of things this book does not do is provide a source for instrument makers, dealers, and suppliers. The omission is intentional and the reason is obvious: these artisans and merchants may no longer be in business or their locations may have changed since the publication of this book. The reader interested in this kind of information, as well as in prices, should contact the office of the society that could most likely provide the answers to such questions (e.g., the American Recorder Society, the Viola da Gamba Society, the Lute Society of America, the Historical Brass Society, the International Society for Early Music Singers, and others) or consult the publications of these organizations. Additional leads may be provided by the office of Early Music America (currently in Cleveland, Ohio) and its journal, *Historical Performance.*

The purpose of all of this, of course, is to arrive at a performance of the music that avoids blatant stylistic incongruities. We perform or listen to the music of this period because we like it, because it communicates something to us, and because it is a significant part of our musical heritage. Since we are dealing with music that does not have a continuous tradition, performers and directors rely on historical information and evidence to achieve an effective performance of the music. Most people have their own idea of what is or is not, can or cannot be considered a "historical," "authentic," or "historically informed" performance, so I won't enter into the matter here. (References to a lively discussion of these "hot" words are listed below.) To be sure, there is a lot that will never be known about this music, but in all fairness should we not make the effort to understand it and have the courage to experiment with it?

I would like to take this opportunity to extend my public thanks to all of the contributors to this book. Their willingness to share their knowledge and experience will doubtless have a positive impact on those who take these offerings to heart and on their performances of early music.

A special word of thanks is due Jack Ashworth, Stewart Carter, Ross Duffin, Frederick Gable, and Herbert Myers, the principal readers of the articles contained in the proto-edition. In most cases they read each article at least twice, and in a few instances three or four times. Readers of individual articles include Frank Hutchison, Edward Kottick, Karyl Louwenaar-Lueck, Willard Martin, Ray Nurse, Ben Peck, and Edward Pepe. I am especially indebted to Herbert Myers, who has been particularly resourceful with his comments and suggestions on the articles in this volume.

I would also like to thank Maribeth Anderson Payne, former editor-in-chief at Schirmer Books, for her willingness to work with Early Music America and me in seeing this effort come to fruition. She was always there with cogent answers when needed and her support was unflagging.

Source List on the Subject of Authenticity

(Complete listings may be found in the Bibliography at the end of the book.)

Boulez–Vestal; Brown–Pedantry; Brett–Text; Crutchfield–Report; Crutchfield–Fashion; Donington–Present; Dreyfus–Early; Kenyon–Authenticity; Kerman–Historical; Knighton/ Fallows(Phillips)–*Companion*; Leech–Wilkinson–Limits; Morgan–Tradition; Morrow–Musicals; Taruskin–Pastness; Taruskin–Tradition; Taruskin–Spin; Taruskin–Limits; Taruskin–On Letting; Taruskin–Musicologist; Temperley–Limits; Tomlinson–Historian.

I

VOCAL/CHORAL
ISSUES

1

The Solo Voice

Ellen Hargis

Taste in voices for Renaissance music has changed frequently in recent decades, with trends swinging from the operatic to the "folksy" and everywhere in between. Currently there seems to be a tendency to consider size as the most important feature of the "early-music voice"; I have often heard singers say, "My voice is too big for early music" or "My voice is small, so I sing early music." However, if we give primary consideration to flexibility, ability to control vibrato, sense of intonation, and intellectual curiosity about the issues of ornamentation and text, we have a much more accurate set of criteria for determining the singer's ability to perform early music convincingly. If the variety among human voices was as great in the Renaissance as it is now, then clearly there is room for most singers to explore this repertory.

A rich repertory it is: like the nineteenth-century art song we are more familiar with, Renaissance art song comprises hundreds of solo songs written to beautiful poetry of great literary merit, set for skillful singers to execute. It is a body of music spanning some two hundred years and nearly every European national style. These songs, along with the devotional music, carnival music, and theatrical music that can also be performed by solo singers, make up a fascinating and varied repertory for the singer to explore.

Voice Types

Renaissance music was composed without designation for specific voice type, so we can choose who sings a piece based on the range, the text, and the melodic style (lyric, florid, etc.). The somewhat narrow melodic range of much Renaissance music, together with the option of transposition, allows nearly all singers of appropriate ability to participate as soloists in an early-music ensemble. Since singers in the Renaissance used their voices in a way that differed somewhat from today's usage, it is best to keep some of these differences in mind when recruiting singers.

Sopranos need to be willing to use the middle and low ranges of their voices, since there is very little repertory that lies mostly above the staff, and they will often have to sing down to c′ and occasionally lower. For those pieces that do go to the top of the staff and above, it is useful to be able to float high notes with ease and without excessive vibrato or volume.

Countertenors who can sing into the tenor range will be very useful for 15th-century Flemish music; chansons of Dufay often range from g to c″, making them too low for most female voices and too high for tenors (presuming no transposition). Female altos or mezzo-sopranos will find that they can manage the cantus line of most compositions quite handily, but must be careful that the text is still understandable in the high ranges of their voices.

Tenors, like sopranos, need easy high notes, but will also often find themselves singing in a range lower than that to which they are accustomed. Tenors can sing much of the music available to upper voices, plus the German Tenorlieder, and particularly the highest of the English lute songs, as the text is easier to hear in the high range of the tenor voice than it is in the corresponding part of the soprano voice.

For solo singing, the bass needs to possess a good baritone range. There is little solo song designated for bass voice, but much of the middle-to-low music is good in the bass voice, provided that the accompanying instruments are low enough to avoid inversions (see Pitch and Transposition, p. 248).

Technique

There is little information in primary sources to give us a clue about vocal technique in the Renaissance, but there are descriptions of good and bad singing that give us an idea about what was prized in a voice (see McGee–*Medieval*: 55–56, Knighton/Fallows (Potter)–*Companion*: 311–16, and other entries in the Bibliography). We can also learn from the sounds of modern copies of old instruments; this, along with current ideas about performance practice, gives us some aesthetic goals to strive for.

Renaissance music calls for purity of tone, a focused, clear sound without excessive vibrato, the ability to sing lightly and with agility, and the command of a wide range of dynamics: loud singing, particularly for church music, and medium to soft singing, to most accompanying instruments. Some of these qualities are natural in certain voices; all are enhanced by good technique. It will be reassuring to the new singer of early music to know that good technique is still good technique. Essential elements include good breath support, well-formed resonant vowels, and focused sound. There is a real danger of singers tending to sing off the support when first encountering early music, in an effort to produce a light and vibratoless tone. The result is flabby sound, poor intonation, and insufficient breath to fill out a phrase. It is important that we stress that "light" singing is not "weak" singing, and that a fully supported, firm, resonant sound is always good style!

When singing Renaissance music, technique takes a slightly different rôle in the complete vocal picture from that in later music: the primary concern of the early-music singer is that technique must serve the music before the voice. This is not to say that a voice need not be beautiful to sing Renaissance music, but to say that it is our concept of beauty that must be considered. Text must be pellucid in Renaissance song; however gorgeous the high notes possessed by the singer, they are inappropriate if they obscure the text. Similarly, brilliant ornamentation, however skillfully executed, must not be allowed to supersede the transmission of the poetry. Occasionally, the voice must join the instruments in untexted sections of a piece (for example, the long melismas at the ends of phrases in Dufay chansons), and then the voice must be spare and agile, to join in sound with the vielles, lutes, organ, or other instruments. Thus, the term "beautiful singing" takes on a multifaceted aspect. We must always ask ourselves: What is my job in this piece? In this phrase? On this word? to really understand how to use our voices intelligently and effectively. It is not that we are unconcerned about vocal sound; on the contrary, we are acutely aware of its importance and of the variety that is available to us.

Vibrato

This is the thorniest issue to confront the singer of early music! The argument about vibrato is probably the primary reason for singers' reluctance to become involved in early-music ensembles. This is a real shame, because it leaves the directors with amateur singers to sing professional-level music and deprives singers of exposure to an enormous part of their repertory.

Thankfully, after years of "straight-tone" singing being the ideal, it is now generally accepted that a gentle vibration of the voice is natural and expressive, and an inherent part of a healthy singing voice. It is really the degree of pressure and pitch obfuscation that is the problem with the modern vibrato; therefore, the argument should be about how much and what quality of vibrato is being applied in a given musical context. Obviously, the effect of vibrato or non-vibrato is highly subjective and depends entirely on execution and context. The only vibrato that is really completely inappropriate to Renaissance music is one with a wide pitch variation, or any vibrato that cannot be consciously altered by the singer. Most singers are challenged and stimulated when asked to experiment with this aspect of their singing.

I have found that a positive approach helps immensely when dealing with a singer new to Renaissance styles. A director does much harm by starting from a rigid platform of "no vibrato!" and grudgingly allowing bits here and there when earned by the dutifully hamstrung singer. Instead, if you provide the singers with something new to do or to think about, you avoid depriving them of an element of singing that they have been programmed to think is fundamentally essential to their technique, expecting them to sing beautifully in spite of it. When vibrato is included in the array of expressive devices available to the singer, there is motivation for the singer to opt out of using vibrato in order to use something more appropriate for a particular effect.

Each singer must experiment and work with his or her teacher to learn to control vibrato. It is essential to maintain firm breath support when singing without vibrato or with reduced vibrato, and also to have very clearly focused vocal tone; otherwise, the sound can seem thin and flat. I work with vibrato control in vocal exercises first, adding vibrato, smoothing it out, increasing and decreasing the speed by changing breath pressure—initially, just exploring the possibilities. When the singer begins to feel in control of these variations, we apply them in a musical context.

Vibrato can warm the tone, adding direction and shape to long notes. It can convey a sense of urgency in the text, when combined with heightened dynamics and bright vocal color. With a dark and warm vocal color, it can help to communicate passion, tenderness, or grief. Starting a note with vibrato and then gradually smoothing it out can create a plaintive, poignant sound. Starting a note without vibrato and then adding it can have the effect of crescendo without the change in dynamics.

Non-vibrato can deemphasize text on multiple repetitions of words or phrases, can sound mournful, angry, exhausted, humorous, stern—the options are endless, depending on its combination with other vocal elements. Rapid diminutions must be sung without vibrato, and tuning at cadences is vastly improved when the vibration is reduced or eliminated.

The bottom line: nobody benefits from non-vibrato singing that results in harsh sound, straining, poor tuning, or vocal discomfort. Remembering that the use of vibrato is just one tool of style, and not the basis of all style, will go a long way in helping singers learn to be flexible and imaginative with this aspect of the voice.

Ornamentation

Use of ornaments is probably the favorite "style-making" device of singers (and instrumentalists) new to early music. To the casual listener, it is the most obvious difference in performance practice and at first glance is the easiest change to make in one's performance of a piece. The important thing is to avoid what I call the "Band-Aid" approach to ornamentation: throwing in a bunch of ornaments to make a piece sound "early." For beginners, less is more; and all ornaments should be added to a piece with good reason.

A piece of music should be well learned before any ornamentation is begun. Once melody and harmony are understood, the text is learned, the phrasing decided, the dynamics sketched out, and the tempo established, *then* ornaments can be added to further embellish and fill out the piece. A good place to begin is at cadences: the singer can be encouraged to decorate final cadential figures, particularly on repeats of sections, with any stylistic cadential formula, or with patterns found elsewhere in the same piece or other pieces of the genre. (Obviously, the greater the exposure to a given style, the easier it is to develop an ear for stylistic ornamentation.)

Next, filling in of intervals, decoration of internal cadences, and ornaments for text painting can be added. Until the singer has been exposed to a sufficient volume of material to develop an instinctive sense, he or she needs rules and guidelines to follow. The best places to find these are in treatises and tutors such as Dalla Casa's *Il Vero modo di diminuir* (1584) or Bassano's *Ricercate, passaggi, et cadentie* (1598), and in written-out examples in other compositions. For instance, one can take a decorated piece and by careful examination "de-compose" it to its basic melodic elements, thus finding ornamental patterns that can be applied in similar places in a similar piece.

Singers often find themselves quite shy about improvising ornamentation so they resort to writing out their proposed decorations in complete detail. While this is fine at first, they must eventually be able to react to others' ornaments and be able to simplify or elaborate upon patterns in the event of a too-quick or too-slow tempo. Part of rehearsal time can be devoted to experimentation with ornaments, with one person producing ornaments for the others to imitate, and then changing rôles so that everyone can try leading and following. I also encourage singers to participate in classes on improvisation. These classes usually seem to be directed toward instrumentalists, but can be of great benefit to singers, too.

Texts and Pronunciation

The issue of historic pronunciation of Renaissance texts is discussed in Ross Duffin's chapter on Pronunciation, as well as in Alexander Blachly's and Alejandro Planchart's chapters, On Singing and the Vocal Ensemble. I add my voice to theirs in support of the attempt to find regional and historic pronunciation systems for performance, however daunting the task may seem. Historic pronunciation affects a vocal piece just as much as the sound of gut strings affects a string piece, or as much as mechanical action affects the sound of an old organ. The rewards of such efforts are immense for both the performer and the audience. I encourage singers to work with coaches in addition to using pronunciation guides. There are some aspects of a language (such as pitch modulation and phrasing) that are difficult to notate, but that affect our singing of the language as much as the individual sounds do.

It is important not to lose sight of the forest for the trees, however. We must remember that most of these carefully pronounced words form poems, carefully crafted (some more, some less) and intended for life outside of a musical setting as well. By learning to appreciate these poems on their own, we bring new insights to our interpretations of the music. Elements such as phrase structure, meter, syntax, and rhyme scheme become clearer, and help us to make musical decisions that highlight or diminish these qualities in the musical setting.

Singers should always look at the text of a piece as written down separately from the music. First, if the piece is not in the singer's native language, a translation must be obtained. It is best to ask first for a strictly literal translation, and perhaps make it more poetic for the program. Translators can be found through most college and university modern language departments, or at language schools. Most Renaissance languages are not difficult for a modern linguist to translate, although some dialects may require a specialist. If all efforts fail, try asking a singer who performs the repertory to recommend a translator. Find out who the author of the text is, if possible, and what form the poem is in (sonnet, octave, *canzona*, etc.). Learn something about that form: Is it fixed or flexible? Is there a standard subject matter for the form, and does your poem conform to it? For instance, the Italian *canzona* nearly always has a light, pastoral content. More serious subject matter is treated in forms such as the sonnet. While the poetic form is not always related to the musical form, it is good to have as much information as is available in order to make a musical interpretation. For instance, if the poem and its genre have many, many verses, that should affect how many of those verses are sung in a modern performance. All too often we eliminate text to shorten a piece if the language being sung is foreign to the audience. However, if length is a salient feature of the poetic and musical forms, that should temper our inclination to edit.

Poetic analysis is something few musicians are trained to do as part of their music education, but singers will find that much of the poetry they want to sing is dense, convoluted, and difficult to understand, and requires some formal analysis to appreciate. Analysis based on the principles of rhetoric that guided writers in the Renaissance can clarify meaning and syntax, explain symbology, and reveal the beauty of language in new and subtle ways. Mary Springfels, Artist-in-Residence at the Newberry Library in Chicago, is working in this field, integrating the study of rhetorical devices into musical and poetical analysis; watch for her lectures and articles on the subject. She recommends several primary and secondary sources for reading; see the Bibliography for these titles.

Transposition

It has become traditional for singers to request transpositions for their solo pieces into keys that "lie better for the voice." While this is certainly a sound historical practice, some basic guidelines should be followed to maintain the stylistic aesthetic the composer may have had in mind.

Singers trained in the modern operatic style tend to prefer music that lies in the mid- to upper ranges of the voice, where they have the most power and brilliance. However, most Renaissance music does not need a lot of power and brilliance to put across the text, overcome a dense instrumental accompaniment, or fill an enormous concert hall. The low and middle parts of the voice are rich in color, sufficiently facile (at a gentle volume), and certainly the best part of the voice for the clear transmission of text. Most of the instruments used to accompany singers have a transparent sound and are soft to moderately loud in volume, allowing the singer great range of expression in terms of dynamics, articulation, and color.

When deciding on a transposition of a particular piece, the technical aspects of the music must be considered first. For example, the madrigal *Ancor che col partire*, with its plaintive, melancholy text, can be beautifully sung in its original range of c′ to c″ by a high or medium voice. However, if one decides to sing the Bassano diminution of the same piece, it might be necessary for the high voice to transpose it to a higher pitch in order to negotiate the runs at an appropriate tempo. If both versions are being performed as an extended form on the program, requiring that they be in the same pitch, the choice of singer becomes crucial. To sing the original madrigal in a higher pitch would call for a voice capable of floating the high parts of the phrases without strain or excessive vibrato, while still bringing out the affect of the text. Alternatively, a low voice with good agility could perform both versions at the original pitch.

An important consideration, too, is the quality of the transposition for the accompanying instruments. A general rule might be to stick to signatures of one or two sharps or flats, to avoid awkward fingerings and tuning difficulties. The tessitura of the piece should also help to determine the key: no instrumentalist wants to play an entire piece at either extreme of the instrument's range, and the piece would sound odd that way (unless one was seeking a special effect, such as low strings in a mournful piece).

Another concern when transposing a piece of music by one octave for another voice range is inversion—a problem when any of the lines go lower than the bass. Some examples from the *Glogauer Liederbuch*: suppose you want to have a tenor or baritone sing the top (melody) line of *Elselein, liebstes Elselein mein*. The cantus, if transposed down one octave, dips below the bass line in four places, causing unstylistic harmonic inversions. A better choice for a tenor would be one of the songs with the melody and the text in the tenor line, such as *In feuers hitz*. However, if you wanted your recorder consort to play this piece, with a tenor singing the melody, you would have inversions again, because the bass recorder sounds an octave higher. One solution is to use recorders with the tenor line sung up an octave by a soprano; another is to mix instruments, and have the bass line played at pitch, allowing the tenor voice to sing the tenor line. This practice, as logical as it seems, has yet to be established as historical, but is certainly useful (and not un-thinkable given Praetorius's comments on transpositions).

Tuning

Most of us grew up knowing about two kinds of tuning: in-tune and out-of-tune. Singers are often frightened by the aspect of alternative tuning systems, and with good reason. Without strings to tune or fingerings to learn, we must depend entirely on our ears to learn new tunings. In the absence of a wide and constant vibrato, tuning discrepancies become all the more obvious and need to be addressed seriously.

The easiest place to start learning a temperament is at the beginning, before the rehearsal of the piece actually begins. Hearing repeated scales played by the accompanying instruments, with an emphasis on leading tones and cadential notes, is very helpful. Next, one can learn to sing carefully tempered fifths and truly pure major thirds, followed by other intervals as they occur in the temperament being used. If a keyboard is being used in the piece, it can be quite instructive for the singer to be present at the tuning session to watch the keyboard and memorize those unequal semitones.

Early in the rehearsal period it is best to sing with reduced vibrato, or if possible, none at all, in order to focus more easily on tuning issues. It is also helpful to sing at a reduced volume, in order to hear the instruments and arrive at good intonation together. In addition, I have found that encouraging the singer to develop a physical sense of tuning is very successful. Singing pure thirds, for instance, feels very "still" compared with the purring vibration of larger thirds. Singers are used to memorizing physical sensation as part of their technique and can use this to help learn new tunings.

Finally, singers must learn to be highly attentive and flexible about their tuning. A piece that might have been accompanied by instruments of one temperament might be played on instruments in a different temperament the next time. There is even a difference in the degree of pitch flexibility between lutes and viols, although they are both fretted strings, and the singer must be prepared to make the adjustments. If we continue to think of tuning as another of our expressive devices, learning to tune can be a welcome challenge. (For further information please refer to Tuning and Temperament, p. 238, and Pitch and Transposition, p. 248.)

Ensembles / Repertory

Renaissance instruments appropriate for accompanying solo singers include plucked strings such as lute, harp, cittern, pandora, and guitar; bowed strings such as vielle, rebec, viol, and violin; soft winds such as recorders, flutes, capped reeds, and sometimes sackbut; and keyboard instruments. In short, just about any consort except the "loud band" or shawms will work.

There is a substantial body of songs written to be sung as solo songs with accompaniment. Italian frottole are a good example; hundreds of songs from Petrucci's publications were arranged by the lutenist Franciscus Bossinensis for solo voice and lute accompaniment. English and Scottish broadsides and other ballads are another example, as are French *airs de cours*, Italian devotional laude, and English consort songs. But there is an enormous amount of polyphonic literature, sacred and secular, of nearly every national style, that can be adapted for solo voice with instruments. This includes Burgundian chansons, German Lieder, Italian madrigals, English carols, Spanish villancicos, and French chansons. Usually the melody is in the cantus, but is sometimes (as in the case of German Lieder) in the tenor. Because of the narrow range of much Renaissance music, the early music director is not restricted to sopranos as soloists, but can assign these pieces to any singer who can accommodate the piece. There is also the option of transposition, as discussed earlier.

To determine whether a polyphonic piece is suitable for performance as a solo song, look first at the text. Make sure that the whole of the text is present in the line to be sung. Often, grammatical phrases are split between voices, and one line completes the sentence begun (but not finished) in another. Even if the text is intact, a piece with a lot of "question and answer" phrasing can sound odd and incomplete. Next, check to see whether the musical phrases match the poetic caesurae of the text in the part to be sung, so that there is a sense of syntactic completeness in the musical pacing. Make sure that the line you have chosen really sounds like a "tune" when sung alone, that it does not cadence to the fifth too often, and that it has sufficient melodic contour (in the context of the piece) to stand by itself. In the end, the judgment is subjective; we have to decide whether a piece is effective based on our own taste.

There is, of course, some music that is absolutely inappropriate for solo vocal performance. For instance, polyphonic Mass settings and motets were almost certainly intended for choral forces, or at least all vocal forces, and we do not benefit from forcing these pieces into another form. With such a wealth of solo repertory available to us, why go looking elsewhere?

Bibliography

Brown–*Embellishing*; Conrad–*De modo*; Dart–How; Edwards–Experience; Finck–*Practica*; Fraunce–*Arcadian*; Gable–Some; Henahan–When; Keyl–*Tenorlied*; Knighton/Fallows (Potter)–*Companion*; Lanham–*Handlist*; Maffei–*Delle*; MacClintock–*Readings*; McGee–*Medieval*; Nurse–Vibrato; Page–Going; Praetorius–*Syntagma*; Ramm–Singing; Rogniono–*Passaggi*; Uberti–Vocal; Ulrich–*Concerning*; Zacconi–*Prattica*; Zarlino–*Le istitutioni*.

Suggested Listening

Adieu, M'Amour: chansons und motetten (Guillaume Dufay). Studio der Frühen Musik, Tom Binkley, director. Reflexe CO 63–30 124 (1974).

Cornago: Missa de la Mapa Mundi. The Newberry Consort with Paul Hillier and guests. Harmonia Mundi USA: HMU907083 (1992).

Goe Nightly Cares: John Dowland's dances from Lachrimae (1604); William Byrd's Consort music and songs. Fretwork with Michael Chance, countertenor, and Christopher Wilson, lute. Virgin Classics 7911172 (1990).

Music from the Spanish Kingdoms. Circa 1500, Nancy Hadden, director. CRD 3447 (1989).

Peasant, Dance, and Street songs in Germany circa 1490–1540. Studio der Frühen Musik, Tom Binkley, director. Telefunken, SAWT 9486A (1967).

Songs for Tenor and Lute (John Dowland). Nigel Rogers, tenor, and Paul O'Dette, lute. Virgin Classics: VC 790726-2 (1989).

2

On Singing and the Vocal Ensemble I

Alexander Blachly

Because instrumental music constitutes only a small fraction of the Renaissance repertory, an ensemble truly interested in exploring Renaissance music must allocate a considerable portion of its energies to vocal works, whether solo (accompanied or unaccompanied), one-on-a-part (polyphonic chansons and madrigals), or choral (most Mass and motet music of the middle and high Renaissance). Written primarily for professionals to perform, vocal music in this period is often of considerable sophistication and difficulty. One might think it appropriate, therefore, for professional singers today to tackle it, but by and large this is not what happens. Professional singers in the Renaissance sang quite differently from modern professional singers; or, to put it the other way around, standard vocal training today often leaves the aspiring professional singer unsuited for Renaissance music. The majority of voice teachers still tend to encourage modern operatic technique as a universal goal for their students, and the high-pressure, high-vibrato style such students use is antithetical to the delineation of counterpoint, to accurate ensemble singing, and to precise tuning independent of instruments. Thus, the "better-trained" singers in a university setting tend to do one of three things: (1) avoid the early music ensemble altogether; (2) create an ineradicable blemish in its sound; or (3) find themselves rejected by the director. As a result, an early music ensemble today typically begins with an ensemble of vocally inexperienced—albeit frequently talented and enthusiastic—amateurs.

Vocal Forces

In a fledgling early-music ensemble with few if any skilled vocalists, rule one is that there is safety in numbers. Twelve or sixteen singers, even if they are insecure and tentative, can still usually manage a pleasing and musical performance of a chanson by Claudin de Sermisy or a madrigal by Verdelot that no quartet drawn from their ranks could negotiate. As the level of execution rises, this rule diminishes in validity, so that with very experienced and competent performers it is easier to create a musically expressive performance with only one singer to a part, especially in more difficult music (such as madrigals by Giaches de Wert or Luzzaschi). Naturally, the ideal would be for the vocal ensemble to match the size and caliber of its pre–Baroque model, with one singer to a part on madrigals and chansons. Choral music generally does not sound as effective with only one singer to a part; moreover, there is internal evidence in the form of *divisis* at cadence points that at least two singers were expected on each line in much of the repertory. But having more than four or five voices per line also has drawbacks, notably in the loss of flexibility that tends to come with the larger forces. A vocal component of between eight and twenty singers would seem to be the ideal size for an early-music ensemble, with smaller ensembles drawn from the larger group when possible for one-on-a-part music.

What types of singers are desirable? Generally speaking, the voices most necessary to perform Renaissance music are those found least often in nature, or at least not very often in the vicinity of early music recruiting stations: namely, high tenors. A vocal ensemble short on tenors will find that it is nearly impossible to function. Countertenors are also extremely useful, although they frequently find that the top line of polyphony is too high and the next highest line too low. Female altos and countertenors combined on the same line can produce a smooth effect that helps keep the individuals in the choir listening to voice-parts other than their own. Basses should ideally be resonant in the bottom range but not boomy, and light in the upper range. (Could he only be enlisted into an early music ensemble, Dietrich Fischer-Dieskau would be perfect.) Sopranos are the trickiest to handle. First, there are usually more of them than one can use. Second, many singers who should properly be classified as mezzos or even contraltos wish to be considered sopranos. What one needs in the highest voice of the choral ensemble is the ability to float high Fs and Gs without strain or excessive volume. Sopranos should also, however, be able to sing comfortably as low as middle C and preferably one or two steps lower.

Vocal Production

In conceiving how to perform Renaissance music, singers and instrumentalists can learn a great deal from each other. It is an immediately perceptible fact, for example, that the individual instruments in a well-balanced recorder ensemble or viol consort produce their sounds with focus and poise and a minimum of vibrato. The same should be true of a vocal ensemble. The type of singing that best matches the nature of the Renaissance repertory is light but clear, yet notable for its pure tone and expressive force.

Gaffurius, in one of the few explicit remarks on vocal production from before the Baroque era, states in his *Practica musicæ* of 1496 that singers should not let their voices wobble because this obscures the counterpoint. He further criticizes "tones having a wide and ringing vibrato, since these tones do not maintain a true pitch."

Solo singers of chansons, when accompanied by instruments, can profit from emulating the admirable qualities in effective solo instrumental performances: conviction, *brio*, and an interpretive point of view. A solo singer, even without trying, automatically commands an audience's complete attention; it is wise, therefore, to limit singers who are placed in such a spotlight to those whose abilities merit the attention. (Few types of music fall flat so fast as poorly sung *formes fixes* chansons, which, after all, tend to be quite substantial pieces when measured by the clock, even if the score fits onto a single page.) What an audience wishes to know is: (a) What is this song about? and (b) Is it a good piece? These questions can only be answered by a performance that conveys meaning and captures the melodic beauty of the music by means of good technique, that is, attractive vocal sound.

It is worth emphasizing that the sound of the voice *should* be attractive. Nowhere in Renaissance literature is there any statement that would justify the cultivation, as the embodiment of some ideal of the time, of a deliberately bizarre or unpleasant vocal production. Like the sounds of the Renaissance instruments with which voices are associated in the documentary evidence—namely, harps, vielles, rebecs, viols, recorders, lutes, and flutes (i.e., the "low" or soft instruments)—voices performing music from the same period should be well proportioned, light, agile, and suitable for small and moderately sized rooms. The qualities praised by Conrad von Zabern in his treatise of 1474 on the singing of plainchant—great resonance in the low register, moderate resonance in the middle register, brightness and delicacy in the highest register—are of paramount importance. So, too, is good intonation, which we will discuss later.

Loud, heavy singing not only violates the spirit of good ensemble music-making, it would also seem to contradict the very essence of the proportion, balance, and "naturalness" that are so clearly idealized in the other arts of the time. This is not to say that Renaissance singing should be consistently soft. Far from it. It should be intense and shapely in both loud and soft passages. Renaissance artists shunned coarseness and aspired to eloquence, but these predispositions in no way imply a taste for weakness of any kind. Michelangelo's art was admired for its inspiring strength, as was Josquin's music. Ockeghem's vocal lines are often of such length that it takes unusual vocal prowess to navigate them properly. The bright colors in Dufay's music and Jan Van Eyck's paintings should provide some clue to the bright, strong (vocal) colors appropriate to the period. People of means found singers in the Renaissance exciting to listen to and worth paying a great deal of money to acquire for their private chapels. The highly competitive arena in which Renaissance singers were traded, bought, and sold should convince us that music-making in this period must have been on a par with musical composition itself and with the creations of painters, sculptors, and architects, that is, consummately polished and intended to be impressive in every way.

Ensemble

The members of a good instrumental ensemble breathe and/or bow either together or in imitation of one another. Singers, too, must learn to produce their tone, phrase the music, and pronounce words identically—especially in the pervasively imitative textures of the later Renaissance repertory. Good ensemble singing is more dependent on the performers' listening to—and precisely imitating—one another than on taking their cues from a conductor. In order to develop good listening habits, it is useful for the director to isolate one or two voice-parts at a time to sing various passages. Another helpful exercise is to have the chorus sing one or two measures repeatedly until all the singers are aware of all the parts.

Importance of the Text

For the vocal repertory to make its full impact, the singing cannot be merely polished and strong. It must also be purposeful and self-aware. That is, the singers must understand the meaning of the words they are singing, and they then must sing those words with untempered sincerity. Singing with a clear projection of the sound and sense of the text is the easiest, most natural, and most obvious way to begin the process of interpreting a piece of vocal music. Yet it is the one most often overlooked, especially by amateurs.

In Mass settings, it is common practice for vocal ensembles today to begin the "Et in terra pax" and "Et incarnatus" softly, and to accelerate or become otherwise more animated at "Et resurrexit tertia die" and at the "Osanna" (just to pick the most obvious cases), and this is entirely appropriate. It is equally important for the singer to adopt a heartfelt musical/interpretive stance for the tragic text of Busnoys's *Seule apart moy* or a jovial one for the amusing Freudian slips in the text of Lassus's *Matona mia cara*. A long theoretical tradition extending back to the ninth-century *Musica enchiriadis* proclaims the importance of matching music with the sense and sentiment of the text; the policy of refraining from doing so—on the grounds that changes of volume and tempo, for example, belong only to Baroque and post–Baroque music—is itself an anachronism, one that fortunately is becoming rarer in performances of Renaissance music with every passing year. Naturally, the degree to which one may wish to approach the more overt and theatrical musical gestures of the seventeenth century will probably vary considerably between a motet by Grenon, at the beginning of the Renaissance, and a lament by Monteverdi, at the end. The degree to which the singer "thinks" the text, on the other hand, should probably not vary much at all, regardless of the age and style of the music.

Since the words are so important to the singer, the vocal director will do well to make it a policy to include a translation of the text in every score he or she hands out. (It is not nearly so important for the audience to know what the words of a piece may mean, although all too commonly in concerts by university early-music ensembles *only* the audience has a complete translation in hand, this having been produced by a specialist in another department of the university just a day or two before the concert.) The most useful aspect of the translation is its conveyance of the general meaning of the text. Nearly as important, however, is that the translation make clear the meaning of each individual word of the original, since the singers will be pronouncing each of the words, even if they are conveying overall meanings. A confusion in the singer's mind about the translation of a single foreign word will manifest itself in a confusion or vagueness in interpretation—that is, in purposeless and directionless phrasing. Thus, an elegant and poetically inspiring translation will often be less useful to the singer than a straightforward but correct one. For the singer, after all, the task is to breathe musical life into the original words themselves, not into their translation.

Pronunciation

As mentioned above, in order to achieve good ensemble, the singers must pronounce the words identically. Ideally, this would match the pronunciation used by those who wrote the music and those who first performed it: recapturing ancient pronunciations can enhance the artistry of the performance, partly because of the added nuance, but also because the original pronunciation makes it easier to hear such elements as rhyme, which are intrinsic to the character of the piece. When old pronunciations are unknown or under debate, it is still important that the singers reach some form of agreement. (Under no circumstances should some of them adopt unusual ideas about the sound of Renaissance French or German or English without troubling to win or succeeding in winning the others over to their point of view!)

It is a rare early-music director who has sufficient command of all the languages found in Renaissance music to be an adequate coach to his or her singers. This is nothing to be ashamed of, but it is important to recognize that the singers will need such coaching. Bringing in a language expert can work wonders quite above and beyond the obvious benefit of achieving unanimity of pronunciation. When the singers focus on the words, which they will do under the tutelage of a language specialist, their ensemble will improve, the phrasing will become more purposeful, and the intonation will immediately begin to ring more true. Even if the language coach is not familiar with Renaissance pronunciations, the presence of a person familiar with modern foreign languages will aid greatly in helping amateur American singers to be conscious of deep-seated habits of pronunciation that, if left unattended, can render the most carefully prepared and solemn performance mildly comical. These habits typically involve all the vowels and usually also the consonants "t" and "r." (For additional information, see Pronunciation Guides, p. 257.)

Phrasing and Editions

In music before Willaert, phrasing often tends to be a subjective decision on the part of the director. My own experience has been that for fifteenth-century music especially, five self-discovered rules of thumb go a long way in helping a vocal ensemble know how to make sense of the many passages where there are few syllables to go with many notes. Rule one is always to *lighten*, or lift, on the dot of dotted notes; this helps the following smaller notes, or following syncopated note, to be sung audibly yet lightly. Rule two is to sing *legato* (and group together) any succession of two or more notes of the same duration, whether these are semibreves, minims, or semiminims. Rule three is to *crescendo* on long notes, but to sing the subsequent note(s) at the volume level with which the long note began (not the louder volume achieved by the *crescendo*). Rule four is to observe *all* punctuation with *at least* a lightening, if not with a complete break, in the sound. Rule five is to treat ligatures (notes joined together in mensural notation) as useful guides to articulation. Interpreting them as if they were slur marks, with the second note softer than the first, helps give the line a convincing contour.

In music of the generation of Willaert and later, many problems of phrasing in vocal music are solved merely by pronouncing the words correctly, and this for the simple reason that after about 1550 most vocal music was written predominantly with one note per syllable. It is here that instrumentalists can learn a great deal from singers about how to bring a melodic line to life. As anyone who is capable of appreciating such things will attest, a vocal melody by Lassus correctly pronounced is a wondrous musical phenomenon. It has variety of color, linear tension, contrast of articulation, directionality—in short, all the ingredients that go into making a performance interesting and coherent. The problem facing the director of a chorus singing Lassus (or Byrd or Willaert) is not so much in getting the singers of an individual line to phrase musically in isolation from the other parts, but in training them to *maintain* their independence—especially when the line calls for a falling-off (*decrescendo*)—at a point where other lines are singing other motives or other words.

Yet this is not the whole story. Even Lassus and Byrd wrote melismatic passages. These are normally best approached using the rules outlined above for fifteenth-century music. More important, the bar lines in modern editions often imply incorrect stress, for the phrasing of Renaissance music is different from music of later times, especially that of the last two centuries. Frequently in editions of Renaissance music, bar lines appear to come at the wrong place, that is, just before the final syllable of a Latin word, which is almost always weak. Some editors have therefore attempted to write irregularly spaced bar lines that are intended to avoid this problem. Others, including some performers, have experimented with editions that do away with bar lines altogether. Both of these approaches, in my opinion, are unnecessary and create new problems in turn. A choir can be taught in a relatively brief time that the words are the proper guides to stress patterns.

The practice of placing bar lines between the staves but not through them also strikes me as a bad compromise. Such bar lines, which the Germans call *Mensurstriche*, are intended to indicate the proper alignment of voices without requiring longer notes to be broken into constituent parts as they cross from one measure to the next. Quite aside from the difficulties posed for the performer when a "measure" begins with a blank space representative of that portion of a long note from the previous measure that crosses the *Mensurstrich*, and then ends with a note that is "too long" (because it crosses the next *Mensurstrich*), such editions must be difficult to proofread, to judge from their many typos.

To say that speech and correct pronunciation are the guiding principles of Renaissance phrasing is to assert the primacy of speech rhythm *over* the apparent bar line stress. Surely singers of Renaissance music are as able as performers of other repertories to master the particular conventions of the music they perform. Learning to overlook the unintended stress implications of modern bar lines is no more difficult than learning the springing rhythm of a gigue or the lilt of a Viennese waltz. As soon as a choir lets the words determine stress, the bar lines become merely visual guides to vertical ensemble and are to all intents and purposes invisible in other respects.

Some editors attempt to indicate the "long-range phrasing" by transcribing Renaissance music in double- or triple-length bars. This strikes me as a mistake on several counts. First, the issue of long-range phrasing is primarily an aural problem rather than a visual one. Second, to write two breves' worth of *tempus perfectum* in a single measure is to confuse the correct stress—it makes no more sense than placing a bar line in an eighteenth-century minuet every six quarter notes. In both cases, the edition would appear to be advocating a pervasive hemiola that is not implied by the original notation. Third, the singers I have worked with find it difficult to read editions that attempt to show the long-range rhythm. The vertical interaction of parts, and sometimes even the rhythmic organization in a single part, becomes so obscured by the excessive information packed between bar lines that the edition actually hampers the singers' ability to read the music. When this is the case, there is no hope for understanding or projecting the larger rhythm. Thus, these efforts seem self-defeating.

What can be learned from singing from part-books? I have found that singers experience a tremendous thrill when they first find they are able to make music reading mensural notation with ligatures. Moreover, singing from part-books frees the ear from the tyranny of the eye and allows the sound of the music as it is happening to serve as the guide to pulse and tempo. On the other hand, reading from part-books greatly slows down the learning process, necessitating more rehearsals to prepare music to concert level. Also, a photocopy of a facsimile of a Renaissance part-book is usually not sufficient for performance. Often the photocopy needs so much editing, primarily in the form of adding missing words, that one is in effect working from a modern edition. If one has the luxury to indulge in the practice, singing from part-books can be a great boon to phrasing, for the ear, following the sound of the other voices, instructs the mind to imitate more effectively than does the eye—a highly desirable thing, inasmuch as imitation forms the underlying basis for almost all late fifteenth- and sixteenth-century composition.

There are so many editions of vocal music from the Renaissance that there would be no practical way to list them all. What is important to the vocal director is to know how slavishly to follow the printed text. Generally, the performer will do well to remember that merely because an editorial decision has appeared in print does not confer on it automatic legitimacy. Even an edition with as respected a pedigree as Lowinsky's *Medici Codex* contains a considerable number of purely editorial decisions that the performer should feel free to question. The two areas in which editors usually have made the most subjective decisions (based upon the least concrete evidence) are text underlay and *musica ficta*. A performer should know that it is his or her right *and obligation* to try to find solutions better than the printed ones (assuming, of course, that the performer is familiar with the historical evidence: "coloring" an edition with purely fanciful accidentals that have no basis in Renaissance theory is naturally a practice to be avoided). To deal confidently with many of the more intractable problems of text underlay and *musica ficta* requires years of experience and experimentation (some detailed studies of these problems are listed below in the Bibliography). Stated in its simplest form, however, most problems of *musica ficta* revolve about when and which of the following rules apply:

1. The cadential octave is to be approached by the nearest imperfect interval (major sixth: hence A–F♯ expanding to G–G, or B♭–G expanding to A–A), as is the cadential unison (minor third: hence C♯–E converging to D, or C–E♭ converging to D).
2. The perfect intervals (octave, fifth, fourth) must not be imperfected, or, in the language of hexachord theory, *mi* is not normally to be sounded against *fa* (hence, E simultaneously against B♭ is forbidden, as is F against B♮), unless the *mi-contra-fa* resolves correctly to a consonance.
3. Rule 2 is also to be extended to melodies in single voice-parts: one nor-

mally adjusts a melody starkly emphasizing the interval F to B to avoid the tritone. A melody passing from F through B and on to C, however, does not require such adjustment.

4. A melody with a single note above *la* in a sufficiently prominent position may adjust this single note to *fa* (sing it as B♭ or E♭).

While on occasion a good idea for *musica ficta* may arise spontaneously from within the ensemble, it is generally not profitable to enter into debates about these topics during rehearsal. Let the director's decision stand, at least until the rehearsal is over.

Most newer editions can be trusted to be more accurate than earlier ones, but performers should always read the introductory material to understand the underlying editorial premises. Volume VI of the *Polyphonic Music of the Fourteenth Century* series may serve as a good example of the potential pitfalls. This anthology presents *trecento* repertory, some pieces of which had already appeared at the time of publication twice or even three times before in other modern editions. In order to make a "contribution," and not merely to duplicate previous efforts, the editor occasionally used sources that had been rejected by earlier editors (including himself), the result being that some of the best-known pieces appear in *inferior* versions.

Most editions contain useful information on sources and the transcription methods employed, but much of this material tends to appear in the introduction or the critical apparatus. A director who takes pieces from a Complete Works without also consulting the editor's explanations of how the edition operates may make serious mistakes when interpreting the transcription at face value. For reasons explained below under Tempo, it is essential, for example, to know the original note values and mensuration signs. (See the chapter Copyright, p. 267 for restrictions regarding photocopying.)

Pitch Level

Since the gauging of "naturalness" by reference to the human form is one of the most widely recognized tenets of Renaissance art, it is only logical for a vocal director to use the comfortable ranges of his or her singers as the gauge by which to pitch *a cappella* vocal music. My own experience has been that Dufay's music often lies well as written (accepting a′ = 440 as the point of reference), but that later choral music (Josquin, Isaac, Willaert, Byrd, occasionally Lassus) tends to work best sung at least a whole step higher than written (although sometimes, as with Ockeghem's *Alma redemptoris mater* and Busnoys's *Victime pascali*, transposition down, by as much as a major third in the case of the Busnoys setting, is necessary). (See the chapter Pitch and Transposition, p. 248.)

It is a common mistake for a vocal director to program a "fascinating" piece that is not suited to the forces at hand. Singers who are forced to sing a line that lies below their effective tessitura cannot help but produce a washed-out, colorless sound. Conversely, a line that lies too high will almost always sound harsh and edgy. "Road-mapping" (switching two or more parts for brief stretches) can sometimes remedy this problem. Another solution is to combine, say, an alto and a tenor on the same line and have them work as a team to cover the entire range of a part with good production (the tenor leaving out the highest notes, the alto pantomiming the lowest).

Tempo

One of the most difficult aspects of performing Renaissance choral music is the uncertainty surrounding the interpretation of mensuration signs. Some editors (especially in the *Corpus mensurabilis musicæ* series) prefer to transcribe passages governed by the signs O and C by reducing the original note values by a 2:1 ratio, while transcribing passages governed by ₵, ⊘, ₵2, or ⊘2 in a 4:1 ratio. Should one disagree with the 2:1 tempo relationship between O and ₵ that is implied in this editorial practice, such editions present very considerable hurdles for the director. My own research and experience over the past fifteen years have convinced me that there is *no standard relationship* between "cut" and "uncut" signs. Therefore, there is no logical or musicologically sound reason to follow the teaching of, say, Sebald Heyden in 1540 (who advocated a 2:1 ratio between all cut and uncut signs in music of the later fifteenth century) rather than the equally forceful advice of Johannes Tinctoris in 1473 (who asserted that the stroke through a ⊘ or ₵ meant simply that the *mensura* should be "accelerated"). All that can be said as a general rule is that the semibreve in the "cut" signs does go faster (never slower) than the semibreve in the "uncut" ones. The most practical policy is to ascertain the original note values and the original mensuration signs, and then to let the semibreve in the "cut" signs go as much faster as feels musically convincing. Generally, I find that the sign O is likely to be an *andante*, frequently of a somewhat "majestic" or "noble" character (though pieces like Dufay's *Navre je suy* and *Se la face ay pale* are unmistakably of a more rapid, sprightly type). The sign ₵ tends to be a *moderato* (often with the beat shifting to the breve in the early fifteenth-century repertory; in the later fifteenth century and throughout the sixteenth century the sign ₵, which is used almost universally for all sacred music, requires a beat on the semibreve).

It should be self-evident that any single sign used for a large and varied repertory over the span of more than a hundred years could not always have been meant to indicate exactly the same tempo. Experience suggests strongly that such a sign may not even necessarily indicate the same tempo within a single piece. Works like Ockeghem's *Missa Au travail suy* and Dufay's *Missa Sancti Antonii de Padua* (published as the *Missa Sancti Antonii*

Viennensis in Besseler's edition of the Complete Works) show considerable variety of character and texture among passages notated under ¢ (in the Ockeghem) and O (in the Dufay). Numerous examples from the sacred works of Josquin, Willaert, Lassus, and Byrd could be adduced to demonstrate the same principle. In the secular realm, flexibility in tempo is even more in evidence. Consider, for example, the way in which madrigals of the later sixteenth century are meant to adjust their tempo in response both to the words and to the composer's setting of them. In humorous pieces like Lassus's moresca *O Lucia, miau, miau,* where contrasts of tempo may be quite extreme, one may draw an important conclusion from the fact that the entire piece is written under a single mensuration sign.

What evidence is there against a "subjective" interpretation of tempo that responds to the words and to the music, in favor of an interpretation in which the beat remains unvaried from first note to last? It must suffice here to note that the explicit injunctions for the *tactus* to remain constant throughout a piece are found only in some primers by German schoolmasters of the early sixteenth century and in treatises by their followers. All of the more sophisticated commentaries on musical practice, such as Gaffurius's *Practica musicæ,* Glarean's *Dodecachordon,* or Zarlino's *Istitutione harmoniche,* carefully avoid rigid generalizations about tempo.

Tuning

Training a choir or small vocal ensemble to sing in tune can be the most difficult challenge facing the director of the early-music ensemble. (Occasionally, the singers will sing in tune to begin with, and then practically no training is necessary. Or perhaps a single individual will be responsible for leading the entire ensemble flat or sharp; that person must then be dealt with independently of the others.) Most singers of even moderate experience have fairly specific, if unarticulated, ideas on how to sing in tune; yet very few know how to correct a problem that arises gradually during a performance. My own observation from directing vocal ensembles during the past eight years is that Just Intonation produces a more satisfyingly in-tune result, and produces it more consistently, than the "high major third/high leading tone" system most singers have been taught. Just Intonation requires a low major third, a low leading tone, a high minor third, and a high minor sixth—or, as most singers will complain when they are first advised to try it, the exact opposite of what they have been taught and have (successfully) practiced for years. The key to making Just Intonation work is to insist that the fifth of the chord be a full (perfect) fifth away from the final. Most singers, when they attempt to adjust a major chord that seems out of tune, will think first to raise the third; but in fact what is normally required is to raise the *fifth* and to *lower* the third. Singing a chord without its third will often make this fact dramatically clear to everyone.

The underlying difficulty in tuning is that very few singers have a concrete notion of how the scale works (though they are usually surprised to find this out). Many singers therefore do not know where adjustments can be made in the scale without all the relationships being so thrown out of adjustment that everyone is left in a state of intonational dissonance with everyone else. In most of the Renaissance repertory, the key signature typically has either no flats and sharps, or only one flat. This simplifies the task of conceptualizing the scale, for most Renaissance scales are closely related. To determine the rôle of any given step in the scale, observe its relationship to the note a third above and a third below. If the note in question is F, it lies a major third below A, and should be thought of as "high" so as to keep the major third small. F also lies a minor third above D, and should be thought of as "high" so as to keep the minor third large. For any given key signature there are three notes that are the bottom notes of major thirds and simultaneously the top notes of minor thirds. These are the three "high" notes of the scale. The three notes that are the top notes of major thirds (A, E, B in the scale with no flats or sharps) are the "low" notes of the scale. One note is a minor third above a note and simultaneously a minor third below another note (D in the scale with no flats or sharps), and the rôle of this note varies according to context.

Another way to approach the issue of Just Intonation is to perform all notes solmized as *mi* as "low" notes (thus, B, E, A in the Guidonian hand), all notes solmized as *fa* as "high" notes (thus, C, F, B♭ in the Guidonian Hand). Though useful, this method is incomplete, for it leaves out of account the notes G and D. Still another approach is to perform melodic half steps as "large" intervals and melodic whole steps as "small." Again, this approach cannot be applied to two of the five whole steps of the scale, namely, the two that are "neutral" (F–G and A–B in the scale without sharps or flats). Nevertheless, this rule of thumb is useful, especially in singing the *subsemitonium* and *finalis* at cadences.

It is only fair to note that singers initially tend to resist Just Intonation with truly impressive persistence, and it will often require great determination on the part of the director in order to achieve success. (See Tuning and Temperament on p. 238 for a technical discussion of Just Intonation and other Renaissance tuning systems.)

Conclusion

The challenges facing those who wish to sing Renaissance music are not to be underestimated—we should not forget that for professional singers half a millennium ago mastering these pieces was a full-time job—but the rewards are great. The high points of the Renaissance vocal repertory, after all, belong among the treasures of Western culture.

Bibliography

Atlas–Paolo; Bent–*Musica*; Bent–*Resfacta*; Berger–*Musica*; Besseler–*Bourdon*; Bowers–Performing; Bray–Interpretation; Dahlhaus–*Zur Theorie*; Doe–Another; Harrán–New; Harrán–Pursuit; Herlinger–Review; Hoppin–Partial; Hughes–*Manuscript*; Knighton/Fallows (Meconi)–*Companion*; Lowinsky–Treatise; Wegman–What.

Suggested Listening

Amarilli mia bella. Max van Egmond. Etcetera KTC 1056.

Antoine Busnoys: In hydraulis and other works. Pomerium, Alexander Blachly, director. Dorian DOR-90184.

Codex Chantilly; airs de cours. Ensemble Organum, Marcel Pérès, director. Harmonia Mundi France HMC 901252.

A Song for Francesca. Music in Italy 1330–1430. Gothic Voices, Christopher Page, director. Hesperion CDA 66286.

John Taverner: Missa Gloria Tibi Trinitas; Leroy Kyrie; Dum transisset sabbatum. The Tallis Scholars, Peter Phillips, director. Gimell CDGIM-004.

Una 'Stravaganza' dei Medici. Taverner Consort/Choir/Players, Andrew Parrott, director. MI Reflexe CDC 7 47998 2.

3

On Singing and the Vocal Ensemble II

Alejandro Planchart

The director of the early-music ensemble has become a relatively common member of the music faculty in most American colleges with a music program. This position is still a relatively new one, and one that often cuts across several areas of activity that in the teaching of the common practice repertory are often more compartmentalized. This requires an uncommon amount of care and sensitivity on the part of the director and an interest in the work of his or her colleagues. Moreover, it necessitates an effort, no matter how arduous, in drawing their interest and cooperation toward the enterprise of the early-music ensemble and toward the idea of historically informed performance; these attributes will be a benefit to the entire institution as well as to the ensemble. Much of what I have to say here is addressed to the early-music director in the early stages of his or her career. Experienced directors and mature artists need no advice from me; they have found their own solutions to all the points raised here. Despite the strident "neo–philistine" tone of much recent criticism of the historical performance movement, it would be imprudent to lose sight that what it offers is an imaginative reconstruction of past styles, a reconstruction that is enlivened, among other things, by historical information that has come down to us about the music and its performance traditions and by our own interest in these aspects of the artistic object we seek to reproduce. But ultimately it is our own sense of the beauty of the music we recreate, and our ability to communicate this sense, that lends "authenticity" to our activity. In this respect the attitude of a performer who is interested in historical performance or in performance practice is not that different from the attitude of a number of thoughtful performers who work within what may still be called "mainstream" tradition, and a young director of an early-music ensemble may find in such colleagues both support and inspiration for his or her work. In the case of vocal ensemble music, the early-music director will have to cross the path of the voice teachers and the choir director most often. In many instances the beginning director can profit from the experience of colleagues in choral conducting, for a great number of them are people of great talent, with extraordinary ears for intonation, blend, and balance, and who, increasingly, have a reasonable knowledge of (if not always a taste for) music before 1600. In the same manner, the basis of most modern vocal teaching at the undergraduate level remains the Italian seventeenth- and early eighteenth-century repertory, and younger voice teachers are increasingly curious about the stylistic and artistic context of this repertory. Any common ground that the director can map with other colleagues will help both with recruiting and with the status of the early-music ensemble as a recognized, viable ensemble.

Thus, even though the majority of voice teachers have (with reasonable justification) an operatic voice and career as their ideal, there is an increasing number of younger teachers who are sympathetic to, if not always knowledgeable about, early-music performance. And in any event, there are in any vocal program a number of well-trained students who have naturally light voices and who do not use an excessive amount of vibrato (sometimes because they simply have not yet learned how to do that). Among them may be the new generation of early-music singers, and the director who does not recruit them and encourage them is missing a very good opportunity. We must remember that the early-music ensemble often has two functions: to give performances of early music that are as good as the talents and knowledge of the performers and the director allow, and to provide serious music students with exposure to and experience in the early-music repertory as living music. The kinds of voice production that many voice students in their late teens and early twenties will use (with the approval of their own teachers) for some of the simpler Italian arias that are so often chosen as teaching pieces, the Lieder of Mozart, and even the French mélodie repertory (I am thinking mostly of the very subtle songs of Fauré), will serve them well as a point of departure in an early-music ensemble. In all of these cases a young singer with an undamaged voice seldom uses an obtrusive vibrato and yet is very conscious of proper vocal support and focus of tone. Encouraging such singers to join the ensemble and also emphasizing the common ground—primarily matters of vocal support and relaxation, focus of tone, and good intonation—between modern and early-music singing will often create an atmosphere of cooperation rather than one of confrontation between the voice faculty and the early-music director. This also may lead some of these voice students to become interested in a repertory that they did not know and help prevent the "tunnel vision" that afflicts so many performers (modern and early alike).

Vocal Forces

With young and stylistically inexperienced singers, three to four voices to a part allows an ensemble to produce a beautiful sound without losing much flexibility and lightness. When I say "without losing much flexibility" I mean this in terms relative to what such singers would do when singing one to a part. The flexibility of one-to-a-part singing one hears in most of the outstanding professional ensembles is predicated on excellent technique and years of experience as solo and ensemble singers on the part of each member of such an ensemble. It also should be remembered that one of the rôles of the early-music ensemble is to provide experience in performing early music to as many students as practicable within the relatively short time of a college career, since such experience will create not just performers of early music but "mainstream" performers who will never have the distrust of early music that was almost a matter of course a generation ago. Such experience will also create an enlightened audience. The young non-music major who could only be a rank-and-file chorister in an early-music ensemble will be the best kind of audience and patron that the early-music profession may hope for, provided that the early-music ensemble is well run and does music that is varied, challenging, and interesting to sing. At the center of all of this is the fact that an early-music ensemble is not one thing but several: a performance ensemble that gives concerts, a performance laboratory where students need to try to learn unfamiliar repertories and techniques (not to speak of new instruments), and also something of a "music appreciation" experience directed not necessarily outward to the public but inward to the members of the ensemble. After all, they need to acquire in a short time the understanding of these repertories that they have gained in the case of the standard repertory as a matter of prolonged exposure. The early-music ensemble should allow as many students to perform as much music as possible.

This being said, it is important at the same time to begin giving students as early as possible experience in singing repertories such as the madrigal and the chanson with only one on a part. Recent research has shown that in certain institutions the sacred choral repertory was sung with only one singer to a part. Singing some of the sacred repertory with one singer to a part, when the students can do it well, should be considered. The matter of size in fifteenth-century vocal ensembles may be something of a historical mirage. We know, for example, that the vocal forces of, say, the Burgundian chapel had a disproportionate number of soprano singers, who were adult falsettists. Now, the Latin term used for falsetto in dozens of documents from Burgundy and Cambrai is *voce submissa*, which had a long-established and firm technical meaning: "soft voice." It would thus appear that, at least in northern France, the remarkably strong falsetto that some modern singers have been able to develop was either not known or not wished for. If this is the case, then the result of the uneven number of singers for the different parts would be an even balance of the parts with regard to volume. Any combination of singers that would achieve such a balance now is thus acceptable. This would appear to be something of a "long way around" to come to a conclusion that could be dictated by common sense, that is, that any composer who spent the time and effort to write inner voices as beautiful and well crafted as those of Dufay, Ockeghem, Obrecht, or Busnoys would want them to be heard clearly. But common sense, guided only by our own experience of the vocal power of modern falsettists (themselves largely part of the historical performance movement) could just as easily decide that, given the vocal disposition of the Burgundian chapel in 1477 (six trebles, three contratenors, two tenors, and three basses), the Masses of Busnoys were meant to be heard as soprano solos with a contrapuntal background.

Vocal Production

We might as well begin by saying that we have no evidence of what the vocal production of any period was like before the existence of recordings. Logically, singers can begin by listening to and imitating the qualities of the consorts of soft instruments from the period, though it is also worth noting that beginning in the sixteenth century some choral singing was done to the accompaniment of sackbuts and cornetts, and that the cornett was often likened to the human voice. Ultimately, for fifteenth- and sixteenth-century polyphony, the ability to hear each line clearly delineated, even when it is background rather than an important motive, is essential. For that a focused and unforced tone appears to work best.

The matter of vibrato should be mentioned here. In dealing with young singers the early-music director will often face three kinds: (1) the untrained voice, often without a vibrato and equally often without focus; (2) the trained voice with a small vibrato; and (3) the trained voice where one can hear the vibrato and a constant high wind-pressure tone production. This last category has no place in an early-music ensemble, even when the ensemble is doing music as late as Mozart or Haydn. Of the other two, an untrained voice without focus adds very little to an ensemble, but can be used if the person reads very well and has a really good sense of pitch and rhythm. Often such non-singers manage to learn relatively quickly how to focus their voices (and the early-music director should encourage them to seek instruction in this) and become good choral voices. The well-focused but untrained voice and the trained voice with a small and unobtrusive vibrato will be the best resources an early-music director may have. Short of a specialist ensemble, a combination of such voices will virtually always produce good results. The director would be well advised, however, not to try for an absolutely vibratoless sound from such an ensemble. The reason for this is that most young singers without training or with only the beginning of a modern vocal training (and here I am assuming the beginnings of a very good and relatively broad-minded modern vocal training) have little or no control over their vibrato, and any attempt on their part to iron it out will produce tense and colorless singing and tire their voices. If the director emphasizes a relaxed vocal production, a light and unforced tone, focused singing, and the use of absolutely pure vowel sounds, then the mixed group of untrained and trained voices described above should be capable of delineating all of the polyphonic lines of a fifteenth-century Mass or a sixteenth-century motet with remarkable clarity and ease. Should the director not have had extensive vocal or choral experience before, this is one field where there is much to be learned from a good choral conductor, and he or she should not be at all shy to seek assistance from a colleague if the school has a good concert choir, or even better, a good chamber choir.

Ensemble

Ensemble warm-ups are one of the places where a director can promote good ensemble while at the same time encouraging good tone and good intonation. The director can easily devise warm-up exercises in which, in addition to limbering up the range of the individual voices, special attention is paid to vowel sounds or to the proper tuning of intervals (for example, the use of Just Intonation, which goes contrary to what most modern singers practice), leading singers to begin to hear the resonance that will guide their ears toward correct intonation.

With regard to phrasing it is particularly useful to isolate a problematic passage and then have the entire ensemble sing through each part of the passage, taking care to phrase the motives in the same manner, and then to let them sing through the polyphony until they can hear how their part fits in the texture. Of course, no one can do this with every difficult section of every work in an entire program, but enough insistence on the students working out on their own similar passages, and pointing out to them the recurrent motives in a work and the clichés of a style, begins to build rather quickly an awareness of style and an instinct for listening that results in good ensemble.

Other useful procedures practiced by numerous choral directors with other repertories involve having the singers rehearse in "cells," where each cell has only one singer to a part, and having the ensemble stand in a full circle, everyone singing toward the center. With an inexperienced vocal group this procedure helps to speed up the singers' ability to hear the other parts and phrase accordingly.

When dealing with passages where there is a *ritardando* (all the more so if there is a return to the main tempo after it), an *accelerando*, or a change of tempo, it is extremely useful to have the ensemble attempt it several times without any conducting, to the point where the group develops a collective sense of where and how the tempo fluctuation happens. This will prevent the slightly ragged ensemble that one usually hears in such cases. Occasionally this approach will also point out a "stumbling block"—something in the music itself that interferes with the tempo fluctuation coming off smoothly, which can then be worked out or worked around by beginning or ending the tempo fluctuation in a different and often unexpectedly more logical place.

Importance of the Text and Pronunciation

The importance of singers knowing what it is that they are saying when they sing cannot be emphasized strongly enough. Translations of the texts—as literal as possible—should be handed out the same day as the music, and the singers should be encouraged to begin thinking not only about the meaning of each word they sing but also about the rhetoric and syntax of the different languages. In this way the often convoluted pronunciation (by modern English standards) of Italian madrigal and aria poetry, for example, begins to feel like familiar ground.

Uniformity of pronunciation will also be greatly aided if the director has insisted from the beginning on setting diction standards for the ensemble. The use of a language expert or a native speaker to demonstrate or to coach pronunciation is essential. In dealing with the secular repertories of the late Middle Ages and the Renaissance it is also essential that the singers achieve not only unanimous and correct pronunciation of the text, but also a sense of the implied large-scale rhythmic patterns of the text as declaimed poetry. For example, in the line

Dúe róse frésche / e cólte in paradíso

the first half of the verse moves toward the first syllable of *frésche*, and the second half moves toward the third syllable of *paradíso* with a small *ritenuto* at *cólte* and an equally small *accelerando* between *"col"* and *"di."* What I have indicated as a cæsura, of course, is a syntactical break that is actually elided in declaiming the poem, but creates a moment of rhythmic repose on the prolonged "e" vowel. All this directly affects the way Andrea Gabrieli and Luca Marenzio set the text; it is something that comes as second nature to cultivated Italian speakers and should be understood by the singers who sing either madrigal. Explaining just one line takes a bit of time, but the principle remains operative for virtually all poetry everywhere. Once the singers know that, they can begin to sense these rhythms if they do speak the language, or perceive them when they hear a language specialist or a native speaker declaim the poem. A good policy in dealing with these repertories is to have a language expert declaim—that is, "perform"—the poetry, line by line, into a cassette tape that may then be put on reserve for the members of the ensemble to listen to in the music library or the language lab. If singers are to sing a madrigal or chanson as soloists or one-on-a-part, they should be able to recite the poem as a poem, comfortably and with correct line stresses, long before they perform the piece in public.

A serious problem concerning words is presented, however, by what should be the easiest language to sing: Latin. Simply stated, in virtually every edition of music with a Latin text written between approximately 1400 and 1550, the early-music director will find dozens of infelicities of text underlay, where the way the text is set to the music not only does violence to the word declamation, but also obscures the musical phrasing, plays havoc with cadences, and so on (sometimes this is due simply to the composers actually "hearing" Latin with their own regional accent). The causes of this are many, and the first may be called the "fatigue factor." Text underlay for much of the music from Dufay to Gombert presents fierce problems, and it is usually one of the last tasks an editor undertakes. Then, the sources are often uninformative, careless, or contradictory, and one senses that at the time considerable latitude existed in these matters. Faced with this, editors tend to be literalist and unimaginative, often with unmusical results from even the very best of them. We must realize that the judgment exercised by the Burgundian chaplains, steeped in tradition, was very different from that employed by a twentieth-century editor who has to justify everything and face reviewers who will complain about "arbitrary" decisions.

Well in advance of distributing the music to the singers, the director will be well advised to take a close look at the text underlay in order to determine where each phrase is going, and if the words, as set, help it. Such a review will almost always turn up dozens of places where shifting a word or a phrase by a note or two or sometimes by a measure or two, or adding a repetition of a word or a phrase, in one voice or another will yield unanimity of declamation that clarifies a cadence, makes the pronunciation of the text easier or clearer, and saves a great deal of time in rehearsals. In these revisions, which are often necessary in virtually all editions of sacred music written between 1400 and 1550, a good rule of thumb when adding a repetition of a word or a phrase to break up a melisma that appears clumsy or uncomfortable, or to achieve unanimity of text at a cadence point, is to think in terms of oratorical rhetoric. For example, in the following verse from Vulgate Psalm 88

Domine Deus virtutum, quis similis tibi?

if there was an articulation point at *virtutum*, and the director felt that two or three extra syllables would help one of the voices to phrase into the articulation better, it would be better to expand the phrase by repeating the word "*Deus*" rather than the word "*virtutum*," for the first would create a recognizable grammatical and rhetorical declamation:

Domine Deus, Deus virtutum, quis similis tibi?

Pitch Level

My experience with pitch level differs only slightly from that mentioned by Blachly in the previous chapter in that for all *a cappella* music between 1400 and 1600 I find that an a′ at about 415 leads to a more relaxed and better sound in most cases. Works such as Dufay's *Missa Se la face ay pale* (not entirely an *a cappella* piece, since the tenor is an organ part and should not be sung) and *Missa Ave regina* sound very good at "written pitch" when one uses A-415 and a mixture of altos and tenor for both the contratenor and the tenor parts. At A-415 a high-tessitura work such as Ockeghem's *Alma redemptoris mater* can be sung at written pitch, but pieces like Josquin's *Missa Pange lingua* may need transposition up a tone (with male voices in all but the top) or even a major third (for an SATB ensemble). This pitch level will also allow most mixed ensembles to negotiate well the "high-clef" music from Clemens and Morales to Lassus and Palestrina (the four-voice cleffing being G2, C2, C3, F3) as written, while the "low-clef" music of the same period (C1, C3, C4, F4) would require a transposition up by a step, since young bass voices seldom have much resonance for the low F (at A-440), much less for the pitch near modern E produced by A-415 as written F. It may be nothing more than an old wives' tale, but my own experience with college singers confirms something that a number of choral conductors have told me over the years, and that is that singers seem to stay on pitch much easier when singing in "black note" keys.

Depending on the ensemble, a work like Obrecht's *Salve Crux* can be sung effectively at two pitches: as written, if one has a first-class male ensemble, or up a fourth with an ensemble of SATTB. Here the fourth-transposition switches the piece to a "slot" where a great deal of music by Clemens and Gombert lies, so that if Obrecht's motet was still sung in the 1530s it is not unlikely that it was sometimes sung at the pitch suggested here. And indeed this is what happens to Willaert's *Veni sancte spiritus,* as a comparison of its publication in 1545 with the *Medici Codex* shows, although in this case the later print has the piece down a fourth. Obrecht's motet was indeed sung in the 1530s, and ensembles of men and boys were capable of transposing it at sight, and would certainly have transposed it up a fourth. I invite the reader to think about what happened to this music as the decades went by and suggest that transposition by a fourth or a fifth was, in fact, common. In a concert of music by Clemens, for instance, I realized that the transposition I had chosen simply "locked" into a set of ranges common in five-voice music used in Obrecht's own homeland at a time when his music was still being sung. This fact, in and of itself, interests me and feeds both my imagination and my curiosity—all the more so since such a transposition will not work for a piece such as Ockeghems's *Missa Ecce ancila.* I had a similar revelation with the transposition of the above-mentioned motet by Willaert. I pass the information on to my readers in the hope of stimulating their curiosity and research. I would be equally fascinated (though for different reasons) if I could find how an Obrecht work of any kind was done in the 1560s or in the 1760s. How Obrecht was sung at Ferrara would also be of great interest and would deserve emulation, if we could find out and reconstruct a Ferrarese event.

Tempo and Proportions

Developing a sense for the tempo and the tempo relationships in this music is greatly hindered by the often tacit shifts in reduction of note values found in most modern editions. Although there apparently was no standard relationship between *integer valor* and *tempus diminutum* in the Middle Ages and the Renaissance, if one studies the music carefully one begins to develop a sense of what O and ¢ meant in Dufay's music of the 1430s or the 1450s, which is not quite the same tempo that Ockeghem had in mind for his own works of the 1450s, and so on. One goes at this the way one goes at music of later times: *Allegro con brio* means different things in the music of Mozart, Mendelssohn, or Brahms. Even in the work of a single composer and within a narrow stylistic band, O will mean one of a number of tempos within certain limits, not a specific tempo in terms of beats per minute.

Nonetheless, there are certain inviolable rules: in any work where the composer goes from an uncut sign to a cut one or vice versa, he is indeed telling you "go faster" or "go slower" in no uncertain terms. Recent recordings of Josquin's Masses in which the tempo at ¢ is markedly slower than that in O are simply being perverse, no matter how beautiful the singing or phrasing. A case in point is a recent recording of Heinrich Isaac's *Virgo prudentissima* in which the music goes from O to O2 in all voices except the tenor, so that a sharp acceleration of the free voices by a factor of two is spelled out unequivocally, and yet the performers take the tempo of O2 at a slower pace than that of O. The result is that despite the exquisite singing, the work dies on its feet just when it should literally be racing ahead. To be sure, any performance of a piece is at the same time a critique of it, but there is a point at which the critic takes over, and we cannot quite hear the composer's own voice. This is something that performers have done for centuries and composers have lived with in varying states of annoyance, depending on their temperament. In the case of Renaissance music, reversing the basic meanings of cut and uncut time is, in fact, a major distortion of the work.

Composers and performers in the fifteenth and sixteenth centuries were trained to think of tempo relationships as mathematical proportions, so when we change tempo within a work in response to the presence of a new mensuration sign it behooves us to seek, within the range of tempos that we feel are appropriate, one that is related in a simple proportion to the previous tempo. The most common such shift in fifteenth-century music is one from O to ₵; its interpretation is still the subject of debate among scholars, although the theoretical traditions give strong evidence of two main interpretations: (1) a 1:2 shift at the semibreve level, and (2) a 3:4 shift at the semibreve level. Thus, these may perhaps be the first two avenues one should explore when encountering such a change of signs. In the sixteenth century an even more common shift is from ₵ to ₵3 (or simply 3). Here the theoretical tradition is virtually unanimous in calling for a 2:3 shift at the semibreve level, although at the beginning of the seventeenth century such a change in signs may mean a 1:3 shift at the semibreve level. In the end the early-music director cannot escape doing a fair amount of reading on tempo and proportions, even if the literature on this topic is immense, full of dogmatic statements by modern scholars, and on occasion bordering on lunacy.

Tuning

Given the tenacity of the resistance of modern singers to Just Intonation, a tenacity reinforced by their voice teachers (if they are voice majors), it is well to be prepared for slow progress in this area, but the director should ultimately neither give up nor let up. It is a frustrating experience, since every new singer in the ensemble will disturb the intonation for a time, and each year one begins almost from scratch. The tuning of open fifths, however, is the place for an ensemble to start to hear the correct tuning of Just Intonation, and if one can get the ensemble to tune perfectly a $\frac{6}{3}$ chord using a kind of *fauxbourdon* pattern, where a chain of $\frac{6}{3}$ sonorities begins and ends with a $\frac{5}{8}$ for a warm-up, is a good way to allow a group of students that has been singing and playing in equal temperament for most of the day to lock into Just Intonation at the start of the rehearsal. Further, intonation exercises may be profitably included in any warm-up routine used for the ensemble; during a warm-up of some five to ten minutes, devoting a little time to hearing the tuning of long-held chords, or hearing the interval sizes in a slow but steadily moving scale will begin creating habits of singing these intervals that will gradually break down resistance to Just Intonation. Compounding the problem is that occasionally, for expressive purposes, a high leading tone may be what one wants. Few college singers develop their ears quite to the point at which they can play with shades of intonation the way some of the best professional early-music singers can so well.

One bit of perhaps obvious advice is that in music that does not use *continuo* or concerted instruments, the director should rehearse without recourse to any instrumental assistance from the start. Even playing a single line on a keyboard to help out a voice part will interfere with the intonation. Once a choir can sing with Just Intonation it can begin to adjust to other temperaments when singing with instruments, since their ears will have become far more sensitive to interval sizes and shades of tuning.

Phrasing

We are almost entirely in the dark concerning phrasing in the vocal ensemble music of the thirteenth and fourteenth centuries, but a good place to start is the conductus repertory of the thirteenth century and the works of the Italian *trecento* where all parts have text. In both repertories one can see at the outset that the text is preeminent in determining the sense of phrasing in the music, and that in a number of instances the composers are playing a subtle game where the textual prosody seems to color the groupings inherent in the melodic and rhythmic surface of the music in ways not immediately obvious from the music alone. The operative word here is "subtle." Any wrenching contradiction between the text phrasing and musical phrasing in these repertories is uncharacteristic and could be the product of scribal error or a less than first-rate composer. In the long melismatic passages characteristic of fourteenth-century French and English music, as well as the rapid coloraturas of the Italian *trecento*, the performer needs to be acutely aware not only of the melodic shape and the interval sizes (often we tend to use large intervals as points of demarcation in phrasing, but ligature writing in the manuscripts would suggest *legato* singing of many of these), but also of the relationship of the part one is singing to the structural parts in the polyphony.

Fifteenth- and early sixteenth-century music poses in some ways even more difficult problems, since in certain repertories, such as the Mass Ordinary and the Votive motet of the late fifteenth century, the relationship between text and music seems to be, at first sight, much looser than in earlier and later repertories. In the previous chapter Blachly offers five rules of thumb for phrasing fifteenth- and early sixteenth-century music that coincide almost exactly with what I have found useful. I do, however, prefer to make a small *crescendo* into a dot if at such point there is a dissonance with another voice, and then lighten up the resolution. In any event, these rules also hold for much of the early Baroque choral music, particularly the dense polyphony of the large-scale works of Schütz and his school. One phrasing mannerism that is to be avoided at all costs, however, is an abuse of the *messa di voce* in polyphonic music of the sixteenth century. It would be entirely appropriate in the solo voice repertory, but for a time it was fashionable to use this technique in works such as the five- and six-voice madrigals of composers like Marenzio and Wert. The result destroys the polyphony and the linear drive that govern virtually all of their music, though it can be used in passages, frequent in Wert and Monteverdi, that amount to ensemble recitative, if all the singers phrase with absolute unanimity.

As noted above, developing a sense of the large-scale rhythm of text phrases will also contribute to correct phrasing and will create a sense of linear direction. In much late sixteenth-century music there is a broad rhetorical structure in which the repetition of certain phrases such as the "miserere nobis" in the Gloria or the Agnus Dei are treated by composers as variations of a given set of motives (this is the case, for example, in a great deal of Byrd's music, notably in the *Mass for Four Voices*). This "macro-phrasing" is crucial to the sense of progression of the music.

Some of Blachly's rules, particularly numbers one, three, and five, can be easily incorporated into warm-up exercises, so that the ensemble members begin to respond to such phrasing situations instinctively. In working with undergraduates I find that they tend to view each instance of something that happens in the piece itself as unique (at least at first) and need to be encouraged to begin taking the step of phrasing similar figures in a similar way. I would add a rule concerning the performance of fifteenth-century music: major color, that is, the hemiola of three imperfect breves over two perfections, is virtually always used by Dufay, his English contemporaries, Ockeghem, Obrecht, and even Josquin and Isaac in ways that demand a slight *crescendo* over the course of the entire pattern and a minute accent of each major note of the figure (e.g., the *Superius* hemiola at the beginning of the first four-voice section in the Kyrie of the English *Caput Mass* and the large cadential hemiolas in the tenor pattern of the same work).

Editions

It is crucial that the director of the early-music ensemble not be intimidated by the printed text of an edition. Problems of text underlay will very often sabotage the best efforts of an ensemble, particularly in fifteenth- and early sixteenth-century music (text underlay becomes much clearer after around 1550). Editors are often extremely timid in matters of text repetition or moving the text as set in the source a few notes or bars to one side or another; and a number of modern editors—some with the most exquisite musical credentials—turn a curiously deaf ear to the natural rhythms of spoken language that very often suggest sensible solutions to problems of text underlay. The difficulties, of course, are based on the nature of the fifteenth-century scribal traditions and will never vanish, but indeed, the best training that a future editor of vocal music may get in dealing with these problems is long experience as a singer in an early-music ensemble. After carefully studying a given work, a director may decide that the number of small text adjustments needed is so large that making his or her own performance edition of the piece is a necessity. The same applies to considerations of *musica ficta*. Such editions, even when the source is not the original but a critical edition in a set of complete works, eventually save an immense amount of rehearsal time. In any case, the director should take great care that the text underlay and the *musica ficta* in any music given to the ensemble come as close as possible to what he or she actually wants. Inevitably some changes may suggest themselves in performance, but extensive changes during rehearsals are time-consuming and waste a great deal of energy.

Long arguments on text underlay or on *musica ficta* can be a waste of rehearsal time, although the occasional suggestion is sometimes helpful. But the director should encourage the members of the group to think about these matters and to call to his attention possible solutions to difficult problems. This is all the more important because certain matters of text declamation and melodic and harmonic direction can often be perceived differently from "inside" the work; thus, in some cases the individual singers do have a privileged view of the music.

It cannot be emphasized strongly enough how important it is for the director to understand the editorial procedures and assumptions that underlie any edition being used for a performance, and how carefully one must read the introduction and even the critical notes of the edition of any work that is being prepared. It is also important that the director begin to train the performers to sing at least some pieces from original notation as early as possible. This is well worth the initial extra time and frustration with regard to the sense of linear independence and of engaging the tonal and rhythmic ear of the singers in the ensemble. It will also give the students crucial experience of what the editor of this music faces in producing a modern score. The ultimate goal of the ensemble, it must be remembered, is the musical and intellectual growth of the students, a growth that comes from preparing performances as polished and beautiful as possible—performances in which, ideally, every member of the ensemble knows why things are being done the way they are. In a very real sense, virtually all music up to the end of the Baroque is chamber music, and the "anonymous soldier" has no place in it.

II

WIND, STRING, AND PERCUSSION INSTRUMENTS

4

Recorder

Herbert Myers

Of all the early winds the recorder is surely the most familiar. In fact, for many it stands as a symbol for the whole of early music, for until not so long ago it seemed that the recorder movement and the early-music movement were almost synonymous. Fortunately for both, that day is now past. In many an early-music ensemble, however, the recorder ensemble still provides the main (if not the only) opportunity for students to become acquainted with an early wind. This modern emphasis on the recorder is not without some historical justification, particularly for Renaissance music, since it is evident from the sixteenth-century treatises of Virdung, Agricola, Ganassi, and Jambe de Fer (whose principal readership was undoubtedly the literate bourgeois citizen) that the recorder was often the primary woodwind of the musically cultivated amateur. Then (as now) its value as a pedagogical tool was recognized; Virdung specifically mentions that what is learned through the recorder can be applied to learning the other woodwinds, and the same thought appears to underlie the method books of Agricola. The recorder was also one of the instruments upon which the professional wind player was expected to double; some, like Ganassi himself, may have specialized on it, and his own method attests to the high level of performance attained by some players. However, it is worth remembering that the ultimate achievement of the professional musician of the Renaissance was not playing any one instrument but several, and that those woodwinds that commanded the most respect were not the recorder but the shawm (in the fifteenth century) and the cornett (in the sixteenth). Thus, a student with the interest and aptitude should be encouraged to look beyond the limitations imposed by the recorder and to explore other avenues of Renaissance performance as well.

Nevertheless, it should be stressed that for many the recorder is an ideal medium through which to experience Renaissance music. Since (as instruments go) it is comparatively easy to learn, it can serve as a common meeting ground for players of diverse musical backgrounds. Players of other woodwinds have a decided advantage in picking it up, of course, and since it requires no special embouchure, it is not perceived as a threat to their modern technique. Its rather limited dynamic range encourages a concentration on subtleties of intonation and articulation, while its "cool"—some would say impersonal—tone color can help inspire a less driven style of musical expression than that typical of contemporary orchestral instruments.

However, the *modern* recorder is far from the ideal tool for Renaissance music. Recorders come in a variety of types and styles, but the one most common today is based loosely upon Baroque models, particularly regarding its basic internal and external shape. (It normally consists of three joints—a head joint with cylindrical bore plus a body and foot with contracting conical bore.) Its standardized range of two octaves and a tone and its fingering system (with some minor exceptions) are likewise a Baroque legacy, as is the basic layout of the family. Five sizes are in common use: sopranino (in f″), soprano (in c″), alto (in f′), tenor (in c′), and bass (in f); a sixth size—great bass or contrabass (in c)—is somewhat rarer. (In Britain the soprano is called the descant and the alto, the treble. Note that for recorders the expression "in f" has a meaning different from that for modern orchestral and band instruments. For the latter it implies a transposing instrument, on which a written "C" would result in a sounding "F." For recorders it merely signifies the specific pitch of the bottom note. Octave displacements aside, recorder music is generally written untransposed; the player is expected to make the appropriate adjustments in terms of "C" or "F" fingerings.) Unlike most Baroque recorders, the modern instrument is usually intended to play in equal temperament at a′ = 440. When well conceived and executed, it is an excellent all-purpose design. However, it should be clear from the following historical discussion that it represents a concept very different from that of the Renaissance recorder.

Description and History

The recorder is a member of the family of duct flutes, which also includes the three-hole tabor pipe, flageolet, penny whistle, and various related folk instruments that share its method of tone production. A built-in duct or windway defines the entering air stream and directs it across an aperture or "window" and against a more or less sharp edge, thus causing the air column to vibrate. As in all woodwinds the frequency of vibration (and thus the pitch) is controlled by the effective length of the air column, determined by the opening and closing of fingerholes by the player. Thus the tone-generating geometry of the duct flutes is fixed at manufacture; it is out of the direct control of the player, who is able to regulate only the breath itself.

By contrast, the player of the transverse flute forms the duct with the lips, controlling both its size and direction as well as the proximity to the edge; regulating these parameters provides the flutist with independent control of pitch, volume, and tone color. The resultant flexibility is not without its price, of course, since much effort and experience are required to develop the correct embouchure. Moreover (following the principle that "from him to whom more has been given, more will be expected"), builders of early transverse flutes relied heavily on this flexibility, requiring the player to compensate for defects of intonation inherent in the design of the instrument. On the other hand, the inflexibility of the tone generator of the duct flute seems to have inspired makers to seek solutions to these defects, at least in the case of the recorder. As a result, for some time (through the Renaissance and into the Baroque) the transverse flute lagged behind the recorder in the sophistication of its acoustical design.

The design features of the recorder separating it from the other duct flutes are subtle in nature but crucial to its unique development as an instrument for art music; it is not "just another whistle." Both surviving museum artifacts and present-day folk derivatives attest to the variety of medieval European duct flutes.[1] The recorder can be distinguished from the others by its fingering system, having seven fingerholes and a thumbhole. (On early recorders the lowest hole was often duplicated in order to accommodate all players regardless of which hand they held lowermost, the unused hole having been plugged up with wax; the resulting total of nine holes gave rise to the Renaissance French term *flûte à neuf trous* for the recorder.) Comparing the recorder to, say, the penny whistle, we see clearly the advantages conferred by the recorder's thumbhole. On the penny whistle, overblowing is achieved simply by increasing breath pressure, causing the high notes to shriek while the low ones are barely audible. Because of its thumbhole, the recorder's registers are more equal in volume. The thumbhole has two functions: it serves not only as a tone hole (extending upward the fundamental scale), but also as an aid to overblowing (much as the register keys on modern woodwinds). By partially uncovering it while fingering one of the lower notes, the player is able to ensure overblowing without greatly increasing breath pressure. Furthermore, the bore of the penny whistle must remain fairly narrow in order for it to overblow easily; the bore of the recorder can be made fatter, giving a rounder, fuller timbre and a more telling bottom register.

It is difficult to determine just when the recorder was invented. Iconography is of little help here, naturally, since the crucial element—the thumbhole—is usually hidden from view. Among the few surviving medieval instruments is the famous recorder excavated from the moat of a fourteenth-century castle near Dordrecht, Holland. This instrument, now in the Gemeentemuseum, The Hague, has been the subject of various reports; estimates of its date of provenance have ranged from the thirteenth to the fifteenth century.[2] Despite this uncertainty, however, it establishes that the recorder as we have just defined it was known from the earliest period we can legitimately call the Renaissance.

The Dordrecht recorder is (in modern terms) a soprano; its bore is a simple cylinder of comparatively narrow diameter (11mm).[3] Without keywork, successful cylindrical recorders can be made down to about the size of a modern alto. In order to overblow accurately they demand rather large fingerholes, particularly at the lower end; with instruments larger than an alto, the holes become impractically large and the finger stretches impossible. The solution, seen on the majority of surviving Renaissance recorders, is to constrict the lower bore, allowing smaller fingerholes with closer spacing. This solution then makes the larger sizes of recorder practicable. The constriction is rarely sudden; the bore profile generally begins to contract near the upper tone holes, reaching its narrowest dimension near the lowest ones. From this point to the bottom end the bore flares out again, attaining nearly the diameter of the top of the instrument; to the casual observer such instruments may even appear cylindrical—and have often been so described by those who should know better. A further benefit of this "choke bore" (as it has been called) is the effect it has on timbre; as pointed out by Bob Marvin, the choke seems to deemphasize the second harmonic of the lowest tones, taking away the "honking" quality characteristic of cylindrically bored recorders.[4]

Unfortunately (and somewhat inexplicably) Renaissance makers did not always exploit the full potential of the complex bore to solve intonation problems; few of the surviving examples live up to what we might expect of professional instruments. (This is not to say that Renaissance recorders cannot be *played* in tune, but that doing so often demands considerable effort.) Typically ●●●/●●○○ overblows as a wide octave, and ●●●/○○○○ sometimes overblows as a narrow one; these problems can be cured by a judicious profiling of the tapered section of bore, as shown by Bob Marvin in building his improved reproductions. We can never know, of course, whether the surviving instruments represent an accurate sampling of those available to Renaissance musicians; quite possibly the best ones were literally used up. But one still has the impression that the achievement of a really good example was to some extent fortuitous.

The Renaissance recorder was clearly developed as a consort instrument for playing vocal-style polyphony. The performance of such music on recorders is documented unequivocally from the second half of the fifteenth century, beginning with the celebrated recorder quartet (dressed as wolves and playing a chanson!) at the marriage of Charles the Bold of Burgundy to Margaret of York in 1468. The practice is undoubtedly even older: a quartet of recorders also performed at the Banquet of the Vow (or Feast of the Pheasant) given in 1454 by Charles's father, Philip the Good, and a set of four recorders (along with four shawms and four douçaines) were ordered by Philip in 1426 to be sent to the Marquis of Ferrara.[5] The first depiction of a set of recorders playing together seems to be the trio (of three distinct sizes) in the Flemish painting "Mary Queen of Heaven," circa 1485, by the Master of the St. Lucy Legend (National Gallery, Washington, DC).[6] No hard evidence has yet been discovered attesting to the development of a bass recorder in the fifteenth century, although the musical repertories of the late fifteenth century would seem to demand one.

The first solid evidence of the bass recorder is in the *Musica getutscht* of Sebastian Virdung (Basel, 1511).[7] (Although Virdung's crude illustrations do not give us the absolute sizes of the instruments he treats, the fact that his largest recorder has a key suggests that it is significantly larger than a tenor recorder—a size rarely provided with a key in the Renaissance.) Three sizes of recorder are mentioned by Virdung: *discant* in g, *tenor* in c, and *bassus* in F. (These represent the *written* pitches of the lowest notes, the *sounding* pitches being an octave higher.) His nomenclature is thus similar to ours, except that his smallest recorder would be called an alto (or treble, in Britain). A set of recorders, according to him, could include four or six; the latter would consist of two of each size (including bass). For four-part music—the norm at that time—one would usually need a *discant*, two c tenors, and an F bass; this is the consort he illustrates. However, an unusually high *contratenor altus* part might demand a second *discant* recorder in place of one of the tenors, as he points out. The same three sizes of recorder (g, c, and F) are mentioned by Martin Agricola (*Musica instrumentalis deudsch*, Wittenberg, 1529 and 1545[8]), Sylvestro di Ganassi (*Fontegara*, Venice, 1535[9]), and Philibert Jambe de Fer (*Epitome musical*, Lyons, 1556[10]). Conspicuously absent from any of these discussions is any mention of a soprano (British descant) recorder in the modern sense; clearly there is some discontinuity between the early sixteenth-century practice and that represented by the Dordrecht recorder discussed above. The first sixteenth-century citation of such an instrument is found in the manuscript writings (ca. 1546) of the scientist, mathematician, and amateur musician Jerome Cardan.[11] Cardan is aware of Ganassi's experiments with expanding the high range of his *soprano* (i.e., alto) in g, but he himself prefers instead to use one yet a fifth higher (in d') to cover that range.

By the seventeenth century the family of recorders had expanded considerably. Michael Praetorius (*Syntagma Musicum* II, Wolfenbüttel, 1619)[12] lists eight sizes: *klein Flötlein* or *exilent* in g''; *discant* in d''; *discant* in c''; *alt* in g'; *tenor* in c'; *basset* in f; *bass* in B♭; and *grossbass* in F.[13] Thus, only the tenor retained its original name, the *discant* and *bassus* having been renamed (and their old names having been reassigned to the sizes next further out in the system). Just when this expansion took place is uncertain, but it cannot have taken place overnight. On this question the didactic sources must be supplemented by other sorts of information, such as inventories, extant instruments, iconography, and documented performances. Collectively these confirm that the larger sizes of recorder were available (to the nobility and more affluent institutions, at least) by about the middle of the sixteenth century.[14] Information regarding the smaller sizes is less abundant, in part because they are simply less remarkable as objects. Again, however, inventories—such as those of the Graz *Instrumentenkammer* (1577) and the Berlin *Hofkapelle* (1582)—are of some help; although terminology is sometimes debatable, they do establish that smaller *discant* recorders had become normal members of the consort by the last quarter of the century.[15]

It will be noticed that Praetorius's pitch designations are an octave higher than those given in the sixteenth century; he has the credit for mentioning in print what some must already have known: that recorders and flutes normally sounded an octave higher than written (at 4-foot pitch, in organists' terminology). He mentions that the tenor recorder or tenor crossflute can serve either as *discant* at written pitch or tenor sounding up an octave. Undoubtedly the larger recorders had for some time been used to play at written (or 8-foot) pitch. However, the traditional use of the smaller recorders and flutes at 4-foot pitch seems to have continued long into the seventeenth century.

Surviving instruments present a somewhat more complex picture than that given by Praetorius. To be sure, several among them attest to his scheme of pitches, assuming a reference pitch of about a′ = 460 (almost a semitone above a′ = 440; see Pitch and Transposition, p. 248). But many do not fit this scheme. Some would appear to be alternative sizes a tone above those he mentions: *bass* in c, *basset* in g, tenor in d′; these are quite numerous in museum collections and would have been handy when playing the large recorders at 8-foot pitch (being an octave below the normal tenor, *alt*, and *discant*). However, these could be regarded instead as "standard" sizes (as defined by Praetorius) conforming to a reference pitch a whole tone higher than a′ = 460, although there seem to be no surviving *grossbass* or *alt* sizes at this pitch to confirm such a notion. A few recorders (those in modern e♭, b♭, f′, and c″) could best be explained as instruments built at a pitch standard about a tone below a′ = 440 (i.e., about a′ = 392); if Praetorius's reference pitch was indeed about a′ = 460, these would then represent a pitch standard a minor third lower, which he says had been common for winds in England and was still common in the Netherlands. Finally, there are a few surviving recorders which play at about a′ = 440 (although among these some of the essential sizes are missing), plus a few "leftovers" that do not fit any of these standards.

Modern Reproductions: Selection and Use

What does all this information mean for the modern practitioner of Renaissance music? Obviously it would be very impractical—not to mention expensive—to have recorders at all of these early sizes and pitches; some choice is necessary. Furthermore, modern versions of "Renaissance" recorders are available in a bewildering variety of models. Among these, the most carefully conceived and executed are produced by individual builders, who naturally charge fairly high prices and commonly have long waiting lists. Factory-built products tend to be more loosely based on historical examples and more often have additional non-historical keywork and other compromises aimed at pleasing a more general clientele. (Exceptions are to be found in both categories, however.) Given the variability of such a market, it would seem most helpful here to discuss the factors to be considered in choosing makes, sizes, and pitches, rather than to make specific recommendations that may soon be rendered obsolete. First of all, priority must be given to the 4-foot pitch set. Praetorius's *bass* and *grossbass* recorders were developed comparatively late and must have been rather rare in their own era. Thus, as lovely and wonderful as an 8-foot-pitch set is, it must be considered a luxury; we need not fear we are misrepresenting Renaissance timbres if it is lacking. On the other hand, the addition of a single *bass* (greatbass, in modern parlance) to a 4-foot-pitch set can be a considerable boon, particularly for the performance of the later repertory in which the bass parts often descend below F. Such an instrument can also allow the transposition of some pieces down a fourth or fifth, giving some relief from the stridency of the 4-foot set. (It is only with a *bass* in B♭ rather than c that the transposition down a fifth could be made automatic by having the players merely shift down a size, as explained in "Pitch and Transposition." At the present time, however, such a *bass* in B♭ is extremely rare; it is offered by few makers.) Instruments smaller than Praetorius's *discant* also appear to have been rather late developments, lying outside the realm of the normal recorder consort. (They are not included in the various quartets suggested in his chart of ranges. He does mention the use of a *klein Flöitlein* to double a cantus line in the *tuttis* of a large concerto;[16] this use recalls Monteverdi's employment of a *flautino* as an orchestral "color" instrument in *Orfeo*. However, these uses reflect more a Baroque than a Renaissance aesthetic.)

Perhaps a more difficult—and certainly a more binding—decision concerns the pitch standard. (One can always buy additional instruments later; changing pitch, however, demands replacing those already purchased.) As we have seen, there was clearly considerable latitude in pitch among the surviving antique instruments. We cannot regard any one pitch as more "correct" or "authentic" than another; again, we are not "misrepresenting the Renaissance" by choosing, say, a′ = 440 over a′ = 460. There are, however, clear physical advantages to a higher standard. It is difficult, for instance, to make a keyless Renaissance tenor at a standard lower than a′ = 460; most makers building Renaissance-style recorders at a′ = 440 resort to a key for the bottom note of the tenor. Still, most people will find that the practical benefits of adhering to modern standard pitch outweigh the drawbacks of the larger dimensions.

The ranges of Renaissance recorders are generally smaller than those of the normal modern instrument. Most Renaissance sources specify a range of an octave plus a sixth or seventh; Jambe de Fer is unusual in specifying two octaves. In all cases the high-note fingerings (those for notes above ⌀ ● ● ○/○ ○ ○ ○) differ from the standard, Baroque-derived modern ones, and the latter do not work on surviving Renaissance examples. The modern high-note fingerings depend on the short, contracting foot of the later design; the expanding lower bore of the Renaissance design (which is responsible for its fuller low register) is proportionately longer, causing them not to work. A further restriction in range is to be encountered in some modern Renaissance-style recorders, particularly those (by several makers) based on the superb designs worked out by Bob Marvin. Here priority has been given to the tone and intonation of the middle and lower registers; as a result, the fingerings for notes above ⌀ ● ● ●/○ ○ ○ ○ are often quite tricky and do not follow the dictates of any historical chart.

Given these restricted ranges, it is particularly important in dealing with Renaissance recorders to have the proper alto—meaning one in g′ rather than in f′. (The question of the d″ or c″ soprano is less crucial, partly because of the specific part ranges involved.) The superius parts of many sixteenth-century pieces fit beautifully on an alto in g′ but are just a little too high for an f′ alto of Renaissance design; if the latter is the only one available, the only solution is to use a soprano instead, giving rather the wrong timbre to the ensemble (especially for the earlier literature). Not surprisingly, having just the right instrument is often the best guide to its own historically correct employment.

The intonation system is also extremely important. Despite their reputation for being easy to play, recorders are actually quite difficult to play in tune, especially with each other. Playing in tune is aided immensely when the instruments themselves are tuned to a system using just or "pure" thirds instead of equal temperament; in practice, this means something resembling meantone temperament. (See Tuning and Temperament, p. 238, for a theoretical explanation.) Most makers of handmade Renaissance-style recorders are aware of this fact and are happy to oblige; they are frequently frustrated by the reluctance of their customers to "experiment" with systems they fear are odd or unnatural. Such fear is ill-founded, however, since the whole point of tuning an early wind with pure thirds is to ease the task of intonation, not to make it more difficult. Furthermore, the reasons to use equal temperament—playing together with modern instruments or playing in keys far removed from C major—simply do not apply to Renaissance recorders; the probability that one would ever be called upon to play in F♯ major with a piano accompaniment is slight indeed![17]

Closely allied with the question of intonation is that of so-called "combination" tones—buzzing sensations in the ear resulting from the interference of two or more soundwaves. These subjective phenomena are particularly noticeable with recorders (and flutes, as well) because of the high pitch. They are also called "difference" tones, since it is the numerical difference in frequency between pairs of actual sounding tones that determines their pitch. For the simple musical intervals formed by adjacent members of the harmonic series, the difference tone is the fundamental of that series. Thus, with the major triad c″–e″–g″ (when played perfectly in tune) the fifth c″–g″ produces the difference tone c′, and both the major third c″–e″ and the minor third e″–g″ produce c. (Changing the voicing of the chord will still produce "Cs," but at different octaves.) With a major chord, then, the difference tones serve to strengthen the root; with a minor chord, things are not so simple. In the case of the minor triad c″–e♭″–g″, the fifth again produces c′, but the minor third produces A♭ and the major third, e♭—altogether a rather cacophonous jumble. No wonder it is often so difficult to tune a minor chord, when even the best intonation still produces a dissonant effect!

Fortunately, for an audience difference tones are less noticeable the farther one is from the source. To the player, however, they can be extremely useful indicators to help achieve better intonation. In playing harmonic (i.e., simultaneous, as opposed to melodic or successive) intervals, one often has difficulty identifying the direction of any mistunings; that is to say, the effect is rather similar if the interval is slightly too large or too small. The difference tone, however, is an immediate and unfailing guide; if it is too low, the interval is too small; if too high, the interval is too large. As an indicator it is surprisingly sensitive; moving from a pure major third to an equal-tempered one raises the difference tone by more than a quartertone.

This brings us back to the importance of pure-third-oriented intonation on recorders. It is here, in my opinion, that we sense the greatest failure of the modern, equal-tempered recorder as a consort instrument. However, with some judicious tinkering with tone-hole sizes one can often work wonders with inexpensive instruments if they are cleanly voiced and have fairly accurate octaves. An early-music ensemble could do far worse, while waiting for its "ideal" set of Renaissance recorders, than to acquire a set of cheap recorders and "have a go" at improving their intonation; the experimentation is itself instructive.[18] This is in no way to be construed as an open invitation to butcher fine instruments, but it is based on the experience that most of what one might reasonably do to change the size of tone holes is reversible, as long as one is fairly neat about it. With inexpensive recorders the potential musical and pedagogical benefits will outweigh the dangers.

Hole sizes are only part of the answer; in order to play really well in tune on any recorder one must be willing to experiment with—and use—alternative fingerings. In particular, one must find flatter fingerings for sharps and sharper fingerings for flats. This, of course, means differentiating between common enharmonic pairs, such as "G♯-A♭," finding a fingering for the "G♯" that makes a pure major third with "E" and one for "A♭" that makes a pure major third with "C." In searching for the proper fingerings it is often helpful to make use of partial coverings, even as part of cross-fingerings. The modern recorder has been designed from what we might call a "digital" (i.e., all-or-nothing) approach to fingering, in which the only adjustable covering is done by the left thumb. Partial coverings, however, formed a regular part of the fingering technique of earlier recorders, Renaissance and Baroque. Ganassi stresses the need for such shaded fingerings both for good intonation in normal playing and for soft expressive effects. Perusal of his charts shows that the sixth finger in particular was often required to make a partial covering of its hole; this is because on Renaissance recorders the modern second-octave fingerings ø•••/•○•○ and ○○••/•••○ are usually too flat and ⌀●●●/○●○○ is too sharp, so that ⌀●●●/●○⌀○, ⌀●●●/●●⌀○, and ⌀●●●/○●⌀○ were used instead (at least by Ganassi).[19] Modern versions of Renaissance recorders often demand the same treatment. One may also find that ●●○●/○○○○ is too sharp and ●●○●/●○○○ is too flat, in which case the "analog" solution ●●○●/⌀○○○ may be less awkward (and more transferable between instruments) than a "digital" solution involving some lower hole.

Mention should be made of the so-called "Ganassi" recorder offered by some makers. Ganassi's regular fingering charts give an octave plus a major sixth for all sizes, a range he claims is normal for most players. However, in addition, he gives special charts for high notes—his own invention, he says—extending the range of his *soprano* (alto) in g yet another octave. There are three of these special charts, which are "brand specific" (carrying the makers' marks "B," a stylized "A," and a trefoil; the latter two marks have been found on surviving instruments). Unfortunately, however, these high-note fingerings do not work on most Renaissance originals; in fact, only one promising instrument seems to exist—an atypical alto in Vienna with a cylindrical bore terminating in a short flare.[20] Using this design as a point of departure, various makers have developed instruments that respond to Ganassi's extended-range fingerings. By a similar process of extrapolation from a fingering chart, makers have also endeavored to fill in another important gap in the recorder's history by producing a "van Eyck" recorder. In some copies of Jacob van Eyck's *Der Fluyten Lusthof* (Amsterdam, 1644–ca. 1655) are included fingering charts (for soprano in c′, written pitch) in which the high-note fingerings are those of later Baroque recorders; the instruments illustrated, however, are of one piece and have the plain outline of the Renaissance design. To date, no example has been found of an original with Baroque bore and Renaissance appearance, although there do exist a few "transitional" instruments with Baroque bore, one-piece construction, and some ornamental turnery.[21]

Historical Technique

Most of the sixteenth-century method books have little to say about recorder technique beyond fingering. Again Ganassi stands out as the great exception, although there are a few helpful remarks about articulation to be found in the 1545 edition of Agricola. From the latter we learn that the basic tongue stroke for slower notes is "de de de . . . ," well coordinated with the fingers; this implies what we might now call "tongued legato." For faster notes one is to employ a kind of double tonguing, alternating "di" and "ri"; players disagree, he says, on whether to use single or double tonguing for medium-fast notes. His practice thus differs from the modern one in two significant ways. Modern double tonguing alternates "t" and "k," to the exclusion of other consonants, and it is usually employed only when the notes are so fast as to make single tonguing impossible; one normally attempts to equalize the sound of the two consonants, so that alternating them at a slower speed would be meaningless. Agricola's examples thus imply both a smooth connection and a subtle distinction between alternating tongue strokes. For the fastest ornamental notes, he says, some use a "flutter tonguing," which he spells "tellellelelle. . . . " Since a literal repetition of l's produces almost no effect on a recorder, it has been suggested that the intended effect is akin to that of the "diddle" or "tootle" tonguings described in the eighteenth century.

Double tonguing is also of primary concern to Ganassi. His patterns range from the sharp "teche teche" (essentially the modern form; Italian "ch" = English "k") to the smooth "lere lere" (which is hardly articulated at all, he says); between them stands "tere tere" (similar to Agricola's "diri diri"), which is a mixture of sharp and smooth. (Note that the "r" of both Agricola and Ganassi is most probably a single "flip" of a rolled "r"; it is certainly not North American English "r"!) Ganassi suggests experimenting with different vowels ("tara; tere; tiri; toro; turu"; etc.) in order to find out which is personally most conducive to speed. The purpose of these different articulations is clearly to provide the largest possible range of expression for the divisions that make up the bulk of his *Fontegara*. In fact, for him imitation of the singer's full range of emotional expression is the chief task of the recorder player. Bound up with imitating the artifice of the singer are *prontezza* (breath control) and *galanteria* (the art of making *tremoli*, or trills); both are to be varied in their effect from *suave* (tender) to *vivace* (lively). Ganassi provides a chart of trills in which those marked with a "V" (for *vivace*) produce larger intervals and those marked with an "S" (for *suave*), smaller. The former are commonly as large as a third and the latter as small as a diesis (about a quartertone), the exact size depending on how far the trilling finger is removed from the hole.

Jerome Cardan confirms much of Ganassi's information about recorder technique and expressive effects. He is particularly enamored of the tremolo of a diesis made by barely lifting the finger from the hole. (It should be noted that this effect is the opposite of the *flattement* of the French Baroque, in which a finger beats against a lower hole; in the latter case, the microtonal fluctuation is below the note, not above.) He does, however, mention two techniques not described by Ganassi. One is making the tremolo (a specific ornament, not a constant vibrato) by means of the breath as well as the fingers; the other is extending the lower range by a tone or semitone by resting the end of the recorder against the leg and abating the breath.[22]

Repertory

Music appropriate for Renaissance recorders encompasses virtually every genre, vocal or instrumental, from the late fifteenth to the early seventeenth century. (One might point to intabulations for, say, lute as an obvious exception but for the fact that scholars have occasionally reconstructed plausible original polyphonic versions of such pieces.) As one of the first instruments to have been developed as a family, the recorder is certainly suitable for the many Franco-Flemish compositions preserved in manuscripts of the late fifteenth century. Although much of this repertory was originally vocal, the fact that it was often transmitted in untexted form points to a penchant for instrumental performance at the time; in addition, many of the pieces do seem to have been conceived originally for instruments.[23] In the early sixteenth century the secular songs of France and Germany appear to have been vehicles for performance on consorts of recorders, and there is no reason to exempt the parallel literature from other countries. Although recorders are perhaps not the most effective dance instruments, they would probably have been the first choice of amateurs playing the many printed sixteenth-century dance collections; they are mentioned by Arbeau as possible instruments for playing pavans and basse dances.[24] Recorders were also important elements in the various mixed consorts of the sixteenth century, whose documentation starts with the Messisbugo "cookbook concerts" of 1529.[25] Recorders (including a set of large ones) were used by Lassus in performances at the Bavarian ducal court in the 1560s.[26] A professional recorder consort was employed in the English royal court beginning in 1540, when five Bassano brothers were imported by Henry VIII from the Venice of Ganassi. Much of the surviving literature composed by members of this long-lived ensemble would appear to have been intended for recorders.[27] In selecting vocal music for performance on recorders one should bear in mind that the word-paintings (so-called "madrigalisms") characteristic of the late sixteenth and early seventeenth centuries often create interesting motives and textures that are effective instrumentally. However, those pieces that rely mainly on the expressive pronunciation of actual words or that feature vocal exclamations (*ahi!* or *Ohimé!*, for instance) seem especially unsuited to recorders. Similarly, those instrumental works from the same period that depend for their effect more on sonority and less on contrapuntal interest are often less satisfying on recorders (particularly at 4-foot pitch).

Modern practical editions of the repertory for recorders constitute an embarrassment of riches; just playing through all that has been published could take years. Much of it is now available in quasi-scholarly editions, in which the editors have taken some pains to distinguish their own contributions from those of the original text without losing the "user-friendly" feel of the practical edition. (See Resource Materials, p. 235, for a discussion and listing of performance editions.) In general, the main fault of such editions is that they still have the modern recorder family in mind, meaning that pieces in the "high clefs" (see Pitch and Transposition, p. 248) almost always appear at their original pitches. Such pieces usually require transposition downward (usually by a fourth) in order to fit on the F-c-g consort of the early sixteenth century; even those from a later period (when a soprano is appropriate) could often benefit from downward transposition so that they might lie in a more sonorous range. The same pieces would, of course, appear at their original pitches in scholarly editions, too. The best solution, short of writing out a transposed version, is to learn to transpose, imagining different clefs (including the various "C" clefs) and sometimes different fingerings. Such a process will work out better for some players in an ensemble than for others. For instance, transposing a part in treble clef down a fourth on an alto in g' is simple; one need only read it as a soprano in c". Unfortunately, the solutions for the other parts are not as straightforward.

Suggested Listening

There are, to my knowledge, no available recordings of original Renaissance recorders, as there are of Baroque examples. However, several excellent recordings have been made by the Wiener Blockflötenensemble using a set of Renaissance-style recorders (at a' = 460) by Bob Marvin. These include *Blockflötenmusik der Renaissance: Italien* (Teldec 6.42033, 1977); *Blockflötenmusik der Renaissance: England* (Teldec 6.42356, 1979); *Blockflötenmusik der Renaissance: Niederlände* (Teldec 6.42635, 1981—reissued by Musical Heritage Society as *Renaissance Recorder Music from the Netherlands,* MHS 7191Y, 1985); and *Blockflötenmusik der Renaissance: Deutschland* (MHS 512326W, 1977). Using sizes from F *grossbass* to c' soprano, they demonstrate almost the full range of Praetorius's expanded consort. From the standpoint of sheer sonority the low (8-foot pitch) grouping is especially compelling, even when its use for the earlier repertory is historically questionable. Recordings featuring mixtures of individual Renaissance-style recorders with other instruments and with voices are somewhat more common. A fine example (again using recorders by Bob Marvin) is *Au verd Boys! To the Greenwood* by the New World Consort (Collegium Records COL 8407, 1985, reissued as a CD by Musical Heritage Society—MHS 512326W, 1989). As more instruments of this type become available—and as players come to appreciate their special qualities—we can look forward to their increased use in both concerts and recordings.

1. For a tabulation and analysis see Moeck–*Typen.*
2. See Fitzpatrick–Medieval and Weber–Recorder for divergent opinions as to the age of the Dordrecht recorder. Fitzpatrick claims that radiocarbon dating of items found with it "proves" a date of ca. 1250; other circumstantial evidence suggests a later date (the castle itself was inhabited from 1335 to 1418).
3. The articles cited in the previous note document two different approaches to making reconstructions and reproductions of this precious find. The instrument is apparently miss-

ing a lower appendage, since (in reproductions) the bottom note is sharp to the rest of the scale. Fitzpatrick has opted for a short foot joint providing a cylindrical extension, while Weber (after trying that) contrived an even shorter foot, which makes a sudden constriction of the bore; the latter solution is based on certain antique and folk examples and is, according to Weber, the superior one for timbre and intonation. Be warned, however, that the acoustical explanations of both authors are as fanciful as their practical insights are valuable!

4. See Marvin–Recorders for a list of surviving Renaissance and Baroque recorders, their physical and musical characteristics, and information he has gleaned from making reproductions of them.

5. Marix–*Histoire*; the word *fleutes* (or *flustes*) employed in Burgundian records can be taken only to mean recorders, given the lack of evidence for transverse flutes in fifteenth-century Europe.

6. Remnant–*Musical*: 115–17.

7. See Hettrick–Sebastian: 100–04.

8. See Hettrick–Martin: 108–09 and 141–45.

9. See Ganassi–Hildemarie. It is unfortunate that these modern editions print Ganassi's fingering charts without including his pitch designations (except for the charts included in the appendix showing a few facsimile pages). The texts, too, leave much to be desired and are in need of thorough revision.

10. Jambe–*Epitome*: 53–55 and (unnumbered) recorder fingering chart.

11. See Cardan–*De Musica*: 68–69.

12. Praetorius–*Syntagma* II: 33–34.

13. A ninth instrument—described and illustrated with the recorders but not listed with them—is his *gar kleine Blockflötlein* with d‴ as its bottom note. Some three or four inches long, this is not, properly speaking, a recorder, since it has but three fingerholes and a thumbhole. The modern "garklein" offered by some makers is usually, in fact, a tiny recorder—a "supersopranino" in c‴—that is so small as to be barely playable by most adults.

14. For instance, the famous *grossbass* (with extensions down to C!) now in the Vleeshuis Museum in Antwerp was part of a chest of recorders (now dispersed) once belonging to the Hansa House of that city. The instruments were probably purchased between 1569 and 1591 and were made by the Hamburg builders Hans Rauch von Schratt (fl. 1535) and Casper Rauchs Schrattenbach (fl. 1570). A matching *bass* in c (with extensions to G) now in Munich is signed "Hans Rauch von Schratt" and was probably once part of that same Antwerp set. (See Lambrechts-Douillez–contrabas.) The Accademia Filarmonica of Verona was another institution that owned numerous recorders; their *flauti grosse* were mentioned as early as 1552. (See Woodfield–*Early*: 188.) In fact, there is evidence suggesting that some of the large recorders still in Verona (including one *grossbass*) were part of a collection predating the foundation of the Accademia in 1543. In any case, we can be certain that by 1562 the deepest recorders owned by the Accademia were larger than *basset* size, since the inventory of that year mentions "three crooks for playing the basses"; such crooks were generally used only on *bass* and *grossbass* recorders in the Renaissance. (See Di Pasquale–strumenti: 8.) What appears to be a *bass* (blown through a crook) is shown in the hands of one of Lassus's musicians in the famous Hans Mielich miniature (1570) depicting the Bavarian court "orchestra."

15. The Graz inventory lists a set of recorders containing "two basses, four tenors, four discants, and four smaller discants, plus two very small recorders"—thus five sizes in all; see Schlosser–*Sammlung*: 19. The Berlin inventory lists one set made up of four sizes (*bass, tenor, alt, discant*) and another of five (the same four plus a *klein discant*); see Sachs–*Musik*: 200.

16. Praetorius–*Syntagma* III: 173.

17. If called on to play with equal-tempered Renaissance instruments (specifically, fretted strings) one still has enough flexibility through breath pressure to make the necessary accommodation.

18. A useful publication when making such modifications is Brown–*Recorder*. Brown has little to say about intonation systems per se, but the physical principles involved in tuning are universally applicable. Of the natural scale one must raise by increasing amounts "Gs," "Cs," and "Fs" and lower (again by increasing amounts) "As," "Es," and "Bs," leaving "Ds" alone. One can either do this "scientifically," using a tuning meter, or purely by trial and error.

19. The less sophisticated charts of the other sixteenth-century authors are "digital" in nature and do not show the partial coverings recommended by Ganassi.

20. See Morgan–Making: 19–20 and Loretto–When: 64–66.

21. See Griffioen–*Jacob* for a discussion of the recorder appropriate for this repertory.

22. Cardan–*De Musica*: 62–71.

23. See Lockwood–*Music*: 266–77.

24. Arbeau–*Orchésographie*: 67.

25. See Brown–Cook's: 233 and 238–40 and Brown–*16th-Century*: 61, 67–68, 97–99, and 104–07.

26. See Baines–*Woodwind*: 256–7 for a partial listing.

27. See Lasocki–Recorder: 94–100.

5

Renaissance Flute

Herbert Myers

The Renaissance transverse flute remains one of the more neglected instruments in the revival of early music; it was, by all accounts, much more important in the period than its modern use would indicate. The consort of flutes appears to have been developed in the first decades of the sixteenth century. Transverse flutes had been in common use throughout Europe in the Middle Ages but seem for some mysterious reason to have suffered a marked decline in popularity near the end of the fourteenth century, and little evidence exists of their use throughout the main part of the fifteenth. The flute first reappears near the end of the fifteenth century as a fife, played in association with the side drum for dancing and in military contexts. Virdung (*Musica getutscht*, 1511) makes casual reference to this military use, which seems to have been the origin of the appellation "German flute," which continued to distinguish the cross-flute from the recorder long after the flute had become a chamber instrument. (Within Germany itself, however, soldiering was associated specifically with the Swiss, giving rise to the term "Schweitzer Pfeiff" found in German sources.) Perhaps surprisingly, the first evidence of the development of flute consorts is to be found within this outdoor, military setting: the fife cases carried by Maximilian I's fifers (Plates 3 and 4 of the *Triumphzug*, ca. 1519) were clearly designed to carry instruments of at least three different lengths. This evidence is soon followed by the first known illustration of a flute consort "in action"—a pen drawing (1522/23) by Urs Graf showing a quartet of flutes being played out-of-doors by four Swiss soldiers (reproduced in the article by Anne Smith cited below).

By the second quarter of the sixteenth century the playing of flute consorts had caught on with amateurs and "civilian" professionals, as we can gather from the more extensive treatment of the flute in Martin Agricola's *Musica instrumentalis deudsch* of 1528 (fully revised in 1545). In France, flutes were given equal status with recorders in Attaingnant's famous chanson collections of 1533, in which several of the pieces are annotated as to their appropriateness for one or the other (or for both). The flute consort received equal treatment with the recorder consort in the *Epitome musical* of

Philibert Jambe de Fer (Lyon, 1556). Most later sources (Zacconi, Virgiliano, Praetorius, Mersenne, and van Eyck) have more to say concerning one particular size of flute (usually the tenor), and it is a single tenor flute that figures prominently in the English "broken" consort of Morley and Rosseter. However, it seems clear that the idea of a consort of flutes of different sizes remained viable well into the seventeenth century, although authors from the late sixteenth century onward mention replacing the bass flute with a stronger instrument such as the sackbut, curtal, or serpent. The Renaissance flute was finally eclipsed by the one-keyed Baroque flute developed in France in the second half of the seventeenth century.

At least forty specimens of the Renaissance type survive, giving a clear picture of the instrument's physical and musical properties. In design it is a model of elegant simplicity, appearing on first glance to be a mere cylindrical pipe, open at both ends and provided with a mouthhole and six fingerholes, but no keys. More careful examination reveals that although the bore is indeed cylindrical, the exterior profile tapers slightly from the mouthhole to the last fingerhole, causing a small but significant change in wall thickness. Concealed inside, just above the mouthhole, is a plug whose lower surface defines the top of the air column; the extension of the tube upward past the plug has no acoustical function but helps balance the instrument both physically and visually. Most surviving examples are of one piece, except for bass flutes, which were often provided with one tenon-and-socket joint (strengthened by either a metal band or a localized swelling of the wood around the socket). The size most often depicted in the hands of Renaissance musicians is the tenor, whose pitch approximates that of the modern (soprano) flute, "six fingers" producing roughly the same d′ on both instruments. According to the majority of relevant sources, however, this was nominally the d an octave lower, so that the flutes, like the recorders, generally played at 4-foot pitch. (Unless otherwise noted, subsequent references will be to nominal, or written, pitches rather than to sounding pitches.) The tenor in d also served for alto parts; following Renaissance principles of consort design, the other members of the flute family radiated in fifths from the tenor, producing a bass in G and a descant in a. Flutes, however, seem to have remained limited to just these three sizes (in contrast with recorders, which had expanded to at least seven sizes by the beginning of the seventeenth century). In compensation, the flutes have a very large range by Renaissance standards—two and a half octaves or more on the tenor, and two octaves on the bass.

Although the pitches as just outlined—G for bass, d for (alto-)tenor, and a for descant—were those generally agreed upon in the sources, other pitches were given as well; a short review may be useful. Assuming that the physical size of the flutes remained relatively constant, these resulted in different transpositions. Agricola presented three different schemes of pitches: D-A-e, C-G-d, and G₁-D-A (the first in 1529 and the other two in 1545). The last, which he characterized as the "regular," easiest, most common, and most comfortable one, is yet another octave below the sounding pitch of the flutes; taken literally, it means that they regularly played at 2-foot pitch. This is puzzling information, since it would mean that they constantly played in their highest, shrillest register, using their most awkward fingerings; at the same time, their bottom octave would have remained almost totally unused since such low notes are rarely to be found in music of the time. (It is perhaps more reasonable to assume that his pitch notation is off by an octave.) The first two schemes (D-A-e and C-G-d) would seem much more practical, since they often place the music in the most effective range (avoiding both high and low extremes of register). Of these two schemes, the second (C-G-d, which in effect transposes the music down a fourth from 2-foot pitch, or up a fifth from 4-foot pitch) has the advantage, since here prominent notes are less likely to fall on the difficult half-hole fingering ●●●/●●∅.

Jambe de Fer's flute consort, by contrast, clearly played at 4-foot pitch. It differed from Agricola's additionally in consisting of only two sizes—the Frenchman's flute quartet was made up of a bass in G and three tenors in d. His recorder consort, like Virdung's and Agricola's, was made up of three sizes (F, c, and g); for the descant of the flutes, however, the third size was unnecessary, as he explains, because of the flute's larger range. Unfortunately his fingering chart for the tenor flute has not survived, but from his description we know that the range was nineteen notes, from d to a″. Exactly the same range was given by Virgiliano (*Il Dolcimelo*) in a chart for tenor flute. Virgiliano's chart is further annotated with clefs for transposition up by a fourth and downward by both a fourth and a fifth. Also in agreement concerning the nineteen-note range for the tenor flute is Praetorius (*Syntagma* II and III), who chose, however, to report it in terms of its actual sounding pitch (d′ to a‴). He specifies altogether three different uses of the tenor flute: first, as a descant at 8-foot pitch; second, as a tenor at 4-foot pitch (apparently the most common use); and third, as a tenor at 2-foot pitch (effective when the part lies too low to be heard at 4-foot pitch, but only when other parts are not being played—or doubled—at 4-foot pitch). He also gives illustrations and ranges of the bass flute in g and descant flute in a′.

Mersenne's information (*Harmonie*) is somewhat enigmatic. He provides two charts for the flute, one starting on d′ and one on g. These have often been understood as charts for tenor and bass flutes at sounding pitch, despite the fact that the nineteen-note range for the g-flute is impracticable on a bass. It seems much more likely that a descant in g′, such as the one illustrated as an alternative to the c″-soprano recorder in some editions of van Eyck's *Der Fluyten-Lusthof*, is actually intended. Like the Baroque c″-soprano and f′-alto recorders, such a g′-descant flute is a tone lower than its closest Renaissance equivalent.

Renaissance flutes are by nature difficult instruments, a fact that more than any other accounts for their current neglect. The need for a special embouchure is an obvious impediment for amateurs, but it is intonation that remains the greatest problem for all players. The tuning difficulties are inherent in the basic design—cylindrical bore with small fingerholes. As one ascends the scale in the second register, the overblown octaves of the fundamental notes are increasingly flat. The historical solution, as seen in fingering charts, was to switch to overblown twelfths partway up the scale. Thus there is a discontinuity between overblown ● ● ●/○ ○ ○ (g′ on the tenor) and ● ● ○/● ● ● (a′—a twelfth above the low d), since the first of these is naturally flat and the second is naturally sharp. Considerable embouchure correction (uncovering the mouthhole more to sharpen the g′ and covering it more to flatten the a′) is therefore required to play this part of the scale in tune. Virtually every modern maker of Renaissance flutes has been asked by customers to improve upon the early design, and some makers have responded with remodelings that (regardless of their virtues) are fundamentally different in character from the original concept. For instance, a tapered bore (as found on the recorder and Baroque flute) will help to open out the compressed octaves but produces a different timbre. Larger fingerholes, too, will overblow more truly but will make cross-fingering less effective. The fingerhole layout of the originals is actually the result of quite sophisticated compromise, given the constraints of the cylindrical bore.

Even flatter than the second-octave ● ● ●/○ ○ ○ is the second-octave ● ● ●/● ○ ○ (the semitone just below—f′-sharp on the tenor). This fingering requires extreme embouchure correction to play in tune (unless the maker has enlarged the fifth fingerhole, in which case ● ● ●/● ○ ● is rendered ineffective as a cross-fingering—a large price to pay!). A possible historical solution is found in Jambe de Fer's chart for the bass flute, in which b-natural is fingered ● ● ●/○ ● ø instead of the ● ● ●/● ○ ○ found in the charts in other sources. However, this cross-fingering tends instead to be sharp, requiring a strong act of will on the part of the player to be played in tune. Requiring a similar act of will (and skill) is the note ● ● ●/● ● ø (e♭′ on the tenor). While undeniably difficult, this note *can* be produced; it is not impossible, as suggested by some modern writers. The trick is not to depend solely on the finger to flatten the pitch, but to help it out both by covering with the embouchure and by abating the breath.

The question of pitch standard represents a greater problem for flutes than for most other early instruments. Renaissance flutes were, as a rule, built to pitches lower than a′ = 440 (in contrast with recorders and most other Renaissance winds, which were usually built to standards *higher* than modern pitch). In scaling flutes to play at a′ = 440, one loses much of the telling quality of the low-pitch original, particularly in the low register. One solution is to build the flutes at a whole tone below a′ = 440, thus in effect striking an average among the low pitches of surviving flutes; the resulting consort (in f, c′, and g′, sounding pitch) is then able to possess both the character and behavior of the originals. The flutes then have to transpose upward, of course, when playing with other instruments. There is an additional disadvantage for the player of the bass flute, since it becomes ever more unwieldy and tonally uneven as it is made longer.

For the beginner who has had no experience with flutes the first task is acquiring an embouchure. Here, in the absence of a specialist in the early flute, an open-minded teacher of the modern flute can be of immense help, since the lip formation is similar in principle. For the modern flutist coming to the Renaissance flute for the first time, the primary concern is the reordering of musical priorities, placing intonation ahead of power—or even beauty—of tone. One of the best exercises is to alternate (overblown) ●●●/○○○ and ●●○/●●● (g′ and a′ on the tenor), exaggerating the pitch corrections mentioned above in order to produce too "small" a melodic second. This not only focuses one's attention on intonation, but makes producing the melodically correct interval almost easy. All of this energy expended on correcting intonation and equalizing an uneven scale tends to limit dynamic flexibility. One must nonetheless learn to counteract this limitation and to exploit the expressive possibilities of the flute, which represent, after all, its primary advantage over the recorder. Without dynamic expression the flute remains a mere alternative timbre to the recorder, on a grand scale only subtly different (and requiring a great deal more work!).

Perhaps the repertory most effective for a consort of flutes is that associated with them historically: the quartet chansons and Lieder from about the first half of the sixteenth century. This is not intrinsically difficult music, but it may nonetheless represent a real challenge to perform well on flutes. Players wanting to reduce some of the difficulties may wish to begin with pieces with fewer parts (*bicinia* and *tricinia*), which abound in sixteenth-century prints. By contrast, Franco-Flemish music of the fifteenth century is often more complex and engaging; although it predates the development of the flute consort, much of it was recopied and reprinted in the sixteenth century, attesting to its continued popularity among later performers (who would have had no qualms about adapting it to flutes). Much of the vocal music of the second half of the sixteenth century lends itself better to performance on the more lush mixtures of instruments and voices (typical of Italian practice) than to performance on pure consorts of flutes; flutes were, of course, regularly employed in such grand consorts, often playing inner lines at 4-foot pitch. Some of the instrumental styles that matured in the latter half of the sixteenth century—*ricercare* and *canzone*—are suitable for performance on flutes. As these forms developed further in the next century, however, there came to be such an emphasis on the violin and on the *basso continuo* that the flute consort was pushed more and more out of the picture. The flute itself then reemerged (along with the other remodeled Baroque winds) as something of a "surrogate violin."

The most thorough examination of sources for the technique and repertory of the Renaissance flute is Smith–Renaissancequerflöte. The fact that it is in German may be daunting to many, but the several charts and tables (including a composite table of fingerings) are intelligible to anyone who

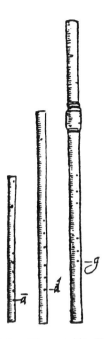

FIGURE 5.1 Complete set of flutes: Discant, Alto-Tenor, Bass
Praetorius, *Syntagma musicum* II, Plate IX

can remember that German "B" means B-flat and "H" means B-natural. A somewhat more cursory treatment of the same material (but in English) is Smith–Renaissance, in which the composite table is reprinted. A similar review (with composite fingering charts) is Godwin–Renaissance. Bernard Thomas in his article of the same title (Thomas–Renaissance) suggests (on the basis of both the pitch of surviving instruments and a questionable reading of Praetorius) that early flutists invariably transposed up a step; experience shows that such a transposition is often very useful, but that just as often it creates more problems than it solves. In Brown–Notes the various transpositions implied by Agricola's charts and their possible implications for Attaingnant's 1533 chanson collections are examined; however, I believe he has slightly misinterpreted some of Jambe de Fer's information, which may actually be more relevant than Agricola to Attaingnant. Finally, for those interested in the period of transition between the Renaissance and Baroque flutes, the available evidence concerning this still somewhat murky area is to be found in Bowers–New.

It should come as no surprise that recordings of flute consorts are hard to find. One of the few available is the recent CD *Flute Music of the 16th and 17th Centuries*, directed and performed by Nancy Hadden with the Renaissance Flute Consort (Hyperion CDA66298). This presents several French chansons, German Lieder, and the Senfl four-part "Tandernaken" played on a quartet of flutes; it also includes pieces for solo flute as well as flutes mixed with other instruments. Other recordings of single flutes participating in mixed instrumentations are the pieces for English consort performed by The Musicians of Swanne Alley (*Popular Elizabethan Music*, Focus 822, 1982, and *As I Went to Walsingham*, Harmonia Mundi HMC 5192, 1987) and the various earlier mixtures of instruments and voice represented by the group Circa 1500 (*Renaissance Music from the Courts of Mantua and Ferrara*, Chandos ABTD 1110, 1984, and *The Flower of All Ships: Tudor Court Music from the Time of the Mary Rose*, CRD Records CRDC 4148, 1987).

6

Crumhorn

Jeffery Kite-Powell

If we were to give the crumhorn a name in English that most aptly describes its appearance, we would probably call it "the curved horn," as did the Germans (*Krummhorn, Krumbhorn*), the Italians (*storto/storti* or *storta/storte*), and the French (*tournebout*—first used by Mersenne in 1636). Rather than refer to the instrument in such a descriptive manner, the Spanish word *orlo* may simply be a translation of the German word for horn, but it could also be a general name for a double reed instrument.

Not only does the curved lower end of the crumhorn give it an unusual appearance, but the sound produced by the instrument is quite striking as well—rather like that of a kazoo to the uninitiated listener. It is referred to as a capped double reed instrument, because the reed is enclosed in a small chamber by a windcap and is never placed directly into the mouth or touched by the lips. There is a small slit in the end of the windcap through which the player blows, sending the air through the reed and causing it to vibrate. This technique of setting the reed in motion is most likely derived from the bagpipe and bladder pipe tradition beginning in the thirteenth century.

The country of origin of the crumhorn is not certain, but the first written record of the instrument is in Berlin, Germany, in 1486; the first pictorial evidence is found in Bologna, Italy, two years later. It is reasonable to assume that the crumhorn was in use a few decades prior to its appearance in the 1488 painting, but it would be inappropriate to use it in music written before 1450, as there is simply no documentation of its existence. After 1500, records of the crumhorn's use and whereabouts are plentiful in both sacred and secular settings, as demonstrated by the following testimony from 1500 (Boydell: 16): " . . . the singers . . . sang two Masses with the help of the organ, three sackbuts and a cornett, and also four crumhorns with the positive organ which were quite joyful to hear." Proof of its popularity is seen in the frequency of organs containing a crumhorn stop, particularly in Germany and the Low Countries. Frequent encounters in church and court inventories in Italy, Germany, and the Low Countries suggest that the crumhorn enjoyed a considerable amount of popularity—indeed, the title page of a publication by the Antwerp printer Tielman Susato gives his address as "near the new weighbridge at the Sign of the Crumhorn." The crumhorn was also used in Spain and, to a much lesser extent, England and Poland. France may have had crumhorns, but it is unknown exactly when they were introduced or what they were called. Decline in the use of the crumhorn occurred in most countries shortly after 1600, but not until after 1650 in Germany.

Standard sizes for the crumhorn are soprano, alto, tenor, and bass, and all are played at 8-foot pitch (no octave transposition necessary). The range of the standard sizes is a major ninth:

soprano: c′–d″
alto: f–g′
tenor: c–d′
bass: F–g

Variations on this include the g-alto (actually the original pitch of the alto), the extended tenor, the extended bass, and the great bass. On the extended bass, an additional key (below the low F) can be preset by means of slider keys to produce an E, D, or C. Changing the preset note requires a short pause in the player's part. There was no upward extension on the crumhorn, even though many makers misrepresent the range of the original crumhorn on their modern replicas by adding two keys on the upper end of the horn, thereby providing a few extra notes. This misleads modern performers into thinking they can play music that has a range of an eleventh, which would have been unthinkable, not to mention impossible, in the sixteenth century. It should be pointed out, however, that having an upward extension key on an f-alto crumhorn enables those who don't have a g-alto or who don't wish to learn a new fingering to play the g-alto line.

If a particular work you would like to perform does not exceed the range of a ninth in any of the parts, but is pitched too high or too low, you might try transposing it down a fourth or up a fifth, a common practice of the period. Additionally, the standard configuration SATB will not work for all pieces, and you may have to try SAAT, SAAB, STTB, ATTB (by far the most typical arrangement of the period), or some other combination. It is always good to have an extra alto or tenor crumhorn lying around.

Reeds are made of cane or plastic. Cane reeds are obviously more appropriate, and they tend to produce a louder, more robust sound with more pitch stability. Plastic reeds have the advantage of being more economical, as they can last for a very long time if well cared for. Students should be given very careful instruction on how to remove the reedcap so that the reed is not damaged in the process. Many a reed has been destroyed by the careless or hasty removal of the reedcap; also, crumhorns should never be carried by the reedcap, as it is prone to come off, damaging the reed or the instrument in the ensuing fall.

Because of the similarities in fingering, crumhorns are often the first instrument recorder players turn to when looking for an alternative early instrument. It should be stressed, however, that the two instruments are quite different in every other respect; in fact, the crumhorn was always a professional—never an amateur—instrument in the Renaissance. Crumhorns are more difficult to play in tune, and because of the reed's greater resistance to wind pressure (as opposed to the whistle of the recorder), one's endurance is greatly diminished. The inexperienced player loses his embouchure altogether after only a few minutes of playing, while the practiced performer will surely experience lip exhaustion at the conclusion of a few pieces. Articulation on the crumhorn requires a lot more energy, too. The initial sound of each note must be made with a sharp attack of the tongue, almost an explosive effect, while the end of the note must have a crisp, clean release. Be creative with your articulation by giving stressed notes their full value while shortening other notes somewhat. The way you articulate a piece—particularly one that is homorhythmic—can enhance it tremendously. Dynamic shading, vibrato, and slurring should not be attempted on the crumhorn.

Tuning crumhorns is achieved primarily by breath pressure. Generally speaking, a considerable amount of air is needed to obtain the proper sound (and pitch) on the crumhorn, depending, of course, on the type of reed you are using. There is very little tuning latitude when inserting the reed's staple into the instrument, so it is imperative that one learn the particular idiosyncracies of one's instrument; for instance, some pitches may need more breath pressure than others to make them higher, while one or two pitches may need less pressure than the average pitch to lower them somewhat. As a reminder, it sometimes helps to put little upward or downward arrows over the notes in the music for the troublesome pitches. Intonation can also be affected by the reed aperture; opening it slightly will lower the pitch, while squeezing it just a bit smaller will raise the pitch and make it a bit easier to blow. Great care must be taken not to damage the reed during this procedure.

The last point to be made with regard to intonation concerns the general maintenance of the horn. A periodic check of the fingerholes (usually quite small on most modern crumhorns) may reveal that natural skin oils have combined with dirt and grime to clog a hole or make it smaller by collecting around the rim of the hole, causing the pitches depending on it to be somewhat flat.

The beginning crumhorn player should start out by playing scale passages in whole notes, perhaps using just the left hand at first. When good intonation and steady breath pressure have been achieved, the right hand may be added. Continue by playing the same scale in half notes, two halves for each pitch, and then quarters, repeating all four before moving to the next pitch. All the while care should be taken to start and stop the tones with a firm tongue, which should make direct contact with the reedcap opening or the roof of the mouth with each attack. When playing in a group you should establish the habit of tuning the octaves and fifths (both pure or beatless) to the bass crumhorn; add the third (also pure) only after the octaves and fifths are perfectly in tune. And remember, the more you play the stronger your embouchure will become and the more endurance you will have. The sound of a well-rehearsed, in-tune consort of four to eight crumhorns is nothing short of awe-inspiring.

Many editors of Renaissance music give the range of each voice part at the beginning of the piece. This makes life much easier for those looking for music that is suitable for a consort of crumhorns, and there is truly a wealth of music available (both sacred and secular) that fits the limited range of this consort. There are several publications containing works that either fit the crumhorn's range as written or that have been adapted to fit it. The most important of these are:

> *Music for Crumhorns* 1. 43 pieces in 4 parts. London Pro Musica Edition, LPM MCR1.
> *Music for Crumhorns* 2. 24 pieces in 5 & 6 parts. London Pro Musica Edition, LPM MCR2.
> *Music for Crumhorns* 3. 33 pieces in 3, 4, & 5 parts. London Pro Musica Edition, LPM MCR3.
> *Crumhorn Consort Anthology* (Vols. 1–3). 43 pieces for four instruments. Musica Rara, MR 1902, 1903, 1565.
> *Music for Crumhorns.*15 pieces in 4–6 parts and *Crumhorn Collections* (3 vols.). 31 pieces for ATTB, ed. David Hogan Smith. The King's Trumpetts and Shalmes Music Editions, 1720 19th Avenue, San Francisco, CA 94122.
> *At the Sign of the Crumhorn: Anthology for an Ensemble of Crumhorns, Recorders, Shawms, or Curtals* SATB, N.M. 148, ed. Block & Nothnagle. London: Nova Music, 1980.
> *Crumhorn Consort Music.* Vols. I, II, III (Harriman), and IV (Neumann) for SATB. Musica Sacra et Profana (out of print).

Many of the Susato dances and pieces from Michael Praetorius's *Terpsichore* fit a crumhorn ensemble, but transposition is often necessary. It should also be noted here that Praetorius occasionally recommends pieces with ranges that are not always obtainable on the crumhorn, suggesting that adjustments must have been common at the time.

Large-scale polychoral works are also quite effective when one of the choirs is performed on crumhorns. Many of the compositions by Italian composers of the late sixteenth century, as well as by the Germans who were influenced by them, work well with crumhorns in combination with choirs of sackbuts, viols, curtals, flutes, recorders, and voices.

Mention should be made of two other members of the capped reed family, both restricted to German-speaking lands: the Kortholt or Kurzpfeif (meaning "short wood" or "short pipe") and the Schreierpfeife (appropriately, shouting or shrieking pipe—also spelled Schreyerpfeife).

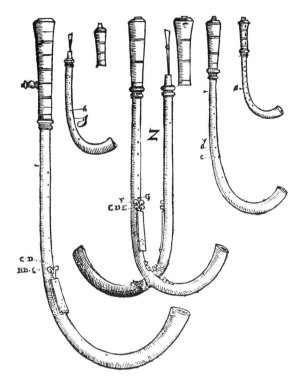

FIGURE 6.1 Crumhorns
Praetorius, *Syntagma musicum* II, Plate XIII

As in the case of the crumhorn the Kortholt gets its name from its appearance. It is a short "woodwind" instrument, but its size, like that of the racket, is deceiving, for inside the wooden cylinder the tubing doubles back on itself, thus causing the sound to be decidedly lower than expected. The Kortholt has twelve open fingerholes and two closed (keyed) holes for upward extension by two pitches. The tips of the fingers and thumbs are used to cover ten of the open holes, and the sides of the index fingers must be employed to cover the remaining two holes. Praetorius depicts only one Kortholt in his *Syntagma Musicum* II, but it is included with a set of Sorduns—a seemingly identical instrument, but without the windcap—and in the range chart for Sorduns as well. Based on this slim evidence, modern makers have extrapolated a family of Kortholts. The sound is soft and pleasing, and because of its extended range, it can serve as the 8-foot foundation of a recorder choir or play a part a bass crumhorn could otherwise not play.

The Schreierpfeife dates from the end of the fifteenth century and is nothing other than a capped shawm. It is an excruciatingly loud instrument due to its expanding conical bore and the fact that you have no choice but to blow as hard as you can in order to attain some semblance of intonation. "Strong and fresh" are the adjectives Praetorius uses to describe the sound, but "loud and raucous" or "coarse and strident" might be more appropriate. There are seven fingerholes and a thumbhole, and the range is basically a ninth, but by leaking the index finger on the left hand a bit, it is possible to increase the range by as much as a fourth. These must have been popular outdoor instruments, as their use has been documented into the late seventeenth century. It should be pointed out that prior to Boydell's exhaustive study of capped-reed instruments, the Schreierpfeife was known as the Rauschpfeife. It is also interesting to note that Praetorius's depiction of Schreierpfeifen seems to have been a mistake, since it does not square with the rest of the evidence.

Bibliography

Baines–*Woodwind*; Bartlett/Holman–Giovanni; Boydell–*Crumhorn*; Hantelmann–*How*; Hunt–*Crumhorn*; MacMillan–Crumhorn; Meyer–*Crumhorn*; Smith–*Reed*; Stanley–Reed; Thomas–Introduction; Thomas–Playing; Wells–Crumhorn.

Suggested Listening

Music of the Middle Ages and the Renaissance. David Munrow. Angel Records SBZ-3810 (1976).

Praetorius: Terpsichore. New London Consort, Philip Pickett, director. L'oiseau-Lyre CD 414 633–2 (1986).

7

Shawm and Curtal

Ross W. Duffin

Perhaps the first and most important point is that the shawm was through-out its history the property of the professional, specialist player. Its value was its thrilling sound, audible even at crowded indoor gatherings and large outdoor events. Its exclusivity was probably due to the sheer difficulty of playing—something that has served to keep it out of most modern early-music groups in spite of its importance. This is not the kind of instrument that can be picked up easily in the middle of a concert by a student player who has just put down a recorder. Nevertheless, the sound of a shawm band perfectly in tune is one of the most satisfying musical experiences a wind player can have, and the instrument's resurrection by conscientious directors and courageous students is to be hailed as long overdue.

Generally, smallish shawms are shown in depictions as early as the thirteenth century, such as in the *Cantigas de Santa Maria*, but the pictorial and documentary evidence points to the middle of the fourteenth century as the beginning of the instrument's heyday. The glory days lasted until about 1500 when the supremacy of the shawm band began to be challenged by the more refined cornett and sackbut band. Shawms underwent the same kind of size development enjoyed by other instruments in the sixteenth century but at the high end they began to lose ground to the more agile cornett, and at the low end to the more portable dulcian or curtal (see below). As instruments of the town bands (which also sometimes played in the churches), they lasted well into the seventeenth century in some places, notably Spain, Germany, and England.

The function of the shawm band was to play for dancing, banquets, ceremonies, processions, and so on. The greatest difficulty in reconstructing what they played is that the bulk of the repertory during the heyday of the instrument seems to have been improvised. This is evident, for example, in the dozens of long-note tenor melodies of the fifteenth-century *basse danse*. We have a few reports of them playing part music too, including motets and chansons, so these are the starting point for the written repertory, although presumably performances of these normally vocal forms were probably purely instrumental when shawms took part. The exception to this rule was in Spain where shawms were respected denizens of the choir lofts of the great cathedrals, and thus likely participants in all the music making that took place there (more on this subject in Kreitner–Minstrels).

The following are typical trio combinations for shawms in consort and with associated instruments:

pre–1400
    treble, straight trumpet, drums
    2 trebles, 1 bagpipe
post–1400
    3 equal (trebles or altos)
    2 trebles, one alto (most likely a fifth below)
    2 trebles, one slide trumpet
    1 treble, two altos
    1 treble, 1 alto, 1 slide trumpet (after ca. 1470, a sackbut)

Four-voice combinations in the early decades (to ca. 1450) are complicated by the apparent use of a spare fourth player, clearly shown not playing, who must have alternated with one or more of the other players for reasons of endurance. This fourth player adds a treble, an alto, or a slide trumpet to any of the ensembles in the post–1400 list above. In fact, this supernumerary principle seems to have lasted into the sixteenth century, since Keith Polk's study of Flemish wind bands shows almost invariably one more member of the ensemble than was the standard number of parts in written music at the time.

One problem of terminology related to sizes of instruments is in the use of the designations "alto" and "tenor." Instruments larger than what we now call the alto were rare before 1500, but the term "tenor" occurs from the early fifteenth century to describe the alto shawm (also known as the "bombarde" or "Pommer") because of the function that the instrument filled in the ensemble. This confusion persisted throughout the sixteenth century in some places. The true larger sizes began to appear in the early sixteenth century, and by about 1550 there seems to have been a proper bass (in F with extension keys down to C). With such an instrument, or perhaps a basset (a tenor in C with extension keys down to G), a fully equipped shawm band might consist of one or two trebles, one or two altos, one or two sackbuts, and one basset or bass shawm. This combination should work well as a resource for all otherwise suitable ensemble music up to six voices written to around 1600. (Praetorius also includes a *klein discant Schalmey*, which is a fifth higher than the treble). I might mention also at this point the reason for combining brass instruments with shawms in the loud band: there is something about the brass that "knits" the ensemble sound together and makes it easier to tune. Obviously, since a brass instrument regularly joined the band from an early date, late medieval and Renaissance musicians thought so, too.

Such an ideal shawm band may not have been a frequent occurrence in the Renaissance because in the early sixteenth century cornetts and Schreierpfeifen (windcap shawms, often formerly referred to as Rauschpfeifen) began to make appearances in the loud band. The former work very well if a balance can be achieved, but the latter invite disaster, in my view. The tone color and tuning of Schreierpfeifen are not easily matched with shawms in spite of their ostensible similarity as loud double-reed instruments. A more successful double-reed newcomer was the dulcian or curtal, introduced in the second half of the sixteenth century and serving in the shawm band as a kind of "folded" bass.

Of all problems in making a shawm band work (after the reeds are adjusted and functioning), the most fundamental is that of ensemble pitch. I'm not talking about a' = 440 versus a' = 460 or any such pitch standard. I'm talking about standard transpositions. Baines, Polk, and Myers have established that the shawm band, by convention, transposed all its written music up a whole step or a perfect fifth. This is related to the pitches of most of the surviving originals, which tend to be in D for the trebles and G for the altos. Thus, if you have shawms at those pitches, you will find that in order to accommodate the ranges of the instruments, you must follow one or the other of these transposition formulas or almost none of the music fits: it goes one or two notes too low, or seems to require a larger size of shawm. Not all modern makers produce D trebles and G altos, however. If you have C and F instruments, you will still find that much repertory will open up if you cultivate the ability to transpose up a fourth, particularly for the period up to 1500. (If you have some odd combination of D & G and C & F instruments, I doubt if you can make it work.) Sackbut players will get used to whatever transpositions you use regularly; they're a durable breed, already used to reading three or four different clefs anyway.

One advantage of shawms is that they are fairly tough compared with other Renaissance woodwinds; the great wall-thickness means that cracking is rare. The obvious difficulty is in the making of reeds. Modern shawms vary a lot in design and therefore in the reed design required to get the best out of the instrument. The best idea is to follow the maker's advice, using any supplied reeds as a model for future efforts. (Try not to modify a maker's reed that works as advertised, and by all means, don't throw it out when it dies!) Unlike oboe reeds, shawm reeds can last a long time (months or years) if nursed along. When the time comes to make new ones, find a clever bassoon reed maker if you are not experienced in this yourself. Bassoon reed makers tend to be especially adept at experimenting, and are used to working with the larger sizes of cane normally required for shawms. (One useful tip for the reed maker is to try a thinner gouge.)

There is no easy way to prepare shawm players except to get them to play a lot. Endurance is the main thing. Fingerings are not a problem for someone already used to playing other Renaissance woodwinds, but for the inexperienced player, chops give out sooner in performance than in rehearsal. The repertory can encompass the same range as that of the Renaissance recorders (i.e. about a thirteenth per part), although the instruments are most comfortable up to about an eleventh or twelfth. Virtually all sixteenth-century dance collections up to Holborne's work well. I do not recommend Brade or Praetorius simply because too many of the phrases are uncomfortably long for loud wind players. The early sixteenth-century chanson, Lieder, and frottola repertories are also fertile territory. Perhaps the most exciting and idiomatic but also the most challenging possibilities are in the late fifteenth-century Franco-Flemish instrumental *carminum* repertory for three to four voices (sometimes five). Written pieces in an improvisatory style are probably the relics of what shawm bands did most up to the early sixteenth century.

Curtal

Curtal is the sixteenth-century English name for the instrument the Germans knew as the Dulzian and which has therefore been commonly known as the Dulcian, without any historical foundation whatever. Other sixteenth-century names for the same instrument include the fagotto (Italy), the Fagott (German), the basson (French), and the baxon or bajon (Spain). The curtal seems to have originated around the middle of the sixteenth century although the exact time and place are obscure. Like other Renaissance instruments, it achieved a complete family of sizes. Praetorius (*Syntagma* II) gives several sizes, the smallest with a sounding length approximately equal to the alto shawm but much smaller in overall length due to the fact that the bore doubles back on itself. The largest instrument he mentions is a *Fagotcontra*, with a sounding length twice as long as the bass shawm. In spite of this size proliferation, there was really only one size in general use: what Praetorius calls the *Choristfagott*—a bass with a bottom note of C (two octaves below middle c, the same bottom note as the bass shawm). This helps to explain why, as mentioned above, one of the uses of the curtal was as the bass of the shawm band: it was more portable. This was an important consideration in a band whose duties often took it outdoors!

But the curtal was capable of a much more subtle sound than the bass shawm, and for this reason it found a place, not just in the shawm band, but also in the cornett and sackbut band, in mixed ensembles with strings, as a foundation doubling the lowest sounding voice in choral groups, and ultimately as a popular continuo instrument, particularly with organ. Its use in these capacities lasted well into the eighteenth century, although no examples are known to have survived dated after circa 1707. By that time, the curtal was beginning to be supplanted by its jointed successor, the bassoon, which had a larger serviceable range over a sounding length that was only slightly larger.

There are two basic categories of curtal: open (*offen*) and stopped (*gedackt*). The stopped instrument has a perforated cap in the bell at the top of the instrument, giving it something of the appearance of an overgrown pepper shaker. This has a softening effect on the sound, although curtals have a good dynamic range anyway as is evident in the variety of their uses. Probably as significant in terms of tone is the variance in bell size, some of which are fairly conical and others substantially flared. The choice of instrument for your ensemble should, to some extent, take into account its intended use: conical/stopped for softer uses; flared/open for louder ones. Basically, the message is that the curtal in its most common size, the *Choristfagott*, is an extremely useful addition to any instrumentarium for performance of music from circa 1550 to circa 1650 and beyond. Of course, many performers, including some professionals, use the curtal for earlier repertory as well, rationalizing that it is a bass shawm substitute.

Like any instrument with a bocal, there is potential for swift and irreversible disaster through mishandling. The bocal is the most sensitive acoustical part of the instrument; a poorly designed bocal can ruin the tone, tuning,

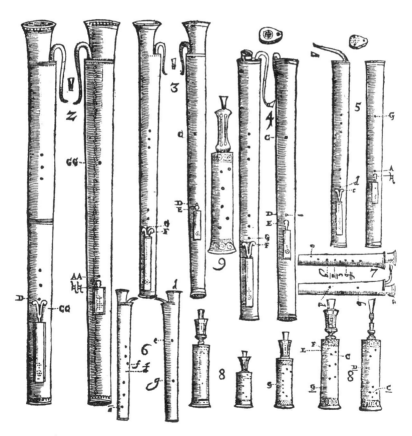

FIGURE 7.1 Curtals and Rackets
Praetorius, *Syntagma musicum* II, Plate X

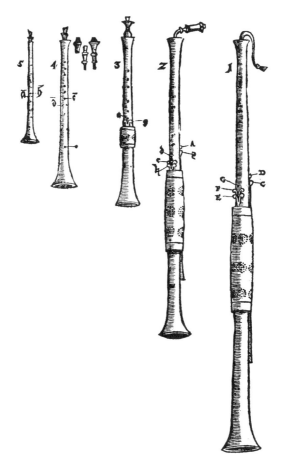

FIGURE 7.2 Shawms
Praetorius, *Syntagma musicum*, II, Plate XI

and articulation of an otherwise well-constructed horn. The curtal's reed design is even closer to the modern bassoon than to that of the shawm, so bassoon reed makers will easily succeed once they learn to make the reeds big enough. Bassoon players make excellent conscripts as players, by the way, finding their way around the double-bore fingering system with ease, and reveling in the simplicity of the keywork.

Bibliography

There are few books and articles about the shawm and curtal, and what exists are sometimes difficult to obtain.

Baines–Shawm; Langwill–Bassoon; Lorraine–Handbook; Myers–Practical; Myers–Musical; Polk–Flemish; Smith–*Reed*; Stanley–Reed; Stanley-Lyndon-Jones–*Curtal*.

Suggested Listening

The material for listening unfortunately matches that for reference in terms of availability. Aside from a few selections in instrumental survey recordings and elsewhere, for shawm band I recommend:

Italienische Instrumentalmusik der Frührenaissance. Schola cantorum Basiliensis Documenta. Alta capella und Citharedi der Schola cantorum Basiliensis. German Harmonia Mundi 1C 065 16 9558 1.

Ménéstrels Hauts et Bas: The Renaissance Wind Band in the Age of Josquin. Boston Shawm and Sackbut Ensemble. Privately produced commercial recording available from Dan Stillman, 32 Corinthian Road, Somerville MA, 02144.

These are the only two that passed the test of unlimited repeated hearings by a certain three-year-old fanatical shawm connoisseur. For curtal, good recordings include:

Heinrich Schütz: Symphoniæ Sacræ, Op. 6 (1629). Selections. Musicalische Compagney. Arion ARN 38604, or MHS 4703F. There are other fine recordings of seventeenth-century works by this group, including MDGG 1229 and MDGG 1230.

Kammermusik am Hofe Kaiser Leopolds I. Concerto Castello. EMI Reflexe 1C 069 1466971. (Mid-17th century)

Lo splendore d'Italia. The Whole Noyse. Intrada 11 58602 (1993). Look for a release of the same title from Musical Heritage Society. This is the only group I know that uses curtal with cornetts and sackbuts in the performance of late Renaissance repertory; other combinations include recorders, Renaissance flutes, and different mixtures with viola, shawm, and gittern—not at the same time, of course.

8

Racket

(Rackett, Rankett [Ger.], Cervelas [Fr.], Cervello [It.])

Jeffery Kite-Powell

Relatively little is known about the history of the lowest woodwind family of the Renaissance. The common practice of Renaissance organ builders to copy the actual sound of real instruments provides us with the first evidence of the existence of the racket in 1564, the date of an organ with a register called *Rancket*. The instrument must have existed prior to this date, however, in order for its sound to have been copied, but there is no factual account of it until Praetorius's description of the family in his *Syntagma musicum* II of 1619. The racket is found on inventory lists in the last two decades of the sixteenth century, and it is pictured being played in an illuminated manuscript of Lassus's "orchestra" from about 1570 and in an ivory carving dating from 1618 to 1624.

For its size the racket produces perhaps the most surprising sound of all the Renaissance instruments. The largest racket, the contrabass, is shorter than an alto recorder and about the same size around as a bass recorder, but the lowest sound it produces is that of the contrabassoon—a sub-contra B♭ (an octave lower than the B♭ below the bass staff). It seems impossible that an instrument so small can emit such low tones, but appearances can be deceiving. Inside this nearly foot-long cylinder peppered with holes all around it is a labyrinth of tubing, which, if stretched out, would reach approximately nine feet in length. The tubing—nine sections in all—is cylindrical in bore and connected alternately at the top and bottom. Holes must be carefully drilled in the wall of the outside container so that they penetrate the proper tube at the correct location and thereby produce the desired pitch—an unusual demonstration of Renaissance technological "know-how."

Its German name (Rankett, from *ranken* to wind around) may be an attempt to describe its inner workings. Its nickname, "sausage bassoon," derives from the Italian *Cervello* and the German *Wurstfagott*.

Praetorius's account of the racket family is hardly flattering. He complains about its sound as comparable to a comb kazoo and states that as a consort, there is no special charm. Combined with viols, however, the sound is pleasing, especially a single bass racket in the hands of a master, together with other winds or strings.

In all, he discusses and depicts four sizes (*Syntagma* II, p. 39 and Plate X: Curtals and Rackets [see page 73 for Plate X]). Modern rackets have the following ranges:

cantus F–d′
tenor/alt B♭–g
bass F$_1$/–d
great bass B♭$_1$–G

It only takes a few moments to become accustomed to the fingering system of a racket, once you realize that your hands must be *next* to each other and not *one above the other*. As with other Renaissance wind instruments, recorder fingerings, with occasional modifications, will serve you well on the racket. If you have experience with the extended notes on the curtal, kortholt, and extended shawms, you will have no trouble playing the lower notes on the racket. If this should all be new to you, a fingering chart and a bit of practice will be necessary.

Perhaps the most unusual aspect of racket finger technique is the need to utilize the sides of both index fingers as well as the pads. Altogether there are twelve fingerholes on a racket, so unless you have two extra fingers, you will need to cover the added holes (fitted with small protrusions called "tetines" or "teats" on most modern instruments, but which originally were found only on Baroque rackets) with the sides of your index fingers in a wrapping maneuver, keeping the ends or pads of the fingers on their holes all the while.

Unlike the Baroque racket the Renaissance racket was provided with a pirouette. This differed in construction from that of the shawm, however; because of the racket's much larger reed, its pirouette envelops proportionately more of the reed blade, placing the embouchure at an optimum position for control. In fact, an experienced player using a good reed can extend the range upward by a third or fourth by regulating embouchure pressure on the reed.

For someone just beginning a double-reed instrument, the first several practice sessions should be devoted to playing long, sustained notes. Do not attempt to play the lowest notes until the left-hand notes can be played with ease. Once this has been accomplished, you can begin adding the notes of the right hand until eventually you can play all notes, including those in the extended range. Never let the fingers stray too far from the fingerholes, lest you have difficulty finding them quickly when you need them. More difficult material should only be attempted after an acceptable tone quality has been achieved, and no music written prior to about 1550 should be played, as the instrument would not have existed. Music written after the mid-seventeenth century is best played on a Baroque racket (which was in fact a bassoon in the shape of a racket, developed by J. C. Denner at the close of the seventeenth century).

As with any reed instrument, the reed must be soaked in a small container of water for a few minutes before being used. If it is not soaked sufficiently, the blades may not vibrate freely enough to produce the proper sound. In addition, a lack of water absorption may cause an air leak along one of the sides, which will result in faulty tone production. Playing on a dry reed may cause it to crack or split, rendering it unfit for further use. Making, repairing, and adjusting double reeds requires special tools and materials and is best left to those who work with reeds on a regular basis such as bassoonists and oboists (see Smith–*Reed*).

The fact that the racket is not an open-ended instrument means that water condensation collects inside the tubing and cannot run out freely. After long periods of playing, an annoying gurgling sound may occur. The best way to purge the instrument of this water is to remove the reed, cover all the fingerholes except the upper left tetine, hold the instrument upside down, and blow into the center hole where the reed staple goes. (Be prepared for a shower!)

The contrabass or bass racket is a wonderful instrument with which to double a bass line for additional weight and support in the performance of polychoral or otherwise large-scale works. If you should have a consort of rackets (and the players to match), the four-part hymns by late Renaissance and early Baroque composers provide ideal literature. (In particular, see M. Praetorius's *Musæ Sioniæ*, Teil VI.)

The only method book for rackets on the market at the present time is by Steinkopf/Kernbach–*Directions*. Further information can be obtained from the article on the racket by W. Waterhouse in the *New Grove Instrument Dictionary*, 3: 185. (See the Crumhorn chapter for suggested listening.)

9

Cornett

Douglas Kirk

During its heyday, the high Renaissance and early Baroque, the cornett was considered the wind instrument of choice for virtuoso treble parts. It possessed a flexibility of color, dynamic range, and expression then unmatched by any other wind instrument except perhaps the trombone, its usual partner in the tenor and bass registers. A hybrid of brass and woodwind characteristics, the cornett is sounded by the player buzzing his lips into a mouthpiece (either separable or inseparable from the rest of the instrument) connected to a conically bored wooden tube vented by seven fingerholes. Like most other instruments during the Renaissance, the cornett customarily came in a family of different sizes. However, unlike other families of instruments, the cornett also appeared in three different forms, each with particular sonic and regional patterns of use. Nearly all modern discussions have concentrated on the most common modern form, the curved cornett, to the relative exclusion of the straight cornett (*cornetto diritto*) and the mute cornett (*cornetto muto*). Thus, the following brief historical survey, while not attempting to replace standard organological texts, will attempt to redress the imbalance somewhat.[1]

Historical Survey

Up to the Early Sixteenth Century

From early times through the Middle Ages, horns crafted from animal horns or ivory tusks were played. These are depicted frequently enough in art through the fifteenth century (Virdung even shows one in 1511) to assume that they must have been used at least occasionally for serious music making. At some time during the fifteenth century a craftsman (probably in southern Germany)[2] designed a more sophisticated version of the fingerhole horn, probably straight (and therefore turnable on a lathe), with a longer body and seven fingerholes so that it possessed all the diatonic and chromatic notes up to the overblown octave. What is not clear from fifteenth-century representations is the nature of the mouthpiece—whether it was carved into the end of the instrument like that of the sixteenth-century mute cornett or whether it was detachable. And to further confuse the picture, curved varieties are also seen, although they sometimes have irregular numbers of fingerholes.

The *cornetto diritto* maintained its popularity in northern Europe, especially Germany, until well into the sixteenth century. It is clearly illustrated by Virdung and others.[3] Although the *cornetto diritto* is almost totally absent from collections of surviving historical instruments, this should not prejudice us against using modern reproductions in early sixteenth-century repertory. This absence is more likely a result of the early form gradually wearing out and being replaced by the next developmental stage.

Sixteenth-century Developments

This next stage was represented by the curved instrument, the "classical" cornett that survives in instrument collections today. The famed Nuremberg instrument maker Jorg Neuschel referred to these instruments in a letter from 1541 as "*welsche krumme Zincken,*" as if he thought them to be of French or Italian origin. My own theory is that they were a development of Venetian workshops, most likely that of Hieronymus Bassano, probably working together with the noted *piffaro* of the time, M. Andrea, whom we know as the source of at least some of the cornetts in the Accademia Filarmonica collection in Verona. Certainly by the mid-sixteenth century, Venetian cornetts were famous all over Europe and had revolutionized the standards of instrument making and playing.

However, the curved cornett was not the sole member of the family during this time. The mute cornett was produced alongside it and was presumably played by the same players, although in different instrumental settings. While curved cornetts were played with sackbuts and other loud instruments alone or *colla parte* with voices, mute cornetts were much more likely played with strings (either plucked or bowed) or harpsichords. Although infrequently used in modern concerts, mute cornetts were common at the time, as evidenced by the major instrument collections in Brussels, Leipzig, Berlin, Paris, Verona, and Vienna, where there are almost as many surviving mute cornetts as curved ones.

By the mid-sixteenth century the normal cornett (Italian: *cornetto*; German: *Chorzink*), which was usually pitched in g, had been extended downward by a tone to produce an instrument in f and downward by a fifth to produce the lowest member of the family. The English called it "lysarden" because of its S-shaped, lizard-like form, without which the notes of the right hand would be unreachable.[4] And even with the curve, many lysarden were fitted with a key at the lower end to facilitate the playing of the lowest note (c). During most of the sixteenth century the lysarden was considered the lowest member of the cornett family and is referred to by Italian instrument makers as a *cornetto basso*. However, by the early seventeenth century, the family had clearly been completed with a true bass cornett (as distinct from a serpent, which with its much wider bore and different fingering system differs considerably from the cornett); two surviving bass cornetts may be found in the Paris Conservatory collection. Coming as it did near the end of the cornett's Italian heyday, we cannot be sure how widely used the bass cornett was. However, there is ample evidence that the tenor cornett (also called a lysarden or *cornetto basso*)—referred to by Praetorius and Mersenne (although the latter calls it a bass instrument)—was not just a curiously shaped, out-of-tune joke. First, as with the mute cornett, a lot of them survive in European collections, particularly those with strong ties to Italian origins, such as Brussels and Verona. Second, there are actual reports of its ownership and use by serious musical organizations of the sixteenth century, like the Norwich and Exeter waites, and at the Medici court in Florence. Third, there is the musical evidence of scores known to have been played by unspecified sizes of cornetts that are simply too low to have been played by the normal *cornetto*. Here we might list pieces that specify "Zink" in the partbooks from the Danish court (ca. 1540), several parts in the various Florentine *intermedi*, reported to have been performed by cornetts,[5] and even musical works originating in the Veneto region of Italy. For example, the third cornett part in Monteverdi's *Vespers* of 1610, when the "Magnificat" is transposed down a fourth, features prominent low gs.[6] Thus, the second (and certainly any third) cornett of the standard Italian wind ensemble around 1600 was probably either an "alto" cornett in f or a *cornetto basso*. It was this sort of group, composed in part of Girolamo dalla Casa, Giovanni Bassano, dalla Casa's two brothers (one on trombone), and others, that was active at San Marco in Venice all through Giovanni Gabrieli's career there.[7] A few years later the German wind ensembles replaced the low cornett on the alto voice-line with an alto sackbut, providing a brighter sound; the Italians, on the other hand, seem to have preferred more mellow scoring. Other Italian preferences that emphasized mellow, softer timbres will be discussed below under Embouchures.

When one reads reports of sixteenth-century performances or archival material on English waites and German Stadtpfeifer, the striking impression is just how conservative tastes were and how late instrument acquisitions often came. Certainly, it is clear that the primary instruments for loud outdoor playing—particularly of dance repertory—remained an ensemble of shawms and sackbuts until after the middle of the sixteenth century. Cornetts may have participated here, and doubtless sometimes did, but their usual documented use was accompanying voices, playing motets and chorales, or accompanying other polyphonic liturgical music.

Golden Age of the Cornett in Italy

The real golden age of the cornett in Italy was brief: approximately 1575 to 1630. It was during this time that nearly all the flashy canzona repertory so often associated with the cornett was composed. Impressive though this repertory is, it is important to keep in perspective how small the group of real virtuosi was. They were nearly all active at San Marco in Venice or San Petronio in Bologna, and there was only a handful of them. Even at that time, the Italians often preferred the viola bastarda or the violin for real displays of virtuosity. In Venice, particularly, the use of the cornett declined relatively early, after the deaths of Dalla Casa (1601) and Bassano (1617). By the 1640s, it had been absent from San Marco "for some time,"[8] although the instrument was reintroduced later in the century, and a certain amount of difficult music was written for it.

The Cornett Outside Italy

The cornett was also actively cultivated until the early eighteenth century in Germany, England, and Spain and its Latin American colonies. In England, it was popular at the royal court, in the cathedrals and collegiate chapels, and among city waites until the reign of Cromwell effectively silenced music-making. It appeared again after the Restoration and saw some use until about 1700. In seventeenth-century Spain the cornett continued to be used, along with the vihuela, harp, sackbut, organ, and especially the curtal, for the support of choirs in cathedrals and monastic churches. However, it does not seem to have been used much for popular, semireligious music like the sacred villancicos. In any case, the shawm remained the most popular instrument for church and minstrel use.

In Germany the situation was different. Here the cornett was widely employed by the Stadtpfeifer as a treble instrument in the company of sackbuts. In large part this was because it could sound trumpet-like and yet play diatonically in a lower register than the natural trumpet in use at the time. Even more important, it was not subject to the severe playing restrictions that court trumpet charters placed on trumpet players. The Stadtpfeifer and the Italians of the time approached the instrument in the same manner they approached the trumpet. Compositions of this period placed much more emphasis on trumpet-like arpeggiations than did earlier works, and they were written much more often in the clarino register. Whereas Italian compositions between the years 1580–1620 keep the instrument mostly within the range of c'-a" (never ascending higher than c'''), Praetorius (1619) lists the instrument's range as ascending to d''', and says that some players could reach a''''! The cornettino (in c or d, a fourth or fifth higher than the standard cornett) is also associated particularly with Germany. While it may have been known in Italy, it is never called for or referred to there. References to it and scores calling for it become rather frequent in seventeenth-century Germany, and its bright, almost shrill sound seems to be better suited to that repertory than to the mellower earlier Italian scoring. The Germans also made use of the mute cornett, although usually in a rather more Italianate mixed scoring. There are also surviving mute cornettini.

Although the German repertory includes some wonderful literature for the cornett, after 1700 the instrument is rarely called for in a solo capacity. Pieces such as the Fux *Sonata a quattro* of 1708 and the obbligato part in J. S. Bach's *cantata No. 118* are real exceptions. Otherwise, the instrument returns to its original function of accompanying choirs (for example, in Bach motets or in *cantata No. 4*) or playing tower music. Even this came to consist more and more of chorales, instead of the virtuoso *Turmmusik* of Pezel and his contemporaries. It finally fell into total disuse in the nineteenth century.

Range

Praetorius gives the following ranges for the various members of the cornett family:

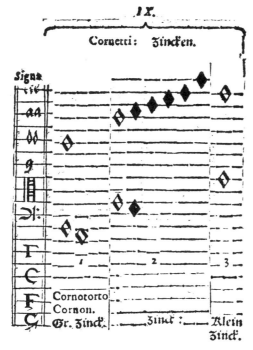

FIGURE 9.1 Cornett ranges
Praetorius: *Syntagma musicum* II, p. 22

The modern cornettino is built in c instead of d. This means that its lowest fingered note is d′ and not the e′ that Praetorius shows. The modern-day cornett, however, corresponds exactly to its seventeenth-century counterpart in range. The low g shown by Praetorius is (as described by him) a falsetto note below the normal range, produced by a very focused embouchure and air stream. Practicing this note, and even others below it, is very beneficial to the embouchure generally, and is something that should be incorporated into the daily workout of all cornettists. The notes from a″ to c‴ are called for in the more virtuosic repertory from Giovanni Gabrieli onwards. The d‴ becomes important in the German seventeenth-century repertory or in untransposed performances of the Monteverdi *Vespers*. Notes above that should be practiced as a means of increasing the player's control over the high register.

Mute cornetts are built both in g and f (with a and g respectively as their lowest notes), and Praetorius shows no special range for them. While both original instruments and modern reproductions will play notes above the staff, the fingerings often become highly irregular above g″ or a″ because of the conical, horn-like bore. This is not really a problem because the register most suited to their real repertory lies well below this (usually up to e″ or f″), and it is in this lower and middle range that they produce their most characteristic sound.

The *cornetto basso* range shown by Praetorius is duplicated by modern reproductions, with the exception of a small-bore "tenor" in resin (formerly made by Christopher Monk), which does not come close to producing all of the lower notes. Indeed, that instrument has so many peculiarities that players would be well advised to avoid it altogether. However, the large-bore instrument by the same maker is very good, if not often somewhat sharp in overall pitch.

Tuning

Instruments with Adjustable Length

For all cornetts with separable mouthpieces, the only tuning adjustment is by positioning the mouthpiece farther out in its receiver to compensate for sharpness of pitch, or closer in if the instrument is flat. However, one cannot adjust very much in this fashion before the instrument goes out of tune internally (that is, some notes of the scale will be affected more than others), as is the case with all other woodwinds.

Tuning isolated notes that are out of tune with respect to surrounding notes in the scale is accomplished by increasing or decreasing the size of fingerholes (usually the first open hole nearest the mouthpiece). However, one can quickly make drastic changes in an instrument by modifying the holes, and it is not recommended unless the person plays well himself or is working with someone who does. A word of caution: unlike recorders, cornetts are not improved by substantial undercutting of fingerholes because this destabilizes the pitch on expanding conical bores. Some slight undercutting is beneficial for reducing turbulence in the airstream where fingerholes meet the bore, but one should beware of instruments with "dished out," highly undercut fingerholes because the maker is trying to compensate for a faulty bore profile.

Questions of Temperament

Cornetts are usually tuned with equal temperament in mind. They often benefit, however, if the maker is capable of tuning the instrument in meantone or Just Intonation. The g♯′ is nearly always flat, and by tuning the f♯′ slightly flat, one will help insure that the f′ does not come out too sharp. C♯′s and d♯′s can be controlled through the amount of fork-fingering used, but one should take special care that c′ and c″ in the first two octaves are not sharp with the unforked fingering (•●●●/●○○). Having to add a fork (•●●●/●○●) is deleterious to the tone quality of the note. The notes e′ and e″ should not be tuned too flat (as pure major thirds above c′ and c″), for this will make them more difficult to play as pure fifths above a and a′. Also, in the case of e″, this will widen an already wide half-step between the e″ and f″ (the latter played •●●●/●●● or •●●○/●●●). Even though this harmonic fingered f″ tends to be rather sharp on most modern reproductions (the result of improper scaling of the bore from higher-pitched original instruments), it is aurally preferable to the very dull sound of •●○●/○○○ in that octave. (Note that this is not necessarily the case on mute cornetts.)

Tuning Mute Cornetts

Mute cornetts present somewhat different problems, since they don't have separable mouthpieces with which to adjust the pitch. They really need to be built in-tune; out-of-tune instruments (sharp instruments in particular) are worthless in the heat of performance. Lowering the pitch of a sharp instrument can be accomplished by having the cup of the mouthpiece deepened by two or three millimeters. If the instrument is very sharp, or if the player is inclined to use mouthpieces of larger internal rim diameter on his curved instrument, one can have the mute cornett mouthpiece deepened at the throat and enlarged at the rim at the same time. This can bring down the pitch of the instrument by 5–10 Hz, depending on the amount of modification. Individual notes can be tuned by adjusting the first open hole for the particular fingering. One should beware of drastic undercutting to raise pitch, as the undercutting will greatly destabilize the instrument.

Mouthpieces

Probably the greatest single source of problems with cornetts is not related to the instruments themselves, but to the mouthpieces. Unfortunately, bad mouthpieces abound—particularly with instruments more than a few years old. The kinds of problems caused range from merely an unfocused sound to wide octaves—that is, flat low-register and sharp high-register notes. The only solution for a bad mouthpiece is to replace it with a good one. Every player needs a choice of mouthpieces. This is just as true for cornetts as it is for modern brass instruments; in fact, probably more so. If your cornett was made by Christopher Monk (whose shop has now been taken over by Jeremy West), whose resin mouthpieces are easily available and inexpensive, order at least ten with the instrument (twenty or thirty if possible) and then take your time sampling them all. Forget the compromise trumpet and horn cups. They never produce a good, focused sound. Instead, request a sampling of his various "acorn" cup models. Other good mouthpiece makers for cornett include Graham Nicholson (Basel), Bruno Tilz, and John McCann.

Care and Precautions

Plastic Instruments

The plastic (resin) instruments are exceptionally durable, and should last a lifetime when given the slightest amount of care. They should *never* be dropped or struck on anything hard, or exposed to heat (such as leaving them in the sun in a closed car or on a heater). Also, students should *never* be allowed to leave mouthpieces in the instruments between playing sessions, and in the interest of good hygiene, the instruments should be swabbed out after playing. For this, trimmed-down recorder or bassoon swabs work well for the instrument and pipe cleaners for the mouthpiece throats and backbores.

Incidentally, I would recommend buying plastic instruments with a leather covering rather than without. The leather gives a less slippery surface and thus a more secure grip and also imparts some additional strength to the resin in case the instrument is dropped.

Wooden Instruments

It should be obvious that instruments made of wood need somewhat more care than those of plastic. They should be swabbed out religiously after playing and lightly oiled periodically. Just how often this should be done is the question. Generally, one should follow the directions of the maker; however, my view as a player is that it is not hard to tell when the instrument needs oiling. It will tell you itself by producing a slightly more diffuse sound and by being more prone to water absorption. I usually oil more in winter than in summer because that is when wood tends to dry out most. Use a light oil, such as almond or peanut oil, rather than something like linseed oil, which leaves deposits in the bore, and let the instrument dry out for a day (no playing) before oiling it.

Since wooden instruments are traditionally made of two lengthwise halves glued together, one needs to do everything possible to maintain the strength and integrity of the glued joint. Never use a swab that is too big for the instrument, never force the mouthpiece into place, and never subject the instrument to extremes of temperature that will crack the wood (especially, never allow the instrument to freeze).

Leather can be maintained just like fine shoes: use a dubbin compound or even black shoe polish from time to time.

Mute Cornetts

Mute cornetts require one special bit of attention that is critical. Since their mouthpieces are a part of the instrument and are fragile, they must be protected—particularly the rim. It is worth the trouble to make a protective cap (I hollow out champagne-bottle corks for this) to put over the end of the mouthpiece when the instrument is not being played.

Otherwise, care is about the same as for wooden, curved instruments: swabbing and oiling. The swab for the mouthpiece end of a mute cornett will need to be very small. I find that bassoon bocal swabs are perfect for this (although they sometimes need to be trimmed down in diameter). Don't neglect oiling the mouthpiece cup.

Basic Technical Considerations

Embouchure

It is important to the cornettist of today to consider the kinds of embouchure used by cornettists historically, as they had a substantial impact on playing technique.

There is ample pictorial evidence and one surviving treatise of Italian origin that discusses cornett technique; these indicate that Italian players generally played the instrument from an embouchure at the corner of the mouth (which corner and how far into the corner were probably left to the player's discretion, depending on the structure of his teeth). This is also recommended by various German writers, notably Daniel Speer, although he is more equivocal about it.[9] Indeed, the evidence from pictures and the large diameters of most surviving mouthpieces suggests that the situation in the North was much more split between players who adopted a side embouchure and those who preferred a central one. Although there are not enough modern-day side embouchure players for us to be too categorical about the relative merits of one position over the other, my own experience in playing for several years from each position leads me to the following conclusions:

A chief advantage of the side embouchure is that response is very fast, due to the thinness of the lips. This aids the delicate articulation of the Renaissance (*lingua riversa*—"te re le re," for example), and makes the fast scales and *passaggi* of late sixteenth-century Italian ornamentation easier. Another advantage is that the cornett lies very comfortably in the hands, in much the same position as a transverse flute.

One disadvantage of the side position is that sustained, loud playing is not accomplished as easily as with the front position, since the mouthpiece for the side embouchure is smaller than the front position mouthpiece. Of course, this is really a curse for the front embouchure, since beginning cornett players (especially converted modern brass players) tend to play much too loudly anyway, and the emphasis in good cornett playing should always be on obtaining a sweet, voice-like sound. But there are occasions when volume is needed, and it is harder to produce from the side position.

Another advantage of the side position is that it is totally independent of the front embouchure, in terms of the demand placed on the muscles. This means that it is of great convenience to players doubling on other instruments, since crumhorns and shawms (instruments that can really tire a cornett player's front embouchure) have little or no effect on a side embouchure. And it can be an advantage to a modern brass player who, obviously, has to use a different size mouthpiece on the cornett from his modern mouthpiece. The only disadvantage inherent here is that the player will need twice as much practice time because he has two embouchures to maintain.

It has been my experience that about the same amount of time is required to build up either kind of embouchure, if one is starting from scratch. Even though modern brass players usually prefer to play with their normal embouchures, they should be advised that using compromise trumpet or horn cup cornett mouthpieces can make achieving a good, characteristic cornett sound more difficult.

Articulation and Fingering

In his 1677 treatise on playing cornett and other wind instruments, Bartolomeo Bismantova recommends that persons wishing to become cornett players should first study singing (to learn phrasing, musicality, and breath control) and then recorder (to learn fingering and articulation). I can only second this. However, in our more impatient world, we are often not able to accommodate these preliminaries, regardless of their importance. Today's beginning cornettists are generally university brass players, who come to the instrument with at least some idea of how to approach a brass instrument. They usually have no idea of woodwind finger technique, however, and all too often they try to play the cornett as they would a marching band instrument, with heavy articulation and much too much air pressure. To combat these tendencies, get them to play scalar exercises of increasing speed and range with frontal double tonguing (trombonists know these as "doodle tonguings"). But make them start *slowly*, only progressing in speed when the notes are very even. For developing good tone, have them imitate a good, natural-voiced soprano, playing *colla parte* (double) with the sopranos (maybe at first, the altos) in your vocal ensemble. *Don't* plop them in with the shawms and sackbuts immediately or you will never get anything sensitive out of them later. Never stop reminding them that a good cornett player should be capable of as much expression as a good singer singing without text.

To find technical studies for developing cornettists, one can look at those presented in the thesis by Gouse. My favorite exercises, however, are those given at the beginning of the treatise of dalla Casa, which even provide suggested articulation syllables for practicing *lingua riversa*. These patterns can then be applied in *bicinia* and the various ornamented settings of chansons and madrigals by Bassano and dalla Casa. The treble ricercare by Ortiz are wonderfully musical also (although the version of "*Douce memoire*" is better transposed up a fourth if performed on the ordinary curved instrument). Don't forget ornamentation studies. Have the student practice the cadential ornamentation patterns of Bassano, Ganassi, Ortiz, and dalla Casa. The list of possibilities is very long indeed. For all-around good technical material to develop range and agility, one can hardly do better than study the études in Arban's *Complete Conservatory Method for Cornet* (*cornet à pistons*), substituting *lingua riversa* for the long slurs in the scalar exercises. After the student can play anything in the first 100 or 150 pages of Arban fluently, he will also be able to do well with seventeenth-century music. (See also the collection of exercises by Michael Collver referred to in Basic Exercises on p. 92: *215 Chop-busters for the Cornetto*.)[10]

Tuning

Along with proper ideas of tone production, the first thing to emphasize to a new cornett player is the importance of consistent, good tuning, for without that, all his music-making will be compromised. Unfortunately, the cornett can be a devilishly hard instrument to play in tune. This is especially true of the instruments made back in the 1960s and 70s, when bores were particularly unsophisticated. Even now, with the state of the art continually advancing, cornett bores necessarily incorporate some compromises in the correct tuning of certain notes. Thus, no matter how sophisticated the instrument, it is probable that players will always have to know how to "lip" a note slightly sharper or slightly flatter.

The best way of gaining the ability to play in tune is by the constant use of a pitch reference while practicing (especially during the early stages of learning the instrument, with frequent use thereafter). This can be a tuning or pitch meter or an organ with a note sounding as a drone (a small weight on a key serves nicely for this). Pitch meters, like the Korg models, that "read" pitches played to them and show the amount of deviation from the nearest equal-tempered pitch are very useful—especially for actually tuning an instrument. For the purposes of learning control over the instrument, however, it is better to use the meter as a pitch generator, which develops the ear and thus ear-lip coordination rather than eye-lip coordination. Although I would hate to do without my pitch meter, I still prefer to use an organ whenever possible because it gives a real, musical sound. I set it to play the tonic or dominant for an étude or passage and then tune constantly to it.

When one first starts learning an instrument, it is better to believe that the tuning of the instrument is correct; playing against a drone is probably the best way to learn how it works. One should also try to get advice from a teacher or more experienced player as soon as possible in case there are problems with the instrument or the beginner's embouchure. Although there are general tendencies among various makers' instruments, one very quickly realizes that every instrument is distinct, with its own behavior patterns. This is even true of the molded resin instruments that one would expect to be as nearly identical as possible. Wooden instruments can vary greatly, even within a single maker's production. Furthermore, as was mentioned earlier, the player's choice of mouthpiece will have a great effect on the behavior of the instrument, both in terms of the tuning of individual notes within a register, and of the general tendencies of registers themselves (the high register may tend to be sharp if the cup is rather shallow, or flat if it is too deep, etc.). Thus, it is probably not worth attempting to list possible problems here. The perceptive player will soon have made his own list—an important part of learning one's instrument.

Once the player gets beyond the rudimentary stages and is able to play simple pieces relatively well in tune, he should be challenged to start thinking in a more sophisticated harmonic sense. That is, he should start recognizing when his "b" is a major third in a G-chord and when it is a fifth in an E-chord. And he should learn where to place the note so that it is a pure third (either major or minor) or a pure fifth. This has relevance on almost every note of the instrument, but is especially important on those that already lie a little bit flat or sharp, because they will then have to be "lipped" more in one direction or the other. For example, f' is often a bit sharp, which may be fine if it is the third in a D-minor chord, but it may need some adjustment in a B♭ chord. On the other hand, B♭ is often the flattest note on the instrument, and it will seem very different in a G-minor chord than in an E♭ or B♭ chord. The player will also need to notice the difference between the forked fingerings used for C♯s and E♭s in the first and second octaves (generally, one needs less fork in the second octave, but cornetts are very idiosyncratic). Again, the key to developing this kind of knowledge is constant tuning to a drone and then sensitive ensemble coaching.

Weak Embouchure

Most beginning cornett players will have to contend with the difficulties of developing a strong embouchure. Certainly this is true of beginners who have not played a brass instrument before, but even many modern brass players discover in coming to the cornett that their normal embouchure does not possess exactly the strength they need for the cornett.

One goes about building embouchure strength in about the same way for any brass instrument. First, it is necessary to get the embouchure to "focus," that is, to work as efficiently as possible. Then one can develop control and stamina. Although these are largely interrelated processes, we will consider them briefly as separate traits in order to prescribe exercises for the development of each.

The musculature involved in the embouchure consists of a ring of muscles running below the nose and around the corners of the mouth, which serves rather like support pillars for the embouchure. Sheets of muscles extend down in different planes to constitute the actual muscles for vibration in the lips. It is these muscles that must be trained to vibrate selectively and with very predictably controlled rates as we play cornett. Buzzing with or without the mouthpiece is the best way to refine the behavior of these muscles. Another way is to play "pedal tones" below the normal fingered notes of the instrument. Have the cornett player produce a descending c-scale down from c′, playing g, f, e, d, and c with all the fingers closed on the fingerholes. Do this slowly, using no mouthpiece pressure, and trying to hold each note as steady in pitch as possible. Repeat the scale, ascending and descending, for several minutes each day. Embouchure focus will improve, not overnight, but within a few weeks. After the player is more advanced, this exercise is still beneficial as a warm-up or to relax after fatiguing high-register playing.

Stamina is best improved through long tones, played in all registers. Each tone should last about ten seconds and, to develop the utmost control, one should vary the dynamics with the duration of the tone. Start the tone without the tongue, *pianissimo, crescendo* (always maintaining good tone) to *fortissimo* (a cornett *fortissimo*, not a symphonic trumpet one), and then *decrescendo* again. Try to end the note so softly that it is hard to tell exactly when it has stopped. Long tones can be done as slow scales, either diatonic or chromatic, ascending and descending, or as regular or irregular intervals moving all over the range of the horn. Overall range is best increased by playing scales in half or quarter notes at slow to moderate speed. Try to play higher than the notes called for in any music you are currently performing. If one needs to play a g″ reliably in a concert piece, then exercises for practice should include b″ and c‴. If one needs to play d‴ in concert, then he should be able to play three or four notes higher than that in practice. I believe this is the point of Praetorius's description of certain German cornett players playing up to g‴ and a‴. It wasn't that they were playing these notes in concert necessarily, but they probably did need a strong c''' and d'''. It is very likely that high scales and long tones, plus pedal notes gave them this extraordinary command of the high register.

Basic Exercises

An excellent source of exercises assembled by a virtuoso player is *215 Chopbusters for the Cornetto*.[10] Good sources of other material have been mentioned earlier; and, of course, the practice should also include study of real pieces of music. Early on this might best consist, as it did in the sixteenth century, of *bicinia* that gradually increase in difficulty. Later the player will move to solo ricercare and diminutions on chansons and madrigals. Vocal pieces, played as expressively as possible, should always be included in the study session. These can be taken from the sixteenth-century sacred or secular repertories, and the player's consideration of them will include such things as phrasing (parallel with text phrasing), articulation (to match word accent or lack thereof, as in melismas), dynamic variation, and ornamentation (as added by the player).

FIGURE 9.2 The Concert
Italian (Emilian), second quarter of 17th century oil on canvas: 99.7 × 146.7 cm
Courtesy of The Fogg Art Museum, Harvard University, Cambridge, Massachusetts (The Francis H. Burr Memorial, Alpheus Hyatt, Louise Haskell Daly. Richard Norton, and Gifts for Special Uses Funds)

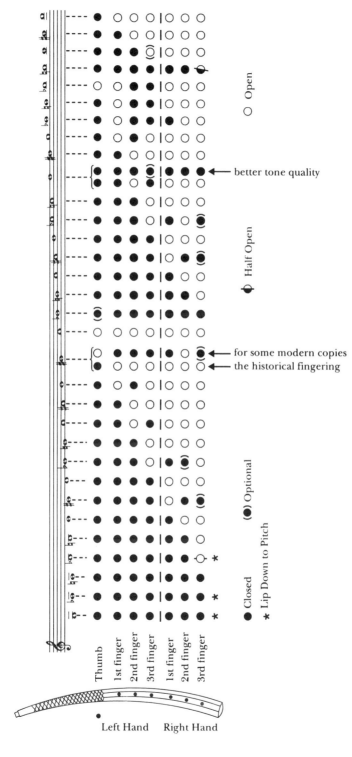

FIGURE 9.3 Fingering chart for Cornett in G

Suggested Repertory

In addition to the more generic pieces referred to in the preceding section, any player will want to study the music actually written with the cornett in mind. There are many such items in the Italian and German repertories of the early seventeenth century, and even a few English pieces have survived destruction. A complete listing of them is obviously much beyond the scope of this chapter, so I will only give a few for ensembles of cornetts. Source lists are readily available for both modern editions and historic collections, and all interested players and teachers are encouraged to make use of them.[11]

Bicinia

Preeminent among sixteenth-century *bicinia* collections are those of Orlando di Lassus, with those of his associate, Francesco Guami, probably next in line. All of these are for unequal voices and thus best suited for cornett and sackbut. Collections of equal-voiced *bicinia* more for cornetts are canons on the church modes by Johann Walter (*Hortus Musicus* edition 63); *bicinia* by Michael Praetorius (scattered throughout the *Musæ Sionæ* in his collected works; the old Bärenreiter publication of just the *bicinia* is now long out of print), and Johann Vierdanck's Capricci *à* 2 of 1641 (*Hortus Musicus* edition 21, now out of print). An English collection of simple duets is Thomas Whythorne's *Songs for two voyces* of 1590 (unpublished, but available from this writer).

Tricinia

For three cornetts, try the pieces for three high voices in the Lassus collected works, or those of Praetorius. The Vierdanck collection mentioned above also contains two trios for cornetts or violins.

Quartets

The principal quartet for cornetts is Samuel Scheidt's *Canzona for Four Cornetts* (available from Robert King Music Co., North Easton, MA) or in the Scheidt collected works.

Quintets

In his *Harmonie Universelle* of 1636, Mersenne reproduces a "*Phantasie à cinq parties composée par le sieur Henry le Jeune, pour les cornets.*" This is also reproduced on page 332 of the 1981 *Basler Jahrbuch für historische Musikpraxis*. If the piece is transposed up a whole step, it is playable on four treble cornetts and one *cornetto basso*. Other than this, the only probable quintets for cornetts known to me are the five *fugæ ad equales* in the partbooks of the Royal Danish court band, circa 1540. (Some of these are playable as they stand on *cornetti alti*, and others seem to be more for *cornetti bassi*. However, they are all very playable on treble instruments if the low pieces are transposed up a fourth.) These can be found in the first volume of the Dania Sonans edition of the manuscript, Copenhagen KB 1872–4°, or from me (in a suitably transposed edition).

Sextets

There are at least two sextets for cornetts (or playable by them). One, specified for the instruments, is that of Wilhelm Lichtlein, circa 1610 (his *Capriccio*), published by the firm Hans Gerig, Cologne. The other, for six treble instruments, but written at a time when the cornett would have been the most probable selection, is William Daman's *Fantasia di sei soprani*, published by Mapa Mundi Editions, London.

NOTES

1. There are too many discussions of the cornett to attempt a complete list here. Kärstadt–Zur is the first important one. Others include Baines–*Woodwind*; Munrow–*Instruments*; Gouse–*Cornett*; Heyde–*Hörner*. Very useful articles in journals include Dickey–Decline and a series of four articles on the cornett, its repertory, and technique by Kaye–Cornett. The most useful, balanced, concise account of the cornett family is that of Anthony Baines in the *New Grove*. See the articles "Cornett" and "Lysarden."
2. Recent discoveries about Augustein Schubinger, the first major cornett soloist, would seem to place the cornett's early development in the area of Augsburg. See Polk–Augustein.
3. See, for example, the German woodcuts from A. Schlick of 1511 and Georg Pencz of 1531 reproduced in "Cornett" and "Zink" in *New Grove* and *MGG*, respectively.
4. For information about Renaissance pitch standards as related to cornetts, see Kirk–Cornetti.
5. The set of 7 partbooks (Copenhagen, Koneglige Bibliotek, Gl.Kgl.Sml. 1872–4°) contains several pieces with the preferred instrumentation written in by a later hand. Of specific interest to us is a *Laudate Dominum à 8* "*for 4 zincken und 4 pusauns.*" While the sackbut parts are very playable on tenor sackbuts, all four cornett parts are too low to be played on the normal treble instrument. Concerning instrumentation in the Florentine *intermedi*, see Brown–*Sixteenth*.
6. For comments on probable performing pitch for these works, see my article cited in note 4 above.
7. See Selfridge–Field–Bassano and Arnold–*Giovanni*: 128–62. The standard ensemble began at three, expanded to four with the arrival of Giovanni Bassano in 1576, and expanded again in 1582 to six. With the exception of major feasts when other players were brought in, it remained at six throughout most of the seventeenth century. For a large corpus of typical Venetian four-part repertory, playable by two cornetts and two sackbuts, see the *Pelpin Tabulature*, transcribed in volume 8 of the series *Antiquitates Musicæ in Polonia*.
8. See Dickey–Decline: 28.
9. Daniel Speer's comments on playing the cornett from his "*Grundrichtigen . . . Unterricht der Musicalischen Kunst . . . ,*" 1697, pp. 232–33, are summarized along with those of all other early sources on the instrument by Leonards–Historische. See p. 335 for Speer and pp.

350–52 for the comments of Johann Daniel Berlin (1744), who still advocates a right-corner placement but says that one can also play from the front of the mouth.

10. Arban–*Complete*. Collver–*Chop–busters* is very useful and provides excerpts from the best of Arban and Bassano.

11. The Gouse dissertation referred to in note 1 above provides a list of pieces for or playable by cornetts in modern publications up to 1974. A more recent listing of music that specifically mentions cornett is that of Collver/Dickey–Musik.

Suggested Listening

Affetti Musicali. Concerto Castello. Deutsche Harmonia Mundi lC-06599–917 (1981).

Alleluia: Chorale Settings by Michael Praetorius. New York Cornet and Sacbut Ensemble, Ben Peck, director. New Port Classic NC 60021 (CD) (1987).

Claudio Monteverdi: Vespro della Beata Vergine. The Taverner Consort, Andrew Parrott, directing. EMI DSB 3963 (2 LPs or CDs) (1984).

Il Concerto Palatino di Bologna: North-Italian Music for Cornetts and Trombones 1580–1650. Concerto Palatino. *Accent ACC 8861D (1992).*

Giovanni Gabrieli: Canzonas, Sonatas, Motets. The Taverner Consort, Choir, and Players. Andrew Parrott, director. EMI Reflexe CDC 7542652 (1992).

Giovanni Gabrieli: Canzoni e Sonate. DGG Archiv 2533 406. The Taverner Consort, Andrew Parrott, director (1978).

Kammermusik am Hofe Kaiser Leopolds I. Concerto Castello. Bruce Dickey, director. EMI Reflexe. 1C-069–1466971 (1983).

"Quel lascivissimo Cornetto . . . " *Virtuoso Solo Music for Cornetto.* Bruce Dickey, Tragicomedia. Accent ACC 9173D (1991).

"Sonata Concertate in Stil Moderno," *Virtuoso Instrumental Music by Castello and Scarani.* Concerto Palatino. Accent ACC 9058D (1991).

Venetian Music for Brass: 1500 to 1600. New York Cornet and Sacbut Ensemble, Ben Peck, director. Titanic Ticas 150 (cassette).

10

Sackbut

Stewart Carter

Unlike many early instruments that have been revived in the twentieth century, the trombone has remained in continuous use, with relatively slight changes in construction, since its inception more than 500 years ago. The term "sackbut," used today to distinguish the early form of the trombone from its modern counterpart, was current in England from the late fifteenth century to the end of the seventeenth century. Probably the name derives either from the old Spanish *saccabuche* ("draw-pipe" or "pump") or the old French *saqueboute* ("pull-push").

Keith Polk and others have shown that the sackbut evolved from the natural trumpet in several stages. Straight trumpets may have been fitted with rudimentary slides as early as the mid-fourteenth century. By about 1370 an S-shaped instrument had evolved, and around 1400 the folded shape appeared. The true sackbut, with a double-branched slide, appeared sometime in the fifteenth century—perhaps as early as the 1430s, but certainly by the 1470s. In the fifteenth century the sackbut, like the slide trumpet, was often associated with shawms (usually a discant shawm and a bombard) in the *alta cappella* or "loud wind band."

The physical characteristics of sackbuts of the sixteenth and seventeenth centuries have been described by Fischer–*Renaissance* and Smith–*Trombone*. In comparison to their modern counterparts, these instruments had a narrower bore (about 10 mm), a smaller, more funnel-shaped bell with less terminal flare, no slide stocking, no water key, and no lacquer. A few surviving tenor sackbuts have larger bores, approaching those of smaller modern instruments (about 12 mm), but most of these are cut-down basses. According to Smith, the early instruments had thinner walls in the bell section, but thicker walls in the cylindrical sections. Early bass sackbuts often had tuning slides, though tenors and altos did not. Most tenors had flat stays, at least until about the middle of the seventeenth century, but a few had tubular stays, which were usually telescoping. Bass sackbuts had a hinged handle attached to the lower slide stay, to permit full extension of the slide.

In the sixteenth and seventeenth centuries the most popular size of sackbut was the tenor, of which several specimens—mostly by Nuremberg craftsmen—survive. Precise pitch data for some of these extant instruments are difficult to obtain. But while there seems to have been a considerable amount of variation, the fundamental pitch in first position for most antique tenors is roughly modern B-flat. However, early brass instruments were customarily tuned higher than today (often a half-step or more), so this first-position note was conceived as A (see Fischer: 4–7). According to Anthony Baines, this higher pitch standard was sometimes referred to as Cornett-ton.

First-position "A" for the tenor is confirmed by Aurelio Virgiliano, whose *Il Dolcimelo* (ca. 1600) contains the earliest known chart of slide positions (Fig. 10.1). The chart shows only four positions, arranged diatonically: adjusted upward by a half-step to conform to modern pitch standards, these positions correspond to modern first, third, fifth, and sixth positions respectively. Praetorius (*De Organographia*, 1619) shows five positions for the bass sackbut (Fig. 10.2), but if we accept his second position merely as an extension of first, then his slide positions correspond to Virgiliano's. Praetorius indicates only one pitch—f—for this extended first position, whereas the corresponding note—c′—in Virgiliano's chart for the tenor is shown in unextended first position. Obviously this too must be lowered, but Virgiliano does not indicate needed extensions.

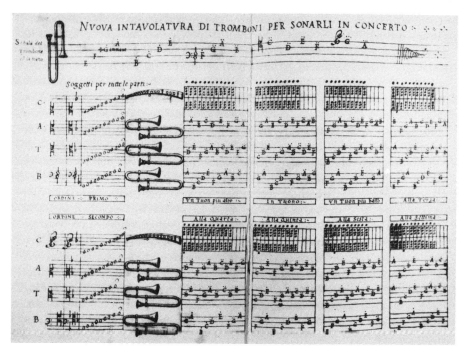

FIGURE 10.1 Aurelio Virgiliano, *Il Dolcimelo* (ca. 1600).
Reprinted by permission, Studio per Edizioni Scelte, Florence.

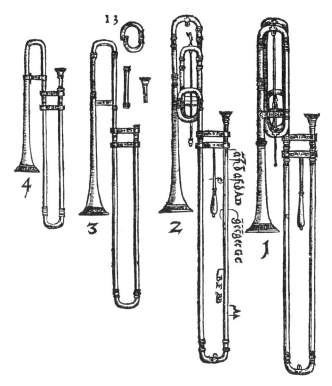

FIGURE 10.2 Sackbuts
Praetorius, *Syntagma musicum* II, Plate VIII

Virgiliano also shows that when playing the sackbut *in concerto* (i.e., in ensembles), the *canto* part is taken by a cornett, and the alto, tenor, and bass parts by tenor trombones. Avoidance of the alto in particular seems to have been typical of Italian practice.

Praetorius describes four different types of sackbut:

1. Alto—*Alto oder Discant Posaun.* Apparently it was pitched in either D or E, its range, B to d″ or e″. Praetorius says this instrument is the natural choice for a high part, but because of its small size its sound is inferior to that of the tenor; furthermore the latter, with practice, can be played as high as the alto.

2. Tenor—*Gemeine rechte Posaun.* It was pitched in A, although notes in "first position" were not always played with the slide fully closed. Praetorius indicates this in another section of *De Organographia* when he recommends using a trombone (especially one made in Nuremberg) with its slide extended by the width of two fingers as the best source for an "a" in "choir" pitch. Variable pitch standards and the absence of a tuning slide apparently necessitated flexible slide positions. The illustrations at the end of the

volume show that the tenor could be fitted with extra lengths of tubing, either straight or coiled, which could probably lower the instrument by as much as a full tone (see Fig. 10.2 on p. 99). The natural range of the instrument is identified in the text as E to f′, but the table on p. 20 (of Praetorius) lists g′ to a′ for the top. The table also shows extensions of this range from A_1 to g″. Factitious tones (false or "bendable" notes), mentioned by Praetorius for the Octav-Posaun (see below), and/or pedal tones must have been used to obtain the lowest notes. The author mentions two virtuosos capable of playing in the extreme ranges of the tenor instrument, one of whom could match the agility of a cornett or viola bastarda.

3. Bass—*Quart-Posaun* or *Quint-Posaun*. These were pitched in E and D—a fourth and a fifth, respectively, below the tenor. In the illustrations at the end of the book, two *Quart-Posaunen* are depicted, varying slightly in size and configuration (see Fig. 10.2 on p. 99). Both instruments are fitted with a push-rod attached to a tuning slide, which was probably capable of lowering the instrument by a step, thereby instantly converting a *Quart-* into a *Quint-Posaun*. The range of the bass is A_1 or G_1 to c′ (extendable downward to F_1 and upward to g′). Praetorius says that a tenor player can learn to play the *Quint-Posaun* by reading bass-clef parts as if they were in tenor clef.

4. Double bass—*Octav-Posaun*. This rarely used instrument plays an octave below the tenor, and the normal range is E_1 to a. The extended range is from C_1 to c′, but the low C_1 and D_1 are described as "falset" notes (factitious tones?), which can be obtained with practice. Praetorius mentions two forms of the instrument: one doubles the tenor in all dimensions while the other, not physically as large, achieves its low pitch by means of crooks and a large bore.

The soprano member of the sackbut family, pitched an octave above the tenor, never achieved widespread use, but it was used occasionally, beginning in the late seventeenth century.

Mersenne's *Harmonie Universelle* shows a tenor instrument fitted with a crook that lowers it by a fourth, thereby converting it to a bass. He also shows that the instrument could be disassembled at several points, since the joints apparently were not soldered. Mersenne seems puzzled by the acoustics of the sackbut, marveling that one can extend the slide some distance and yet obtain the same note, seemingly in defiance of the laws of musical proportion.

During the sixteenth century the sackbut served a variety of functions. It kept its place in the *alta cappella* as this ensemble evolved (see Shawm, p. 69), but with increasing frequency it was teamed with the agile cornett in the cornett-and-sackbut ensemble. The sound of the instrument could be loud, but it could also be subdued enough to blend with softer instruments or voices. Evidence from Florentine *intermedi* indicates that sackbuts combined with voices, and occasionally with such soft instruments as lutes, recorders, crumhorns, and transverse flutes. Infernal scenes sometimes called for sackbuts combined with viols. In church music, sackbuts frequently doubled voices in the lower and middle ranges.

In the seventeenth century sackbuts continued to be used in town, church, and court bands. The loud shawm band, often with one or more sackbuts, gradually disappeared in the seventeenth century, but the cornett-and-sackbut band (now customarily in five parts) saw its finest hour, particularly in Italy, England, and Germany. In church music, sackbuts were used both to support voices and to play independent lines in the new concertato manner. Giovanni Gabrieli called for as many as twelve sackbuts in his sacred works, often with violins or cornetts on the upper parts. Throughout the seventeenth century, sackbuts continued to be associated with strings, in concerted sacred vocal music as well as purely instrumental music. Many Italian sonatas call for one or two violins or cornetts on the top, with sackbut or violone on the bottom, playing a part closely tied to the continuo.

Tuning

Many modern reproductions have tuning slides, which are anachronistic with respect to the tenor and alto. Others have a thumbscrew that allows adjustment of the amount of overlap between bell and slide sections. For more faithful reproductions, tuning bits, which are placed between bell and slide sections (see Fig. 10.2 on p. 99), are the only means of altering the basic pitch of the instrument. Some makers supply these bits with their instruments.

Slide Positions

Modern reproductions of tenor sackbuts are customarily built in B-flat. Basses are in E-flat or F, with altos theoretically an octave higher, though most altos are in the lower key. Table 10.1 gives "modern" positions for tenor sackbut in B-flat, and basses in F and E-flat. Positions for alto may be obtained by octave transposition.

Small adjustments for some notes are normal, and one important advantage of the sackbut is its almost infinite pitch adjustability because of the slide; large adjustments for notes other than those of the seventh partial may indicate a poorly made instrument.

Seasoned sackbut players who would like to reproduce the playing experience of a Renaissance performer as closely as possible are encouraged to learn to play the tenor sackbut in A, with four diatonic positions rather than seven chromatic ones, as indicated by Virgiliano and other writers of the time. Sackbut players who work with an ensemble that performs at $a' = 460$ or thereabouts (see Pitch and Transposition, p. 248) can simply play A in "regular" first position, without recourse to radical tuning adjustments. But in order to make a tenor sackbut pitched in B-flat sound $a' = 440$ in first position, the basic length of the instrument must be extended. It may prove

101

TABLE 10.1 Slide positions for sackbuts in B♭, F, and E♭

1	2	3	4	5	6	7
			B♭ tenor			
B♭	A	G♯	G	F♯	F	E
f	e	e♭	d	c♯	c	B
b♭	a	g♯	g	f♯	f*	e*
d′	c♯′	c′	b	b♭*	a*	–
f′	e′	e♭′	d′*	–	–	–
–	g′**	f♯′**	–	–	–	–
b♭′	a′	g♯′	g′*	–	–	–
c″	b′	–	–	–	–	–
			F bass			
F	E	E♭	D	C♯	C	B_1***
c	B	B♭	A	G♯	G	F♯***
f	e	e♭	d	c♯	c*	–
a	g♯	g	f♯	–	–	–
c′	b	b♭	–	–	–	–
–	d′**	c♯′**	–	–	–	–
f′	e′	e♭′	–	–	–	–
g′	f♯′	–	–	–	–	–
			E♭ bass			
E♭	D	C♯	C	B_1	$B♭_1$	A_1***
B♭	A	G♯	G	F♯	F	E***
e♭	d	c♯	c	B	–	–
g	f♯	f	e	–	–	–
b♭	a	g♯	–	–	–	–
–	c′**	b**	–	–	–	–
e♭′	d′	c♯′	–	–	–	–
f′	e′	–	–	–	–	–

*   denotes common alternate positions
**   denotes seventh-partial notes, which must be raised slightly
*** seventh position is very difficult to obtain on most basses

difficult to lower the instrument a half-step with the most common tuning devices—tuning bits, or (anachronistically) a tuning slide or screw mechanism—but a good brass repairman could lengthen the tubing, as suggested by Smith. However, thinking of the instrument as keyed in A rather than B-flat is inconvenient, to say the least, for players who must switch back and forth from sackbut to modern trombone. My personal preference is to tune the instrument so that first-position B-flat is extended slightly—perhaps half an inch. This expedient permits upward adjustment of the slide for characteristically flat notes, and virtually obviates the need for fully closed notes, which can cause problems on an instrument without cushion springs on the slides.

Care and Precautions

Care of a sackbut is the same as that for a modern trombone. The slide must move freely and easily, and should be lubricated with slide cream, available in music stores. Some players spray water on the slide to keep the cold cream moist. Every few months the inside of the inner slide tubes should be cleaned with a "snake"—a long piece of flexible wire, often coated with plastic, with small bristles on either end (available in music stores). Mouthpieces can be cleaned with a mouthpiece brush.

Lacquer finishes for brass instruments are a fairly recent development, and are probably best avoided on historical reproductions, as the lacquer may inhibit vibration slightly. Unlacquered instruments tarnish, and may be polished periodically with brass polish.

Common Problems

It is relatively easy to convert good trombone players to tenor sackbut, although a certain amount of coaching on style will be necessary. They must be taught to articulate properly, and cautioned not to overblow. As the bell of a sackbut is often lower in relationship to the slide than on a modern instrument, modern players who are accustomed to judging third and fourth positions from the location of the bell will need to readjust.

Hand Position

Renaissance paintings and other iconographical sources often depict players with all four fingers of the right hand wrapped around the lower (movable) slide stay, and with the left hand gripping the instrument just below the mouthpiece (see Fig. 10.3), or perhaps with part of the hand around the stationary slide stay. As the grip has no effect on the sound of the instrument, I recommend the more flexible "modern" hand position described below.

For the tenor and alto, the right hand should be held so as to afford maximum wrist flexibility. Grasp the lower (movable) slide stay with the thumb on the side closest to the mouthpiece, with the index and middle fingers opposite the thumb and the ring and little fingers below the lower slide tube. The palm of the hand should face the player so that the wrist can act as a "hinge," thereby allowing maximum flexibility. With the slide held in this manner, the wrist alone can move the slide the distance of approximately two positions. For longer throws of the slide, wrist and arm are used together.

Modern trombonists generally wrap all four fingers of the left hand around the upper (stationary) slide stay (sometimes with the index finger atop the upper slide branch), with the thumb hooked around the nearest bell stay. This method also works for many sackbuts, particularly those with tubular stays. On some modern reproductions this method is difficult

FIGURE 10.3 Hans Burgkmair, *The Triumph of Maximilian I.*
  Reprinted by permission, Dover Publications, Inc., New York.

because the left thumb cannot comfortably reach around the bell stay. This is particularly true for instruments that have tuning bits inserted between slide and bell sections, thereby lengthening the distance between the bell stay and the upper slide stay. In such cases the player generally must wrap the entire left hand around the upper slide stay. Players should avoid grasping the bell itself with the left hand, as this inhibits vibration.

Embouchure

Embouchure development is a difficult and time-consuming process, and for this reason, conversion of musicians with little or no previous experience on a brass instrument requires a great deal of patience. The mouthpiece should usually be placed equidistant laterally between the corners of the mouth, with more of the mouthpiece on the upper lip than on the lower. It is important to keep the corners of the mouth firm while playing. For assistance in embouchure development, the novice sackbut player is encouraged to seek the assistance of a modern trombone teacher.

Tone Production

Because of its generally smaller bore, the tone of a sackbut is more easily "broken" than that of a modern trombone, and the most common problem of a modern player who converts to the early instrument is that of forcing the tone. The sackbut usually requires a smaller volume of air, but diaphragmatic breathing and proper breath support are essential, as with any wind instrument.

Articulation

Several early sources discuss articulation for wind instruments, although none of them specifically mentions the sackbut. By examining sources for cornett and trumpet, however, we probably can gain a fairly clear idea of articulation for the sackbut. Some excellent sources are Dalla Casa's *Il vero modo di diminuir* (1584) and Francesco Rognoni's *Selva di varii passaggi* (1620), which mention the cornett; and Fantini's *Modo per imparare a sonare di tromba* (1638), for trumpet. Dalla Casa mentions three principal types, all illustrated by passages moving in conjunct eighth notes. The first type is the *lingua riversa* ("reversed tongue"), which is further subdivided into three categories, ranging from the very smooth *lere lere*, to the moderate *dere lere* and the harsher *tere lere*. (Both the l and the r are articulated in the front of the mouth, on the hard palate behind the upper teeth, the r being flipped, Italian style.) The second type is the *lingua dretta* ("straight tongue"), *tere tere*. The third type, *teche teche* (the ch sound is hard), is used to sound "frightening." Dalla Casa also mentions two single tongue-strokes, *ta* and the smoother *da*, both appropriate for longer note values.

Choosing an Instrument

The prospective purchaser of a modern reproduction may consult Fischer's Appendix II, in which eleven makers are evaluated, and also my article, "Contemporary Sackbut Makers—an Update" (*Historic Brass Society Newsletter* i [1989]: 9–13). Good reproductions are expensive, and anyone who is tempted to modify a modern instrument for use as a sackbut may be encouraged by Smith's remarks on this issue (Smith: 29).

Choosing a Mouthpiece

Only a handful of antique mouthpieces survive, but perhaps their most important characteristics are a relatively flat rim, a bowl-shaped cup with a sharp-edged throat, and no backbore. As some sackbut makers do not supply historical mouthpieces with their instruments, it may be necessary to have a mouthpiece custom made. Dimensions for historical mouthpieces are given in Fischer: 52 and Smith: 32.

A good instrument is expensive, but the money will be virtually wasted if a modern mouthpiece is used, since it will be very difficult to obtain a good sackbut sound. Smith argues that the sackbut and its modern counterpart represent somewhat different acoustical systems, and therefore a mouthpiece designed to operate with one system is incompatible with the other. A modern trombone player, when converted to the sackbut, will frequently fight against using a historical mouthpiece. The response will prove quite different, and at first it simply will not "feel right." Encourage him or her to take some time to adjust to the unfamiliar mouthpiece.

Exercises

For building tone quality and endurance, long tones are very useful. These should be played in all ranges of the instrument, and with varying dynamic shadings. Lip slurs are excellent for embouchure development and flexibility. Experienced trombonists likely will have committed many such exercises to memory; the novice sackbut player may consult any of several modern method books, such as Fink's *Handbook*.

Scales are good for developing slide technique, and these should be done with a variety of tonguings: the normal *ta* stroke, the gentler *da* stroke, and the multiple tonguings described above. The player who wishes to study genuine Renaissance exercise material is encouraged to explore the multitude of diminutions in the manuals of Dalla Casa, Francesco Rognoni, and other Renaissance authors.

Suggested Repertory

Sackbuts are capable of performing a wide variety of Renaissance music, in an equally wide range of timbral contexts. The instrument combines nicely with the raucous shawms in the *alta cappella*, with medium-loud cornetts in the cornett-sackbut band, and with soft instruments. For fifteenth-century music, one sackbut and two shawms make a good three-part combination (see the chapter on shawms for details). For sixteenth-century music, one or two sackbuts can be used in the expanded *alta cappella*. The cornett-and-sackbut ensemble can be adapted to an enormous range of sixteenth-century ensemble repertory—dances, secular songs, motets. Such an ensemble in four parts most often consists of one cornett and three sackbuts. Five- and six-part music customarily requires two cornetts, with the remaining parts taken by sackbuts. Alto and bass instruments can be used, particularly for late-sixteenth-century music, but much of this repertory works just fine with tenors on all the sackbut parts. Particularly recommended for the cornett-sackbut band are the five-part dances of Anthony Holborne (London Pro Musica Edition), Thomas Stoltzer's five-part *Octo tonorum melodiæ* (*Das Erbe deutscher Musik*, vol. 22), or for simpler fare, the four-part dances of Susato (Schott). It is important to remember, however, that one of the chief uses of sackbuts was to support voices.

From the seventeenth century, the extensive Italian canzona repertory works well for cornetts and sackbuts. Among several works written expressly for the cornett-sackbut band, I recommend in particular nos. 19–21 of John Adson's *Courtly Masquing Ayres* (London Pro Musica).

Good sackbut players should not be too hard to find, but locating shawm and/or cornett players to complement them is another matter. Sackbuts can be joined with softer instruments, but another possible performing outlet is the homogeneous sackbut ensemble. Three or four instruments is the optimum number here, with tenors forming the core, and alto and bass taking the extreme parts if they are available. From the sixteenth century there is a fair amount of four-part literature in ATTB arrangement—French chansons, Latin motets, and the like—which work on four sackbuts. For some of these pieces with a high tessitura, downward transposition by perhaps a fourth or a fifth is a good possibility, particularly if a bass is available. Many three- and four-voice compositions will work with an ensemble of tenors only, but the lead player must have a strong upper range. From the early seventeenth century there is a small body of literature expressly written for sackbuts alone. It includes:

For four sackbuts and continuo
J. G. F. Braun: "Canzonato" (Max Hieber)
Giovanni Cesare: "La Bavara" (Musica Rara)
Biagio Marini: Canzona (Ensemble Publications)

For five sackbuts and continuo
Moritz von Hessen: Pavana (Ensemble Publications)

For eight sackbuts and continuo
Tiburtio Massaino: Canzona (Musica Rara)

An interesting and apparently unique sixteenth-century composition that specifies four sackbuts and solo (alto) voice is Francesco Corteccia's "Vienten' almo riposo," from the Florentine *intermedi* of 1539 (Mitchell/Minor–Renaissance). From the first half of the seventeenth century there are numerous works calling for sackbuts in varying combinations with other instruments and voices. As a seventeenth-century volume is planned for this series, such works will be covered there. However, it is impossible to leave this subject without mentioning—in spite of their late date—two stunning compositions by Heinrich Schütz for bass voice, four sackbuts, and continuo: "Fili mi Absalon" and "Attendite populue meus" (both in Schütz, *Werke*, vol. 14).

Bibliography

Baines–*Brass*; Barclay–*Art*; Besseler–*Entstehung*; Fink–*Trombonist's*; Fischer–*Renaissance*; Polk–Trombone; Praetorius–*Syntagma*; Smith–*Trombone*; Virgiliano–*Il Dolcimelo.*

Suggested Listening

Affetti musicali. Concerto Castello. Harmonia Mundi 065–99 9917.

Alleluia: Weinachtslieder von Praetorius. The New York Cornet & Sacbut Ensemble. Newport Classic, MC: NC 30021; CD: NC 60021.

Giovanni Gabrieli: Sacræ Symphoniæ. A Sei voci and Les Saqueboutiers de Toulouse. Adda 581245.

Music of the Stadtpfeifer. Musica Fiata. Harmonia Mundi 622D.

North Italian Music for Cornetts and Trombones, 1580–1650. Concerto Palatino. Accent ACC 8861.

Venetian Church Music. The Taverner Players. Angel CDC 54265.

A Venetian Coronation 1595: Ceremonial music by Andrea and Giovanni Gabrieli. Gabrieli Consort and Players. Virgin Classics DC, VC 91110–2; cassette, VC 79119–4.

Venetian Music of the Piffari and Canzonas. The New York Cornet & Sacbut Ensemble. FSM/Pantheon 68–905.

11

Bowed Instruments

Wendy Gillespie

The bowed instruments of the Renaissance offer many possibilities of sound, technique, and function. Some bowed strings occur in families, others are specially designed for chordal playing. There are instruments held on the shoulder as well as those supported with the legs. Some bows are held from above the stick, others are held from beneath, as with the viola da gamba family. The following survey of instruments, their technique, and repertory is not exhaustive. Its purpose is to describe the principal bowed strings of the Renaissance in a way that will provoke the curiosity of players, instrument builders, and directors of ensembles. The violin is not discussed here since this *Guide* devotes a separate chapter to it.

Players of modern bowed instruments can quickly acquire a certain amount of facility on many Renaissance bowed instruments. These players especially should be discouraged from approaching Renaissance instruments as crude predecessors of modern ones. It is possible to play the viol just like a modern cello—bowed overhand, without frets, and with almost constant vibrato. Such a playing technique, however, would not capture the essence of the instrument or its music. Varying qualities of sound (such as the chiff of a fat gut string when bowed, or the nasal quality of an instrument without a soundpost) must be appreciated as the nature of the instrument rather than as a defect. Listening to music outside the "classical" tradition will suggest ways to extend one's technical and aesthetic boundaries.

For the non-string player, fretted instruments are somewhat easier to begin with than non-fretted ones,[1] though ultimately they are equally difficult to master.[2] Anything that hurts when playing Renaissance bowed strings should be carefully scrutinized, since playing technique should be based on natural physical motion with minimal stress. Nevertheless, the non-string player can reasonably expect to feel some strain on the left hand at the outset. Common sense suggests a cautious approach, strengthening the fingers (especially the little finger of the left hand) gradually and methodically. Calluses will gradually develop on the pads of the left fingers. The tiny muscles controlling the movement of the fingers must be trained slowly, without causing strain to muscles, tendons, or ligaments that could result in injury.

Live demonstrations can best illustrate the principles of bowing, though one cannot help but notice a certain scarcity of rebec and lirone teachers nowadays! However, an experienced player of any bowed instrument can help the novice with principles of bow speed, pressure, and distance from the bridge. Ian Gammie's *A Book of Bowings*[3] gives general principles to apply to various bowed instruments. The non-string player who wishes to explore subtler aspects of bowing and fingering (articulation, vibrato, ornaments, etc.) also can consult a book such as *The Art and Science of String Performance* by Samuel Applebaum and adapt its instructions, written for the modern string player, to suit the instrument at hand.

In the absence of any assistance in playing bowed strings, the beginner is urged to isolate various aspects of playing. Posture is the first consideration to promote a relaxed and easy technique. For instruments played on the arm one can stand with the feet slightly apart and the knees unlocked. But all Renaissance bowed strings except the very largest can also be played seated. A chair with a flat or slightly forward-pitched seat is best, so that the hips are slightly higher than the knees, and the player feels the weight of the body going into the floor through the feet, which are flat on the ground.

To position a vertically held instrument,[4] sit forward on the chair and place the left foot slightly ahead of the right. Once the seated position is comfortable, with shoulders relaxed and head erect, one begins the process of finding a placement for the instrument that allows access to all the strings with both the bow and the left hand. One strives for a position where the instrument can sit firmly between the legs without having to squeeze them together. Smaller instruments rest higher on the calves than large ones. The playing position will require reevaluation as the technique develops, bearing in mind that the instrument should be adjusted to the body of the player rather than vice versa.

As natural a playing position as possible is also the key to a flexible, supple, strong left hand. Whether the instrument is supported on the arm, shoulder, chest, or leg, one might curve the fingers of the left hand and think of "hanging" them on the fingerboard. This image may help keep the wrist and hand in a neutral position, neither convex nor concave. Efficiency of left hand motion can be achieved through minimal effort, leaving fingers down until necessity causes them to be lifted, and then lifting them only slightly off the string. One should concentrate only on the left hand for some of the allotted practice time. Instead of bowing try plucking the instrument with the finger(s) of the right hand at first, taking care to pluck farther from the bridge than the bow will ever be placed so that oil from the fingers does not interfere with the bowing.

There are many different ways one can hold a bow. Instruments held on the arm are usually bowed with the hand on top of the stick of the bow, while those held with the legs are bowed with the hand facing palm upward underneath the stick. The length and weight of the bow determine how near the end of the bow one should place the hand. With an overhand bow grip one can put the thumb underneath the frog or hair instead of on the stick opposite the fingers. It is useful to think about dropping the elbow and letting the weight of the arm hold the bow on the string. With an underhand bow grip the weight of the arm also keeps the bow on the string, and again there are several possibilities for holding the bow. One way might be compared to holding a pencil with the thumb and the index finger opposing each other, and the middle (and possibly ring) finger actually in contact with the hair of the bow. Another well-documented way of holding a bow underhand involves putting two or three fingers on the stick of the bow, again opposed by the thumb.

However one chooses to hold a bow, the wrist, arm, and fingers must be relaxed but controlled to yield the best result. The wrist leads the arm through the bow stroke in both directions. Its movement must not be floppy or there will be a loss of control at the change of direction, which adversely affects the sound. The elbow must not lead the underhand bow stroke, because it tends to take the weight of the arm out of the sound, which will therefore lose its focus. The fingers must be flexible to control both the tension of the bow hair and the subtlety of articulation and dynamics at any point in the duration of a note. It is useful to remember that the beginning, middle, and end of a note are almost infinitely variable when one can gain control of the bow.

Bow-hair tension should be less if one is playing mostly chords to enable bow contact with several strings simultaneously. It is possible then to increase the tension of the hair to play individual strings, if the finger(s) in contact with the hair pull it taut.

There is nothing quite like the sound of someone learning to bow a string instrument, and the smaller the instrument, the more potential there is for unusual and unplanned sounds. It may help to bear in mind that beginners can only get better, and they will only get better by persisting! Many beginners find that the bow slides around on the string. To help remedy this, imagine that the bridge is a plane, and try to keep the bow parallel to that plane. This will cause it to travel in a track, at a constant distance from the bridge. It is helpful to experiment with the distance of the bow from the bridge. Playing too close to the bridge often produces what might politely be described as overtones, while playing too far away causes the sound to lack focus and can make playing individual strings difficult. The speed at which the bow moves and the weight of the arm, whether above or beneath the bow, also have a considerable effect on the sound. With all these issues to consider, it is readily apparent why beginners should spend as much time as possible simply bowing open strings, using the ear to guide the arm, wrist, and hand.

A clean sound also involves being able to cross strings and change bow direction successfully. One can practice rolling the bow silently over the strings, keeping the arm relaxed, to see how the arm position changes as one goes from the bottom to the top of the instrument. Practice going from every string to every other string without lifting the bow or making unseemly noises, keeping all motions small and relaxed. For bow direction changes, invent repetitive patterns that use combinations of long and short notes in ever-increasing complexity to explore the potential of the entire length of the bow. Fat gut strings are difficult to set in motion and will require a lot of weight from the bow and arm before the note begins. That weight must be released when the bow moves.

The coordination between the left and right hands is unique to string instruments. The left hand must always anticipate the right by a split second. It prepares the note during the bow change. It will be helpful at first to allow extra time between notes for this preparation, which will gradually become automatic. The alert ear can detect problems of coordination that sound as if more than one pitch occurs in a given bow stroke.[5] Plucking before bowing puts the right hand in more direct contact with the string and can help in the learning of this coordination.

The principles of learning any new instrument can be successfully applied to Renaissance bowed strings. Patience is the key. Slow and methodical practice, paying separate attention to the left and right hands at first, will yield the best results. Pluck a melody until the left hand works automatically, then try to add the bow. Practice bowing patterns on open strings, then try to apply the left hand. Begin in the middle range of the instrument, then gradually exploit the more difficult upper and lower reaches. When something doesn't work, let the ear analyze the problem, and break a passage down into component parts. What one thinks is a right-hand problem may be a left-hand problem.

The Instruments

The *medieval fiddle*[6] survived well into the Renaissance. There were amateur and professional fiddlers at all levels of society who played in church, in liturgical dramas, at feasts and entertainments, for dancing, and to accompany song.

The Renaissance fiddle was generally oval shaped, with or without incurved sides. There is a clear demarcation between the body and the neck, and a flat or almost flat back. The fiddle has between three and six strings, one of which might be a lateral drone string that does not pass over the neck. There were probably fiddles both with and without features such as frets, a separate fingerboard, soundpost, and curved bridge. The concept of a family of fiddles does not seem relevant, as the alto-range instrument with a bottom note of perhaps C or D seems to predominate, if the apparent size in pictures is any indication.

Some specific information is available concerning the tuning of the fiddle in the Renaissance. Tinctoris (ca. 1487) refers to three-stringed fiddles tuned in fifths and five-stringed fiddles tuned in fifths and unisons. But the player may decide to choose a tuning that suits the set-up of the instrument,[7] the music in question, and his or her technical skills. Many string players find it useful to begin by tuning and playing their medieval fiddle like a violin or a viola, or, if the instrument has five strings, a combination of both. The more experienced player probably will experiment with alterations to those tunings.

One should explore the use of the fiddle in Renaissance polyphony with singers or with other soft instruments such as the harp and lute. It can play any type of music, but an interesting place to begin is with some of the early Petrucci prints of untexted three- and four-part music, such as *Harmonice Musices Odhecaton A*, and its successors *Canti B* and *Canti C*. Depending on the sound, range, and set-up of the specific fiddle, an ensemble can try different combinations of instruments and many sorts of repertory.

The *lira da braccio* was one of the most important bowed string instruments in the Renaissance and is one of the most neglected today. Associated particularly with Orpheus and Apollo, it was cultivated in Italy during the fifteenth and sixteenth centuries for improvising accompaniment to poetry and was usually played by the poet himself. Though its primary use was for accompaniment of narrative, epic, and all other sorts of verse, it was also specifically called for in dramatic entertainments in Italy and in orchestras for *intermedi* such as *La Pellegrina* (1589).

A successor to the medieval fiddle (or possibly a Renaissance development of it), the lira da braccio is held and tuned similarly to the violin with seven strings tuned (d/d′-g/g′-d′-a′-e″, though Praetorius gives the pitch of the top string as d″.)[8] It looks a lot like a violin but with a wide neck, flatter bridge, and two lateral drone strings. Designed for chordal playing, its bow was either very long or very wide between the stick and the hair to accommodate playing three or four strings simultaneously, as seems to have been the practice.

The surviving music specified for the lira da braccio consists of one setting of the *romanesca* and a bit of a *passamezzo*, which are found in a late sixteenth-century Italian manuscript that also includes several charts showing chord positions. This tiny bit of information suggests that the instrument could play melody on its top two or three strings (the single courses) and accompanying chords on the lower. In its most usual context the lira da braccio might play simple chords and more complex melodic interludes to punctuate sung or spoken verse. As an ensemble instrument it can play a single line, possibly decorated with passage work, adding the odd chord for accompaniment.

The *rebec*, another instrument with medieval origins, survives in various forms even today. Sources that mention the rebec in the Renaissance include Tinctoris[9] (ca. 1487), for whom it and the fiddle were "my chosen instruments, those that induce piety and stir my heart most ardently to the contemplation of heavenly joys"; Virdung (1511); Gerle (1532), who gives several pieces for four-part consorts of rebecs; and Agricola (1545). There is clear evidence of its use in both art and more rustic music well into the seventeenth century. There were rebec players at Henry VIII's court in England. The instrument also appears in Italian painting of the late fifteenth century and French painting of the early sixteenth century—in short, the rebec was in use all over Europe during the Renaissance. It was played by professional musicians in royal courts and noble households, in sacred and secular processions, at feasts, dances and entertainments, and by non-professional players in rustic settings in taverns and at village revels.

In its Renaissance form the rebec is a pear-shaped wooden instrument with a pegbox and a tailpiece much like a violin. It seems to have been used like a violin, and some contemporary uses of the word rebec may actually refer to a violin or proto-violin.[10] There are usually three or four gut strings. Gerle says that the rebec is tuned in fifths, and Agricola gives tunings for four different sizes: a discant tuned g-d'-a', alto and tenor tuned c-g-d', and bass F-G-d-a. (These pitches are relative, not absolute.) There seems not to have been any distinction between bows made for various instruments. Perhaps the particular instrument and the music to be played will suggest an appropriate length, weight, and shape of bow.

During the sixteenth century some rebecs appeared that were narrow in proportion to their length. These easily portable instruments, associated with dancing masters and dancers, became known as *kits* (French: *pochette*). Besides the boat-shaped model derived from the rebec, later kits resemble viols, violins, guitars, or sometimes hybrids of various bowed strings. Instruments survive from all over Europe, some by makers as famous as Antonio Stradivari, some richly decorated, others very simple.

Generally, the kit has a narrow body and a relatively long string length, with three or four strings and no frets. It can be tuned like a violin, or a fourth, fifth, or even an octave higher if it only has three strings. Played on the arm, its bow can be similar to a rebec or Renaissance violin bow. There is iconographic and literary evidence for the kit at all levels of society, though there is no surviving music specifically composed for it. The Renaissance violin repertory of dance music and popular tunes is appropriate for performance on the kit.

The *trumpet marine* (French: *trompette marine*, German: *Trumscheit*, Italian: *tromba marina*) developed in the mid-fifteenth century from the plucked medieval monochord. It had several different shapes and sizes in the Renaissance that gradually merged into a mature form whose period of greatest popularity seems to have been the mid-seventeenth to early eighteenth centuries, beyond the scope of this chapter. The trumpet marine was mentioned by Virdung, Agricola, Praetorius, and Mersenne, among others; there are five surviving sixteenth-century examples in museums today.

The trumpet marine is an open-ended, hollow resonator with an attached neck usually topped by a scroll with a tuning device of some kind. Usually there is only one string, though earlier examples seem to have had up to four strings. It was held either at the shoulder or resting on the ground, depending in part on its size. A striking feature of the trumpet marine is its vibrating bridge; its one string is not centered on the bridge leaving one foot free to buzz against the soundboard. This increases the volume and causes the buzzing or snarling sound that Praetorius says is more pleasant to listen to from a distance.

Individual pitches are sounded by touching the string lightly with the fingers or thumb of the left hand to produce harmonics. The smaller, shoulder-held model was bowed close to the nut and supported by the left hand, a method of playing that limits one's dexterity. Another limiting factor is that harmonics are very close together on a short string length. In its most satisfying form, which evolved in the late sixteenth century, the larger, vertically held instrument can produce all the pitches of the harmonic series through the sixteenth partial. A long string length makes the pitches lie farther apart and therefore easier to find. A skilled player can alternate between letting the bridge vibrate and playing normal harmonics; ornamentation is also possible. In short, the trumpet marine is an unusual specialized instrument that can be a fascinating addition to a Renaissance ensemble.

The *viola da gamba* family is the best known of the bowed strings of the Renaissance. Today it is associated particularly with English music of the late sixteenth and seventeenth centuries and French seventeenth- and eighteenth-century music. But the history of the viols begins in the late fifteenth century and extends all over eastern and western Europe throughout the Renaissance.

Like many other sixteenth-century instruments, the *viole da gamba* (literally, "viols of the leg") are a family of instruments of varying sizes that play in different ranges. They have four to six strings tuned mostly in fourths.[11] Held vertically on the legs or between the calves depending on the size, viols are played with a bow held underneath the stick, "upside down" from a violin-family bow. The viol is traditionally constructed with a soundboard carved or bent to a slightly curved shape, a curved bridge and fingerboard, and seven or eight frets positioned by half-steps along the neck. Until the late seventeenth century the viol was strung in gut, although not enough is known about string technology to say exactly how the strings were made.

In an attempt to simplify a complex history, the viola da gamba family is usually characterized as having three sizes, namely treble, tenor (a fourth or fifth below the treble), and bass (a fourth or fifth below the tenor). This modern terminology is based on the later seventeenth-century English chest of viols, which contained smaller instruments than its sixteenth-century counterpart.[12] Thus one will find, for example, that the instrument known today as the bass viol is called a tenor viol by Praetorius. It may help to think of both sizes of viols and the pitch level to which they are tuned as

115

relative rather than absolute. There was no single absolute pitch in the Renaissance, and viol players transposed pieces to suit their instruments. (See Pitch and Transposition, p. 248.)

Unlike the bowed instruments discussed above, there is a good bit of information available about the playing technique of the viol. This technique was not the same in Italy in 1543 as it was in England in 1659, nor were the instruments themselves the same. The player must decide whether to pursue a single compromise technique on a compromise instrument—which will allow the performance of many different repertories—or else to apply a specific technique to a historically appropriate instrument for a specific repertory. It is difficult to become expert at several different historical viol techniques, as instruments, bow grips, and left-hand fingerings differ significantly from one period to another and one location to another.

In theory, frets make every note sound like an open string, a contraindication for constant vibrato, though vibrato can be a very effective way to grace individual notes. The viol can sustain a wonderful resonance after the bow leaves the strings, and thus the basic bow stroke can be more detached than the basic sound for which one strives on a modern violin or cello. One might think of the way a plucked instrument sustains sound as a preferable image. The left-hand technique reflects this idea and is more closely related to that of the lute than the cello, as it emphasizes horizontal, chordal fingerings and the holding down of fingers for as long as possible after a note is played.

The Bibliography lists several modern instruction books for the viol that are intended for private and classroom instruction with or without an experienced player or teacher, though live demonstration remains the best way to learn the capabilities of any instrument. Interested musicians should also consult historical sources, such as Ganassi, Gerle, Ortiz, Simpson, and Playford, for a glimpse of how people learned to play the viol in the sixteenth and seventeenth centuries. All are available in modern facsimile editions and translation into English where applicable.

Several specialist techniques that apply to the viol as a solo instrument are worthy of mention. One of these is the lyra style, characterized by *scordatura* (i.e., non-standard) tunings for the viol, and music that is usually read from the same sorts of tablature that lutenists read.[13] Chords are an integral part of this style; the concept for them goes back to Ganassi and forward into seventeenth-century England, where one finds a vast repertory of solo and ensemble tablature pieces in a chordal style. Chords on the viol should be played with due attention to sounding the bottom note on its own before rolling the bow to the top note of the chord. Any size viol can play "lyra way," but there are also instruments called lyra viols that are specially designed for this style of playing.

Another special technique is playing the viol *alla bastarda*, which involves virtuosic bursts of quick passagework all over the instrument. This style is manifest in sixteenth-century Italy in solo diminutions on polyphonic pieces. The performer draws on different voices of a madrigal, chanson, or motet and adds to them to the extent that the original polyphony is often obscured.

A third style of playing—improvising on a ground bass—might be compared to improvisatory practices of the twentieth century such as playing the blues. In the sixteenth century Ortiz devoted the second part of his treatise to examples of improvisation on a tenor line (*La spagna*) as well as the standard Italian grounds such as the *passamezzo moderno, passamezzo antico, Romanesca*, and *Ruggiero*. The English translation of this style of playing culminated in the *Division Viol* of Christopher Simpson (1659 and 1665). Simpson describes how to improvise on a ground bass and gives examples of preludes and divisions "for the practice of learners," with the implication that the more advanced player will make his own preludes and improvisations.

Classically trained musicians accustomed to being given exact information about which notes to play and how to play them may be surprised to find that there is a lot more to playing the viol than ever appears on the page. Ganassi tells the viol player that the quality of performance is enriched by ornamentation of a composition, and that one would draw praise from the listener if the diminutions were executed with varied and well-planned *passaggi*. Ortiz devotes the first part of his treatise to embellishment, that is, the filling of intervals in a polyphonic line with improvisation and the decoration of cadences.[14] It is clear that improvisation, on both a large and a small scale, was an integral part of viol playing.

The repertory for the viol is vast and widely available in monuments such as *Musica Brittanica*, collected works of individual composers, and general collections of Renaissance music.[15] In the corpus of music composed specifically for the viol, the English ensemble repertory of the sixteenth and seventeenth centuries is the best known, including instrumental fantasias, *In nomines*, dance movements, consort songs, and verse anthems.[16] But there is also French, German, and Italian ensemble music for viols. Solo music includes the above-mentioned Italian viola bastarda repertory, English lyra- and division-viol music. The Viola da Gamba Society of America is a good source of information about the availability of music for viols.[17]

In addition to music composed specifically for viols, one should not ignore the enormous sacred and secular vocal repertories of the Renaissance, as well as instrumental ricercars, canzonas, fantasias, and dances. Intabulation of polyphonic pieces by a single viol is possible, or one can play individual lines of polyphony in mixed ensembles with voices, keyboards, plucked instruments, soft wind instruments, and other strings. The English consort[18] deserves special mention as a specific mixed ensemble for which there exists a significant amount of music from around the turn of the seventeenth century.

A great deal of viol music is now available in facsimile[19] and on microfilm.[20] Even players of modest ability sometimes find that playing from original partbooks gives them a special sense of continuity with their counterparts from the time the music was composed. Unencumbered by bar lines, rehearsal letters, and scores, the player is forced to listen and learn a piece in a way that may take longer, but ultimately may be more satisfying.

Violone was another word for the viola da gamba in the sixteenth century. The word gradually came to refer particularly to the bass member of a viol ensemble and even to large bowed string instruments in general. A violone might have the size and range of today's standard bass viol, or it can be larger and tuned a fourth, fifth, or even an octave lower. Orlando Gibbons composed pieces for the "great dooble bass" that go down to A and are probably intended for the smaller violone. Though not enough specific information exists to draw positive conclusions, the violone can function at either 8-foot or 16-foot pitch for use in ensembles playing a bass line for polyphonic music or as part of a continuo section.

The *lirone*, or *lira da gamba*, is a larger, fretted, bass version of the lira da braccio that might date back to the early sixteenth century,[21] surviving until late in the seventeenth century. Like the lira da braccio, it is called for in some *intermedi*, but music specifically composed for it does not survive. The lirone seems to have been used mainly in Italy as a proto-continuo instrument, supporting a polyphonic texture or solo song with chords and occasional melodic decoration.

With two drone strings, nine to fourteen strings running along the fingerboard, and a tuning of either ascending fifths[22] or alternating ascending fifths and descending fourths,[23] many players will be daunted at the prospect of playing this instrument, even if an ensemble is lucky enough to acquire one. But with a playable instrument and a bit of experimentation, the intrepid player will discover that one fingering pattern will produce four- or five-note chords in many keys when applied to different strings. The addition of a barré technique in which the index finger is laid across several strings, and one or two other fingering patterns, will yield a great variety of chord inversions and progressions.

Though documentation for bowing technique is lacking for the lirone, an underhand bow grip allows control over the tension of the hair with the middle finger of the right hand. A well-set-up lirone is particularly crucial to the success of the player, as the curve of the bridge must allow easy access to four or five strings at once (but not all fourteen of them simultaneously!), and also the possibility of passagework on individual strings. Without this capability the instrument will be frustrating and ultimately unplayable. But the combination of a reasonable instrument and a performer willing to discover what it does will yield a unique and magical sound which is seldom heard and well worth the effort.

Maintenance

If one is responsible for the maintenance of Renaissance bowed strings, it is useful to establish a good relationship with a violin maker who is sympathetic to early instruments. Such a person can do most of the necessary repairs, though ideally it is best to have the maker maintain the instrument. An inexperienced string player should seek assistance if the bridge warps,[24] the soundpost[25] falls down, or the instrument starts buzzing, changes its sound, or develops bulges, cracks, or open seams.

All wooden instruments are happiest in a humidity-controlled environment. If the atmosphere is too dry (as often happens in heated buildings in the winter) the wood can shrink and develop cracks. The use of instrument humidifiers, which are sold by violin supply shops, should be approached with caution, as over-wetting can also damage an instrument. A room humidifier or even a pan of water set on a radiator can help maintain some moisture in the air. Too much humidity causes instruments to sound soggy and gut strings to disintegrate. The fit of the soundpost is affected by weather changes and sometimes requires adjustment by a professional instrument repairer.

Gut strings, the common denominator of Renaissance bowed instruments, are manufactured by a number of makers in the United States and Europe.[26] One should keep a supply of extra strings for these instruments, especially top strings, which tend to break more frequently than the thicker lower strings. Strings can be changed by the player or ensemble director when they break, lose their sound, or go false (i.e., no longer play in tune) after many hours of play. Attaching a new string is accomplished by first fixing the string to the tailpiece by means of a knot or loop, then feeding the free end through the hole in the peg and winding it on, making sure the string lies in the grooves cut for it on the bridge and nut. Care should be taken not to loosen too many strings at once, as the soundpost may fall over if pressure on the top of the instrument is suddenly released.

Frets must be replaced when they loosen, flatten, or break. A simple way to tie a fret is to make a loose overhand knot in one end of the gut or nylon, pass the fret material around the neck twice,[27] then put the unknotted end through the middle of the knot and pull tight.[28] The positioning of the frets can be done by ear or with the assistance of a tuning machine. There is evidence for various tuning systems on fretted instruments,[29] but most sources agree that the player should use his ear as the final arbiter, and pitches on gut strings, even on fretted instruments, are somewhat adjustable by a skilled player.

Many bows have a screw on the end that adjusts the tension of the hair. One needs to experiment with hair tension. The tension is not high enough if the wooden stick makes constant contact with the strings. It is too high if the bow bounces on the strings. Over-tightening the bow can put undue stress on the stick. The player should loosen the tension when the bow is put away. Bows need rosin periodically, the necessity for which is indicated by the bow sliding around on the string more than usual and the player having difficulty in producing a focused sound. The bow should be smoothly drawn in one direction (lengthwise) across the cake of rosin several times. Bows also need occasional rehairing, something done by a bow maker or string instrument repair person. Players of gut-strung viols are urged to experiment with using some or all black horsehair, which has a coarser texture than its white counterpart. The modern string technician may want to put too much hair on a Renaissance bow and should be discouraged from doing so.

Priorities

Bowed instruments are expensive to purchase, string, and maintain. The best instruments should ideally be given to the least experienced players, as badly made instruments are very difficult and discouraging to tune and play. A good bow can help even a mediocre instrument sound much better. One should consult an experienced player for advice on instruments, bows, and strings. For further information about players, instruments, bows, strings, repertory, and short courses for enthusiasts, contact the Viola da Gamba Society of America.[30]

A logical first instrument for an ensemble to acquire is a bass viol[31] on an English or Italian model from around 1575, which would combine flexibly with other families of instruments and voices. From there the director must

FIGURE 11.1 Title page from Ganassi's *Regola Rubertina*

consider which repertories are most frequently performed by the ensemble. If an ensemble is interested in complete families of instruments and the music of the latter part of the Renaissance period, it will gradually acquire a matched consort of viols (perhaps in the order of tenor, treble, bass, tenor, treble). Alternatively, an ensemble interested in variety of sound and mixed consorts should go in the direction of tromba marina, Renaissance fiddles, and rebecs. If Italian solo singing and proto-continuo playing are stressed, the lira da braccio and lirone are the ideal bowed instruments. The fully equipped ensemble would have a chest of five Italian sixteenth-century viols, six English-style consort viols, three lyra viols, a violone, a trumpet marine, vielle(s), rebec(s), a kit, a lira da braccio, and a lirone. The ideal ensemble would also have enthusiastic virtuosi who could play all those instruments!

FIGURE 11.2 Violas da gamba (1, 2, 3); Viol Bastarda (4); lira da braccio (5)
Praetorius, *Syntagma musicum* II, Plate XX

NOTES

1. One places the finger immediately behind, but touching the fret.
2. Thanks to Jeffery Kite-Powell for noting that guitar players find that the left hand technique of the viola da gamba family comes especially easily, since the tuning is similar to that of the guitar.
3. See Bibliography.
4. For hints on placement of horizontally held instruments, see the chapter on the Renaissance violin.
5. Slurring, the deliberate playing of more than one note in the same bow, is best attempted only after one can play one note at a time.
6. Fr. *vielle*; Ger. *fiedel*; Sp. *vihuela da arco*; It. *viola*.
7. A flat bridge is more likely to want a tuning of unisons, fifths, or octaves, so that the open strings produce a consonance when played simultaneously.
8. According to Ray Nurse these pitches are relative, as there are different sizes of lira da braccio.
9. *De inventione et usu musicæ* (see Bibliography for references to primary and secondary sources).
10. Information courtesy of Ray Nurse.
11. The standard tuning for families of six-stringed viols, which can be substantiated from sixteenth-century Italy through eighteenth-century France (though one would not make any claim for its exclusivity), is all perfect fourths except for a major third between the middle two strings.
12. This statement must be understood to represent the tip of an iceberg. Most of today's viol enthusiasts play mostly English music on mostly English-style consorts of viols. Research on Renaissance viols, spearheaded of late by Ray Nurse, shows that the sixteenth-century Italian consort of viols was very different in construction, size of instrument, and tuning. Rather than becoming discouraged, the reader is encouraged to revel in the variety of sound and color presented by the seemingly endless range of viol shapes and sizes.
13. For further information on tablature, see the chapters on notation and plucked instruments.
14. See Brown–*Embellishing* for more information about this important and neglected subject.
15. For example, London Pro Musica, Antico, and Hortus Musicus editions. All these can be obtained from music shops specializing in early music. (See also the chapter Editions.)
16. Although it stretches credibility to call the seventeenth century the Renaissance, English music in particular refuses to adhere to the stylistic or chronological limits we try to impose on it. Few would describe English viol fantasies of Gibbons or Dowland's *Lacrimæ*, for example, as Baroque music.
17. Desktop publishing helps keep alive the tradition of transmission of repertory by viol players to their colleagues. See, for example, the publications by the Viola da Gamba Societies of America and Great Britain, Dovehouse, Fretwork, and PRB Publications.
18. An ensemble consisting of treble viol or violin, flute or recorder, bass viol, lute, bandora, and cittern, sometimes mistakenly referred to as a "broken" consort.
19. Broude, Scolar Press, Alamire, Garland, Boethius, and SPES publications, for example.
20. The Harvester Microfilm Collections contains, among other things, a large proportion of the English viol repertory in partbooks copied by players of the sixteenth and seventeenth centuries.
21. Once again, thanks to Ray Nurse for the information of a possible mention of a lirone as early as 1505.
22. Praetorius gives a tuning of C♭-d♭ for the drones and A♭-e♭-B♭-f-c-g-d-a-e-b-f♯-c♯ for the fingered ones.
23. Mersenne gives two tunings, the most usual of which is c-c' for the drones, then d-d'-g-g'-d'-a-e'-b-f♯-c♯-g♯-d♯-a♯.
24. The bridge should be examined regularly and carefully straightened if it is leaning toward

the scroll of the instrument. The side toward the tailpiece should be perpendicular to the plane of the belly (at least in traditionally constructed instruments).

25. The vertical wooden dowel inside the body located under the treble side.
26. Consult current early-music shops and journals or the Viola da Gamba Societies of America and Great Britain for sources of gut strings.
27. Make sure to go under all the strings!
28. The fret will cross over itself, but it is easy to adjust the place where it crosses to be out of the way.
29. See the chapters on Tuning and Temperament and Plucked Instruments.
30. This organization, despite its name, has members interested in all Renaissance bowed instruments. Its address is given at the end of this chapter.
31. The d-tuned instrument Praetorius refers to as a tenor viola da gamba, but in modern terminology is called a bass viola da gamba.

Bibliography

Agricola–*Musica*; Applebaum–*Art*; Bishop–*Method*; Brown–*Embellishing*; Crum–*Play*; Dodd–*Thematic*; Gammie–*Book*; Ganassi–*Regola*; Ganassi–*Lettione*; Gerle–*Musica*; Knighton/Fallows (Thomas)–*Companion*; Mersenne–*Harmonie*; Ortiz–*Tratado*; Panofsky–*Bass*; Playford–*Musick's*; Praetorius–*Syntagma*; Remnant–*English*; Simpson–*Division*; Tinctoris–*De inventione*; Virdung–*Musica*; Woodfield–*Early*.

Suggested Listening

Diego Ortiz, Jordi Savall and others, Astre (1984) (music from Ortiz's *Tratada da glosas*) E8717.

Dreames and Imaginations, David Gordon, tenor, with consort of viols, Musical Heritage Society, MHS 512390Y (Elizabethan consort songs, lyra viol music and viol consorts) (1989).

Hearts Ease, Fretwork, Virgin Classics, Ltd., VC7, 90706–4 (Consort of viols playing English sixteenth- and seventeenth-century music) (1988).

Heavenly Noyse, Dowland Consort, BIS CD-451 (English mixed consort) (1989).

Joyne Hands: Music of Thomas Morley, Musicians of Swanne Alley and Red Byrd, Virgin Classics VC7 91214–2 (English mixed consort) (1992).

Renaissance Music from the Courts of Mantua and Ferrara, Circa 1500, Chandos CHAN 8333 (lirone).

Selva di varii passaggi, Ariane Maurette and others, Gallo 30–461 (Italian Renaissance viols, Italian diminutions) (1986).

Una Stravaganza dei Medici: Intermedi (1589) per la pellegrina, The Taverner Consort, Choir, and Players, Andrew Parrott, director, EMI, CDC 7 47998 2 (lirone, lira da braccio, viols) (1988).

For further information:

The Viola da Gamba Society of America
  John A. Whistler, Executive Secretary and Treasurer
  1308 Jackson Avenue
  Charleston, IL 61920–2242

The Viola da Gamba Society of Great Britain
  The Administrator
  Carolyn Wood
  56 Hunters Way
  Dringhouses, York YO2 2JJ
  England

Both of the above organizations publish an annual journal and quarterly newsletters containing articles about instruments, repertory, bibliography, and recent research, as well as reviews of and advertisements for concerts, publications, instruments, bows, and recordings. One also finds information about long- and short-term course offerings for players, builders, and scholars.

12

The Violin

David Douglass

It is still not common knowledge (even among violinists) that the violin family was an important part of the musical life of the sixteenth century. This condition is rarely addressed by stringed instrument educators or even early music programs. This apathy toward the early history of the violin has deprived violinists of an enjoyable repertory. But more important, studying the origin of the violin, understanding and incorporating the techniques of the dance master, and developing an appreciation of Renaissance polyphony will open worlds to be experienced and will also cast a new light on later, more familiar repertories. Fortunately, unraveling the early history of the violin is not an impossible task, as there is sufficient information to assemble an account of the use of the violin during the Renaissance.

Early History

It is impossible to pinpoint exactly when the violin came into being, since bowed-string instruments existed in many forms and were continually evolving. The development of instruments we would recognize as violins occurred at the end of the fifteenth century, an especially active time of experimentation in instrument construction. The violin varied in design throughout most of the sixteenth century, and it coexisted with other bowed-string instruments (such as the rebec) that were tuned likewise in fifths and played on the arm or shoulder. It was not until the mid-sixteenth century that Cremonese and Brescian makers, Andrea Amati and Gasparo da Salo in particular, began producing what we think of today as the "standard" violin model, although with some important differences: the neck was very short (on the violin proper, just large enough to accommodate the hand) and set in the plane of the body, rather than arched backward as the modern one is. Bass bars were at first entirely absent, and the first ones were much smaller than the standard modern pattern.

The proto-violin of the early sixteenth century had three strings, and music theorists of that time indicate that it was tuned in fifths, which correspond roughly to the lowest three strings of modern tunings. The fourth and highest string was added by the mid-sixteenth century. The expanded range improved the violin as a dance instrument, and made the entire family more versatile for the performance of polyphony. The bass of the family came in two sizes, large and small. The first was somewhat larger than the violoncello (which began to supplant it in the late seventeenth century). It was tuned $B\flat_1$-F-c-g, a whole tone below the 'cello; Praetorius (1619) was the first to give the C-G-d-a tuning. The small bass was considerably smaller than a 'cello and was tuned either F-c-g-d' or a tone higher. Lines of polyphonic music that lie at the very bottom of the viola tuned in C would be much more easily played on a small bass in F. Of course, letter names for pitches do not take into account the wide range of frequencies that could sound for each pitch. Since violins often played with cornetts, sackbuts, and other high-pitched winds, they had to match that pitch standard (commonly a' = 460, or even higher).

The first Renaissance theorist to discuss the violin family in a significant way (beyond the basics of tunings) was Philibert Jambe de Fer in his treatise *Epitome musical* of 1556. This short text contains a wealth of information about how and when the violin was played in the sixteenth century. In a comparison of the viol and violin he states:

> The violin [*violon*] is very different from the viol [*viole*]. First of all it has only four strings, which are tuned in fifths . . . and in each of the said strings there are four tones [*tons*] in such a way that in four strings there are as many tones as in the five strings of the viol. The form of the body is smaller, flatter, and in sound it is much harsher [*rude*]; it has no frets [tuning instructions follow] and the French and Italians differ in no way as regards playing the instrument.

> Why do you call one type of instrument viols and the other violins?

> We call viols those with which gentlemen, merchants, and other virtuous people pass their time.

> The Italians call them *viole da gambe* [*sic*] because they are held downward, some between the legs, others on some seat or stool; others [are held] on the knees by the said Italians, although the French make little use of this method. The other type [of instrument] is called violin; it is commonly used for dancing, and for good reason, for it is much easier to tune since the interval of the fifth is easier [*plus douce*] to hear [accurately] than the fourth. It is also easier to carry, a very necessary thing while leading [*conduisant*] wedding processions or mummeries.

> The Italians call it *violon da braccia* [*sic*] or *violone* because they support it on the arm, some with a scarf, strings or some other thing; the bass [member of the family] is very difficult to carry because of its weight, for which reason it is sustained with a small hook in an iron ring or other thing, which is attached to the back of the said instrument very exactly so that it does not interfere with the player. I have not illustrated the said violin because you can think of it as resembling the viol, added to which there are few persons who use it save those who make a living from it through their labour.[1]

Since dance music was the primary repertory of the Renaissance violinist and dancing was an entertainment shared by most segments of society, fiddling was a source of employment as well as an enjoyable pastime. By the 1530s the financial records of courts across Europe show payments to violin bands (a consort of violin family instruments) for both public festivities and private functions, and by the end of the sixteenth century violin bands were a fashionable entertainment medium for anyone who could afford them. One example of the extent to which violin playing permeated society is found in an account of Mary Queen of Scots' return to Edinburgh in 1561 by the sixteenth-century chronicler Branthome. He tells of hundreds of "scoundrels" who disturbed her sleep playing the "retched violins of which there is no lack of in this country" [*sic*]. A few violinists, such as Balthasar de Beaujoyeulx and Antonio Morari, became quite famous and were able to secure high salaries.

The term "violin band" is slightly misleading in that the repertory of the sixteenth century relied heavily on violas. In some instances a violin is not even needed because the range of the music is low and the parts are tightly voiced. Music written with two equal treble parts requiring two violins does not appear until the early seventeenth century. It is best to stay in the upper range of whatever sizes you choose for performing a polyphonic composition, in order to play on the most efficient and responsive gut strings, but some Renaissance violas were very large and can easily manage parts to the bottom of their range.

The fact that Renaissance instruments differed in construction from their modern counterparts should not deter string players from attempting to play the repertory on their twentieth-century instruments. With a few minor changes in equipment most novices can take a big step toward a Renaissance sound. The two most effective changes involve the strings and bow. Renaissance strings were made entirely of gut (specifically, sheep intestine) and provided quite a different sound from modern overspun strings. Determining what size and kind of gut string should be used is not difficult once a few basic concepts are understood. Pitch on stringed instruments is a factor of three main variables: string length, diameter, and density. Increasing the length or the diameter has the effect of lowering the pitch, and decreasing either has the opposite effect. Since the vibrating length of a violin is a fixed distance from the nut to the bridge, the pitch of the instrument is established primarily by determining the proper string diameters. High pitches, such as $a' = 460$, allow the use of relatively thin strings that have the advantage of quick response with a clear sound. Thicker strings are noisier due to the greater friction required to activate them and are slower to respond. In fact, thick gut strings of normal construction are most unsatisfactory as bottom strings. It is suspected that before the advent of overspinning with metal (first documented in the late seventeenth century) string makers improved the response and intonation of the lower strings by imparting greater twist or even using a rope-like construction. Recently a few specialist makers have been applying these techniques to producing middle and lower strings. We may never know for certain whether their "catlines," "lyons," or "pistoy basses" are the same as those mentioned in Renaissance sources, but at the moment they are the only viable alternatives to (clearly anachronistic) overspun strings. It is usually best at first to let a string maker decide what strings should be used (once you inform him of the string length and desired pitches), and then, after you have some experience with them, you can change them to suit your individual needs. There are no hard and fast rules about what is best. Some players prefer thick strings at a high tension, and some prefer the opposite.

The second most important change from modern equipment involves the bow. The Renaissance bow tended to be short, with an outward bend. Bows of this design, when used with the technique of the period, facilitate the clear and quick articulation of gut strings. Renaissance bows had no screws but used clip-in frogs, which, once in place, brought the hair to playing tension. However, high humidity could make the hair too loose, and it would eventually stretch and have to be replaced. One style of Renaissance bow featured hair that was tied at the tip in a way that it could easily be detached and shortened to restore the proper tension—an asset for the professional musician who could thus do his own repair work.

Repertory

Once schooled in the basics, violinists were often taught their parts by rote, almost always playing from memory. Some dance music was improvised around a unifying melody or harmony but the extant music for violin band is vast and indicates the high level of ability that was required of these professional musicians. All of the numerous dance publications of the sixteenth century—by Susato, Gervaise, Phalese, Bendusi, and others—if not written exclusively for violins, are perfectly suited to them. Canzonas, originating in the sixteenth century and popular well into the seventeenth, provide particularly complex rhythmic challenges and help to shatter the belief, often held by modern musicians, that Renaissance music is simple. Another source of purely instrumental music is the ricercar repertory. Composers such as Gabrieli, Willaert, and Cavazzoni wrote their ricercars primarily for keyboard, but indicate that they can also be performed on other instruments. By the early seventeenth century, composers such as Cifra and Trabaci specify that their ricercars are also appropriate for violin band.

The sixteenth-century English fantasy was probably intended for viols, but the early seventeenth-century dances, canzonas, and ricercars of composers such as Dowland, Simpson, and Holborne approach the complexity of the English fantasy and were specifically written for violins as well as viols.

Determining the suitability of a piece of music for violins (as opposed to viols) is complicated by the fact that professional violinists often played viola da gamba as well. There is no evidence to suggest that violins and viols *never* played together, and by the mid-seventeenth century, chamber works were scored for various combinations of the two. Since violins and viols produce different sounds at different volumes and with different articulations, an extra effort must be made to establish a consort with truly equal voices. For dance music, this effort is mostly the responsibility of the gambist, who must concentrate more pressure into the string at the moment of bow-change in order to match the greater volume and more aggressively articulated over-hand bowing of the violin. For other music, such as fantasias, the violinists might imitate the sound of the viols, smoothing out the articulation some-what. Matching the energetic bowing of the Renaissance violin is anathema to many modern gambists whose appreciation of the viola da gamba re-volves around the voluptuous sound and seamless phrasing natural to an underhand grip. Modern gambists have also suffered from an unnatural isolation, for until recently the viola da gamba has been the only Renais-sance bowed string instrument to enjoy a revival. In the sixteenth century, however, the sounds of the violin and its expressive devices were a part of the musical consciousness. One of the most important educational aids for the beginning Renaissance violinist is the alternative experience of the gambist, especially for those whose background has been the equally iso-lated environment of the modern violin. As the nature and capabilities of the Renaissance violin and violin band become more a part of the vocabu-lary of early music (it is, after all, a relatively recent rediscovery), violinists and gambists will incorporate each others' natural strengths to the benefit of everyone, and combining them will be less of an issue.

In the late Renaissance, music for violin band blossomed in variety, quan-tity, and degree of compositional daring, but the basic identity of the violin band remained that of a dance ensemble well into the eighteenth century. The dance music of Brade, Trabaci, Praetorius, Hammerschmidt, and innu-merable others continued to widen the scope of this once-utilitarian music. Even many of the late seventeenth-century dances and consort sonatas of Biber retain the important characteristics of equal-voiced Renaissance poly-phony, and are most fully experienced from the articulate and energetic perspective of the Renaissance violin band. Since music is inextricably en-twined with time and historical context, it can be fully appreciated only from a forward-looking perspective. It is a simple principle that is easy to forget, since we are forced to look backward at this repertory in the first place.

In addition to the many instrumental forms appropriate for the violin, evidence shows that a wide variety of vocal music rounded out the reper-tory for violin band. Aside from the vocal forms that were closely related to instrumental music, such as the *balletti* of Gastoldi and Vecchi or the

Neapolitan canzonas of Willaert, we know that violin bands performed their own renditions of motets and madrigals, particularly the arioso madrigals of such composers as Verdelot, Lassus, and Wert. The account of the 1568 wedding of the Duke of Barvaria to Renée of Lorraine describes violin-band performances of motets by Cipriano de Rore, among others. For modern violinists, playing vocal music is also an effective way of developing an awareness of articulation, by imitating the inflections of words and phrases, and by learning to communicate a sense of sentence structure. To become as subtle and as flexibly expressive as a singer is usually a captivating idea to the novice early violinist whose previous goals as a modern violinist had been the development of right-hand power and the mastery of ever more complex left-hand calisthenics.

Not all of the repertory for Renaissance violin is ensemble music. A large body of virtuoso solo repertory exists in the form of solo renditions of polyphonic works, ornamentations of songs, and improvised variations over ground basses. The Italian practice of division ornamentation—the origin of this solo repertory—can be studied in the treatises of the period, many of which are now available in modern English-language editions. Many ornamentations of madrigals have also been published in easily obtainable modern editions. These may be performed to the accompaniment of violin band or chordal continuo instruments that supply the remaining parts of the polyphony. Amadeus Press has published a wonderful edition of diminutions in which madrigals with all of their extant ornamentations are collected and presented in score. Besides providing a wealth of performance material, this edition is a very good educational tool that allows one to explore the important elements of style by comparing the different ornamentations. The most exciting goal of the modern Renaissance violinist is to be able to improvise new works in the appropriate style.

One long-lived spinoff of Italian ornamentation, the English practice of division playing, was born in the Renaissance and thrived well into the eighteenth century. Violinists of many nationalities gained international fame through their ability to improvise divisions of incredible complexity. The fact that these Renaissance-style works were still in publication at the same time as the new solo sonata repertory in the seventeenth century gives added insight into the ways in which these early Baroque-style works were perceived and played. The legacy of the dance master and his technique lasted much longer and changed more slowly than most violinists would like to admit.

Learning to improvise Renaissance divisions is accomplished by first becoming comfortable with the rules of Renaissance ornamentation (adding notes to an established melody), and then gradually increasing the complexity of the ornamentations. One feature of divisions, a highly specialized form of ornamentation, is that the identity of the original melody is sometimes completely obscured in the most elaborate of the divisions. For example, take the melody to "John come kiss me now":

EX. 12.1 "John come kiss me now"

After stating the theme the division violinist, in this case David Mell as printed in *The Division Violin* in 1684 (which, in spite of its late date, represents an earlier practice), ornamented it in a way that divided the melody (hence the name of the style of playing) into faster and faster note values:

EX. 12.2 Divisions on "John come kiss me now"

Eventually, the melody was left entirely, and he worked solely with the underlying harmony:

EX. 12.3 Improvisation based on "John come kiss me now"

Like improvisors of jazz, Renaissance division violinists develop a vocabulary of melodic devices that can be drawn on spontaneously. But before reaching that point the student of division playing practices by improvising simple variations to acclimate the fingers and ear to the pitches on the fingerboard. More complex divisions should be composed on paper as a mental and creative exercise, and then memorized as a vocabulary of ideas for later use. It is a long and difficult process, but the final result is the most exciting performance practice possible—a living creation rather than a studied recreation.

Technique

What was the technique of the Renaissance dance master? The most important clues for unlocking that mystery are in the iconography of the period. In practically every instance it is easy to see that the instrument is held very low, comfortably nestled in the area of the armpit. Both arms hang in a relaxed position at the sides, and the arms need be raised only enough to make playing convenient. One example of this playing position, and one of my favorites for its simplicity and essence of relaxation, appears in Arbeau's *Orchésographie*, a dance treatise published in 1589. The results, from what seems like a relatively small change in position, are far-reaching. Because the instrument does not need to be held up, neither does the bow arm, and explosive articulations can be made from a sudden and complete release of the weight of the arm. In my opinion, it is the single most important reason that the violin was so highly prized as a dance instrument. Renaissance technique gives the dance master a bow stroke that is impossible to create from a higher-held position because the additional weight of the arm would overpower the string. Trying to imitate the stroke in a higher placement by using a faster bow speed will still betray the tension that exists in the arm from holding the arm up. The dance master's technique allows tremendous freedom, and that freedom can be communicated directly through sound as well as movement. Indeed, some paintings of violin bands in action depict musicians dancing to their own music. The simplicity of sound and the energy of articulation, natural to the bow arm when the instrument is held this low, is equally beneficial to the performance of polyphony for many of the same reasons. It lends a unique sound and an energetic detail to each line.

Since the weight of the arm is not so much a factor on the up-bow with this low placement, differences between up-bow and down-bow are minimized. A passage that might be "corrected" by a modern violinist because it feels backward is more easily played "as it comes" with a lower bow arm. In treatises by Gasparo Zannetti, Richardo Rogniono, and Francesco Rognioni, it is clear that the Renaissance violinist organized his bowing (with a minimum of corrections) so that down-bows fell on strong beats, regardless of whether they were "downbeats." Thus, pieces commonly began or ended with up-bows rather than down-bows because more important notes occurred *after* the first note or *before* the last note. Here is an example of bow markings in a saltarello from Zannetti's *Il Scolaro per Imparar Suonare i violino* (1645):

EX. 12.4   Zannetti: *Il Scolaro per Imparar*

By starting up-bow (rather than down-bow, by convention), every important note of the melody is stressed, and the down-bow on the final note prepares the player for the up-bow on the return without unnecessary retaking. Following this example (Crequillon's *Frisque et Galliard*), a canzona might also begin with an up-bow:

EX. 12.5   Crequillon: *Frisque et Galliard*

An example of an unimportant final note might be the cadence of Anthony Holborne's *Spero*, published in his collection of *Pavans, Galliards, and Almains* of 1599. In the final two measures of the first section the cantus part extends the cadence in a manner that is most expressively bowed with a down-bow on the downbeat of the last measure, rather than last note:

EX. 12.6   Holborne: *Spero*

One other small change necessitated by the different position of the instrument involves the bow grip. When the violin is held on the shoulder and the right arm is raised, the contact point of the index finger on the bow is outside the large, middle finger joint, so that the wrist is at an angle offering the greatest degree of flexibility. When the violin is moved down on the arm, that advantageous contact point moves further into the hand, just inside the middle joint. Even though it might seem inhibiting at first, altering the contact point corrects the forearm and wrist angles and allows them to work together properly.

The large frogs commonly found on Renaissance bows produce a particularly large distance from the stick to the hair, which is often a psychological impediment for modern string players who are used to the feel of bows with smaller frogs. Some pictures show an alternative bow grip in which the thumb is positioned *underneath* the hair. This grip allows more direct control of the hair, which not only satisfies the player, but enhances the bowing of any music requiring aggressive or highly articulate bow strokes. Not surprisingly, this technique is particularly successful for dance music. An additional benefit to this thumb position is that the pressure from the thumb can tighten bow hair that has loosened from humidity or other causes. There is one repertory that in my experience does not benefit from this bow grip: division music. The open hand that results from the grip reduces the flexibility of the fingers, and this flexibility is essential for the subtle phrasing of rapid divisions.

One of the initial responses I get from students when they first attempt to play with low violin placement is that the left hand feels uncomfortable, particularly with the added reach necessitated by the low placement. The short necks of the period instruments are definitely more comfortable physically (and comfort should be a hallmark of any technique), but modern-length necks are perfectly manageable. Complaints about left-hand comfort usually mask the real issue, which is the modern prejudice regarding the need for total left-hand mobility. Doing anything to restrict the freedom of the left hand is considered foolish, and the added responsibility of having to hold the instrument in place seems only to make it worse. The truth is that the left hand is relatively unimportant: all that is required of it is that a finger be at the right place at the right time. Information from a few sixteenth- and seventeenth-century sources tells us that the sound of the open strings was preferred to that of stopped strings, so the fourth finger (the finger most disadvantaged by the position, due to the angle of the hand to the fingerboard) is rarely used. If the fourth finger is called on, as a result of a particular melodic figuration that creates numerous string crossings, it can be aided by dropping the wrist as much as possible. Afterward, the wrist can return to its normal position. Even measured trills (*groppi*) to open-string notes are best accomplished through a rapid exchange of open string and leading tone, instead of fourth-finger and leading tone. The dissonance created from the ringing open string amplified the effect of the ornament.

Shifting through positions up and down the fingerboard is possible, with practice, although most repertory never requires you to leave first position. Even so, we know that many Renaissance violinists (particularly Italians) were famed for playing to the end of the fingerboard. Unfortunately, no modern violinist (myself included) has yet become sufficiently adept at Renaissance technique, or stylistically familiar enough with the repertory, to accomplish such a feat. At first, shifting while holding the instrument in the low position will seem like a physical impossibility, but once a player becomes more relaxed and understands the specific mechanics involved, shifting becomes easier. Shifting is most often accomplished through a crawling motion, traveling through positions one at a time. The thumb remains back in its first-position placement, ready to pull the hand back. Another advantage of the short Renaissance neck is that third or even fourth position, depending on the size of the hand, can be reached with the thumb still anchored to first position. Raising the neck slightly above the horizontal also aids shifting back. Accurate intonation is elusive at first, but it is easy to forget how hard it was to learn to shift accurately using any technique. Since shifting while holding the violin in a low position involves some complicated maneuvers, many students come to the quick and misguided conclusion that Renaissance technique is inferior and unnecessary. However, the primary reason for using Renaissance technique (or for that matter, the technique of any period for the performance of its music) has to do with the way in which the music is expressed. The bow arm is the major source of expression (often a surprising discovery to a modern violinist once vibrato is eliminated as the primary expressive device) and deserves a string player's undivided attention, while the left-hand works unconsciously.

As style evolved from the Renaissance into the Baroque, violin placement rose higher on the shoulder. As the bow arm rose proportionately to accommodate the higher position, the gathering weight of the arm effectively allowed violinists to communicate with the new stylistic vocabulary. The tension that results from constantly carrying the weight of the arm creates the proper circumstances for expressing Baroque music in a way that is natural to the whole body, just as total relaxation of Renaissance technique allows the whole body to perform Renaissance dance music or polyphony (or the early solo sonata, for that matter) in the most effective way. Currently, students of Baroque technique tend to be fanatical about erasing tension, because they know that it is a more relaxed technique than the one they grew up with, but working by gradual subtraction does not necessarily teach the proper rôle of tension and the weight of the bow arm in a style. Coming from the perspective of Renaissance technique, from the near absence of weight and tension, the effect of tension and its rôle in the expression of style are easy to experience and understand. By beginning at the beginning you can learn how to use your body as well as your mind to lead you toward the expressive communication of many different styles of music.

Once the importance of using the appropriate technique is fully appreciated, it becomes necessary to determine the violin's (and the all-important bow arm's) specific degree of elevation. Almost every piece, and certainly every composer, needs to be evaluated individually, and the stylistic requirements of the bow must be weighed against the logistical needs of the left hand. One must not jump to the conclusion that a higher placement is better only because the left hand needs to shift. Moments of shifting are often sufficiently accommodated by rests in the music or strategically placed notes on open strings, and if the character of a piece of music will be best served by a lower placement it is worth working out a few left-hand technical difficulties.

The violin-band repertory is a vast resource of music for viola, especially compared to later string music, and the egalitarian nature of Renaissance polyphony is usually a liberating experience to modern violists, who often see themselves as subservient inner-part players. Violinists who take up the challenge of playing viola will at least widen their marketability, but sensitive players will also deepen their understanding of string mechanics and the expressive use of the bow. There is also a wonderful hidden benefit in learning to adapt to many different string lengths: in order to play in tune you must learn to engage the ear. You might be surprised at the number of string players who have stopped listening to themselves in the process of acquiring proper left-hand mechanics. It is only a short jump, once you are listening, to concentrating on *how* you are playing that in-tune note, and then the path to phrasing, articulation, and effective communication is open.

FIGURE 12.1 Violin family
Praetorius, *Syntagma musicum* II, Plate XXI

My experience has been that only adventurous and curious string players fully accept the challenge of new repertory, instruments, and techniques. It is hard enough to learn to play just one way, and most violin teachers actively discourage any deviation from their own personal method. Often (as in my case) the novelty of other, less familiar Renaissance instruments will lure modern string players into earlier repertories. Then, once convinced that their violin, viola, or cello is also a "period instrument," even if it is not in "period condition," they might be willing to come to grips with the subtleties of Renaissance technique. With the advent of professional violin bands such as the King's Noyse in Boston and the Orpheus Band in Chicago, young instrumentalists can experience this repertory firsthand in concerts and through recordings. Aside from the obvious advantages of seeing and hearing convincing performances of this repertory, students cannot afterward deny the value of early techniques and what they bring to the music. They will have to question the premise that their modern technique can accomplish everything, possibly realizing that all the work involved in exploring different ways of playing is worth the effort.

NOTES

1. David D. Boyden. *The History of Violin Playing* (London: Oxford University Press, 1965), 31–32.

Bibliography

Agricola–*Musica*; Bassano–*Ricercate*; Boyden–*New*; Boyden–*History*; Ganassi–*Regola*; Holman–*Four*; Jambe de Fer–*Epitome*; Mersenne–*Harmonie*; Riley–*Teaching*; Rogniono–*Passaggi*; Sandys–*History*; Van der Straeten–*History*; Zacconi–*Prattica*; Zannetti–*Il Scolaro*.

Suggested Listening

As I Went to Walsingham. The Musicians of Swanne Alley. HMU 905192 (1987).

Christmas Music by Michael Praetorius. Westminster Cathedral Choir and The Parley of Instruments, David Hill, conductor. Hyperion CDA 66200 (1986).

Consort Music by Peter Philips 1561–1628. The Parley of Instruments, Peter Holman, director. Hyperion CDA 66240 (1988).

An Englishman Abroad. The Parley of Instruments, Peter Holman, director. Hyperion CDA 66435 (1991).

In the Streets and Theatres of London: Elizabethan Ballads and Theatre Music. The Musicians of Swanne Alley. VC 7 90789-2 (1989).

The King's Delight: 16th- and 17th-Century Ballads and Instrumental Works. The King's Noyse, David Douglass, director. HMU 7101 (1991).

Music for Prince Charles: Fantasias and Dances by Orlando Gibbons (ca. 1583–1625) and Thomas Lupo (?1571–1627). The Parley of Instruments, Peter Holman, director. Hyperion CDA 66395 (1990).

Musick for Severall Friends: English Seventeenth-Century Theatre Music. The Newberry Consort, Mary Springfells, director. HMU 907013 (1989).

Instruments and Strings

Editor's note: As there is no Society for Early Violin, makers of violins, bows, and strings are listed below.

Instruments

Hansell, Roger. Grace Cottage, Caldbergh, NR Leyburn, North Yorkshire DL8 4RW, England.

Larson, Daniel. 26 N. 28th Avenue East, Duluth, MN 55812.

Pringle, John. 2218 Mount Willing Road, Efland, NC 27243.

Bows

Ashmead, Ralph. P.O. Box 1411, Tuolumne, CA 95379.

Grabenstein, H. F. East Farm, Charlotte, VT 05445.

Larson, Daniel. 26 N. 28th Avenue East, Duluth, MN 55812.

Strings

Boston Catlines. 34 Newberry Street, Somerville, MA 02144.

Damian Dlugolecki. 520 S.E. 40th Street, Troutdale, OR 97060.

Gamut Strings. 26 N. 28 Avenue East, Duluth, MN 55812.

13

Plucked Instruments

Paul O'Dette

The Lute

Of all Renaissance instruments the lute was, in the words of John Dowland, that which "ever hath been most in request." Though one of the best-known Renaissance instruments today, the lute, and especially its rôle in ensemble music, is often misunderstood. It is important to realize that the lute is not just a single instrument, but an entire family of instruments, involving different sizes, tunings, playing techniques, and functions. Thus, the instrument used to perform fifteenth-century chansons is quite a different beast from that used to accompany Elizabethan lute songs or Italian monody. Though few players are able to afford the more than two dozen plucked instruments required to perform music from the fifteenth to the seventeenth century, it is useful to know what instruments were originally used so that, if necessary, intelligent compromises may be reached. In fact much of this repertory can be performed on one or two instruments providing the players understand the techniques involved and are willing to make occasional changes to the stringing of the instruments. While ideally all the instruments discussed in this chapter would become part of an early-music ensemble's instrument collection, even a few lutes can be very effectively used in ensembles with the proper scorings and application.

In the late Middle Ages the lute generally had five pairs of strings, called "courses," the upper three of which were tuned in unison, the lower two in octaves. It is possible that the octaves were added after the introduction of right-hand finger technique, since Tinctoris is the first to mention them, and the brightness produced by a plectrum would have made them less necessary until that time. The highest course, or "chanterelle," was often, though not always, single for reasons of clarity and tuning (it being extremely difficult to get two very thin strings perfectly in tune). The strings were generally made entirely of gut, though Tinctoris mentions the use of brass for the octaves.[1] Notwithstanding that several different tunings were used in the fifteenth century, by the time Conrad Paumann invented

German lute tablature around 1470, the familiar tuning in fourths, with a third between the third and fourth courses, had become more or less standard. Lutes of many different sizes can be seen in paintings and drawings of the period, ranging from small descant instruments to large bass lutes. The keys of early German and Italian intabulations suggest that a tuning in a' or g' may have been the most common, at least for solo playing. (See tuning charts below.)

By 1500 (perhaps even several decades earlier) a sixth course had been added a fourth below the fifth course. Throughout most of the sixteenth century lutes had six courses with the lower three tuned in octaves. These octave strings were not only used to brighten the timbre—the thick gut bass strings of the time probably did not have very good pitch definition—but were also used melodically by such composers as Capirola, Spinacino, Francesco da Milano, and Bakfark. Thus, melodies on the upper strings will sometimes appear to stop in mid-phrase in the tablature, when they merely jump to the octave of the fourth or fifth courses, a situation almost never reflected in modern transcriptions of the music. The octaves also serve to enrich the sonority of the instrument, producing seven-note chords, for instance, when only four courses are played.

A seventh course, and eventually an eighth, became commonplace by the 1590s, while nine- and ten-course lutes had become standard by 1610, with the basses all strung in octaves. The Neapolitan Fabrizio Dentice appears to have been the first continental lutenist to tune the fourth, fifth, and sixth courses in unisons, possibly due to the Spanish influence on Naples[2] (see vihuela below). How far beyond Naples this practice spread is not known; however, from at least the fifth course down, octaves seem to have been standard well into the seventeenth century, with the possible exception of England. Dowland was critical of octave stringing, since it sometimes produced faulty voice-leading. Whether other English lutenists followed Dowland's advice we just do not know, though it would appear that his predecessor John Johnson used octaves.[3] Indeed, they are indispensable for most Renaissance lute music.[4]

Lutes of a variety of sizes are documented in court accounts and required in surviving ensemble music.[5] The most common lutes in sixteenth-century ensembles were trebles in a', altos in g', tenors in f' and e', and basses in d'. A descant lute in d" was used in late Renaissance ensembles, as well as the mandora in g". Praetorius also mentions descants in b' and c", as well as a large octave bass lute in g, an octave below the tenor lute. The reason for the variety of sizes was not only to expand the available range, but to provide more resonance over a wider range. For example, in transposing a soprano lute song for an alto singer (or a tenor song for a baritone), it was common practice to change from a tenor lute to a bass lute, rather than to transpose downward on the smaller instrument. Though most, if not all, of the notes required are playable on the smaller instrument, the effect is not nearly as sonorous as it is on the larger instrument. The reason for this is that gut-strung instruments sound best when notes are produced by the longest vibrating string-length possible. This is because thick gut strings produce a dull, thuddy sound, while thinner strings are brighter and more resonant. In order to use thin strings, however, the string length must be long enough to place those strings at or near their breaking point, the point at which gut strings sound best.[6] While the smaller lute produces low notes on thick, short strings, the larger lutes will produce the same notes on the bright, clear upper strings of the instrument. This corresponds to the Renaissance and early Baroque practice of performing viol consort parts on the strong, resonant treble strings of large instruments, rather than on the middle and lower strings of smaller ones.[7] For this reason, bass lutes were extremely popular ensemble instruments in the sixteenth century since they would project the lower and middle parts of ensemble music more clearly than can standard tenor lutes. One further advantage of transposing by changing lutes is that it enables the player to read from the same tablature part.

EX. 13.1a   Typical Renaissance six-course lute tuning

EX. 13.1b   Typical English eight-course lute tuning

EX. 13.1c   Tuning for bass lute in d

EX. 13.1d   Tuning for Praetorius's French mandore

While the left-hand technique of the lute is quite similar to that of the classical guitar, the right-hand technique, at least in the sixteenth century, was quite different. Until the third quarter of the fifteenth century the lute was played with a quill, restricting it to either single-line passages or strummed chords.[8] Tinctoris reports that some German lutenists in the middle of the century began to play with the right-hand fingers, instead of a quill, in order to perform polyphony.[9] The two styles co-existed into the beginning of the sixteenth century, when the quill was eventually abandoned. (The well-known virtuoso Giovan Maria was heard performing with a plectrum as late as 1526.) It was probably ensemble players who retained the plectrum-style the longest, while solo performers cultivated the new finger-style for its greater flexibility. For single-line playing in fifteenth-century music the plectrum is the most appropriate, while performing two or three parts on one lute, as in playing the lower parts of a chanson, is most easily accomplished using the fingers.

For plectrum-playing, a downward stroke was used for strong beats and an upstroke for weak beats. This sequence was replaced in the finger-style by the alternation of the thumb and index finger. This remained the basis of lute fingering into the seventeenth century, when the middle-index stroke gradually took precedence for much solo playing. Until about 1600 the right arm was held nearly parallel to the strings, allowing the thumb to pass under the index finger, a technique often referred to as "thumb-under" today. The right hand was supported by the little finger, which rested on the soundboard, providing a point of reference for the freely moving arm. In fact, the movement of the arm provides most of the energy for the thumb-under technique, allowing the fingers to relax and concentrate on contacting the strings with as much of the fingertip as possible. This technique provides the ease and lightness required to articulate the rapid divisions of Renaissance lute music. By the early seventeenth century the right arm had been brought around to a more perpendicular position with the thumb moved outside the hand, jutting out toward the fingerboard, a position now known as "thumb-out." While less suitable for early sixteenth-century music, this position is nevertheless more familiar to classical guitarists, most of whom will feel more comfortable beginning with it. The basic thumb-index alternation was maintained for single-line playing even in the thumb-out position. (For a summary of the two hand positions and their use, see Beier below.) The sound produced by the "nibble end" of the fingers was preferred for solo playing, while many ensemble lutenists apparently used fingernails.

The following methods provide much more detailed information about playing techniques, repertory, notation, interpretation of the music, and so forth:

Patrick O'Brien and Paul O'Dette. *The Lute Made Easie: A Tutor for the Renaissance Lute* (in preparation)

Pascale Bocquet. *Approche du Luth Renaissance*, (self-published 1988, available through the Société Française de Luth, 48, rue Bargue, 75015 Paris, France)

Stefan Lundgren. *New Method for Renaissance Lute* (Munich: Lundgren Musik-Edition, 1986)

Diana Poulton. *A Tutor for the Renaissance Lute*, (London: Schott ED 12324, 1991)

Stanley Buetens. *Method for the Renaissance Lute*, (Menlo Park, CA: Instrumenta Antiqua Publications, 1969)

The Use of the Lute in Ensembles

Due to the use of a quill, the lute in the fifteenth century primarily played single lines or strummed chords. Intricate polyphony was not possible on one lute until the adoption of finger technique in the last quarter of the century. Strumming was probably confined to dance music, making monophonic playing the most common for participation in secular art song, perhaps the primary repertory in which lutenists would have taken part. The plectrum produces a bright, articulate sound ideally suited to playing the active contratenor and triplum parts of fifteenth-century chansons.

The upper strings of the lute are generally the strongest and clearest, and it is this register that is usually the most effective in ensemble playing. Slow, sustained parts rarely work well on the lute, particularly in the middle and lower registers. Rhythmically active writing, parts with numerous leaps, or highly florid passages are particularly effective on the lute, since dynamically it is able to dart in and out of the texture as required. When lutenists did perform slow-moving lines, *cantus firmi*, and the like, they tended to repeat notes or to ornament, as can be seen in the tenor parts of Francesco Spinacino's lute duets,[10] intabulations of vocal music, and settings of, for instance, *La Spagna, Tandernaken, In Nomine.* This is important to keep in mind when scoring fifteenth- and sixteenth-century music. Try to choose a part that suits the strengths and characteristics of the instrument. If that is not possible, the player must adapt the part to make it fit the instrument.

From the early sixteenth century on it would appear that lutes most often played in two to four parts. Though there are many examples of very florid single-line lute parts, there is surprisingly little evidence to suggest that lutenists played simple single-line parts in Renaissance ensemble music after about 1526. Without a plectrum it is difficult for a lute to hold its own against other instruments playing only a single line, unless it is either very active or up high on the fingerboard. This is not to say it was never done, but I do not believe it was very common.

Arrangements of four-part frottole, chansons, and Lieder for voice and lute made between 1500 and 1530 indicate that the superius line was sung, while the lute intabulated the bass and tenor with some added ornamentation to assist the flow of the lines.[11] Though occasional chords are filled out with a third voice, the alto part is, for the most part, left out. Even when a flute is added to this ensemble, as in the famous paintings by the Master of the Half-Lengths, it plays the tenor together with the lute. This is probably because most cadences in this music occur between the superius and tenor. If the alto were to be played by the flute, the least important line would become quite prominent, confusing the cadences. Why the lute did not trade the alto for the tenor in this situation is not clear. On the other hand, judging a practice by a few paintings is indeed risky, and there were undoubtedly approaches to this problem we just do not know anything about today. Nevertheless, the type of part found in Bossinensis, Attaingnant, Schlick, and Paris Rés. Vmd. Ms 27. (all available in facsimile editions) gives valuable clues about the style of early sixteenth-century lute accompaniments. Even when all four parts are otherwise covered by voices, viols, recorders, and the like, these slightly ornamented two- to three-part accompaniments work well for the lute. For performances involving two lutes, as was often done, it would seem reasonable to assume that one lute played the tenor and bass, the other the alto and bass.

In Willaert's 1536 arrangements of four-part Verdelot madrigals for solo voice and lute, we find the three lower parts intabulated intact.[12] Still later in the sixteenth century an even fuller texture was used with the soprano part doubled by the lute as well. Many of the accompaniments in the *Bottegari Lutebook*, for example, are essentially full intabulations of the madrigals (complete with ornamentation), which were apparently used to accompany a solo singer.[13] Indeed solo lute intabulations often make good accompaniments to vocal ensembles as well as to solo singers. Sometimes the ornamentation will need to be simplified or the texture thinned out to enable the lutenist to maintain a singable tempo. My own preference, and one expressed by several sixteenth-century authors, is not to double the soprano part, particularly in solo songs. It was nevertheless done by some sixteenth-century musicians.

In vocal ensemble performances, multiple lutes were often employed. The most valuable models for this practice may be found in Verona Accademia Filarmonia Ms.223 and in Emanuel Adriaensen's *Pratum Musicum* of 1584. The former is particularly interesting in that it contains four- to eight-part madrigals with multiple lute accompaniments for instruments in different pitches. Each of the surviving partbooks contains a vocal part with written-out ornamentation, and aligned beneath that, a lute intabulation of some of the lower parts. The soprano part of the four-part madrigals is never doubled in this source, at least not by the lute in the soprano partbook. Unfortunately the manuscript is missing at least one, and possibly several partbooks, so that we cannot be sure how the six- and eight-part madrigals were performed. Each of the singers may have had his own accompanist, or what is more likely, the singers accompanied themselves. At any rate, it is clear that lutes in ensembles of this period played several parts at once, doubling vocal lines and often each other. (In some examples from this manuscript two lutes play virtually the same intabulation, undoubtedly for additional resonance.)

Adriaensen's 1584 settings for four lutes and four voices are somewhat thicker in texture.[14] The lutes are used in the following way:

LUTE 1 (in a′) plays the cantus, adding some ornamentation and filling in chords of three to four parts down to the bass
LUTE 2 (in g′) plays the alto and bass, filling in chords of three to four parts
LUTE 3 (in e′) plays the tenor and bass, filling in chords of three to four parts
LUTE 4 (in d′) plays the bass in octaves and fills in the harmonies

It should be noted that all four lutes are of a different size and tuning, making the sound even richer. Renaissance musicians apparently tried to avoid combining more than two lutes of the same size. Most surviving lute trios and quartets call for three or four different sizes, a practice employed in mixed ensembles as well. Thus, it seems that in large ensembles, lutes usually played two to four polyphonic parts each, not the single lines or block chords heard in many modern performances.

A word of caution: the notated pitch of vocal parts, especially in frottole, vihuela songs, and *airs de cour*, is not necessarily an indication of the pitch of the lute required to accompany them. While in larger ensembles (i.e. Adriaensen, Verona Ms., etc.) the pitch of the lutes does seem to correspond to the pitch of the vocal parts they accompany, often the vocal parts simply indicate the mode of the piece using the fewest sharps or flats, not the actual performing pitch.[15]

Another use of the lute in late sixteenth-century ensembles was as a florid single-line instrument weaving rapid divisions throughout the texture of the ensemble. This technique is most clearly documented by the "in concerto" settings of Terzi[16], the Elizabethan broken consort lute parts,[17] and in the descriptions given by Agazzari and Praetorius.[18]

Perhaps the best way to acquaint oneself with the various approaches to ensemble playing is to play as many of the original lute ensemble parts as possible. While these may not always represent what the finest professional players of the time did, they will nevertheless provide a point of departure. Besides the obvious skills anyone playing in an ensemble must possess, lutenists should become fluent in clef reading, transposition, intabulation, and ornamentation. Of these, intabulation is perhaps the least familiar. It is the art of scoring a vocal or instrumental ensemble piece for the lute, transposing where necessary, thinning out or revoicing chords to make them easier to play or more sonorous, and most important, adding ornamentation to facilitate phrasing and to add variety.[19] This process is described in many sixteenth-century sources, of which Adrian LeRoy's *A briefe and plaine Instruction to set all Musicke . . . in Tableture for the Lute* written in 1574 is the most accessible.[20] The acquisition of these skills will greatly facilitate the lutenist in devising parts to play in ensembles.

(Several of these styles may be heard on the recording *Three, Four and Twenty Lutes* listed below in Suggested Listening.)

Guitar and Vihuela

Appearing in many medieval artworks—often alongside the lute—is a small lute-like instrument, long called the mandora by historians. However, Laurence Wright[21] has pointed out that "mandora" (or its variants) is rare in any language before 1570, and that the instrument we had been calling by that name was most probably known in the Middle Ages and early Renaissance as the gittern or qui(n)tern—early forms of the word "guitar." (Meanwhile, Wright has demonstrated that the holly-leaf-shaped instrument we had been calling the gittern was actually the citole, ancestor of the Renaissance cittern; see below.) The early gittern shares many characteristics with the rebec (see Bowed Strings, p. 109): hollowed-out construction, smooth transition from body to neck, and sickle-shaped pegbox, often terminating in an animal head. (An amazingly well-preserved example, made by Hans Ott in Nuremberg about 1450, is to be found in the Wartburg, Eisenach.) By the time of Praetorius, however, the gittern had acquired the flat back and waisted outline we now associate with the guitar, although the two body shapes undoubtedly overlapped for some time. Adding to the confusion was the advent of the true mandora (mandürichen; bandürichen, pandurina) with its lute-like shape, whose tuning (alternating fifths and fourths), however, represents a real departure from the lute-like tuning (in fourths, with an interior third) of the gittern or guitar.

The four-course Renaissance guitar is an unjustly neglected instrument today. Though its solo repertory is not large, it can be a very useful ensemble instrument, particularly for lighter music such as villancicos, villanelle, dance music, and chansons.[22] The Renaissance guitar was plucked as well as strummed and thus able to play polyphonic as well as homophonic textures. (Plucking refers to striking each string individually with a different finger, while strumming involves sounding several strings with one finger.) The Renaissance guitar is technically not difficult to play but can contribute a great deal of rhythmic verve in the right kinds of pieces. It survived well into the seventeenth century when it was joined by the larger five-course guitar, tuned a fourth lower, which eventually replaced the smaller instrument as the most common type. The five-course instrument, often referred to today as "the Baroque guitar," made its appearance in the late sixteenth century and was extremely popular as a solo and a continuo instrument throughout the seventeenth century.[23] The elaborate right-hand strumming techniques discussed in seventeenth-century sources are reminiscent of many Latin and South American folk traditions and provide much of the character of the instrument. Unfortunately, very few players today have taken the time to learn these sophisticated techniques, many of which were undoubtedly already in use in the sixteenth century.[24]

EX. 13.2a   Five-course Baroque guitar tuning

EX. 13.2b   Four-course Renaissance guitar tuning

In Spain the vihuela, a six-course, guitar-shaped instrument that shared the same tuning as the lute, was played in place of the lute. The primary difference between the vihuela and the lute, besides the shape, is that the vihuela was strung in unisons throughout. This gives the instrument a darker, more somber sound well-suited to the moodiness of its repertory. The Italian Paolo Cortese complained that "the evenness and soft sweetness of the lyra hispanica [presumably the vihuela] is usually rejected by the satiety of the ear, and its uniformity is longer than could be desired by the limits imposed by the ear."[25] Vihuela music was sometimes played on the lute in Italy and Northern Europe and can be executed successfully, particularly if unison tuning is employed. For specialists, however, the characteristic sound of the vihuela is irreplaceable. (For more information about surviving instruments, sizes, shapes, the repertory, etc., see the vihuela article in *The New Grove Dictionary of Musical Instruments*.) Vihuelistas employed a few specialized playing techniques, such as the *dedillo*, a rapid tremolo produced by the back and forth motion of the index finger, a technique not yet convincingly reproduced by modern exponents of the instrument. Other aspects of the vihuela repertory not yet sufficiently explored include the use of left-hand ornamentation, as discussed by several of the vihuelistas and the keyboard players Henestrosa and Tomás de Santa Maria,[26] as well as the use of rhythmic alterations, also encouraged by Santa Maria.

Cittern, Ceterone, Orpharion, and Bandora

Another underused instrument in today's early music groups is the cittern. Its solo repertory is second in size only to that of the lute in the sixteenth century, and as an ensemble instrument it was popular throughout the

Renaissance and early Baroque. The cittern was strung with a combination of iron and brass strings arranged in pairs—some of the low courses were even triple strung with a fundament and two octave strings—and plucked with a quill. Most English and French citterns had four courses, while Italian instruments often had six. The cittern is a chordal instrument fulfilling much the same rôle as a rhythm guitar in a rock band. Because of its "re-entrant" tuning, the cittern lacks a real bass, and produces many chords in inversions. For this reason it is best used in combination with another instrument that is able to provide the written bass line. The cittern was most commonly used in dance ensembles and to accompany broadside ballads. Frederic Viaera's cittern parts, written to fit with Giovanni Pacoloni's lute trios, provide good models for the former.[27] (Some of these may be heard on the recording *Three, Four, and Twenty Lutes* listed in Suggested Listening below.) The cittern is an essential member of the English broken consort and survived in Italy as a continuo instrument. The ceterone, or archcittern, is a large bass cittern with a second neck and pegbox to hold the diapasons. An exquisite original ceterone by Gironimo Campi survives in the Bardini Museum in Florence. A picture of it is shown on page 325 in *The New Grove Dictionary of Musical Instruments*. Monteverdi calls for ceteroni in *Orfeo*, a fact ignored by most recordings of that work to date. The parts were probably similar to that provided by Pietro Paolo Melii in his *Balletto* of 1616.[28]

EX. 13.3a   English cittern tuning

EX. 13.3b   French cittern tuning

EX. 13.3c   Paolo Virchi's cittern tuning

The bandora, or pandora as it is called in some sources, was devised "in the fourth year of Queen Elizabeth" (i.e. 1561) by the viol maker John Rose.

It is essentially a wire-strung bass lute with a scalloped shape, perhaps vaulted back, and often a slanted bridge and nut to increase the length of the bass strings. The surviving music for bandora includes a small but rewarding solo literature, a number a song accompaniments, and several lute duet grounds; it is, however, in the broken consort repertory that the bandora really shines.[29] It is an irreplaceable member of that ensemble, filling a double rôle as continuo and double bass. Together with the cittern, the bandora provides a continuo with the dynamic flexibility required in such a delicately balanced ensemble. Though keyboard instruments such as the virginal and spinet are sometimes shown in paintings of broken consorts taking the place of the bandora, they are rarely mentioned in musical sources and were probably not considered as desirable as the bandora, since they would be the only member of the ensemble incapable of subtle dynamic shading. The bandora is mentioned as a continuo instrument on the title page of numerous seventeenth-century collections including a few published in Germany. Nevertheless, the bandora seems to have fallen out of favor in the 1620s, along with the broken consort, though Roger North mentions bandoras strummed with quills accompanying oboes and violins in late seventeenth-century consort music.

EX. 13.4 Seven-course bandora tuning

The orpharion is a wire-strung instrument with a scalloped outline and a flat, or slightly vaulted back, tuned like a lute. It was played almost exclusively in England and in some parts of Holland and northern Germany. Mentioned as an alternative to the lute on the title pages of several books of lute songs, the orpharion may, because of its tuning, be used to play any English lute music. In fact, in thirty-two household inventories made between 1565 and 1648 the bandora and orpharion occur as frequently as the lute. While music published specifically for the orpharion mostly requires a seven-course instrument, the finest surviving example has nine courses.

Chitarrone, Theorbo, and Archlute

The terms chitarrone, theorbo, and archlute have been a constant source of confusion over the centuries. Though Robert Spencer finally sorted them out more than a decade ago, conductors, scholars, and performers still have trouble keeping them straight.[30] To a non-player the distinctions can seem minimal if not insignificant. To the player, however, the differences are enormous; they have to do with tuning, size, repertory, and playing technique. To begin with, the chitarrone and theorbo are one and the same instrument, the first being the common name from the instrument's invention in the 1580s until the 1640s, the second, a term used from around 1600 to the late eighteenth century.[31] Praetorius distinguishes between the Paduan and Roman "theorba," the latter of which he says is called "chitarrone," but the surviving instruments do not substantiate his account, and his description of two different instruments has resulted in mass confusion in the secondary literature. While undoubtedly much experimentation with different body shapes and sizes, string lengths, tuning, and stringing took place after the invention of the chitarrone in the 1580s (most of which is undocumented; it is clear that most seventeenth-century Italians used "chitarrone" and "tiorba" as different names for the same instrument.)[32] It is likely that what the players in the 1589 *intermedi* called "chitarrone" was different from what Monteverdi or Kapsberger or Piccinini meant by that term, but that was the result of individual preference rather than terminology. Praetorius and Piccinini discuss the use of metal strings on the chitarrone, but gut was probably more common—it is certainly more reliable. The most common number of courses was fourteen, six on the fingerboard, with eight diapasons. The diapasons were tuned diatonically according to key. Some early examples have only twelve courses, while Kapsberger used a fully chromatic, nineteen-course instrument, no example of which appears to have survived. Many modern players compromise by placing seven or eight courses on the fingerboard to access the low G-sharp and F-sharp so crucial for continuo playing, as recommended by some French sources. Surviving instruments and iconographic evidence indicate that some players used double courses over the fingerboard, while others preferred single strings. (The latter are easier for articulating the long, slurred passages called *strascini* so common in solo theorbo music.) The diapasons were always single. The theorbo was the instrument of choice in accompanying Italian monody and early recitative. It was commonly used in early trio sonatas, opera, English and French song, oratorio, and *concerti grossi* well into the eighteenth century.[33] Indeed theorbists played in operas in Berlin, Prague, and Vienna after 1750, though the instrument they used may have been a kind of Baroque lute rather than the seventeenth-century-type theorbo.

EX. 13.5 Typical seventeenth-century theorbo tuning

The archlute, on the other hand, is simply a Renaissance lute with an extra octave of bass strings. The term was not, as suggested in many modern books on musical instruments, a generic term for long-necked lutes. While it is possible that uninformed observers may have used "archlute" or "theorbo" generically in the seventeenth and eighteenth centuries, experienced musicians clearly knew the difference, since parts specifying one or the other are usually idiomatically well conceived. Small archlutes, sometimes called *liuti attiorbati,* usually had double courses in the bass, while the larger instruments had single basses. It is these latter instruments, with their long extended necks, that are most often confused with the theorbo, since their appearance is so similar. (The archlute, in fact, has a smaller body and a shorter string length than most theorbos.) The major difference between the two is that the treble strings of the archlute are tuned in the standard Renaissance lute tuning, while the top one or two strings of the theorbo are tuned an octave lower. Because of this the theorbo has a very full tenor register but lacks a true treble, while the archlute has a bright, clear treble but lacks the fullness of the theorbo. In addition, the basic pitch of the theorbo was usually a step higher than that of the archlute. For that reason the choice between the two instruments was made not only for their tonal characteristics but according to the keys they favored. This is an aspect we do not yet fully understand. While Handel uses the theorbo primarily for flat keys and the archlute for sharp keys, the reverse actually provides more resonant, technically convenient chord shapes. Even though the theorbo was preeminent in the seventeenth century, the archlute seems to have overtaken its larger cousin after 1700, probably because its shorter string length makes for easier playability in a wider variety of keys. Archlutes remained popular into the second half of the eighteenth century.

EX. 13.6   Typical fourteen-course archlute tuning

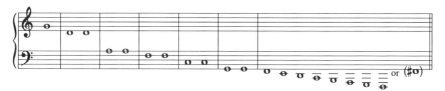

Instrument Priorities

For early-music ensembles the most versatile first lute would be an eight-course instrument with a string length of 58 to 60 cm tuned in g′. If there is more than one lutenist in the ensemble, I would recommend another of the same, this being the size of instrument best suited to the largest portion of the solo repertory, most flexible in ensembles, and most utilized in lute duets. After that, the choice of instruments will be determined primarily by the director's preferences in repertory. For seventeenth-century music, a theorbo is the most suitable, while for the eighteenth century an archlute is the most useful. If one wishes to specialize more in Renaissance music, I would recommend a bass lute in d' (string length of 84–88 cm) or e', an alto lute in a', then a soprano lute in d" (string length 42–44 cm) as the next instruments. Others, such as the cittern, bandora, Renaissance guitar, and the like, can be added according to the number of players available and the requirements of the music. It is worth keeping in mind, however, that Renaissance ensembles often included a large number of plucked instruments. (As many as forty lutes took part in some masques and ballets!) This not only improves sonority and balance, but has the practical advantage of involving a lot of guitarists, both folk and classical, in Early-Music programs.

NOTES

1. Baines–Fifteenth-century: 24.
2. Le Roy–*Briefe* fol. 41'.
3. Nordstrom–Lute: 33.
4. Radke–Beiträge: 34–51.
5. Rooley/Tyler–Lute: 13–24; and Brown–*Sixteenth-Century*
6. Nurse–On the Development: 102–7.
7. Morrow–*Sixteenth-century*: 163.
8. Danner–Before: 4–17.
9. While plectrum players undoubtedly managed to play simple polyphony by damping undesired adjacent strings with unoccupied left-hand fingers, as is done in some types of jazz today, the thicker textures of late fifteenth-century polyphony must have made this increasingly impractical.
10. Spinacino–*Intabulatura*.
11. Arnolt Schlick's settings of *Tenorlieder* in his *Tabulaturen etlicher lobgesang und lidlein* of 1512 are something of an enigma. While the tenor of these songs was commonly the only texted part (in the earlier sources, at least), Schlick has intabulated the tenor and bass for lute, and has left the superius in mensural notation. This leaves the melody in the lute while the accompanying descant line in the soprano is sung or played. Whether this was a common practice or an aberration is just not known. I prefer to believe the latter, and have found that intabulating the superius, altus, and *bassus* of *Tenorlieder* for lute to accompany a tenor singer works very well in much of this repertory.
12. Willaert–*Intavolatura*.
13. Bottegari–*Bottegari*.
14. Adriaensen–*Novum*.
15. Ward–Changing: 27–39.
16. Terzi–Intavolatura.
17. Beck–*First*; Nordstrom–English: 5–22; Nordstrom–Lute: 50–63; and Edwards–Music.
18. See Paul O'Dette, "The Use of Chordal Instruments," this volume, p. 209.
19. Lawrence-King–"Perfect": 354–64.
20. Le Roy–Les Instructions.
21. Wright–Medieval. 8–42.
22. Tinctoris–De inventione.
23. The two types may be heard side-by-side in the closing *Ballo* to the 1589 Florentine *intermedi* recorded as *Una stravaganza dei Medici*, The Taverner Consort and Choir, conducted by Andrew Parrott EMI CDC 7 47998 2 (1989).

24. Weidlich–Battuto: 63–86; Tyler–*Early*: 77–86.
25. Pirrotta–Music: 127–61.
26. Myers–Vihuela: 15–18.
27. Pacoloni–*Longe.*
28. Melii–*Intavolatura.*
29. Nordstrom–Bandora.
30. Spencer–Chitarrone: 407–23.
31. Mason–*Chitarrone.*
32. Spencer–Chitarrone: 407–23.
33. North–*Continuo*: 20–24.

Bibliography

Beier–Right; Brown–*Instrumental*; Brown–*Sixteenth–Century*; Danner–Before; Knighton/Fallows (Smith, Thomas)–*Companion*; Mason–*Chitarrone*; Munrow–*Instruments*; Myers–Vihuela; Nordstrom–*Bandora*; Nordstrom–Cambridge; Nordstrom–English; Nordstrom–Lute; North–*Continuo*; Nurse–On the Development; O'Dette–Some; Pirrotta–Music; Poulton–*Lute*; Radke–Beiträge; Spencer–Chitarrone; Sadie–*New*; Tyler–*Early*; Tyler–Mandore; Tyler–Checklist; Tyler/Sparks–*Early*; Ward–Changing; Wright–Medieval.

Suggested Listening

Alonso Mudarra: Tres libros de musica en cifras para vihuela. Hopkinson Smith, vihuela and Renaissance guitar. Astrée E 8740 (1992).

Dowland: Musicke for the Lute. Paul O'Dette. Astrée COE7715 (1984).

Francesco da Milano: Intabolatura da Leuto. Paul O'Dette. Astrée CD E7705 (1986).

Il Tedesco della Tiorba. Kapsberger Pieces for Lute. Paul O'Dette. Harmonia Mundi 907020 (1990).

In the Streets and Theatres of London. Musicians of Swanne Alley / Paul O'Dette, Lyle Nordstrom. Virgin Classics VC 7 90789–2. (1989).

Italian Lute Duets. Paul O'Dette / Hopkinson Smith. Seraphim S-60361 (1979).

John Dowland: Lacrimæ 1604. The Dowland Consort / Jacob Lindberg. BIS CD 315 (1985 & 1986).

Robin is to the Greenwood Gone. Paul O'Dette. Nonesuch 9 79123–2. (1987).

Three, Four & Twenty Lutes (includes Italian madrigals). Jacob Lindberg, Robert Meunier, Nigel North, Paul O'Dette. BIS CD-341 (1986).

14

Harp

Herbert Myers

The harp is yet another instrument that has not found its rightful place in modern performances of Renaissance music. Held in the highest esteem in the fifteenth century, the harp was a symbol of musical nobility and erudition. (Of course, its biblical association with King David cannot have hurt its reputation!) Entering the sixteenth century as a diatonic instrument, it was increasingly perceived as defective because of its inability to cope effectively with chromaticism. As the century progressed, methods were developed to render it completely chromatic; however, Praetorius in 1619 seems to have regarded the diatonic harp as still the most common type, and such simple instruments continued for some time to coexist with more developed forms.

The graceful shape of the Renaissance European harp is familiar to many from the paintings of the Flemish masters such as Jan van Eyck and Hans Memling whose depictions of angel musicians have appeared on countless Christmas cards. This form of harp is often called "Gothic" by historians to distinguish it from the earlier, so-called "Romanesque" type. The three main elements (body, neck, and forepillar) of the latter were typically about equal in length, producing a fairly squat form. From early in the fifteenth century we see evidence of the elongation of the body and forepillar—presumably to accommodate longer bass strings—producing the taller, slimmer outline of the Gothic design. At the same time the forepillar (often quite outcurved on earlier harps) was somewhat straightened and was carried upward beyond the joint with the neck, terminating in an ornamental, horn-like protrusion; an answering protrusion was often to be found farther back on the neck. Both forepillar and neck were often deeply fluted, evidently in order to reduce mass while retaining strength; the flutings also serve to emphasize the graceful curves. The body was both narrow and quite shallow, expanding rather minimally toward the bottom. The result of these modifications is (visually speaking) an extremely well-integrated design; the Gothic harp appears to the casual eye to have been made of a single piece of wood.

This appearance is, of course, somewhat deceptive; for strength, the grain of the wood must run generally parallel to the length of each principal element, requiring the joining of separate pieces. But in one sense the appearance is quite genuine, for all three elements (including the body or soundchest) were made of a single type of wood. This means that the active acoustical surface—the belly—was, like the rest of the instrument, of hardwood (though the particular species of wood varied among instruments). The soundchest was not so much constructed as carved, being made up of two hollowed-out planks joined at the edges to form an enclosed cavity. Its cross-section (as viewed from either end) was often a flattened oval; three surviving examples from around 1500 (in Nuremberg, Eisenach, and Leipzig) have the latter form, and it is depicted clearly by Hieronymus Bosch in his famous *Garden of Earthly Delights* in the Prado, Madrid. However, many pictures show that the cross-section could also be rectangular or almost so, with a flat back and either flat or bulging belly. (A flat back is a definite advantage when one wants to lay the harp down.)

The choice of hardwood as belly material has considerable acoustical significance, for it is inherently much stiffer than the softwood (spruce or pine) employed for the bellies of the more recent types of harps with which we are familiar (and, indeed, for the bellies of most other stringed instruments, bowed or plucked, from the Middle Ages to the present). The stiffness of the hardwood belly, coupled with its small surface area, makes for a very inefficient radiator, particularly for bass frequencies. However, the Renaissance builder had quite an effective solution to this problem.

Perhaps the most remarkable feature of the Renaissance harp is its use of "brays" (or "bray pins")—L-shaped wooden pegs that served both to anchor the gut strings in the belly (much as modern guitar bridge pins do) and to touch them a short way along their vibrating length, imparting a buzzing quality that amplified and prolonged their sound. They are most efficient at this in the bass, where the amplitude of vibration of the string is greatest— and where, as we have seen, their amplifying effect was most needed. They are clearly depicted in art works from early in the fifteenth century, through the sixteenth, and into the seventeenth; they also figure in illustrations of harps in musical treatises (notably the *Dodecachordon* of Glarianus, 1547, and the *Syntagma musicum* II of Praetorius, 1619). In addition, they are to be found on several surviving instruments (including two of the three mentioned above; the Eisenach example has lost them, it seems). Mersenne (*Harmonie universelle*, 1636) calls them *harpions* and claims that they had gone out of fashion in France; however, they are still present on some later seventeenth-century harps, and their use on the Welsh harp continued into the nineteenth century.[1]

One might be tempted to regard the use of brays as but one of the available options (or a mere fad among certain players) but for the evidence that the nasal quality they impart was then considered characteristic of harp timbre. For instance, in the lute book of Vincenzo Capirola (ca. 1517) we are advised to make the frets of the lute almost touch the strings, so that they will "harp."[2] Similarly, in describing a newly invented keyboard instrument,

Sebastian Virdung (*Musica getutscht,* 1511) says, "This is just like the virginals, except that it has different strings (of sheep gut) and nails which make it 'harp'. . . ." The implication is clear that this was a keyboard instrument meant to sound like a harp. Such instruments may have been more common than hitherto realized; several Italian writers of the sixteenth and early seventeenth centuries distinguish between *arpicordo, clavicembalo,* and *spinetta,* and there is some evidence that the first of these terms referred specifically to a keyboard-harp.[3] *Arpichordum* was, in addition, the name of a stop often applied to Flemish muselars, being a batten (carrying metal hooks) placed next to the bass part of the bridge; it could be moved to bring the hooks close to the vibrating strings, causing them to buzz. Praetorius uses the expression *Harffenierender Resonantz* (harping sound) to describe the buzzing effect of both this stop and the peculiar bridge of the trumpet marine, even claiming that the term had this buzzing connotation for the common man. Finally, "harp" was the name of a Renaissance organ stop consisting of regal pipes (which also, of course, buzz). Given all this evidence for the use of brays throughout the period, it seems odd that they have been so generally rejected by modern builders and players.

Authors throughout the period confirm the basic diatonic tuning of the ordinary, "simple" (i.e., single-strung) harp, although some indicate that "Bs" (and sometimes "Es") might be tuned either flat or natural. Such harps commonly possessed from 24 to 26 strings. Most sixteenth-century sources give either F or G as the bottom note, but Juan Bermudo (*Declaración de Instrumentos musicales,* 1555) says that although some players think of the harp as beginning with F (and some, with G), it actually begins with C. This should remind us that such pitch designations represented concepts more than "actual" pitches in the modern sense, but it is perhaps significant that Praetorius—the first author we can reasonably trust regarding a reference pitch—gives F as the bottom note of his diatonic harp of typical Renaissance size.[4]

The harp figures prominently among the *instruments bas* (soft instruments) in fifteenth-century art works, both of "angel consorts" and worldly ensembles; the combination of harp and lute is particularly common. Some idea of its somewhat lowered position in the early sixteenth century (in certain musical circles, at least) may be gleaned from a perusal of the various accounts of court entertainments listing specific instrumentations; here it had a rather limited showing compared to other chordal instruments, such as lutes and harpsichords, until the final decades of the century.[5] Still, there were some notable virtuosi, for instance the celebrated Ludovico, harpist to King Fernando el Católico; something of his idiomatic style is embodied in the famous vihuela *Fantasia X* of Alonso Mudarra (1546) "which imitates the harp in the manner of Ludovico." According to Bermudo, when Ludovico needed a chromatic alteration, he placed a finger under the string to raise it a semitone; this technique, however, required "great skill and certitude." (Mudarra had mentioned the same technique, adding that the finger was placed "near the wrest-pins.") The alternative, according to Bermudo, was to preset certain necessary leading tones, making them available in one octave but not in another. Either of these techniques could account for the prominent cross-relations (f against f♯) near the end of the fantasia.

The most effective solution, however, was to add extra strings; the problem was to differentiate the added strings from the diatonic row, just as the chromatic notes are differentiated from the naturals on a keyboard. Bermudo proposed adding eight strings for the most-needed accidentals, differentiating them by color. He adds (almost as an afterthought) that this solution was still insufficient for some players, who had added all 19 (or at least 15) chromatic strings to the 27 naturals. How (or if) the added strings were distinguished he does not say, but his remark has been taken to be an early reference to the *arpa de dos órdenes* (harp of two ranks), of which there is clear evidence in Spain from early in the next century. In this instrument the planes of the diatonic and chromatic ranks cross each other, so that the strings of each are available to one hand at the top and to the other at the bottom.[6]

The Italian *arpa a due órdini* represents a different approach, despite its similar name.[7] Here the planes of the two ranks are parallel, and the player reaches through the diatonic strings to pluck the chromatic ones. Since the hands approach from opposite sides, the two ranks actually switch sides about halfway up the scale, so that the diatonic row is closer to the right hand in the treble and to the left hand in the bass. Thus each hand is basically limited to its own part of the range. Possibly in order to overcome this limitation came the invention of the three-rank (or "triple") harp, in which the chromatic row is sandwiched between duplicated diatonic rows. (The extremes of range are, however, often left single.) The term *arpa doppia* could apparently refer to both two- and three-rank harps, possibly because they were "double" in another sense as well, having acquired an extended lower range. The two-rank instrument was known in Italy from before 1581, when Vincenzo Galilei reported that it had been introduced there a few years previously; an extant example (in the Galleria Estense, Modena) appears to be from rather earlier, having been made in France some decades before it was decorated in Ferrara about 1587. The invention of the triple harp followed close behind, occurring just before the end of the century.[8] The triple harp is now associated primarily with Wales, but that association is not documented before the beginning of the eighteenth century.

Coexisting with the gut-strung Continental harps was the wire-strung Irish harp, which represented a completely different concept of tone and performance. Elegant in its own way, it was much more robustly constructed. The joints between its members, rather than being disguised, were emphasized by ornamentation. Its massive soundchest was hollowed out completely from behind to make a deep trapezoidal box whose "lid" then constituted the back of the chest. This back was left removable to allow access to the inside for attaching the strings, which were held in by toggles, never brays. (This remarkable chest often served the itinerant bard as a sort of suitcase.) Irish harpists traditionally played with sharpened fingernails, in contrast with the players of gut-strung harps who used the fleshy part of the finger. The strong, prolonged, and bell-like tone of the Irish harp demanded an elaborate system of damping by the fingers. The use of the Irish harp was confined mainly to the British Isles during the Renaissance, although Continental authors knew of its existence; Dante considered it to have been the ultimate prototype for the harp he knew. There is considerable evidence of the development of chromatic forms of the Irish harp near the end of the sixteenth century. These had some currency on the Continent, and they were known to both Vincenzo Galilei and Praetorius.[9] The Irish harp was quite popular in England in the seventeenth century; recently a case has been made for the use of the chromatic Irish harp in the famous "harp consorts" of William Lawes, long thought to be the province of the gut-strung triple harp.[10]

It should be mentioned that the so-called "Celtic" and "Troubadour" harps offered by modern harp companies are a complete fiction as historical (or at least Renaissance) instruments. Having evolved from some nineteenth-century designs, they generally preserve in their smaller format the acoustical and playing characteristics of the modern concert harp. They are commonly provided with "hooks"—bent wire devices set into the neck of the harp that can be turned quickly by hand to raise specific strings by a semitone. Hook harps were an invention of the late seventeenth century and represent one of the first stages in the mechanical development leading to the modern pedal harp.

Specific information on the technique of playing the Renaissance harp is quite scanty. Iconography suggests the use primarily of the thumb and first two fingers; this is borne out in later written sources indicating that the use of the ring finger was then innovative. (The use of the little finger is still avoided in modern harp technique.) Depictions of Continental harps consistently show the right hand taking the treble and the left the bass (as in modern playing); in traditional Irish (and Welsh triple) harping, the rôles of the hands are reversed. Thus, the harp was always a "two-handed" instrument; it would seem as improbable to restrict it to a single line as to so restrict a keyboard instrument (with the obvious exception of the organetto). In fifteenth-century pieces, therefore, the harp can easily handle two voices or even play an intabulation of the complete texture (*ficta* willing, of course—although one solution to the *ficta* problem is to ignore it). The combination of harp and plectrum lute would seem particularly apt for this repertory, the lute's chromatic flexibility complementing the harp's limitations. Moving into the sixteenth century we are on more certain ground, with some keyboard collections suggesting the alternative use of harp (or vihuela). From early in the next century we even find repertory specifically designated for harp, some of it demonstrating idiomatic techniques. For a discussion of this sixteenth- and seventeenth-century repertory see Morrow–

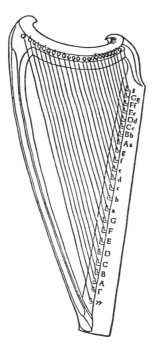

FIGURE 14.1   Glarean's diagram of a diatonic harp from *Dodecachordon*, 1547

Renaissance. A fine general work on the harp is Rensch–*Harps*. Also useful is the entry "Harp" in the *New Grove Dictionary of Instruments*. Excellent performances of sixteenth- and seventeenth-century repertory for various chromatic harps are to be heard on two solo CDs by Andrew Lawrence-King: *Harp Music of the Italian Renaissance* (Hyperion CDA66229, 1987) and *The Harp of Luduvico: Fantasias, Arias and Toccatas by Frescobaldi and his Predecessors* (Hyperion CDA66518, 1992). Lawrence-King has obviously opted for versions of the instruments that eschew brays. Recordings of bray harps are extremely rare; one of the few is to be found on the CD *Forse che sí, forse che no* by the Ferrara Ensemble, directed by Crawford Young (Fonti Musicali—Atelier Danse, fmd 182, 1989); it is track 11, "Giove" by Domenico da Piacenza, performed by Debra Gomez. A Gothic harp with working brays on just a few bass notes is to be heard on the *Harp Collection* (Amon Ra CD SAR36, 1989) by Frances Kelly, second piece on track 4.

NOTES

1. See Hadaway–Re-creation: 61–72.
2. I am grateful to Ray Nurse for pointing me to this reference.
3. See Neven–L'Arpicordo: 230–35.
4. See Pitch and Transposition, p. 248, for a discussion of Praetorius's reference pitch.

5. See Brown–Cook's: 233, 237–41; Brown–*Sixteenth-Century*: 85–135; and Weaver–Sixteenth-Century: 374–78.

6. See Bordas–Double: 148–63; her illustration #3 shows an interesting early seventeenth-century variant in which the ranks diverge rather than cross. This harp already shows considerable enlargement of the soundchest.

7. See Hadaway–Re-creation: 59–62 concerning building a copy of an example in Brussels.

8. However, already in 1511 some form of triple harp was said to be in use in England, according to the theorist Johannes Cochlaeus (*Tetrachordum musices*, Nuremberg, 1511; translated and edited by Clement A. Miller, American Institute of Musicology, Musicological Studies and Documents No. 23, 1970: 30). A 2-rank harp (with parallel string planes) is shown in one Spanish illustration from the late fourteenth century (Remnant–*Musical*: Ill. 6). Adding extra strings is such an obvious invention it probably took place more often than it was documented. Nevertheless, the single harp remained standard until near the end of the sixteenth century.

9. See Hadaway–Knot and Billinge/Shaljean–Dalway for an examination of this evidence.

10. See Holman–Harp.

15

Early Percussion

Ben Harms

The percussionist of today who wishes to play Renaissance music on the appropriate instruments faces two major difficulties: (1) few original instruments survive and (2) very little music survives, if, in fact, it was ever written down in the first place. The only instruments that are datable from about 1600 or before are three field drums (in the Musikinstrumentenmuseum of Basel, Switzerland), while the only music for percussion written before 1600 is contained in Thoinot Arbeau's *Orchésographie* of 1589.

Despite this, things are not totally bleak for a percussionist wishing to play in a historically informed manner. A large number of visual depictions survive—statues, reliefs, paintings, etchings, drawings, woodcuts—that often show percussion instruments and their players in great detail. In addition, there are several treatises on music and instruments that discuss percussion instruments, often in detail: from the sixteenth century Virdung (1511), Agricola (1529 and later printings), and Merlin and Cellier (1575); from the early seventeenth century Praetorius (1619) and Mersenne (1636). Upon studying all of these sources one is struck by how little percussion instruments have changed in construction and playing technique in the centuries since their first appearance.

The kettledrum, consisting of a copper bowl over which a calfskin head is stretched (Virdung), has merely become larger, while the only change in the rope-tension field drum is that a few more snares have been added. The instruments of the pipe-and-tabor tradition remain unchanged, as does their primary function of playing for dancing. Frame drums (the tambourine and hand drum) from 1500 and from 1990 are virtually identical, and the technique for playing them, while altered in the West, remains alive and basically unchanged in the Arab world, much of southern Asia, and Latin America.

A modern percussionist must use discretion about what rhythmic patterns to use when performing ensemble music from before 1650. African-influenced rhythms are clearly inappropriate when accompanying a medieval estampie, as is an Indian raga when performing a piece from Praetorius's monumental dance collection *Terpsichore*—this despite the fact that Praetorius himself depicts a mridangam and timila (Indian drums) in his *Syntagma Musicum* II.

This chapter is divided into two parts. The first part describes the most important percussion instruments in use from the thirteenth through the seventeenth century. The second part provides some practical advice on what instruments to use in a typical concert situation, how to play them, and what rhythms to play.

The Most Significant Percussion Instruments

Kettledrums

Kettledrums (timpani) were used as early as 1500 in conjunction with an ensemble of natural trumpets, providing the bass or fundamental notes— tonic and dominant—for the ensemble. They were well established by the early 1500s, as evidenced by their mention in Virdung, their presence in the Maximilian woodcuts of Dürer (ca. 1515), and engravings of Burgkmair (ca. 1508–1519). The drums were always used in pairs, with individual diameters ranging from about 17 inches (40 cm) up to possibly 26 inches (60 cm) by 1800 (precise dating of antique kettledrums is virtually impossible because dates, makers' names, and other identifying marks are rare). The bowls were usually made of copper (occasionally of silver and brass), and the skins were from calf, goat, or other animals. The sticks were bare wood, though they might have been covered with leather or other material for funerals or solemn occasions, in lieu of placing a cloth on the skin for a muffled effect.

Nakers

Nakers (small kettledrums) are found in some illustrations prior to 1500; related instruments are found today in areas in and around India. Strapped to the player's waist or hung from the shoulders, they were played with sticks. Modern attempts at reproducing nakers with either ceramic or metal bowls have yielded instruments with a tone ranging somewhere between that of bongos and timbales.

Frame Drums: Tambourine and Hand Drum

The wooden frames are usually round (occasionally square or some other shape), two to five inches in depth, six to fourteen inches in diameter (sometimes larger), and covered on one side—occasionally both—with an animal skin. With a hand drum, a snare (strand of gut, silk, or hemp) might be stretched across the skin. With a tambourine, the frame itself was pierced with holes or slits into which metal disks (jingles) and/or pellet bells were placed.

Modern players of the frame drum from all parts of the world possess a technique on the frame drum similar to that encountered in the tabla and mridangam players of India. An amazing variety of sounds and rhythms can be produced on the instrument by using the fingers and various parts of the hand on both the skin and jingles, as well as by shaking it or rocking it back and forth. There seems little reason to doubt that similar techniques were used by the players depicted in European paintings of the medieval and Renaissance periods, who are shown playing similar or identical instruments, held the same way, with the frame upright, perpendicular to the ground.

There are some pictures from the sixteenth and seventeenth centuries showing ladies or nymphs dancing to the accompaniment of the tambourine and other instruments. These tambourines are often held in the more conventional "Western" way we know today. That style of playing, requiring little technical sophistication, will be described later.

The jingle ring, a tambourine without a head, is occasionally encountered before 1600.

The Arabic dumbek should be used sparingly (if at all) and only for medieval music.

Two-Headed Cylindrical Drums: Field Drum and Tabor

Although the field drum and tabor are constructed similarly, they function quite differently. Virdung, Arbeau, and Praetorius all distinguish between them; Arbeau gives sample rhythms for each.

Both drums are made of wooden cylinders (shells) ranging in size from about six inches high and five inches in diameter to 24 inches by 24 inches, perhaps even larger. Across the open ends are stretched animal skins, usually calf or goat. By 1500, possibly even earlier, these skins could be stretched or tightened by wooden hoops that were pulled down on them by means of ropes tightened by leather straps. A snare was stretched across one of the heads and often doubled back.

The field drum is suspended from the shoulder by a strap and is played with two sticks, usually beating the skin without the snare(s). The technique employed on it by the beginning of the seventeenth century was formidable! Both Arbeau and Mersenne notate rhythms that can be played well only by a modern professional in top shape. As early as 1332 an account of a field drum played with a transverse flute (i.e., a fife) appears in the Basel City Chronicles. This fife-and-drum duo appears to have been associated with armies of foot-soldiers—helping them march together as well as signaling maneuvers. By the seventeenth century the field drum was played with shawm ensembles, though how frequently this happened is not clear. A version of the shawm/drum ensemble survives today in the Basque region of

Spain, where two shawms and a field drum are played outdoors and can be heard over long distances.

The tabor can be as tall as a field drum, but the diameter is smaller, because it is played with only one stick, usually on the skin with the snare stretched across it. The tabor is suspended from an elbow, forearm, or wrist of the hand not holding the stick and is most often associated with the pipe (see below), though Arbeau indicates that playing it alone is also acceptable. The tall tabor, called the "tambourin," is found today in the Provence region of southern France and dates from the beginning of the seventeenth century, or possibly earlier.

Pipe-and-Tabor

This "one-man-band" is encountered as early as the thirteenth century in Spain and France; it spread in succeeding centuries to England, the Netherlands, Italy, and the New World. The tradition of pipe-and-tabor playing remains unbroken in today's southern France (Provence region) and northern Spain (Basque area and Catalonia).

The pipe, also called the tabor-pipe, is a fipple flute like the recorder, but is played with only one hand, as there are merely three fingerholes (two on top and one underneath). The other hand plays the tabor, which is suspended on the arm (wrist, forearm, or elbow) that plays the pipe. The playing range of the tabor-pipe is an octave plus a fourth or fifth, within the pitch range of the sopranino recorder. This large pitch range is achieved by blowing various overtones of the four fundamental pitches of the instrument, plus using half-holes.

A considerable amount of secular music from before 1600 is playable on the tabor-pipe. Since it was essentially a folk instrument, it is likely that its importance has not been fully appreciated by modern researchers. For example, of the nine identifiable musical instruments found on the Mary Rose—Henry VIII's flagship, which sank fully loaded and manned in 1545 and which has only recently been excavated—three are tabor-pipes (also two field drums, two fiddles, a bagpipe, and a still shawm). Mersenne praised the virtuosity of the Englishman Jean Price, who played the tabor-pipe as fast and eloquently as the best violinists of the time.

The Strawfiddle

The strawfiddle is a type of xylophone, with only one row of wooden bars placed on a frame. Between the frame and bars is placed braided straw (to support the bars without damping their resonance), whence the name of the instrument. The largest bar is closest to the player's body, and the succeeding bars, laid parallel to the first, extend outward from the player, similar to the modern-band bell lyre. Agricola shows an instrument of three octaves with a basic scale of F major, with an "H" (B-natural) placed between

"B♭" and "C." This is an extremely difficult instrument to play, not only because of the added note but also because there is no exterior point of reference (such as the black keys on the piano) for a player to tell where he or she is.

The Triangle

This metallic instrument is occasionally found in a trapezoidal shape. Many triangles had metallic rings looped around the bottom. How the triangle functioned historically is not clear; it is possible that it had more of a rhythmic function than the modern triangle, which is valued more for its timbre.

Clappers/Castanets

These are pairs of wooden or possibly metal pieces struck together. They are seldom encountered in Renaissance depictions of musical events.

Handbells

Handbells are a dubious part of an instrumentarium for early music. The few historical depictions of this size bell appear to be in the context of describing Pythagorean proportions, not musical performance. In spite of the slim evidence, they are often used in modern attempts to recreate the ambience of a medieval religious setting.

Cymbals

Cymbals were small (six to ten inches in diameter) and appear to have been used either in processions or by singers, who may have punctuated texts with them. They are infrequently encountered, and when they are, usually before 1500.

Basic Percussion for the Early-Music Ensemble

What do the instruments described above have to do with modern performances of Renaissance music? Many of them are capable of providing excitement and variety in a concert. They are also rather strong in character as well as volume and require a certain minimum amount of study and practice in order to be used effectively. Unfortunately, this makes several of them of little practical value to many ensembles simply due to the group's instrumentation—usually consisting of only soft instruments—and personnel, which normally does not include a trained percussionist. Thus, kettledrums, which generally accompany at least two trumpets, are impractical.

The same is true of a field drum, which will overpower most ensembles, unless someone learns to play the fife (two or three sopranino recorders can be an acceptable substitute).

On the other hand, the pipe-and-tabor can be learned fairly easily. The player must first learn to play a tune on the pipe—this is relatively simple for a recorder player—and then add whatever drumbeats are possible, starting with downbeats. This can be a welcome addition to any concert.

The tambourine and hand drum are effective with soft or loud instruments, especially if played in the manner previously described in the description of frame drums. The basics are easily learned, if someone can be found to demonstrate them. Lacking this technique, the tambourine can be played in the more conventional manner (see below).

The Renaissance strawfiddle is difficult to play and hard to find for purchase. It is possible, however, to compromise and use a modern xylophone without resonators. Solo recorder pieces can be quite effective when performed in combination with this instrument.

Cymbals seem out of place in most early music, although they could be effective if used by a narrator or singer in a medieval drama. Clappers and castanets are also of limited use. Handbells, as stated above, appear to have little or no relevance to the authentic performance of Renaissance music. Bear in mind, too, that a triangle (or even the modern finger cymbals) adds a pleasing color when played on downbeats with a recorder ensemble or other soft group, but there is no historical justification for either, as the available literature makes clear.

In an ensemble where no trained percussionist is available, a performer with a strong sense of rhythm should be chosen to play percussion parts. If it comes down to a question of having an inner part of a dance piece played impeccably or having a tempo remain steady, the steady tempo should take precedence; in other words, don't relegate the percussion part to the weakest player in the group.

On the other hand, a serious percussionist with professional aspirations in the field of early music should acquire skills in at least two of the following three categories: historical hand drumming, pipe-and-tabor playing, and early kettledrumming.

*   *   *   *   *   *   *

The recommendations that follow should form a point of departure for percussion playing in an ensemble. They are based on historical considerations as well as this writer's sense of taste.

Instruments

The first two percussion instruments an early-music ensemble should acquire are a tabor and a tambourine. To these can be added a high-pitched hand drum (played with the hand or a stick) and a triangle.

Playing Technique

The basic playing technique for the tabor requires holding a stick in the strong hand (for most people, the right) and the tabor in the other. The stick should be a small snare drum stick; a piece of moleskin—available in a drugstore—can be wrapped around the back (butt) end of the stick, which can be used when a softer attack is desired. The stick is held between the thumb and forefinger, thumb pointing toward the tip, the forefinger opposite it, and at a 90° angle to the thumb.

For historic playing style on the tambourine or hand drum, a specialist in hand drumming should be consulted. Complementing this style (or in lieu of it), the modern Western way of playing the tambourine can be used. The instrument should be held in the left hand (for the right-handed person) at a 45°–60° angle to the ground, with the thumb pressing lightly on the skin, and the fingers curled around the frame. The first three fingers of the right hand should be bunched together with the thumb, and the pads of the fingers should tap on the skin opposite the left thumb, one to two inches from the rim. For louder playing the skin can be struck with the knuckles, a little closer to the middle. The shake, or roll, is made by holding the tambourine upright, at a 90° angle to the floor, with the left hand grasping it at the bottom. Rotate the tambourine on an axis with the hand and the wrist. Most shakes start and finish with a hit of the right palm or knuckles; they are often used at the ends of phrases or the end of a piece. A thumb roll, effected by sliding the thumb lightly around the periphery of the tambourine, is helped by applying beeswax to the skin.

Rhythms

With regard to the rhythms that should be played, the best policy is to establish a basic pattern at the beginning of a piece and maintain it throughout, elaborating on it as the piece progresses. An effective point of departure is Thoinot Arbeau's *Orchésographie* (1589), the only source of percussion music from before 1600. The two rhythms given specifically for *tambour ou tabourin* are:

EX. 15.1 *Tambour ou tabourin* rhythms

In the same section of the book, a few pages later, this rhythm is given:

Although a percussion instrument is not specified in this passage, it may be surmised from the context that this is an appropriate beat for a drummer to use.

From these basic rhythms we may extrapolate additional basic patterns and expand on them by varying them:

EX. 15.2 Basic rhythmic patterns and their variations

These rhythms work especially well for sixteenth- and seventeenth-century dance music (Attaingnant, Susato, Praetorius, et al.). For other music, simpler patterns might even be more appropriate—for example, playing only on downbeats.

Variations in the rhythmic pattern should be made only after the original pattern has been established (16, 24, 32 times) or after the piece, if short, has been played once in its entirety. Additional notes can be used effectively at the end of a phrase, in the manner of a flourish leading to the next phrase.

Dynamics

For variety one may alter the dynamics of a piece within sections or, if the piece is short, when going from one repetition to another. For a typical sixteenth-century dance in which each of three sections (A, B, C) is repeated, the following dynamic scheme is effective:

EX. 15.3 Suggested   a.   A   A │B   B   │C   C   ‖
   dynamic schemes   f   p │f   p   │p   f   ‖

A dance in two sections (A, B), each repeated, might follow this scheme:

                             b.   A   A │B   B   ‖
                                   f   p │p   f   ‖

A *crescendo* can be made in the final measure of a *piano* section (building to *forte*) or at the end of the piece. A *decrescendo* can be made in the final measure of a *forte* section (going to *piano*). (Please note that there is no mention of dynamics in any treatise. General musicianship, however, dictates a certain amount of flexibility in the application of dynamics to the music of any period.)

Starting and Finishing

There are two ways in which an ensemble piece can be started. The usual way is for all players to breathe together and follow a leader's sign or nod. The other way is for the percussionist to play one or two repetitions of the basic rhythmic pattern as a preparation for the ensemble's entrance.

To finish a piece the percussionist should play through the final written measure and conclude on the following downbeat.

Thus, if the final note is a whole note, it should be played:

EX. 15.4 Concluding a piece

a.   (instrument)

       (percussion)   Drum:

If the final note is a dotted half, it should be played:

b.   (instrument)

    (percussion)

When to Play

Secular music that is either monophonic or homophonic/homorhythmic is the most appropriate type of music for using percussion instruments. Once the percussionist has started playing he or she should not stop (an exception is when one verse of a chanson is performed *a cappella*). Polyphonic music should generally be avoided, as it is difficult to give the parts equal justice.

FIGURE 15.1 Percussion Instruments
Praetorius, *Syntagma musicum* II, Plate XXIII

Bibliography

Agricola–*Musica*; Arbeau–*Orchésographie*; Blades–*Percussion*; Blades–*Early*; Blades/Montagu–Capriol's; Merlin/Cellier–*Recherche*; Mersenne–*Harmonie*; Montagu–*World*; Montagu–*Making*; Montagu–Early; Praetorius–*Syntagma*; Virdung–*Musica*.

Suggested Listening

Calliope Dances. Calliope: A Renaissance Band. Nonesuch 79039 (1982).
Calliope Festival. Calliope: A Renaissance Band. Nonesuch 79069 (1984).
Diversions. Calliope: A Renaissance Band. Summit Records DCD 112 (1991).

III

KEYBOARD
INSTRUMENTS

16

Keyboard Instruments

Jack Ashworth

Explanations of pitch reference, tuning, the short octave, and split keys are appropriate for all Renaissance keyboard instruments. These items are grouped together here with an introduction to the topic of early fingerings and a list of general sources of keyboard music.

Pitch Reference

On the organ an open flue pipe sounding c′, or "middle c," is roughly two feet long. The pipe for the note one octave below it, c, is twice as long (four feet), and the pipe one octave further down, C, is twice as long again (eight feet). This eight-foot length has been used as a pitch reference standard since the Middle Ages. Eight-foot pitch means unison pitch: the pitch of middle c played on an 8-foot organ rank or harpsichord register is the same as that of the same key on a piano; c′ in a 4-foot rank will sound one octave higher; the same key in a 16-foot rank will sound one octave lower, and so on. This nomenclature is standard, even though pitches are sometimes produced by strings or pipes shorter than expected. Thus, the lowest pipe in an 8-foot stopped diapason is only four feet long; organ reeds of the *regal* family have very short resonators, or sometimes no resonators at all; and harpsichords and clavichords are scaled in such a way that their strings are not necessarily as long as the pitch would ordinarily seem to require (i.e., the string for c is not necessarily twice as long as that for c′).

Tuning

Although several systems for tuning the twelve chromatic notes of the octave relative to each other were documented in the sixteenth century, *quarter-comma meantone* was probably the one most frequently used. A clear, concise, and not difficult method for tuning a harpsichord in this system appears in Ed Kottick's book, listed in the bibliography. The tunings associated with Andreas Werckmeister and Philip Kirnberger were not in common use until long after 1600.

Short Octave and Split Accidentals

Certain notes in the lowest octave of keyboard instruments were rarely called for in Renaissance music, so builders assigned more useful pitches to these accidentals. This is the so-called "short octave" concept. Here is the typical pattern, with the changes indicated.

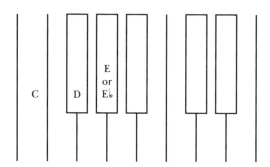

FIGURE 16.1 Short octave and split accidentals

Occasionally builders provided split accidentals, with the back and forward halves sounding different pitches. On the lowest two accidentals this was done to allow access to both the "proper" pitch and the short octave substitute; on others it was devised to offer a given note in either of two versions (e.g., as g♯ or a♭ in meantone tuning; see Tuning and Temperament, p. 238).

Fingering

Keyboard players should experiment with early fingerings to get a sense of how the keys felt under the fingers of their sixteenth-century colleagues. These patterns can be used to create a melodic line that is connected but *non-legato*, acknowledging the uneven stress patterns of recorder tonguings and string bowings called for in various period treatises. Experimenting with the fingerings is useful even if they are not actually applied in practice.

The precise application of early keyboard fingerings is a complex matter, and dangerously prone to oversimplification. An even halfway systematic study well repays the effort, however, because it brings out interpretative possibilities and probabilities that are not readily sensed otherwise. Reduced to simplest terms, what we know of sixteenth-century fingering philosophy indicates that the thumb was not normally used in scale passages except at either end ("thumb under" scales were not used), and that diatonic passages were generally played by repeating patterns of 2–3 or 3–4, or occasionally 1–2, the choice depending on the hand (right or left), the di-

176

rection of the scale (ascending or descending), the country, and any given author whose book you happen to be reading.

Further information can be found in the article on Renaissance Keyboard Fingering by Mark Lindley, p. 189, as well as in works by Schott and Soderlund (see harpsichord and organ bibliographies respectively).

General Keyboard Repertory

Apel, Willi, ed. *Corpus of Early Keyboard Music.* Dallas: American Institute of Musicology, 1963–. About 50 volumes of European keyboard music, including many of fifteenth- and sixteenth-century repertory.

Ferguson, Howard. *Early French Keyboard Music.* 2 vols. (Oxford University Press, 1966).

Ferguson, Howard. *Early Italian Keyboard Music.* 2 vols. (Oxford University Press, 1968).

Ferguson, Howard. *Early German Keyboard Music.* 2 vols. (Oxford University Press, 1971).

Ferguson, Howard. *Style and Interpretation. An Anthology of 16th–19th Century Keyboard Music.* 4 vols. (Oxford University Press, 1964).

The Organ

Pipe Design

Organ pipes work in one of two ways. In *flue* pipes vibrations are generated by directing a stream of air against a sharp edge, as in whistles, flutes, or recorders. In *reed* pipes the generator is a small strip of metal anchored at one end and made to vibrate by the flow of air. In both cases the length and shape of the pipe determine pitch, timbre, and volume.

Types of Organs

During the fifteenth and sixteenth centuries there were four main types of organ: the regal, the positive, the portative, and the large church organ. The claviorganum combined an organ with a harpsichord in one instrument.

The standard regal was a small, self-contained instrument with one keyboard and a rank of 8-foot reed pipes with either very short resonators or no resonators, producing something of a cordial snarl (see Fig. 16.2). Later regals often included additional flue stops, and sometimes strings to be plucked (by means of keys) as well. The instrument was especially popular in Germany, where some late sixteenth-century examples are found disguised as large books (bible-regal). The instrument retained its popularity, especially as a continuo instrument, into the seventeenth century; it was

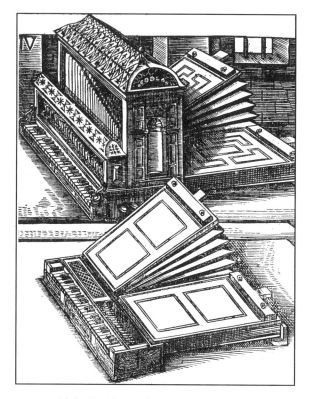

FIGURE 16.2 Positive and regal organs
Praetorius, *Syntagma musicum*, Plate IV

specified by Monteverdi in *Orfeo* (1607) to accompany the not-so-friendly snarling of Caronte, guardian of the ferry across the River Styx.

The portative, or organetto, was a small organ that could be carried and played simultaneously by one person, who played with one hand and pumped the bellows with the other. It had a short range (1–2 octaves) and generally no more than one rank of pipes, the longest of which was about two feet (thereby producing a lowest note of c′). Portatives also occasionally had one or two *bourdons*, or larger pipes, that could be used for droning. When simulating the sound of a portative on a larger organ, play no more than one melodic line; it is unrealistic to expect the possibility of chords on this instrument. Portatives appear frequently in the paintings of Hans Memling (ca. 1430–1495). They were in common use throughout the fifteenth century, although they seem to have passed out of use almost completely by around 1500.

The larger, self-standing positive is also a one-manual instrument, typically (though not exclusively) with a small number of flue pipes—sometimes only a single 8-foot flute (see Fig. 16.2). Though stationary while played, it was designed to be moved to various locations in the church to accompany singing. It was also used in (larger) homes.

By the middle of the fifteenth century the large church organ had one or more keyboards. Its most typical sound was that of the *Blockwerk*, which is not an individual stop but rather an arrangement where any one key controls several pipes speaking at different spots in that pitch's overtone series. This conglomerate of sound lives on in the various mixture stops still found on organs of any size. By the sixteenth century, the *Blockwerk* had been engineered so that players could shut off (stop) individual ranks as desired; the name "stop" was eventually reversed to mean turning *on* a given set of pipes. Of particular importance was the *praestant*, a set of principal pipes placed in the façade, usually at 8-foot pitch. When several lines are played together on a properly voiced praestant, the sound is reminiscent of vocal polyphony.

Finally, the claviorganum was an instrument in which an organ and harpsichord were placed in/on the same case so that they could be played at the same time. On some instruments they could actually be played in tandem from the same keyboard, while on others the "combination" only meant that the keyboards were placed close to each other while the instruments themselves remained independent. The term was also sometimes used to denote the standard organ (i.e., without strings attached), especially as used in the home.

Development

The organ underwent one of its most dramatic periods of expansion and development in the Renaissance period. These activities went on at different rates and with different emphases in different geographic regions, which makes any attempt at giving a brief, uniform account of the development of the organ little short of futile. It is generally true that most builders sought to increase colorful effects, often by trying to copy, or at least to acknowledge, the sounds of other instruments. In most regions, both the regal and other reed stops with characteristic qualities were incorporated into the larger instruments. Indeed, the earliest known occurrence of the term *krummhorn* is as an organ stop (Dresden, 1489), although it must have been named for the wind instrument. The positive was also assimilated into the larger organ, where in many regions it was placed behind the player (hence, *Rückpositiv*).

Registration

A thorough introduction to the intricacies of organ design and registration practices in different countries is beyond the scope of a manual such as this;

pertinent information can be found in various books cited in the bibliography. As general observations regarding the period from 1500–1600, note the following points:

A. Some sixteenth-century organs had pedal divisions comprised of solo stops at various pitches, used to emphasize a *cantus firmus.* Others did not have independent divisions, but had pedal keys that merely operated pipes in a manual division. On a modern organ, when registering sixteenth-century music that does not have a *cantus firmus* in the pedal, it is generally advisable just to couple the manual to the pedal with no separate pedal stops drawn—that is, do not draw a 16-foot stop in the pedal if there is not one drawn on the manual.

B. Single-manual instruments were often built so that the stops could be separately drawn in either the treble or bass, with the break coming somewhere in the vicinity of c′. Thus, even though many Renaissance instruments are known to have had only one keyboard, the possibility of solo-and-accompaniment effects should not necessarily be ruled out.

C. Many organs currently found in churches or college auditoria will have a very heavy sounding 8-foot diapason on the great. It is a sound unlike anything a sixteenth-century organist would ever have heard. When registering sixteenth-century music on such instruments, it is best to substitute a different 8-foot stop for the great principal. Sometimes a lighter 8-foot principal can be borrowed successfully from another division; sometimes an 8-foot flute (gedackt, etc.) will work; often an 8-foot gemshorn or viola works best. In general, sixteenth-century organ sound was fairly top-heavy by modern standards; late nineteenth- and early twentieth-century organs (meaning many instruments in the United States) are decidedly bottom-heavy, and compensation must be allowed for this. At the same time, overly thin or harsh sounds must also be avoided. Take care to find sweet, rich, singing registrations.

D. Use of the swell pedal and combination pistons is anachronistic in sixteenth-century music, which should be played at one dynamic level on any given manual in any given passage. Stop and/or manual changes can be made at major divisions in the piece, but it is inappropriate to make them *en passant.* On some organs, a cluster of characteristic stops was found in the *Brustwerk*, a small division often sequestered behind doors which the player could open or close. But it hardly seems likely that these doors would be moved while a piece was actually being played.

Common Problems

Volume and articulation. When accompanying, organists must be constantly alert to problems of balance. In addition to selecting stops carefully, it is also helpful to play with a more detached touch, particularly when playing dance or dance-style music. This both adds rhythmic verve and cuts down on the amount of sound. Solo polyphony should be rendered in a more connected style, although it should not be played completely legato, either. Organists should avoid the substitution fingerings taught as a matter of course in modern organ technique.

Exercises

With regard to the feet, sixteenth-century organists used only the toe and not the heel. Doing this virtually guarantees a detached line in the pedal, for obvious reasons. Use of the heel was not unknown, however; for instance, pieces published by Arnolt Schlick (1511) require four simultaneous voices from the pedals.

Repertory

> England: *The Mulliner Book*, Thomas Preston, John Redford, William Byrd, John Bull
> France: Jean Titelouze, Pierre Attaingnant
> Germany: Hans Buchner, *The Buxheim Organ Book*, Conrad Paumann, Arnolt Schlick
> Italy: Claudio Merulo, Giovanni Gabrieli, Girolamo Diruta, Marco Antonio Cavazzoni, Girolamo Cavazzoni
> Spain: Tomás de Santa Maria, Antonio de Cabezón

Bibliography

Knighton/Fallows (Thomas)–*Companion*; Mountney–Regal; Owen/Williams–*Organ*; Soderlund– *Organ*; Williams–European; Williams–*New*.

Suggested Listening

Froidebise, Pierre. *Music from the Chapel of Charles V.* One side includes organ pieces by Arnolt Schlick, including "Ascendo ad patrem meum" with four voices in the pedals. Nonesuch, H-71051, n.d.

Hogwood, Christopher. Pieces played on regal, positive, and large Spanish church organ (1562), on record set accompanying David Munrow's *Instruments of the Middle Ages and Renaissance.* Angel, SBZ-3810 (1976).

Tachezi, Herbert. *Orgelmusik der Renaissance.* Ebert-Orgel, Innsbruck. Pieces by Tomás de Santa Maria, Antonio Cabezón, Paul Hofhaimer, Hans Kotter, and others. 16th-century organ in original condition, including meantone tuning. Das alte Werk, 6.42587 AZ (1980).

Tramnitz, Helmut. *Orgelmusik der Schütz-Zeit.* One side is devoted to repertory performed on the Compenius organ described by Praetorius in *Syntagma musicum* and now located in the Fredericksborg castle in Hillerød, Denmark, tuned in meantone. Deutsche Grammophon Gesellschaft/Archiv, 198 350 (1964).

Vogel, Harald. *Die Spätgotische Orgelkunst.* Includes selections by Buchner, Kleber, Kotter, Paumann, and Schlick, as well as pieces from Attaingnant and the *Buxheimer Orgelbuch.* Recorded on the organ in Rysum, originally from 1457 and now restored to its 1527 state, with tuning after Schlick. Organa, ORA 3001 (1981).

Vogel, Harald. *The Fisk Organ at Wellesley College.* Includes pieces from the manuscript of Suzanne van Soldty, late sixteenth century; organ tuned in meantone. Organa, ORA 3005 (1982).

The Clavichord

The clavichord was developed in the late Middle Ages and remained popular, especially as a domestic instrument, through the sixteenth, seventeenth, and eighteenth centuries. The key of the clavichord has a small piece of brass, called a *tangent,* lodged in the back. Depressing the key brings this tangent into contact with the string, setting into vibration that portion of the string between the point of contact and the bridge. The remaining length of string is damped by strips of felt, called *listing,* which also damp the entire string when the key is released and the tangent falls away.

Clavichord design differed from south to north, with builders favoring certain construction principles in line with those practiced on their harpsichords (e.g., inner/outer case design and thin case walls on Italian clavichords). On all instruments, notes were generally double-strung.

One peculiarity of clavichords is the idea of *fretting,* whereby one string is made to serve for two or more pitches. This is possible because more than one tangent can be assigned to any given string since different pitches will be created by stopping it at different points. For example, the oldest extant clavichord has forty-five keys but only twenty-two strings. The German term *gebunden* is applied to a clavichord built in this way, as virtually all were until the eighteenth century. Of course, one string cannot produce two or more pitches simultaneously (see Common Problems, below).

The clavichord is a venerable instrument; its direct ancestor is the monochord, which was used to demonstrate the translation of number into sound, the basis of medieval music theory. The instrument first appeared in the early fifteenth century; it is pictured in the same fifteenth-century treatise by Arnaut of Zwolle wherein are found harpsichord and organ designs. A clavichord is pictured in Sebastian Virdung's *Musica getutscht* of 1511, as well as in various other instrument treatises throughout the sixteenth century. An instrument by the Italian builder Domenico da Pesaro appears to be the oldest surviving example (1543). Clavichord cases could be plain or decorated; the inside of the lid often had a scene painted on it, or a Latin inscription.

Range

Arnaut's fifteenth-century clavichord shows a nearly three-octave compass (B–a″); by 1618, Praetorius notes that a compass of C to f ‴ is standard.

Common Problems

The key action on a clavichord can be problematic to the uninitiated at first, since it so exactly mirrors the motion of the player's hand. It takes time to acclimate one's technique to the fact that the tone is both generated and held captive by the tangent, meaning that the finger must be "playing" at all times. Too light a touch produces an inadequate sound; one too heavy may result in an unpleasant brashness. Watchwords are firmness and strength of touch, the correct degree of which will vary from instrument to instrument.

On a fretted clavichord it is obviously impossible to play two pitches generated by the same string at the same time. Fretting was and is designed to accommodate this responsibly; for example, no builder would make an instrument with both middle c and the e′ above it produced by the same string. Indeed, fretting is generally planned so that only pitches a major or minor second apart are played on the same string; if these are required as simultaneous notes, they must be rolled very slightly.

One problem in using a clavichord in performance is volume, or, rather, the lack of it. The clavichord is simply a very soft instrument. Ideally a clavichord concert should not be given in a large hall; it if is, amplification will be a virtual necessity, but it must be done very carefully so that no distortion results. Clavichord concerts are often most successful when the audience is seated on the stage, a few feet from the player. If you are the player, this naturally takes some getting used to.

Similarities to Other Instruments

Clavichord technique is unlike that of any other keyboard instrument, but facility on the organ, harpsichord, or piano will naturally stand a clavichordist in good stead.

Repertory

There are no known pieces from the fifteenth or sixteenth centuries that are actually specified for the clavichord, but much keyboard repertory from that period works well. See *Repertory* in the Organ, Harpsichord, and Keyboard introduction segments.

Bibliography

Munrow–*Instruments*; Neupert–*Clavichord.*

Suggested Listening

Benson, Joan. *Joan Benson, Clavichord.* Repertoire Records, RM 901 (1962).
Brauchli, Bernard. *Renaissance Clavichord.* Titanic, 10.
Brauchli, Bernard. *Renaissance Clavichord II.* Titanic, 27.

The Harpsichord

History

The word "clavicembalum" is found in an Italian source in 1397, while the first physical representation of a harpsichord followed about thirty years later (1425) in an altarpiece found in northern Germany (Minden). Many of the early pictorial representations show small instruments, probably built at 4-foot pitch. The oldest dated harpsichord is an Italian instrument by Vincentius, begun in 1515. This instrument, currently in the Accademia Chigiana, Siena, is described in Wraight–Vincentius. An undated clavicytherium (harpsichord with vertical soundboard) in London's Royal College of Music is thought to be from about 1480.

By the end of the sixteenth century most harpsichords were built according to one of two basic patterns, "Italian" or "Flemish." The Italian-style instrument was actually the representative European harpsichord for most of the century, with the Flemish design offering serious competition only after about 1580. The outer appearance of both types is superficially the same: a wing-shaped outline, with a single manual at one end. Otherwise, the instruments are quite different.

Italian Style

Sixteenth-century Italian harpsichords were generally built with one set of strings at 8-foot pitch, although some had two, generally at 8-foot and 4-foot. The familiar Italian set-up of two 8-foot registers plucking in unison was known in the late sixteenth century but not common until the seventeenth; many instruments were converted to this disposition from earlier ones that had been built with either a single 8-foot register, or registers at 8-foot and 4-foot. Period instruments with the 2×8-foot disposition, which is the common one in "Italian copies" today, did not have stop levers that could be controlled from outside the case. Usually one of the two registers could be controlled individually by reaching underneath the jackrail, but this was only to make tuning easier; both registers were almost certainly intended to remain on at all times while playing. In the Italian design the relative lengths of the strings approximate what one would expect from their relative pitches; that is, the string for c'' is roughly half the length of that for c', which is itself about half the length of that for c. This just curve creates an elongated shape with a pronounced bentside. The case of an Italian harpsichord was very thin and light; for protection, it was generally placed in a second, outer case. The inner case was not painted, but rather left in natural wood (typically cypress). The outer case was generally decorated, usually with paint or sometimes a tooled leather cover; the underside of the lid was often decorated with a painting or Latin inscription. Under the soundboard the Italian instrument had a distinctive pattern of many right-angle knees joining the bottom with the sides, in addition to struts connecting the top of the bentside with the case bottom on the opposite side.

Flemish Style

The late sixteenth-century Flemish-style harpsichord had the same basic outer design as the Italian. The stringing was not laid out according to the just curve that typifies Italian instruments, however, resulting in—among other things—a less pronounced bentside curve. The case walls of northern instruments were thicker and they were never placed in a separate, outer case; the interior bracing was also done differently. The outside was painted, frequently with a wide band of simulated marble finish on the cheek and bentside; the inside, around the keywell and on the case sides above the soundboard, was decorated with fanciful block-printed papers, often in a "seahorse" design; the inside of the lid was either covered in ash-grain paper with a Latin epigram in large block lettering, or displayed a painting; and soundboards were decorated in tempera paint with fruit, flowers, birds, and insects. These instruments had two registers, 8-foot and 4-foot, with the register slides protruding through the right side of the case so that they could be controlled individually by the player. Flemish builders also provided a two-manual instrument, but it is not what you might be thinking: the keyboards were set up to sound a fourth apart, ruling out both manual coupling and solo-with-accompaniment effects. The reason for this design is not documented. While the most obvious reason would be for downward transposition by a fourth, it may have been used for other reasons as well. (See Shann–Flemish.)

In addition to these basic types, both Italian and Flemish workshops produced spinets or virginals, sometimes at 8-foot pitch and sometimes one octave higher (the *ottavino*). The typical Italian model was an irregular polygon, with the keyboard protruding from the center of the long side and the strings lying more or less perpendicular to the keys. This instrument was generally placed in a rectangular outer case. Early Flemish virginals were also polygonal, but later ones were most often rectangular, with a keyboard recessed into the long side; its position (right, left, or center) determined the timbre. Instruments with keyboards on the left or in the middle were called *spinets*. Having the keyboard on the right moves the plucking point towards the center of the string, creating a distinctive "fluty" sound; instruments of this design were later called *muselars*. In one design, called "Mother and Child," the keyboard could be on either the right or left; a compartment is on the other side where a smaller octave virginal is stashed. This can be placed on top, and the two instruments played together as a two-manual instrument, with the keys of the lower instrument operating the jacks of the top one (after the lower jackrail has been removed). This was not a common model, however, and only appeared late in the sixteenth century.

Lute Stop and Buff Stop

Confusion persists regarding two special effects available on some harpsichords, the buff stop and the lute stop. Most modern Flemish (and French) design instruments have the first, which is a bar with small pieces of felt attached that can be moved so that the felts are placed against one set of strings to dampen them so that they do not ring when plucked. It was also common on period Flemish instruments, where it was often divided into two halves so that the treble end of the keyboard could be played with a timbre different from the bass. Italian instruments did not generally have buff stops.

Today this is often mistakenly referred to as a "lute stop." In fact, the lute stop is an extra set of jacks positioned closer to the nut, producing a more nasal sound than the standard jacks operated by the same keys.

Until the mid-seventeenth century the English generally called all plucked keyboard instruments by the name "virginal," with the term applied to wing-shaped and box-shaped instruments indiscriminately. The rectangular version was based on the spinet, rather than the muselar, design.

Range

There was no absolute standard for keyboard compass on the sixteenth-century harpsichord. Hubbard (see Bibliography) gives ranges for many instruments from Italy and from the Ruckers workshop in Antwerp, which reveal an average range of about four octaves. Most harpsichords are tuned at "unison pitch"; that is, the keys govern pitch in the same octave as do the corresponding keys on a piano. Small virginals and spinets are tuned one octave higher. In the sixteenth century, harpsichords were built in a variety of sizes, resulting in a variety of pitch ranges; for example, the key for c′ might sound at what we would call f′.

Pitch

The issue of sixteenth-century harpsichord pitch is still a controversial one, there being at that time no standard pitch level in Europe either for musical instruments or for anything else (see Pitch and Transposition, p. 248). The choice of pitch for a harpsichord is a strong factor in determining its character, since the optimal sound for a given string is achieved by tightening it as closely as is practical to its breaking point. (Compare the injunction found in period instrument tutors such as Thomas Robinson's *Schoole of Musicke* for the lute: "First set up the Treble, so high as you dare venter [venture] for breaking. . . .")

Exactly what the pitch in use on any given instrument was (that is, its measurement in cycles per second) would depend on variables including the choice of string material (brass or iron) and the scale (a measurement related, at least nominally, to the proportional lengths of the strings relative to that of the longest unison pitch string at c″). Recent scholarship has suggested that the key lever for, say, a′ on a sixteenth-century harpsichord could have sounded anywhere from "modern" a′ = 440 to a minor sixth lower (c♯), with most instruments speaking either at approximately modern pitch, or about one fourth lower.

Care and Precautions

A harpsichord is sensitive to variation in humidity and temperature. Increasing humidity will cause the action to stick and the soundboard to roll and buckle, while a change to dryer air may cause cracks to open up in the soundboard. Frequent changes in humidity will cause both of these effects *and* make the tuning extremely unstable, as the instrument tries to compensate for the various strains on its system. Harpsichords should be kept in stable climatic conditions.

Common Problems

The soundboard. A few small cracks in the soundboard are almost inevitable. They should not cause undue alarm and ought only to be fixed if they cause buzzing, or show signs of extending out of control.

Voicing and action. Kottick's book, listed in the bibliography, should be consulted about these two points. Here, it will suffice to say only two things. First, by far the vast majority of instruments have plectra made of Delrin or a similar plastic. A curious idiosyncrasy of these plastics is that they set up (i.e., get harder) with use, meaning that many harpsichords will need at least one revoicing after about a year of use, because the plectra have actually gotten harder. Revoicing is a tricky business, but people with the responsibility for keeping an instrument in shape must come to terms with either having it done or doing it themselves.

Second, at some point in your harpsichord's life, its action may stick and/or clatter and/or miss the string, depending on climate conditions and maturity of the instrument. Builders generally make allowance for this: for one thing, most register slides can be set at both ends to define the amount of bite the plectra will take out of the string. Keep the temperature and humidity in the harpsichord's room as stable as possible.

Similarities

Harpsichord technique bears a superficial resemblance to piano technique, although the harpsichordist must play with considerably less arm weight and depend more on suppleness and flexibility in the fingers. It is perhaps more similar to organ technique, especially that used on tracker (mechanical action) instruments, although harpsichordists playing music from the sixteenth century and before should not use the substitution fingerings taught as part of nineteenth-century organ technique.

Suggested Repertory

There is an abundance of printed music for the harpsichord. One series including a number of pieces from the Renaissance is the *Corpus of Early Keyboard Music*, for which full information is given at the end of the Keyboard Introduction.

Bibliography

Boxall–*Harpsichord*; Ferguson–*Keyboard*; Hubbard–*Three*; Jorgensen–*Equal–Beating*; Klop–*Harpsichord*; Kottick–*Harpsichord*; O'Brien–*Ruckers*; Russell–*Harpsichord*; Sadie–*Early*; Schott–*Playing*; Shann–Flemish; Wraight–Vincentius.

Suggested Listening

I only list representative recordings (from the many available) on which each of the various types of harpsichords discussed above may be heard.

Double virginals: *Music for Virginal.* Played by Colin Tilney on a double virginal of 1580 by Martin van der Biest and a 1697 harpsichord by Carlo Grimaldi. Archiv, 2533 379 (1978).

Flemish harpsichord: Froberger, Johann Jacob. *The Sound of the Early Harpsichord.* Played by Gustav Leonhardt on a Jan Ruckers instrument (Antwerp, 1640). RCA Records, VICS-1494 (1970).

Recordings of an anonymous Italian seventeenth-century harpsichord and a modern copy of a virginal of 1611 by Andreas Ruckers, both played by Christopher Hogwood, are included among the recorded examples in David Munrow's *Instruments of the Middle Ages and Renaissance.* Angel, SBZ-3810 (1976).

Virginals and organ: Byrd, William. *My Ladye Nevells Booke.* Recording of the entire 1591 collection by Christopher Hogwood. L'Oiseau-Lyre, D29D 4 (1976).

17

Renaissance Keyboard Fingering

Mark Lindley

A keyboard player who is most at home with modern techniques may find Renaissance fingerings uncomfortable at first, and it should go without saying that a good performance with modern fingerings is preferable to an awkward one with early fingerings! However, a player who takes the trouble to become perfectly at home with early fingerings, and with the choreographies of the hand that they entail, will gain entry into a different and very rewarding world of articulation and rhythmic inflections.

From sixteenth- and early seventeenth-century Germany we have two discussions of fingering, two sets of exercises, and two pieces that are almost completely fingered in the original sources. From Italy and Spain during this period we have very little music with fingerings, but several discussions of keyboard technique in tutors and prefaces. From England we have no keyboard tutors, but hundreds of fingerings in late sixteenth- and early seventeenth-century manuscripts.

Before surveying the evidence from these various countries it seems best to mention, as a general principle, that if one hand had to take two parts, the same finger was very likely to play two or more successive notes in a line (see Exs. 17.1–17.5, where the fingerings are, as in all the examples cited here, from the original sources).

EX. 17.1 Buchner, "Quem terra pontus," (*CH-Bu* F.i.8a, f.), bars 31–33

EX. 17.2 Erbach, Ricercar (*D-Mbs* mus 1581, nr 151), bars 15–18

EX. 17.3 Banchieri, brief examples from *L'organo suonarino* 2/1611)

a.

b.

EX. 17.4 Anonymous seventeenth-century voluntary (*GB-Lc* 2093, f. 45), bars 7–9 and 21–23

a.

b.

EX. 17.5 Anonymous voluntary (*GB-Lc* 2093, f. 40), bars 19–22

Several tutors imply that each kind of harmonic interval or chord was always to be played with the same fingers no matter what the context. Such rules were probably oversimplified for beginners (Correa de Arauxo gave more elaborate rules in 1626), but since there is no evidence at all from before the eighteenth century for substituting fingers on a note, it seems clear that (a) this aspect of Renaissance technique was simpler than that of the nineteenth century, when substitution fingerings began to be used as a matter of course, and (b) legato playing was not as legato as in Romantic organ and piano music.

The oldest fingering rules for fast notes, summarized in Example 17.6, are from a manuscript of Hans Buchner's *fundament buch* dated 1551 (some thirteen years after his death).

EX. 17.6 Summary of the rules for quick notes in Buchner's *fundament buch*

Did Buchner really reserve 3 for weak notes, or is it only that none of these groups begins in the middle of a three-note span? Fortunately, the manuscript gives the fingering for an entire piece. There we find that 3 takes all the notes that have a mordent, and various half notes weak or strong, but is otherwise generally reserved for *weak* quarter, eighth, and sixteenth notes. In Examples 17.7 and 17.8, the actual duration of the first bass note (which completes a phrase) has to match the quarter note or eighth note in the middle voice.

EX. 17.7 Buchner, "Quem terra pontus," bars 4–5

EX. 17.8 Buchner, "Quem terra pontus," bars 15–19

If several other half notes (elsewhere in the piece) are not also to be truncated drastically, the hand must perform some rather strange gymnastics. Probably the sixteenth notes in Example 17.9 want to be played with a high wrist, with the backs of the fingers facing left, with the tips touching the keys as indicated in Figure 17.1, and with distinctly more weight on the first of the four notes than on the others.

EX. 17.9 Buchner, "Quem terra pontus," bars 8–9

FIGURE 17.1 Finger placement on keys (Buchner passage)

Some experts have said that in order to use Buchner's fingerings, "one needs an extra hand (or nose),"[1] or that the fingerings in the manuscript indicate, not how Buchner would play the piece, but which fingers he would *avoid* using.[2] The problem is aggravated by the mistake shown in Example 17.7, where a low C was overlooked and middle C was accordingly fingered 2. The proper emendation is to play the octave with 5 and 1, like all the other octaves; but B should still be played with 3, as in the next bar. In such passages the hand tends to render the metrically weak eighth notes (played with 3) slightly shorter than their neighbors (played with 1 or 2) and thus make an effect not unlike *notes inégales*. Skeptics should reserve judgment as to whether Buchner used such fingerings until they understand firsthand why it is more feasible to play such sixths and sevenths with 5 and 3 than to play simultaneously two notes an octave apart with 5 and 2.

A ricercar by Christian Erbach is preserved with fingerings in a Bavarian manuscript of the 1620s. Here also, 3 has mostly weak eighth and sixteenth

EX. 17.10 Erbach, Ricercar, bars 2–3 (r.h.), 6–7 (l.h.)

notes (Ex. 17.10), but at the same time there are some rather unsystematic fingerings (as in Ex. 17.11, where the right hand's 4 on D gives rise to a cadential rubato and a relatively deliberate articulation).[3]

EX. **17.11** Erbach, Ricercar, bars 13–14

In Example 17.10 it is obvious that to slur all those notes that can most readily be slurred when the wrist is in a normal modern position would often make a silly "hiccuping" effect (as in Ex. 17.12).

EX. **17.12** Unlikely phrasing for part of Ex. 17.10

Some alternatives are: (a) to detach all the notes, (b) to slur them all by "walking" with a high wrist and with the backs of the fingers facing the direction of the melody at each moment; and (c) to slur in pairs within the beat, using a hand position such as described under (b). I would recommend a subtle and fluctuating compromise among all three possibilities, with occasionally a phrasing and with the opportune use of "backward" steps (i.e., not changing the orientation of the hand) when the melody zigzags as in the last bar of Example 17.10. The high wrist—perhaps only momentarily so, but in that case nicely prepared—facilitates the turning of the hand where the melody changes from a downward to an upward scale as in the middle of the first bar of Example 17.10. The high wrist also facilitates some of the other fingerings, such as $\frac{5}{4}$ for harmonic thirds in Example 17.13; such

EX. **17.13** Erbach, Ricercar, bars 19–21

a wrist can be seen in the lower left corner of the full-page illustration (perhaps depicting Erbach himself) to the article "Augsburg" in *New Grove*.

In Elias Ammerbach's two sets of fingered exercises (1571, 1583), 3 is used on weak or strong notes indifferently (Exx. 17.14–17.15) and the left

EX. 17.14 Ammerbach, exercise (*Orgel oder Instrument Tabulaturbuch*, 1583, preface)

EX. 17.15 Ammerbach, exercise (*Orgel oder Instrument Tabulatur*, 1571, preface [excerpt])

thumb is applied to the last note of certain groups (Exx. 17.15–17.16)— even if it may be a flat. (The right thumb is not called for in any German Renaissance source.)

EX. 17.16 Ammerbach, scale (1571, 1583, prefaces)

Ammerbach may well have used a moderately low wrist as in Figure 17.2. At any rate he fingered most groups independently of each other and thus the same finger may have the last note of one group and the first of the next (as happens once for each hand in Ex. 17.15); perhaps in such cases the weak note was played with merely a finger motion, but the following strong note with a hand motion.

Our only sixteenth-century Italian source of information, part 1 (1593) of Girolamo Diruta's *Il transilvano*, prescribes that the wrist be "a bit high" ("*alquanto alto*") to keep the hand and arm level. Diruta dwelt on the importance of a quiet hand—relaxed as if caressing a child—except that in dances one might instead, if playing on the harpsichord or virginal, "leap and hit with the fingers." He also said that the arm should guide the hand, and the fingers should be "*alquanto inarcate*," which various translators have rendered as "slightly," "somewhat," or "rather" curved, according to their own preferences.

Diruta was the disciple of a famous virtuoso, Claudio Merulo, yet it is hard to get a clear picture of contemporary practice from his book. He found that in right-hand scale passages moving away from the body, 2 (with no notes to play) tends to become straight and stiff ("*sforzato*"), and the thumb also stiff under the hand, and 5 rather drawn in; and he said that many organists had accustomed the hand to these defects, to the detriment of their playing; but he did not say whether they were well-known performers or nonentities. He reserved 3 for weak notes ("*note cattive*"), but all the

FIGURE 17.2 Ammerbach *Orgel oder Instrument Tabulaturbuch* (1571), fol. i^v

later Italian writers, including Banchieri in 1608, gave the strong notes to 3 or were indifferent. He said that for scales the left hand should descend (2)3232 . . . even though "many eminent men" preferred to descend with 4, and he said either hand should move toward the body (4)3232 . . . even though many eminent men preferred to ascend with 1 and 2 in the left hand. He said weak notes that leap should be played with 3, or could be played with 1 or 5 if the leap is larger than a fifth; but since none of his examples is fingered it is not clear whether a weak note before a large leap should ever be played with 3, or whether a weak note after a leap might ever be played with 1 or 5.

Diruta said that diminutions must be played "cleanly, that is, not pressing a key down before the finger is lifted from the previous one, moving up and down at the same time." However, his examples of diminutions include sevenths for which 2–5 would be the smoothest fingering that unquestionably conforms with his rules; so at least in the case of such leaps his phrase "at the same time" should be taken to allow a slight margin of detachment.

The rules given in five sixteenth- and early seventeenth-century Spanish treatises and prefaces (Bermudo 1555, Henestrosa 1557, Santa María 1565, Hernando Cabezón 1578, Correa de Arauxo 1626)[4] show that scales were taken with various fingerings. Bermudo prescribed 4321 4321 and 1234 1234. Cabezón recommended for beginners (in his edition of the music of his brother Antonio): r.h. up 343434 and down 323232; l.h. up 4321 4321,

TABLE 17.1 Santa Maria's fingering suggestions

	Toward the body:		Away from the body:
Right hand:			
♩ (or ♪)	(4) 3232...	♩ or ♪	(12) 3434...
♪	(3) 2323...		
♪(or ♩)	(4) 321321...*		
♪	4321 4321...		
	3, 4 or 5 43 2132 1 or 3 ♩ ♫ ♭♬ ♩		
Left hand:			
♩	(43) 2121...	♪	(12) 3434...
♪ or 𝅘𝅥𝅯	4321 4321...	♪ or 𝅘𝅥𝅯	1234 1234...
	543 2132 1 ♩♫ ♬ ♩		1 12 3434 5 or 3 ♩ ♫ ♬ ♩

*with 3 and/or 2 on a chromatic note

but down 1234 3434. A preference for paired fingering away from the body is evident also in Henestrosa's advice (again for beginners) that the l.h. go up 4321 321, but down 1234 3434, and the r.h. go down 4321 3 . . . (or perhaps it might start with 5), but up 3434 (once 4 has been reached after starting from 1 or perhaps 2 or 3). Santa María's suggestions were the most elaborate. Table 17.1 summarizes some of them. For all fingerings alike, Santa María said the hand should point toward the keys to be played next, and the finger that has just played should be lifted before the next one plays. (So if the thumb followed 4 in a scale away from the body, the hand was turned outward and the thumb would approach its key just as 4 was releasing its hold.) However, Correa de Arauxo warned against releasing one note before coming upon another in the same voice-part, a defect he said he had found particularly in the playing of nuns. He said that for runs on all-diatonic notes the r.h. should normally go up 3434 . . . and down 2323 . . . , the l.h. up 2121 . . . and down 3434 . . . ; but for "extraordinary runs"—that is, those involving chromatic notes—the r.h. might better go up 234234 . . . or 12341234 . . . (perhaps ending on 5), the l.h. 321321 . . . or 43214321. . . . He recommended practicing such fingerings even with all-diatonic notes, and he gave some examples with the runs shown in Example 17.17 (where neither 1 nor 4 takes a chromatic note).

EX. 17.17 Correa de Arauxo, "extraordinary runs" (*Faculdad organica*, 1626, ff. 23–34)

In a brief survey such as this, it is better to deal with the English evidence by means of examples than by a detailed discussion. In manuscripts from the late sixteenth and early seventeenth centuries, scale passages fingered as in Examples. 17.18 and 17.19 are commonplace and show that for scales, 3 would most often play the strong notes except that when the left hand had an ascending scale, 2 would routinely cross over 1.

EX. 17.18 Bull, Preludium (*GB-Lbm* add 31403, f. 3), bars 4–5 (r.h.) and 7–9 (l.h.)

EX. 17.19 Gibbons, Preludium (*F-Pc* res 1186 bis i, p. 5), bars 21–22

In various other contexts as well, 3 would take metrically strong notes (see Exx. 17.20–17.24); but contrary examples can also readily be found (as in Exx. 25–30).

EX. 17.20 Gibbons, "The woods so wild" (*GB-Lbm* add 36661, f. 41v), bars 25–27

EX. 17.21 Bull, Prelude (*GB-Lbm* add 31403, f. 4), bars 4–5

EX. 17.22 Gibbons, Fantasia (*F-Pc* res 1186, bis ii, p. 44), bars 29–32

EX. 17.23 Anonymous, "The buildings" (*GB-Och* mus 431, f. 4v), beginning

EX. 17.24 Bull, Fantasia (*GB-Lbm* add 36661, f. 48), beginning

EX. 17.25 Anonymous seventeenth-century voluntary (*GB-Lc* 2093, f. 44), beginning

EX. 17.26 Byrd, "Qui passe" (*My Lady Nevell's book*, no. 2), bars 48 and 62–64

a.

b.

EX. 17.27 Byrd, "The march before the battle" (*My Lady Nevell's book*, no. 3), bars 41–43

EX. 17.28 Gibbons, "The woods so wild," bar 41

EX. 17.29 Bull, "Miserere" (*GB-Och* 1207; *F-Pc* res 1186 bis ii, f. 54), bars 2–3

EX. 17.30 Bull, Galliard (*GB-Lbm* add 36661, f. 50v), end

Repeated notes would most often be taken with changing fingers (as in Exx. 17.25, 17.27, and 17.29).

Some good modern sources for more detailed information on Renaissance fingerings are the anthologies of music marked with an asterisk in the bibliography (except that Le Huray's transcription of Bull's "Miserere" is quite inaccurate)[5] and the anthology, marked with a cross (+), of keyboard tutors and prefaces (or pertinent excerpts) in English translation.

NOTES

1. Sandra Soderland in her organ tutor (see Bibliography).
2. Harald Vogel in his lectures.
3. I used to think the "4" on middle D was due to a mistake, but now I like the musical effect—provided the hand position is managed suitably.
4. Barbara Sachs and Barry Ife in their anthology, and (for Correa de Arauxo) Jon Holland in his thesis (see Bibliography).
5. For details see *Early Music* 12/1 (1989): 65–66.

Bibliography

Boxall–English; Boxall–Girolamo; Boxall–New; *Boxall–*Harpsichord*; Holland–Francisco; Koopman–*My*; *Le Huray–*Fingering*; Le Huray–English; Lindley–Early-Selected; Lindley–Early English; Lindley–Early-Editing; Lindley–*Ars*; *Lindley/Boxall–Early; Parkins–Keyboard; Rodgers–Early; +Sachs/Ife–*Anthology*; Soderland–*Organ*.

IV

PROTO-CONTINUO

18

Overview and Practical Applications

Jack Ashworth and Paul O'Dette

In most history books the *basso continuo* is said to be one of the musical innovations that distinguishes the Baroque era from the Renaissance. But was the *basso continuo* such a new thing in 1600, and was it practiced in a significantly different manner from the accompaniment styles of the sixteenth century? In fact the *basso continuo* was nothing more than a new method of notating a practice that had been in existence since at least the late fifteenth century, the practice of providing a simple harmonic accompaniment to a solo singer or ensemble. What was new about the *basso continuo* was that instead of writing out the accompaniment in lute tablature or organ score (*partitura*), only a bass line was provided, often with figures added to indicate the chords to be realized above the bass. This saved the player the trouble of intabulating all the parts, a lengthy and not altogether artistically satisfying process. As Agostino Agazzari suggested, "If [an organist] were to put into tablature or score all the works which are sung in the course of a year in a single church in Rome . . . he would need to have a larger library than a Doctor of Law."[1] Indeed, one suspects that the better musicians of the sixteenth century were able to accompany from a bass line long before Viadana's coining of the term *basso continuo*, by applying their knowledge of counterpoint and the standard harmonic progressions, much as was done with the unfigured bass parts of the seventeenth century.

Chordal accompaniment before 1600 is found in four main textures: solo melody with accompaniment, accompaniment of larger ensembles, English mixed consort music, and late sixteenth-century organ scores.

Melody with Accompaniment

The recitation of poetry to music remained popular from the Middle Ages into the Renaissance. On the Italian peninsula it was especially popular to sing verses such as *terze rime, ottave rime,* sonnets, and the like to simple melodic patterns (e.g., *aria de Romanesca*) repeated over and over. Much of the time these would have been sung to improvised accompaniment, first on the lira da braccio and later on other instruments. An example occurs in Giambullari's printed account of the entertainments for the marriage of Cosimo I de' Medici and Eleonora of Toledo in 1539. At the wedding banquet, figures representing Apollo and the muses sang for the royal couple. Apollo entered carrying a lyre and a bow, performing several stanze in *ottava rima* during the ensuing interval. He is described as singing and playing, yet no music is given. Since music is given for all other parts of the production, including the canzone sung by the muses accompanying him, it seems clear that Apollo was expected to sing and accompany himself in the traditional formulaic manner. Examples of such formulas survive in some frottola collections and in the Bottegari *Lutebook* entitled, for example, "Aria per sonetti," "Aria da ottave rime." For an idea of how this might have sounded on the lira da braccio one may consult the single known sixteenth-century piece for the instrument, a setting of the *Romanesca* found in a manuscript source of lute music (Pesaro, Biblioteca Oliveriana 1144, *olim* 1193.) A transcription of the tablature is printed on pages 224–25 of Brown–*Sixteenth-Century*. An effective example of this recitation style with lute accompaniment is the lauda "Se mai per maraviglia," found in Franciscus Bossinensis's *Tenori e contrabassi*. While this stark declamatory style is well suited to some kinds of texts, it has been suggested that poetry was also sung to the popular ground basses of the day such as *Romanesca, Passemezzo antico, Folia.* This would not only be extremely easy to improvise, but would also be more appropriate for lively texts than the more serious declamatory style. Popular tunes were also accompanied by chordal instruments. Ciro Spontone reports (1589) that the "Girometta" tune was sung to lute, viol, and/or harpsichord accompaniment,[2] and another reference describes Orlando di Lassus accompanying himself on the lute—possibly strumming chords?—while singing Azzaiolo's popular *"Chi passa per questa strada"* during the wedding festivities of William V of Bavaria and Renée of Lorraine in 1568.

Lutenists also participated in the performance of vocal polyphony, but here they actually played the vocal lines instead of fashioning any kind of separate "accompaniment" part. These performances could either be rendered as solos for individual voice(s) with the lute providing the remaining lines, or the lute could double the voices while the lines were all sung. (The pieces could also be done as lute solos; see the discussion of intabulations under Lute, p. 139.)

In the early sixteenth century, at least three books of frottole were published in arrangements for solo singer and lute, which played two of the four original polyphonic lines (the other voice was omitted). Similarly crafted arrangements of twenty-four chansons for solo voice and lute, based on preexisting polyphonic vocal chansons, were printed by Pierre Attaingnant in his *Très brève et familière introduction* (Paris, 1529); these pieces also appeared as lute solos. Later repertory was treated similarly, as in the case of Adrian Willaert's "lute-song arrangements" of Verdelot madrigals, and Willaert's own *villanesche* as arranged for singer and vihuela by Diego Pisador. Around 1570, Vincenzo Galilei wrote out several lute-song arrangements of madrigals and other works, with the bass line of the model taken as a solo and left in the bass range. (See Palisca–Vincenzo.)

In his *Tratado de glosas* of 1553, Diego Ortiz gives written musical examples of various ways for the viol to play with harpsichord accompaniment. These accompaniments range from simple, repeated four-part chords as used in the examples of playing divisions on grounds, to full polyphonic textures in examples of the suggested ornamentation design for madrigals and chansons.

Between 1580 and 1600 Simone Verovio published several collections of polyphonic vocal pieces in the format of score on one page and both keyboard and lute intabulations on the facing page. These intabulations could have been used as either solos or accompaniments.

In 1601, Verovio's firm published Luzzascho Luzzaschi's *Madrigali per cantare e sonare*, selections from the virtuosic repertory of the "Three Ladies of Ferrara" compiled some fifteen to twenty years after the three ladies had taken their final bow. The published format includes a written-out harpsichord part, often assumed to be indicative of what Luzzaschi would have played in performance. These parts consist of straightforward, four-part realizations of the harmonies; the right hand includes the notes of the vocal line(s) virtually all of the time. There are also many passages where the bass repeats a note several times in quick succession (quarter-note motion in the modern edition) and the right hand is given a chord for each one, resulting in the quick repetition of many identical chords—which comes across as somewhat jarring in practice. While these accompaniments may hold true to Verovio's concept of what a good accompaniment should be, and possibly reflect what many musicians thought was proper in accompanying polyphony, one must bear in mind the difference between accompanying polyphonic pieces and virtuoso *solos* such as these. One suspects that when he was actually playing them, Luzzaschi provided a much more sensitive, less repetitive accompaniment to his solo singers. And we must also keep in mind that the three ladies accompanied themselves on the lute, harp, and viol together with Luzzaschi, meaning that if everyone were to have played the published accompaniment the result would have been very thick and choppy indeed. Agostino Agazzari, writing in 1607, gives a detailed account of what was undoubtedly a common late-sixteenth-century accompanimental practice in northern Italy, if not elsewhere. He specifically cautions players to avoid "too frequent repercussions while the voice executes its passage, and expresses some kind of emotion, so as not to interrupt it" (trans. F. T. Arnold in *Art of Accompaniment . . .* , p. 70). For a substantial account of this work, see the section on chordal instruments below.

Music

Attaingnant, Pierre. *Très Brève Introduction.* Ed. Lionel de La Laurencie, A. Mairy, and G. Thibault in *Chansons au luth.* Paris: 1934, 1–51. (See discussion in Heartz, *Preludes . . .*, listed below.)

Bossinensis, Franciscus. *Tenori e contrabassi intabulati col sopran in canto figurato per cantar e sonar col lauto: libro primo.* Venice: Petrucci, 1509. Reprint. Geneva: Minkoff, 1977.

Canzone villanesche alla napolitana and villotte: Adrian Willaert and his Circle. Ed. Donna Cardamone. Recent Researches in Music of the Renaissance 30. Madison, WI: A-R Editions, 1978. (Diego Pisador's arrangements of three polyphonic pieces by Willaert for solo voice with lute accompaniment are found on pp. 77–84.)

Luzzaschi, Luzzascho. *Madrigali per cantare e sonare, a uno, due e tre soprani* (1601). Ed. Adriano Cavicchi. Monumenti di musica italiana, ser. 2: Polifonia. 2. Brescia: L'Organo, 1965.

Ortiz, Diego. *Tratado de glosas* 1553. Ed. Max Schneider. Kassel: Bärenreiter, 1936. An English translation by Peter Farrell of most of the commentary is found in the *Journal of the Viola da Gamba Society of America* 4 (1967): 5–9.

Bibliography

Arnold–*Art*; Bottegari–*Lutebook*; Bottrigari–*Il Desiderio*; Brown–*Sixteenth–Century*; Brown–Lira; Brown–Psyche's; Brown–Petrarch; Einstein–*Italian*; Heartz–*Preludes*; Palisca–Vincenzo.

Suggested Performance

Solo singing of repeated, formulaic melodies was originally accompanied by a lira da braccio or lute playing simple chords, while solo performances of frottole, villancicos, chansons, madrigals, and other similar repertory of that period could be accompanied by a lute, vihuela, Renaissance guitar, or keyboard playing the lower two or three parts.

Larger Ensembles: The Intermedi

The musical *intermedii* written by Francesco Corteccia for Antonio Landi's *Il Commodo,* presented during the marriage festivities of Cosimo de' Medici and Eleonora of Toledo in 1539, document what was undoubtedly an already established practice of including instruments in the performance of texted polyphony. Although the exact arrangements are not specified, a published description of the event reports that Dawn sang the prelude (*Vattene almo riposo*) accompanied by *un gravecembalo a duoi registri sottovi or-*

gano, flauto, arpe, et voci di uccegli et con un violone. Howard Brown suggests that this probably means the use of a rather elaborate claviorganum, complete with harp and nightingale stops—this is theater music, after all—with a bass viola da gamba playing the bass line (Brown–*Sixteenth-Century*: 89. For an alternate interpretation, see Minor/Mitchell–*Renaissance*: 229). The second *intermedio* (*Chi ne l'ha tolta ohyme?*) includes three lutes, and the third (*O begli Anni del Oro*) features an evidently solo performance by the main character (Silenus), who accompanies himself on a "violone" (probably a bass viol played lyra way). A few years later (1543), Silvestro Ganassi published such a song-with-solo-viol accompaniment in *Lettione seconda*, the second part of his viol treatise, which provides a good model for this style of playing (see pp. 80–81 in the Peter edition). Though playing chords on the viol "lyra way" is usually associated with English music, these references indicate that it was already practiced in Italy by the 1530s, if not earlier. Each of these pieces is printed as a polyphonic madrigal with text in each line, although nothing is said in either the first or third about more than one singer; the second example, scored in six voices, stipulates three female singers.

The practice is seen on an even grander scale in accounts of Florentine *intermedi* in 1565 and 1589, when harpsichords, lutes, harps, and viols are included in the performance forces for various texted pieces. It seems reasonable to assume that such instruments would spend at least part of the time playing chords or melodic figuration based on the harmonies, rather than limiting themselves strictly to the given polyphonic lines; such chordal playing would correspond nicely to the practice of accompaniment by "instruments of ornamentation" and "instruments of foundation" as described by Agazzari (see below).

Bibliography

Agazzari–*Del sonare*. Commentary in several places, including Arnold–Accompaniment l: 67–74 and Borgir–*Performance*. Brown–Psyche's: 1–27. Includes Brown's transcription of, and suggested instrumentation for, the one piece known to remain from the 1565 Florentine *intermedii*—a piece later published by Vincenzo Galilei as a vocal solo with lute accompaniment. Brown–*Sixteenth-Century*; Ganassi–*Lettione*; Minor/Mitchell–*Renaissance*; Walker/et al.–*Musique*.

Suggested Listening
Firenze 1539: musiche fatte nelle nozze dello illustrissimo duca di Firenzi il signor Cosimo de Medici. Centre de musique ancienne de Geneva and Studio di musica rinascimentale di Palermo, directed by Gabriel Garrido. Tactus TC 53012001 (1987–88).
A Florentine Festival. Musica Reservata, directed by Michael Morrow, conducted by John Beckett. Argo, ZRG 602 (1970).
Una 'Stravaganza' dei Medici: Intermedi (1589) per 'La pellegrina.' The Taverner Consort, Taverner Choir, and Taverner Players, directed by Andrew Parrott. EMI Reflexe, CDC 7 47998 2 (1988).

Suggested Performance

Chordal accompaniment of sixteenth-century Italian madrigals may be provided by lute, viol, harpsichord, organ, or harp, with harmonies derived from a short score of the parts.

English Mixed Consort Music

Music was performed on stage in sixteenth-century English theaters with groups of plucked instruments participating, suggesting a chordal texture. For instance, Gascoyne's *Jocasta* (1566) had a "dumb show" before each act featuring "viols, cythren, and bandores" in addition to various wind instruments and drums. These house bands were to coalesce into the famous "Morley Consort," or English mixed consort. This group does have a written repertory from as early as the 1580s, but there is evidence that it was used both for incidental theater music and to accompany stage jigs, which suggests at least an element of improvisation. The standard instrumentation for English mixed consort music includes treble viol or violin, flute or recorder, bass viol, cittern, bandora, and lute; such groups are depicted in some pictures, mostly Dutch and German, with the cittern and bandora replaced by a spinet. And later, when describing what "the English call . . . a 'consort,'" Michael Praetorius provides a list that includes each of the above instruments and also others, such as harp, trombone, and racket (*Syntagma musicum* III [Wolfenbüttel, 1618], p. 5). Whatever the make-up of the group, the chordal instruments are used to provide a kind of late sixteenth-century proto-continuo (see Mixed Ensemble, p. 217).

Bibliography

Edwards–*Music*; Morley–*First*; Nordstrom–Broken; Nordstrom–Cambridge.

Suggested Listening

In the Streets and Theatres of London. The Musicians of Swanne Alley, directed by Paul O'Dette and Lyle Nordstrom. Virgin Classics VC7 90789–2 (1989).
Joyne Hands: Music of Thomas Morley. The Musicians of Swanne Alley, directed by Paul O'Dette and Lyle Nordstrom. Virgin Classics VC7 907168 (1992).

Organ Scores

In church music, scores used by an organist to accompany the choir appear in manuscript as early as 1587 and were printed from at least 1594. The early organ scores took three forms: the organ part could consist of the entire piece transcribed in full score; a piece could be reduced to short score, either as the top and bottom voices or as a three-voice reduction of a bigger work; or, in a multichoir work, the organist's part could be a composite of the lowest sounding notes at any given time selected from all the choirs.

Lodovico Viadana's *Cento concerti ecclesiastici* (1602), an early source describing *basso continuo* realization, reflects an extension of this practice, but it is different in that the bass line and its figures represent harmonies not always otherwise present in the counterpoint. As such, it marks the first use of a true and independent *basso continuo* part—although Viadana suggests that organists write out the parts they will play, rather than improvise them. Soon after, of course, accompanists were expected to improvise from bass lines, with or without figures.

Bibliography

Arnold–*Art*; Horsley–Full; Lawrence-King–"Perfect"; Williams–*Figured*.

The Use of Chordal Instruments

So how were chordal instruments used in the Renaissance and how did this change in the seventeenth century? The basic approach to accompaniment in the sixteenth century was to "intabulate" the piece of music—a process in which the bass, along with other selected parts of a polyphonic composition were set into tablature (for plucked and keyboard instruments), or into score (usually for keyboard instruments only). The number and distribution of the parts intabulated depended on the number of instruments involved, the practice of the specific repertory at hand, and the ranges of the accompanying instruments. In some cases the alto line was left out altogether and replaced with ornamentation; in other cases the lower voices were intabulated leaving the soprano line to a vocal or instrumental soloist, while at other times the soprano line was doubled in the intabulation.[3] Other practices included the doubling of the bass line an octave lower (particularly in the second half of the sixteenth century), the insertion of ornamentation in any or all of the parts (as in solo lute and keyboard intabulations), the addition of new contrapuntal lines (as in Diego Ortiz's *"quinta boz sobre el misma madrigal"*),[4] and the introduction of a style of ornamentation known as *alla bastarda*. This practice, which was performed on the viol, lute, harp, trombone, and bass voice(!), involved ornamenting each voice in turn, connecting the phrases with virtuoso scales to indicate the transition from one voice to the next.[5] *Alla bastarda* ornamentation was generally added only to pieces in which all of the lines were already covered, either by an organ, lute, vocal ensemble, or a larger group of voices and instruments.

Models for ensembles involving two to four lutes have been discussed in the chapter on plucked instruments.[6] It is generally not recognized (or perhaps just not practiced today) that large ensembles of Renaissance instruments, including numerous keyboard instruments and as many as twenty plucked instruments, appeared throughout the sixteenth century.[7] Although there are few models to guide us, what is known about lute ensemble practices combined with the descriptions of Agazzari in his *Del sonare sopra 'l basso* of 1607 (later borrowed by Michael Praetorius in Book III of his *Syntagma Musicum*) provide a good basis for getting the maximum contribution from the assembled forces.

First, a variety of sizes and pitches of each of the chordal instruments is essential. Five lutes of the same size and tuning will not produce nearly the effect of five lutes of three or four different sizes.[8] The same is true of keyboards, harps, and guitars.[9] Second, each instrument should have its own function. Not everyone should play four-part chords all of the time. Some instruments can be responsible for rhythm, others for sonority, and others for texture and filigree. That is to say, the practices outlined above, along with those described by Agazzari (quoted below) may be divided up among the different instruments.

Third, experiment with different types of articulations. Lutes, harps, and guitars can be strummed as well as plucked, each instrument providing its own rich vocabulary of plucking, strumming, and arpeggio techniques, as well as the amazingly effective block chord. The sequence of block chords, arpeggios, and strums is essential to the character of Renaissance "continuo" playing. Harpsichordists steeped in the French Baroque tradition of rolling chords nearly all of the time will take a little time getting used to this approach, but it is simply part of a different sound-world.

Fourth, using the right kinds of keyboard instruments for Renaissance music is extremely important, if the right balance and timbres are to be achieved. Spinets, virginals, and Italian harpsichords combine with lutes, harps, and guitars much more effectively than do, say, eighteenth-century-style double-manual French harpsichords. Similarly, sixteenth- and seventeenth-century chamber organs tend to be more focused and transparent than many of the dark, woolly-sounding continuo organs made today. The latter tend to thicken the texture undesirably and obscure plucked instruments. Of course, a playing style that provides some space between the notes will also help in providing an appropriately transparent texture.

Finally, the total effect of ensembles with lutes and keyboards will be much greater if the instruments are very well in tune, and meantone temperament is employed.[10] Despite the highly publicized and exaggerated paranoia of a few late Renaissance and early-Baroque theorists regarding unequal temperaments on fretted instruments, they were, in fact, widely used and are not at all difficult to achieve.[11] Experience has shown that even quarter-comma meantone can be very effective once the frets have been properly set, and the players learn which fret produces which accidental.[12] Using split frets (as recommended by Christopher Simpson),[13] or just adding extra frets to provide the most critical accidentals ($g\sharp$-$a\flat$, $c\sharp$-$d\flat$) will take care of all but the most remote chords, which are undoubtedly meant to sound tense anyway.[14] The new Korg multitemperament tuner can be a great help in setting up an unequal temperament, since the open strings must be correctly tuned as well as the frets placed properly. The problem in the past with using meantone temperament on fretted instruments has been that players set up the frets appropriately, but persist in using their usual method of tuning the open strings. The open strings must also be tuned to meantone!

Though his famous treatise was published in 1607, Agazzari was writing about the performance of late-sixteenth-century concerted music. In it he divides instruments into two classes, those "like a foundation" (including the organ, harpsichord, lute, theorbo, and harp) and those "like ornaments" (including lute, theorbo, harp, lirone, cittern, spinet, chitarrino, violin, pandora, etc.). The foundation instruments he called "perfect" in that they can provide a complete accompaniment consisting of the bass with harmonies. The lirone, cittern, and chitarrino are able to provide only an "imperfect harmony," since they do not have true bass strings and produce most chords in inversions, while the "viola," violin, and pandora have "little or no harmony," since they cannot play chords.[15] It is interesting to note that the lute, theorbo, and harp are placed in both categories since they are able to play chords as well as ornament in various ways.

Agazzari continues:

> The instruments being divided into two classes, it follows that they have different functions and are differently used. An instrument that serves as foundation must be played with great judgment and due regard for the size of the chorus; if there are many voices one should play with full harmonies, increasing the registers; while if there are few one should use few consonances (i.e. thinner chords), decreasing the registers, and playing the work as purely and exactly as possible, using few runs and divisions, occasionally supporting the voices with low notes, and frequently avoiding the high ones which cover up the voices, especially the sopranos or falsettos. For this reason one should take the greatest possible care to avoid touching the note which the soprano sings, or ornamenting it with a division, in order not to duplicate it or obscure the excellence of the note itself or of the passage which the good singer executes upon it; for the same reason one does well to play within a rather small compass and in a lower register . . . [the foundation instruments] must maintain a solid, sonorous, sustained harmony, playing now *piano,* now *forte,* according to the quality and quantity of the voices, the place, and the work, while, to avoid interfering with the singer, they must not restrike the strings too often when he executes a passage or expresses a passion.

> The decorating instruments, which are combined with voices in various ways, are in my opinion so combined for no other purpose than to ornament and beautify, and indeed to season the consort. For this reason, these instruments should be used in a different way from those of the first class; while those maintained the tenor and a plain harmony, these must make the melody flourishing and graceful, each according to its quality, with a variety of beautiful counterpoints. But in

this, the one class differs from the other; while the instruments of the first class, playing the bass before them as it stands, require no great knowledge of counterpoint in the player, those of the second class do require it, for the player must compose new parts above the bass and new and varied passages and counterpoints.

For this reason, he who plays the lute (which is the noblest instrument of them all) must play it nobly, with much invention and variety, not as is done by those who, because they have a ready hand, do nothing but play runs and make divisions from beginning to end, especially when playing with other instruments which do the same, in all of which nothing is heard but babble and confusion, displeasing and disagreeable to the listener. Sometimes, therefore, he must use gentle strokes and repercussions, sometimes slow passages, sometimes rapid and repeated ones, sometimes something played on the bass strings, sometimes beautiful vyings and conceits, repeating and bringing out these figures at different pitches and in different places; he must, in short, so weave the voices together with long *groppi, trilli,* and *accenti,* each in its turn, that he gives grace to the consort and enjoyment and delight to the listeners, judiciously preventing when there are other similar instruments, a thing to be avoided, these embellishments from conflicting with one another and allowing time to each, especially in my opinion, unless they play at a great distance or are differently tuned or of different sizes.

And what I say of the lute, as the principal instrument, I wish understood of the others in their kind, for it would take a long time to discuss them all separately.

But since each instrument has its own peculiar limitations, the player must take advantage of them and be guided by them to produce a good result. The player of the lirone must bow with long, clear, sonorous strokes, bringing out the inner parts well. The theorbo, with its full and gentle consonances, reinforces the melody greatly, restriking and lightly passing over the bass strings, its special excellence, with *trilli* and *accenti muti* played with the left hand. The arpa doppia, which is everywhere useful, as much so in the soprano as in the bass, explores its entire range with gentle plucked notes, echoes of the two hands, *trilli,* etc.; in short, it aims at good counterpoint. The cittern, whether the common cittern or the ceterone, is used like the other instruments in a playful way, making counterpoints upon the part.[16]

It is clear from these passages that Agazzari's "ornamental" instruments do not simply add divisions and arpeggios (which would be impossible on the lirone for instance). Rather, they embellish the music with color and character, however each instrument is best able to achieve that. It is striking that Agazzari's list of instruments corresponds closely to the forces used in the Florentine *intermedi* of 1589.[17] It is also likely that his descriptions of the instruments' functions closely mirrors the approach taken on that momentous occasion.

That is, of course, the same tradition that inspired Monteverdi's *Orfeo* of 1607, Praetorius's *Polyhymnia Caduceatrix et Panegyrica* of 1618/19, the fascinating scorings detailed in the same author's *Syntagma Musicum* III, the large lute bands of the English masque and French *ballet de cour,* the Roman "blank passage" practices described by André Maugars,[18] and the lavish forces convened for Luigi Rossi's magnificent *Orfeo* of 1647. The use of these large ensembles of plucked instruments, and the richness and beauty they provide, is one of the most exciting aspects of late Renaissance performance practices, one all-too-rarely experienced in today's concert halls.

NOTES

1. Agazzari–*Del sonare*: 71.
2. Palisca–Vincenzo: 351.
3. See discussion in Paul O'Dette, Plucked Instruments, p. 139.
4. Ortiz–*Trattado*: 83–85, 103–106.
5. Gutmann–Viola bastarda: 178–209; Paras–Music: 1–49. See also the *"in concerto"* pieces by Giovanni Antonio Terzi from his *Intavolatura di Liutto . . . Libro Primo* (1593) and *Libro secondo* (1599), facsimile edition (Florence, 1981).
6. O'Dette–Plucked, p. 139.
7. Elsner–*Untersuchung* is full of references to sixteenth-century ensembles many of which have large complements of chordal instruments. See also Brown–*Sixteenth-Century*; Newcomb–*Madrigal*: 32–46, 264; and Praetorius–*Syntagma* III: 168.
8. O'Dette–Plucked, p. 139.
9. Some seventeenth-century treatises recommend the use of several sizes of guitars in guitar consorts. See O'Dette–Plucked, p. 138. Thus the four guitars used to accompany Euridice in the Ciaconna *"Al imperio d'amore"* in Act 2 of Luigi Rossi's *Orfeo* in 1647 were undoubtedly of at least two, if not three, different sizes and tunings.
10. See Ross Duffin, Tuning and Temperament, p. 238.
11. Most surviving metal-fretted instruments of the time (citterns, orpharions, chitarre battente, etc.) are in unequal temperaments, usually a modified meantone of some sort. Also, the numerous mixed consorts involving fretted instruments, such as the Elizabethan broken consort, must have employed a type of meantone temperament, since virtually all surviving transverse flutes are tuned unequally as were the citterns and bandoras. The warnings of Ercole Bottrigari and G. B. Doni against combining keyboard instruments, which they said were in meantone tuning, and fretted instruments, which they claimed could not be, just does not correspond to the numerous documented situations in which the two were combined. Modern experience shows it is not that hard to do successfully.
12. Recent recordings of fretted instruments in 1/4 comma meantone include *Monteverdi Balli and Dramatic Madrigals,* Red Byrd/The Parley of Instruments (Hyperion CDA66475), in 1/5 comma meantone; *John Jenkins Late Consort Music,* The Parley of Instruments (Hyperion CD A66604), in 1/6 comma meantone; *William Lawes Consort setts for 5 & 6 viols and organ,* Fretwork (Virgin Classics VC 7 91187–2).
13. Simpson–*Division*; also the discussion in Crum–*Play*: 155–63.
14. Lindley–*Lutes*: 18.
15. In this case "viola" is probably a generic term referring to "bowed strings." What the "pandora" refers to here is something of a mystery. It probably has nothing to do with the Elizabethan pandora, which was primarily a chordal instrument!
16. Agazzari–*Del sonare*: 67–69.
17. Walker–*Les Fêtes.* This work has been recorded as *Una stravaganza dei Medici,* The Taverner Consort and Choir conducted by Andrew Parrott, EMI CDC 7 47998 2.
18. MacClintock–*Readings*: 116–26.

V

PRACTICAL
INSTRUMENTATION

19

Mixed Ensembles

James Tyler

This chapter is about ordinary, everyday, small-scale music making, both courtly and domestic, for non-specific instrumental ensembles: the sort of music making in which the majority of modern players of Renaissance music are likely to be most often involved. It is not about the ensemble music performed in the lushly scored, magnificently splashy court and civic entertainments of the sixteenth century, the Renaissance festivals, royal weddings, Florentine *intermedi,* and the like, about which quite extensive eyewitness coverage survives, and several excellent studies have already been written (see Brown–*Sixteenth-Century* and Bowles–*Musical*).

The sixteenth century produced great quantities of music originally conceived for instrumental performance. Unfortunately, specific instrumentations were rarely given, which might explain why this body of work has yet to be dealt with comprehensively in terms of performance practice. Because modern writers have tended to concentrate on the extraordinary, exceptional, and hence, well-documented musical events and have dealt so little with the music that is the subject of this chapter, it is easy for modern players to make the mistake of assuming that practices that applied to the exceptional and the extraordinary also applied to everyday music making. The aim of this chapter is to provide ensemble directors with whatever information can be gleaned from the writings of contemporary theorists, the few scattered references to specific instruments in actual music sources, and pictorial evidence, in order to help them make decisions on the instrumentation of sixteenth-century "chamber" and dance music that are both practical and appropriate.

In the recent past our perception of the sounds of sixteenth-century music has often been distorted by the recordings of well-meaning, but misguided early-music ensembles, recordings that present some repertories, especially dance music, replete with a whole range of exotic and inappropriate wind instruments and percussion. Intended to charm and evoke "olde" times, this toy-shop approach, which was first taken thirty or forty years ago (and to a certain extent still persists to this day), has resulted in the trivialization of much fine music and, ironically, was probably inspired by one of the most important theorists of the late Renaissance, Michael Praetorius. Volume II of his famous treatise, *Syntagma Musicum* (1619), with its abundance of information, some misinformation, and scale drawings of instruments, has been available to us for many years in facsimile edition, has been widely read, and has motivated many a modern ensemble director to create what amounts to an organological fantasyland.

Let me explain: Praetorius's *Syntagma Musicum* is encyclopedic; systematically and for the sake of completeness, he has included everything—that which is contemporary, that which is historical, that which is theoretical, and that which is mere guesswork and hearsay. Users of the work must first be able to distinguish between what was normal instrumental usage in the early seventeenth century, and what was theoretical (or rarely ever used). Unfortunately, many directors have not always been able to make those distinctions, which has resulted in there being many more greatbass, soprano, and sopranino recorders; rackets; bassanelli; soprano curtals; and cornamuses and the like in the world today than ever existed in Praetorius's day.

Moreover, directors of ensembles performing sixteenth-century repertories must realize that some of the instruments discussed by Praetorius for use in seventeenth century music were not yet in common use in the sixteenth century. These include the sopranino recorder, the soprano recorder in c″, and the various sizes of greatbass recorder—instruments routinely used in today's performances of sixteenth-century music. It may be difficult for modern players to accept, but all known sources of information throughout the sixteenth century (Virdung, 1511; Agricola, 1529 and 1545; Ganassi, 1535; Cardan, 1546; Jambe de Fer, 1556; Zacconi, 1592; and Virgiliano, ca. 1600) confirm that the recorders in common use were the bass in f, the tenor in c′ (used for playing both tenor and alto lines in part music), and the alto recorder in g′ (which played the top line in a recorder ensemble). All three sizes of recorders read part music at written pitch, but actually sounded an octave higher. Thus the alto in g′ was actually the "soprano" recorder of the sixteenth century and covered much of the actual sound range of today's soprano recorder (Hettrick-Sebastian: 104; Hettrick-Martin: 80/109 and 82/145). Though common in today's recorder consorts, a soprano recorder was referred to in only one source in the entire sixteenth century (Cardan, 1546), and that was a soprano in d″, not in c″.

For this reason I have decided to concentrate exclusively on the information available to us from the sixteenth century (Brown/Sadie–*Performance*, "Bibliography of Sources"), and to use only the instruments (and sizes of instruments) that were commonly used in the performance of part-music of that century.

Other instruments that did not exist at all in the sixteenth century (and were not even mentioned by Praetorius), but that are regularly used in today's performances of sixteenth-century music, are alto recorders in f′, soprano flutes in g′, and alto crumhorns in f.

The most common wind instruments were recorders, flutes, shawms, cornetts, trombones, crumhorns, and curtals. Other winds, such as sorduns, cornamuses, doppioni, rackets, and Schreierpfeifen, were very rare or only regional instruments. Instruments such as the trumpet (used only for military and ceremonial purposes during this period), bagpipe, gemshorn, hurdy-gurdy, and jew's harp (used mainly for folk and popular music, which was not written down), *lira da braccio,* and *lirone* (highly specialized use mainly in recitations of humanistic poetry and in experimental "new" music) will not be employed here. Because there is no compelling evidence that percussion instruments were used in ensembles during this period, even in dance-music ensembles (see Neumann–Kompt), they, too, will not be used. (Although contemporary visual art sometimes depicts either a pipe-and-tabor player or a fife and military drum combination in the same picture as a "dance band," these were regarded as separate units. The pipe-and-tabor player (or the fife and military drum players) did not perform as a member of the dance band, but apparently alternated with it.

Although few standard conventions for instrumental combinations can be drawn from contemporary sources, what does emerge helps to establish some guidelines. One early convention, which carries over from the late fifteenth century into the early sixteenth, is the combination of two shawms and one trombone for a dance ensemble playing the *basse danse* repertory. This was an improvisatory tradition with little or no genuine, written-out part-music surviving; however, the convention can be applied to similar "art" versions of the *basse danse,* such as the various "La Spagna" settings that survive in some of the earliest sixteenth-century prints. This combination probably resulted from the ability of these two types of instruments to match each other in volume.

Another convention is that of three different-size members of the same family of instruments playing four-part music. Thus, a recorder quartet would consist of an alto in g′, two tenors in c′, and a bass in f to play SATB part music. A crumhorn quartet would consist of one alto in g, two tenors in c, and a bass in F (Hettrick-Martin: 80/109 82/145). Due perhaps to their basic range of only a ninth, other sizes of crumhorn were also known, including a soprano crumhorn in c′ and various additional bass sizes, though these seem to have been less common.

The most common configuration for a viol quartet throughout the sixteenth century was the "low consort" consisting of a tenor (top string a′), two basses (top strings d′), and a large bass (top string a or g). Of course, these are modern designations; in the sixteenth century an instrument was named according to the line it played in part-music, not according to its size or specific pitch. Hence, the three sizes of instruments playing four-part music just described would have been called (in English) treble, alto, tenor, and bass, respectively.

Although the "low consort" may be a difficult concept for modern viol players to accept, the following sources all confirm the "low consort" tunings: Florence, Biblioteca Nazionale Centrale, MSS Magl. XIX, 165; the bass part-book to the set 164–167, circa 1520 (Woodfield–*Early*: 240, fn.8); the Weltzell manuscript of 1524 (Woodfield–*Early*: 108); Agricola (1529 and 1545); Gerle (1532 and 1546); Ganassi (1542, *quarta regola*); Zacconi (1592); and Virgiliano (ca. 1600). The Weltzell and Gerle books contain four-part French chansons and German Lieder intabulated for three sizes of viols (side by side with staff notation in some cases). The precise nature of tablature notation coupled with the tuning information given in these sources shows unequivocally that the "discant" part is played on a tenor viol (modern terminology) with a top string tuned to a', the "altus" and "tenor" parts on two basses (top strings d'), and the "bassus" on a large bass viol (top string a).

A "high consort" using the familiar treble viol (top string d"), two tenor viols (top strings a' or g'), and a bass viol (top string d') configuration was also known (Lanfranco, 1533; Della Viola, ca. 1560; and Marinati 1587), but seems to have been less common. Ganassi, the great exponent of the viol, advocated the "high consort," yet acknowledged that most players used the larger (lower) instruments. The illustration on the title page of his 1542 publication shows large instruments, as do most contemporary pictures (Woodfield–*Early*: 151). This pictorial evidence coupled with all of the tuning information given above and the rarity of surviving treble viols from the sixteenth century (there is one), in comparison to the great number of large viols from that century, supports the idea that the "low consort" was more commonly used.

The large bass viol (in a or g) was known even earlier than 1523. (Slatford-Double–*New Grove* includes a German drawing from 1518 and Slatford-Double–*New Grove Inst.* has a Tyrôlean painting from about 1570 copied after a German painting of 1516.) It played at 8-foot pitch, as did the higher members of the family. Probably only toward the end of the sixteenth century was a true, six-string, double bass viol (contrabasso, *"violone in contrabasso"*) developed that was large enough to have strings capable of sounding at 16-foot pitch throughout its range. (A surviving example is an instrument by Linarol dated 1585.) Banchieri (1609) seems to have been the first writer to give a tuning for a *"violone in contrabasso"* with a top string of d, an octave lower than today's bass viol. His *"violone da gamba"* was an ordinary large bass viol tuned to g and played at 8-foot pitch.

Another important convention was that of transposition. The most basic and essential information given by writers on instruments of this period (e.g., Agricola, Jambe de Fer, Ganassi, Virgiliano, et al.) includes either transposition charts, verbal instructions, or a choice of clef for the same line of music. Although the ranges of a great many pieces of part-music from the first three-quarters of the century are such that they can be played by the three-size instrument combinations described above without having to resort to the transposition techniques of the time, if parts were too high for the instruments, contemporary wind and string players were expected to transpose the music down (often by a fourth) so that it fit the instruments better. (For an invaluable discussion of transposition practices, see Brown–Notes–Viol and Brown–Notes–Flute, and Pitch and Transposition, p. 248 in this *Guide.*)

Yet another convention is the combination of a cornett and three tenor trombones, which became so established by about 1600 that Virgiliano could give a chart and tablature for playing trombones in "concerto," illustrating a consort of three tenor trombones and a cornett without need for further comment (see Sackbut, p. 98 for the facsimile of this chart). The tenor and bass of the trombone family were commonly employed during this period; the alto did not come into general use until the next century. The cornett and trombones combination, like that of viols or viols with a violin, is appropriate for huge quantities of sixteenth-century chamber and dance music.

The use of the violin at this time was primarily as an instrument for dance music. Indeed, it was regarded as the preeminent instrument for dance music in professional ensembles because one of the early violin's chief characteristics was its ability to employ the crisp, clear rhythmic articulations essential to the performance of practical dance music.

A final convention was the usage of both viols and trombones for music of a dignified or somber character. For such music, trombones and viols sometimes were used in combination. Of course, in order to play chamber music and be in balance with stringed instruments, it is essential that modern early-trombone players use reproductions of the relatively lighter, original instruments and avoid using modern instruments with sawn-off bells and modern mouthpieces, which produce a loud, opaque sound inappropriate for chamber music.

Before decisions on instrumentation are made, the ensemble director should first answer the following questions about each piece that he or she is orchestrating: (1) What is its country or region of origin? (2) What is its date? (3) Who is likely to have performed it (amateurs or professionals), and under what circumstances? (4) Under what genre does it fall? (5) What are the ranges of each part?

Why must these questions be answered? Because some instruments were known in some countries or regions and not in others, and because some instruments either were not used at all in the sixteenth century, or were not introduced until the middle or the end of the century. Also, if a performance of music by amateur musicians is being recreated, then certain instruments, such as the violin, cornett, crumhorn, trombone, and curtal, are to be avoided, since they were the instruments of professionals; whereas, if an ensemble of professional musicians is being recreated, the choice is far wider. Certain basic instruments, such as viols, recorders, flutes, lutes, and other plucked instruments, were used by professionals and amateurs alike.

We are now ready to decide on suitable and effective instrumentations for specific pieces. The first musical example is a four-part dance published in Paris in 1530 by the printer Pierre Attaingnant entitled "La Scarpa"

(LPM, *The Attaingnant Dance Prints*, AD1, p. 4). As is the case with most prints of dance music, this was probably intended for the amateur market. With its typically narrow ranges for the four parts (first line d' to c"; second line g to g'; third line f to g'; fourth line G to g), "La Scarpa" could be played as it stands by a viol consort consisting of tenor, two basses, and a large bass. (A third bass viol could play the bottom line, but as it would have to stay mainly on its lower strings, its sound might lack the strength and brilliance required to balance the other viols.)

A whole consort of recorders—g' alto, two tenors, and bass—could also play the piece as it stands, all parts, of course, sounding an octave higher; or the recorders could all double the viols on repeats; or just the top line, the tune, could be doubled by a g' alto recorder, which could also embellish the line. Alternatively, a tenor flute at the octave could double the tenor viol on the top line. Flutes have more dynamic control than recorders and can play high notes softly. This dynamic flexibility, coupled with a tonal character that enables it to blend and balance with other kinds of instruments, makes the flute a good choice in an ensemble with viols. For rhythm, a lute could play the appropriate chords from the bass line, divide up dotted half notes into three quarter notes, play through all rests, and fill in the final notes of phrases. (Citterns and guitars were not widely known yet in France at the time of this publication.)

A professional French ensemble would likely have had many more possibilities for instrumentation, although since the violin family probably was not widely known in Paris until the 1540s, viols would still have been the first choice for indoor performance, with one or more lutes to help rhythmically.

Alternatively, a soprano rebec could be used on the top line (sounding an octave higher) with viols beneath, or a whole consort of rebecs: a soprano, two tenors, and a bass. The sharp, penetrating sound of the rebecs makes them ideal for dance music ensembles, and since Gerle (1532 and 1545) gave a clear illustration of this archaic instrument, as well as some four-part music for three different-sized rebecs, we can assume that they were used in ensembles at least through the first half of the sixteenth century. To judge by the numerous French literary sources and payment records for rebec players in France at this time (Downie–Rebecs and Dobbins–Music), the rebec was popular there as well as in Germany, and it is conceivable that some French rebec players, like the German, might have played in whole consorts.

Agricola (1529 and 1545) gave the tunings—entirely in fifths—for the three rebecs: the three-stringed "discant" (tuned to a', d', g), the three-stringed "Alt" and "Tenor" (the same instrument played both part ranges, tuned to d', g, c), and the four-stringed "Bassus" (tuned to a, d, G, F in the 1545 edition). The rebec ensemble tablature given by Gerle confirms this tuning. Taken literally these pitches in these octaves seem impossible on what were, to judge by pictorial evidence and surviving examples, inherently small instruments. The "Bassus" pitch would seem especially unlikely; the rebec tuned to that pitch would have to have been the size of a modern cello in order to derive any musical sound from its gut strings. Such a large instrument could hardly have been carved from one piece, played on the shoulder, and called a *"kleingeigen"*!

My theory is that Agricola's charts show the notes as they would be read in staff notation, not the actual pitches, and that the actual pitches are an octave higher. In fact, Agricola uses this very same method in his charts for wind instruments (Brown–Notes–Flute). If I am correct, the rebecs read at one pitch level, but actually sounded an octave higher than written, just as recorders commonly do. Then, too, the bass rebec would only need to attain a size similar to that of a viola.

To recreate an outdoor performance by a professional French ensemble, such as the musicians at the Parisian court of François I, the top line of the piece could be played as written on a g alto shawm or a cornett. The second line could use a g alto shawm (assuming a good instrument and a good player), a tenor cornett, or a trombone. The third line could employ a g alto shawm, tenor cornett, or trombone. The bass line could be played on a trombone. Since the music would have to be repeated several times to fit the choreography, and since the wind players probably would have needed to rest their embouchures, it is conceivable (though not documented) that the wind band could alternate with another dance unit, such as a pipe-and-tabor or a fife-and-drum. Similarly, if the ball were held indoors, the wind band could still be employed, and for the same reasons could alternate with a string band. It would not have been unusual to find an ensemble of eight or more musicians employed at a royal court.

We have been discussing "La Scarpa" as it might have been performed in France, but as it was originally an Italian dance, it could also be performed reflecting northern Italian practice, which would allow for additional performance choices. For example, crumhorns, not used in France, were common in Italy. Hence, a soprano in c′ could play the top line, a g alto the second line, and a bass the fourth line. The third line could also employ a g alto if the one note that goes below its range is changed. Although no sixteenth-century writers discuss this practice, there are indications that musicians occasionally resorted to altering notes, as is shown by comparing Morley's printed parts (1599), marked for flute, with the same parts in the manuscripts (1580s), marked for recorder, in some of the repertory for English mixed consorts. In the manuscript recorder parts, not only are single notes changed, but often entire passages are put into another octave in order to fit the range of the recorder.

The violin family, though not widely used in France until the 1540s, was developed in Italy in the 1520s and thus is appropriate for an Italian performance of this piece. A viola could be used effectively for the top line as written, or, transposing the piece up a fifth, a violin and two violas could be used for the top three lines, as could a mixture of viols for the lower lines and a violin on top.

A greater variety of plucked instruments was also in use in Italy in 1530. For example, the small diatonic harp with its single row of strings and L-shaped "bray pins" (used both to secure each string to the soundboard and, when carefully adjusted, to produce a softly buzzing, semi-sustained sound), could double another instrument on the second line, since no chromatic changes are required. One or more four-course guitars could provide a rhythmic, even strummed, accompaniment. Strumming was a fundamental and unique feature of the guitar from its earliest history. Normally all of the courses were struck in rhythmic patterns that probably were similar to the ones finally notated by guitarists in the late sixteenth century. (For further details, see Tyler–*Early*: 25–34, 82–86.)

The cittern, too, could serve a rhythmic function in this piece, or it could play the "lead" melody line with chords beneath it. In this latter rôle it has several advantages: its range is just about the same as the violin; with its plectrum technique it can play highly virtuosic embellishments to melody lines with relatively little difficulty; and, whether playing single-line fashion or chordally, it has (assuming proper plectrum control) a very wide dynamic range from soft, warm, and shimmering to extremely bright, pungent, and robust. The range and "key" of "La Scarpa" are perfect for an arrangement with cittern lead, and this and scores of similar dance pieces were published later as cittern "solos" (Harwood/Tyler–Cittern–*New Grove Inst.*).

A second musical example is from the late sixteenth century. This is an "Intrada" by Alexander Orologio, published in northern Germany in 1597 (LPM, *German Instrumental Music*, GM4, no. 3). An intrada is a formal, ceremonial piece, often written in a solemn style, partly homophonic and partly carefully controlled, cautious polyphonic movement. As its name suggests, its use is likely to have been in court or theatrical ceremony as an entry piece. Given this background information, a wind band capable of making a richly sonorous sound is a natural performance choice.

The piece is in five parts (cantus g' to g", quintus g' to g", altus e' to c", tenor g to a', and bassus A to c'). With these ranges and the fame of German wind players in mind, a first choice for instrumentation would be three cornetts and two trombones, as the editor of the modern edition correctly suggests. These instruments would produce the desired sonority in perfect balance, but there are other valid choices. A string band consisting of two violins, viola (or tenor viol), bass viol, and large bass viol would have been commonplace at the north German courts. The bass violin probably would have been less common than in Italy or France at this time. However, to produce a sound as ceremonially grand as that of the cornett and trombone ensemble, it probably would be necessary to employ more than one string player to a part, and perhaps to have the bass line doubled by a trombone or bass curtal. The curtal's dynamic range makes it equally suitable for chamber music with strings and wind band music.

Yet another possibility would be to transpose the piece down a fifth and use crumhorns: two c' sopranos, an alto in g, and a tenor, with a curtal on the bass line. This combination could be used effectively alternating with or combined with a string ensemble. As a ceremonial entry piece, it probably would have been repeated several times in order to accommodate the exact length of the procession. The practice of alternating (or combining) ensembles, though not documented, would—then as now—provide wind players with opportunities to rest their lips. On a piece of this kind, an organ doubling most of the parts would contribute greatly to the sonority. This use of an "organ bass" is documented in Williams–Continuo–*New Grove Inst.*

By way of contrast the third musical example is real chamber music and from the very beginning of the sixteenth century. "La Guercia" (LPM, *Art of the Netherlanders,* AN2, no. 4) is from a manuscript copied in the Netherlands for a north Italian patron around 1508. The four-part piece, in Franco-Flemish style, appears to be an early example of purely instrumental part-writing; imitation is used throughout and is distributed equally between all the parts. This suggests that no single part should be allowed to stand out, and, as in the later English viol consorts, that the balance between instruments should be carefully maintained. Doubling of parts in this context would be out of the question.

Given the musical genre, writing style, and the sort of instruments that are most likely to have been used in the home of an Italian connoisseur around 1508, a viol quartet consisting of a tenor, two basses, and a large bass is the likely first choice. Although this is a very early date for the large bass viol, the fact that viols as we know them were developed in Italy in the late fifteenth century (Woodfield–*Early*: 119), and that we have the previously mentioned visual evidence of the large bass viol from a 1516 German source, it is reasonable to assume that this instrument was known in Italy around 1508. Although the fourth line is also within the range of an ordinary bass viol, during this period viols typically had only five strings, hence, this viol, in order to play the bass line, would have to remain in its weakest, least resonant register (the low G being its bottom, open string, and a gut string at that), while the other viols would be playing in their best registers. The balance between the instruments would be lost. The sixteenth-century practice of viols playing in their best registers (on their upper strings) is important to remember when scoring for viols.

Another possible instrumentation is a lute quartet playing in the old-fashioned, but still-employed, plectrum style. The ranges of the four parts (first line, b to d"; second line, A to g'; third line, c to g'; and fourth line, G to d') would present no problems even on lutes of all the same tuning. Another balanced instrumentation would be a recorder consort of g' alto, two tenors, and a bass, though the second part has one note below the tenor range, which would have to be changed.

The final musical example is Anthony Holborne's almaine "The Honiesuckle," published in London in 1599 (LPM, AH1, no. 60). This piece is from his famous collection entitled *Pavans, Galliards, Almains and other short*

Aeirs both grave and light in five parts, for Viols, Violins, or other Musicall Winde Instruments. The publication was probably intended for both the cultivated amateur market and the municipal musical organizations of several cities (hence the reference to violins and wind instruments).

Elizabethan ensemble music often had quite colorful instrumentations, such as the well-known combination of violin (treble viol for publications intended for the amateur market), flute, bass viol, lute, cittern, and bandora, as exemplified by Thomas Morley's Consort lessons of the same year (Beck–*First*). Since Holborne himself was an excellent player of all three of the plucked instruments in this combination, it seems appropriate to suggest a similar type of instrumentation for "The Honie-suckle." The ranges of the parts are first line, a' to g''; second line, d' to d''; third line, g to a'; fourth line, c to g'; and fifth line, G to a. The two top lines and the bass contain the essential musical material, while the third and fourth lines are less important. Indeed, if one were to make a Morley-type arrangement of the piece, as was done at the time to a few of the other items in Holborne's collection, they could even be eliminated.

Here, however, all five parts will be employed. If one thinks of this almaine as a practical dance piece, a violin for the top line is appropriate. The second line could be played by a viola or a tenor viol, the third and fourth lines by bass viols, and the fifth line by a large bass viol, a bass violin, or a curtal. If the melody line, played by a single violin, is overbalanced by the four lower instruments, it could be doubled by a g' alto recorder (which, you will remember, sounds an octave higher and if historically constructed, has a range g–g'' or a''). This doubling need not inhibit ornamentation, provided that the players do not ornament simultaneously, and are sufficiently skilled at doubling and improvising. Although there is little written discussion of dance music performance practice from this period, we should consider what can be gleaned from similar techniques in the unwritten tradition, since these might be possible survivals of an older practice. For example, to this day players of traditional dance music from Dublin to Palermo manage to double and to improvise brilliantly while doing so (as can be heard on the many available recordings of so-called "ethnic" music).

Although plucked instruments are not mentioned on Holborne's title page, it was common practice in Elizabethan England to arrange five-part ensemble music to include plucked instruments. Morley's five-part "Sacred End Pavan" and "Southerne's Pavan" were also arranged and published by Rosseter for mixed consort (including lute, cittern, and bandora). In the same Rosseter publication is found "Infernum" for mixed consort, an arrangement made of a piece from the very same Holborne publication that contains "The Honie-suckle."

A bandora would add a rich and sonorous bass- and baritone-range chordal accompaniment to the ensemble. According to extant tablature parts, it functions almost like a proto-continuo instrument, doubling the composed bass line mainly at the lower octave, while also playing low chords above its own bass line. (A bass lute in d′ could also provide this continuo-like function.) For rhythm, a cittern could play a continuous series of chords, making certain it never duplicates the treble or bass rhythms, and breaks every half note into two quarters. A lute in g′ could be used, both as a rhythm instrument and, more important, to provide embellishment (divisions) based upon the second line and fill-ins for the final bars of each section, while also incorporating as much as possible of the bass line. These techniques can be learned by studying the scores to some of the English mixed consorts (Beck–*First* and Edwards–*Music*).

If the forces are available, a wind ensemble comprising cornetts on the first two lines and three trombones on the remaining lines could alternate with the string ensemble or be used in its stead.

Another wind option is an ensemble consisting of a g′ alto recorder on the first line, a g′ alto recorder or flute (sounding an octave higher) on the second line, a flute (sounding an octave higher) on the third line, and tenor and bass recorders on the fourth and fifth lines. For this instrumentation, the bass could be reinforced by an instrument at 8-foot pitch. This combination is especially effective in conjunction with the aforementioned plucked instruments.

Bibliography

Beck–*First*; Bowles–*Musical*; Brown–*Instrumental*; Brown–*Sixteenth–Century*; Brown–Notes–Viol; Brown–Notes–Flute; Brown/Sadie–*Performance*; Dobbins–Music; Downie–Rebecs; Edwards–Music; Harwood/Tyler–Cittern–*New Grove*: 379–86; Hettrick–Sebastian; Hettrick–Martin; Munrow–*Instruments*; Neumann–Kompt; Praetorius–*Syntagma* II; Praetorius–*Syntagma* III; Slatford–Double Bass–*New Grove*: 5/585–589; Slatford–Double Bass–*New Grove–Inst*: 1/590; Tyler–*Early*; Williams–Continuo–*New Grove*: 1/478–9; Woodfield–*Early*.

20

Large Ensembles

Jeffery Kite-Powell

Performances by a large group of recorder or viol players (or any other group of like-sounding instruments for that matter) are not what is meant here by "large ensemble." In a large recorder ensemble for instance, players are often required to play a line that is being played by at least one other player. This is rarely very rewarding for anyone involved, except perhaps for the pedagogical assistance a lesser player may receive by doubling a more accomplished player. Tuning problems are inevitable, articulation is difficult to coordinate, and the playing of rapid passages is often unclean—and these are areas that are difficult enough when there is only *one* player on a part! Doubling a player at the same octave by the same instrument in a performance situation just is not a sound idea and should be avoided at all costs. It is highly unlikely that parts would have been doubled in this manner in the Renaissance, and it is not necessary that it be done now either. If you have four recorders, play a four-part piece that fits the range of the instruments you have; if there are five recorders, then find a five-part piece—and so on until you are playing pieces (by Gabrieli, for example) for eight, ten, or twelve instruments. Your group will find this much more enjoyable and challenging, as each player is responsible for his or her own part.

A large ensemble may be constructed in a variety of ways. In fact, there is no set instrumentation for a large ensemble. Generally, this kind of group involves either a mixture of instruments that are well suited to each other or a combination of two or more consorts of instruments and voices (if appropriate). In the latter case polychoral compositions in which two to possibly six four-part choirs alternate and combine with each other work well.

These large, polychoral compositions require a large and diverse collection of instruments, and only the wealthiest courts and churches of the sixteenth and early seventeenth centuries could have come close to having an instrumentarium consisting of consorts of recorders, flutes, crumhorns, curtals, shawms, Schreierpfeifen, violas da gamba, violins, and an assortment of cornetts and sackbuts; in addition, there would have been a variety of plucked strings (lutes, theorbos, citterns, guitars, vihuelas, bandoras) and several kinds of keyboard instruments (small organ, harpsichord, clavichord, virginal, regal). Some courts may have even had several kortholts, cornamuses, sorduns, and rackets at their disposal. It goes without saying that not many twentieth-century early-music groups can afford such a large collection of instruments either.

When considering which instruments are going to play a polychoral work together, great care must be taken not to mix loud and soft ensembles. The two predominately loud consorts listed above are the shawms and Schreierpfeifen, but the cornett and sackbut ensemble can sometimes be used as a loud consort as well (see Shawm and Curtal on p. 69). There is a great deal of freedom in working with soft ensembles, as almost anything goes well with anything else (including voices). Just remember that an SATB recorder consort sounds at 4-foot pitch; in this regard, it is often quite effective to use a low recorder consort (TTBGb or TBBGb—assuming there is no pitch lower than c when covering one of several choirs in a polychoral work precisely because it is playing at 8-foot pitch. Another point to remember is that the greater the distance (within reason) between each consort, the more striking and impressive the contrast in sound will be. This is the Renaissance equivalent of the modern-day stereophonic (or quadraphonic) sound system. One drawback to having widely spaced ensembles is the difficulty of coordinating them all. Indeed, Praetorius suggests:

> . . . . songs [hymns & *Sonaten*] should be arranged in such a way that five, six or seven trumpeters, together with an optional timpanist, can be put at a special site just outside the church. This is to prevent their sound and its reverberation from overpowering the music, which would happen if they were placed inside the church. In this way each part may be heard properly. With the help of the thoroughbass, the choirmaster, or whoever is responsible for keeping the beat, must lead the group of musicians in the church and the trumpeters outside the church, especially the person playing the *Quint* or, as it is usually called, the *Principal.* All members must be able to see him and follow his lead. (Editor's translation of Praetorius–*Syntagma*-III, p. 170)

Further evidence of the effort to coordinate two or more ensembles may be found in the frontispiece of his *Theatrum instrumentorum* appended to *Syntagma* II, which depicts three ensemble conductors. André Maugars, in a somewhat later reference (1640) to conductors, reports of eight conductors coordinating their groups (four on either side of the nave) with the conductor of the main choir at the Santa Maria church in Rome (see MacClintock–*Readings*: 118).

In the large-scale, multichoir vocal/instrumental works of Venetian and other late Renaissance transitional composers (in particular, Germany's Michael Praetorius, among others), you might try placing one or two singers in some (or all, if you like) of the instrumental consorts. They may double instruments in the consort in which they are singing, or they may take the place of instruments on those lines. A variation on this idea might be to assign solo singers to one whole consort, a keyboard instrument to another, and winds and strings to the remaining consorts. As you can see, there is a great deal of latitude here; the only limitations in orchestrating these pieces are those of imagination and instrumentarium. There was generally more money allocated for instrumentalists and singers to perform on feast days than on regular days of the week, and it may be that your performance is supposed to reflect just such a festive occasion.

Just because Renaissance instruments come in all sizes does not mean you have to play all three-, four-, five-, six-, seven-part (etc.) compositions on like-sounding instruments. Yes, it is effective, and it certainly has its hallowed place in the scheme of things, but a mixed consort can also produce highly satisfactory results. Many of the *quodlibets* and *ensaladas*—medleys of popular tunes of the time—by Ludwig Senfl and Mateo Flecha, among others, provide a wonderful opportunity to use a mixed consort. Also quite effective are the multipart works (four parts and more; sacred, secular, and instrumental) by the Flemish composers, as they frequently divide into groupings of 2+2, 3+2, 3+3 or 2+2+2, or some similar arrangement of voices. This is often the case with the late Italian madrigal as well. In these situations it is appropriate to arrange contrasting instrumental sounds for each grouping. Generally, it is the provenance and character of the piece, and the ranges of the parts, together with the meaning of the text (if any) that will provide the clues on instrumentation. The preceding chapter by James Tyler provides specific suggestions for orchestrating a few select pieces, and much more advice on what to do and what to avoid.

Another type of music that lends itself well to instrumental contrast is that based on a *cantus firmus* or a popular "tune" that remains in an inner voice. These works are substantially enhanced when the "tune" is played by a contrasting instrument. Along the same line, a simple frottola, chanson, or villancico is very effective when the top part is sung and the others are played on like-sounding instruments.

And finally, large ensembles may be employed in the performance of compositions that are divided into sections (Isaac's *A la Bataglia* comes to mind here). These kinds of composition almost cry out for variety and contrast, which may be provided at each change of section (e.g., Section A on viols, Section B on recorders, and Section C *tutti*—viols and recorders together).

This kind of alternation has been employed in recent years in performances of Renaissance dances, although there is no iconographical or other evidence that this was originally practiced. Loud consorts performed these dances at court, generally employing only small groups of performers. Later, dances were played in chambers—in some instances by professional players, in others by non-professionals—by mixed or closed consorts of diverse players on soft instruments.

The repeats of sections in dances are best varied by improvisation and ornamentation, techniques known to have been used. The top line should receive the most adornment, but other parts may also substitute appropriate figuration for long notes and fill their skips with divisions. Another possibility could be reducing the number of lines actually sounded by the consort instruments, while other lines are harmonically covered by a continuo instrument. The full consort then plays on the repeats. A historical clue to this technique is the *quinta pars* terminology used in the printed editions. It is known that whole lines were added to works by composers, each complementary to the bass and other lines. There is room for much inquiry and experimentation here.

There are many ways to achieve variety, but one must be careful to strike a good balance and not attempt to do too much; employ only one or two techniques on any given work—they are, after all, quite short pieces. Utilize other techniques with different instrumentation on the next dance so that each work can display a truly different character. Certainly avoid any sectional changes that involve quick passes of an instrument from one person to another, or even one person covering a part with a quick change of instruments at a repeat. Alternation works only when done in great moderation.

Finally, the great experimenter, Michael Praetorius, suggested that a bass line doubled by one or a variety of instruments at 16-foot pitch can add a great deal of excitement to polychoral works, as can the addition of a soprano or even a sopranino recorder (in the hands of a master) at the upper octave on repeats of sections.

There is an enormous quantity of music appropriate for the large ensemble available both commercially and in library sets and collections (see Performance Editions on p. 263).

Remember, there is no single, correct instrumentation for the individual parts of most compositions written in the sixteenth century. Indeed, as the years go by you may well have to rethink the instrumentation of pieces you have done in the past, due to the comings and goings of your players, or simply because you want a change—the same reasons used by players and ensemble leaders in the Renaissance!

Bibliography

Arnold–*Giovanni*; Bartlett/Holman–Giovanni; Bowles–*Musical*; Bowles–*Musikleben*; Brown–*Instrumental*; Brown–*Sixteenth-Century*; Carver–*Cori*; Keyl–*Arnolt*; Keyl–*Tenorlied*; Knighton/Fallows (Welker, Jones, Segerman)–*Companion*; Polk–Vedel; Polk–Voices; Salmen–*Musikleben*; Selfridge–Field–*Venetian*.

Suggested Listening

Canzoni da Sonare of Giovanni Gabrieli, Guiseppe Guami. Hesperion XX. EMI Reflexe. 1C 065–45 646 (1979).

Dances and Motets by M.P.C. David Munrow. EMI CDM 7–69024–2 (1974/85).

Giovanni Gabrieli: Canzonas, Sonatas, Motets. The Taverner Corsort, Choir, and Players. Andrew Parrott, director. EMI Reflexe D 135132

Heinrich Isaac: Die Kunst der Niederländer I. The Hilliard Ensemble & Kees Boeke Consort. EMI Reflexe 1C 069 k1466921 (1983).

In Dulci Jubilo: Polychoral Music from Venice & Germany. Winchester Cathedral Choir and the London Cornett and Sackbut Ensemble. Martin Neary, director. EMI 8701 DP (1987).

Keeping the Watch. The Philadelphia Renaissance Wind Band. Joan Kimball and Robert Wiemken, directors. Newport Classic NPD 85527 (1991).

Michael Praetorius. Huelgas Ensemble. Paul van Nevel, director. Soni Classical SK 48039 (1992).

Music of the Renaissance in Naples. Hesperion XX South German Polychoral Music. Pro Arte. Pal 1047 (1984).

Praetorius: Terpsichore. New London Consort, Philip Pickett, director. Loiseau-Lyre CD 4l4 633–2 (1986).

Praetorius Christmas Music. Choir of Westminster Cathedral. Parley of Instruments. David Hill, conductor Hyperion CDA 66200 (1986).

Schütz: Christmas Story / Praetorius: Four motets from Polyhymnia Caduceatrix et Panegyrica. The Taverner Consort, Choir, and Players. Andrew Parrott, director. EMI CDC 7 47633 2. (1987).

Venetian Church Music. The Taverner Consort, Choir, and Players. Andrew Parrott, director. EMI CDC 7 54117 2 (1991).

A Venetian Coronation 1595. Gabrieli Consort and Players. Paul McCreesh, director. Virgin Classics LC7873 (1990).

VI

PERFORMANCE
PRACTICE

21

Resource Materials

Frederick Gable

General Guides to Style and Interpretation

Two recent practical guides on performing Renaissance music (and medieval as well) can be highly recommended: Timothy J. McGee, *Medieval and Renaissance Music: A Performer's Guide* (Toronto: University of Toronto Press, 1985), and Elizabeth V. Phillips and John-Paul Christopher Jackson, *Performing Medieval and Renaissance Music: An Introductory Guide* (New York: Schirmer Books, 1986). All but the most experienced performers will profit from the study of these comprehensive books. On the subjects of style and interpretation, the sections and pages in McGee's book, "Basic Musical Problems" (pp. 20–53) and "Techniques" (pp. 147–212), will be especially helpful. From the Phillips and Jackson book the sections that pertain most to style are "General Guidelines for Early Music Performance" (pp. 17–60) and "Pronunciation Guides" (pp. 283–87). Both works treat the standard topics in some detail: *musica ficta*, tempo and rhythm, use of editions, instrumentation, ornamentation and improvisation, articulation and phrasing, text underlay, pitch and tunings, and pronunciation. The Phillips and Jackson book is especially concise and practical in its format. [Editor's note: *Companion to Medieval & Renaissance Music* edited by Tess Knighton and David Fallows must be added to Professor Gables's list of practical guides. It appeared too late to be considered in detail, but it, too, will provide valuable information to those seeking information on performance practice. See the Bibliography for details.]

The sections on Renaissance performance in the general survey articles by Howard M. Brown, "Performing Practice," *The New Grove Dictionary of Music and Musicians* (New York: Macmillan, 1980), Vol. 14, pp. 377–83, and *The New Grove Dictionary of Musical Instruments* (New York: Macmillan, 1984), Vol. 3, pp. 42–48, have recently been superseded by *Performance Practice: Music before 1600*, ed. Howard M. Brown and Stanley Sadie (New York: Norton, 1989). The essays in this volume offer the best summaries of the topic to date and deserve a separate listing: Brown–Introduction; Reynolds–Sacred; Fallows–Secular; Newcomb–Secular; Haar–Monophony.

The two additional essays on *musica ficta* and Tempo and Proportion are listed below under the specific topic. As in the *New Grove* articles, however, practical solutions to the problems are not always offered; look to the McGee and the Phillips and Jackson books cited above for more practical help. These, together with the Brown and Sadie *Performance Practice* and the present *Guide*, must now be considered the most essential resources for Renaissance performance practice.

More personal and limited treatment of Renaissance performance may be found elsewhere. While Thurston Dart's *The Interpretation of Music* (London, 1954; reprint New York: Harper and Row, 1967) remains remarkably perceptive and helpful, some ideas and ideals have changed since then. For the most part, the books by Robert Donington pertain primarily to Baroque music, in spite of their general title. The section "Renaissance Music" in John Caldwell's *Editing Early Music* (Oxford: Oxford University Press, 1985), pp. 45–68, discusses performance problems and solutions in the course of describing editorial practices. Two guides based on extensive experience as conductors of ensembles performing Renaissance music are those by Denis Stevens and Josef Mertin. Part Three of Stevens's *Musicology: A Practical Guide* (New York: Schirmer Books, 1980) called "Applied Musicology" voices his distinctive views on most of the standard problems of Renaissance performance. *Early Music: Approaches to Performance Practice* (New York: Da Capo Press, 1986) by Mertin offers his personal answers to a narrow selection of performance questions.

Access to translations from selected primary sources on performance is provided by Carol MacClintock's Readings in the *History of Music in Performance* (Bloomington: Indiana University Press, 1979). Important treatises from the Renaissance occupy pages 12–101, but several items from the seventeenth-century section also pertain to late sixteenth-century performance styles.

A growing number of music journals devote space to specialized articles on performance practice. Among the most significant are *Early Music* (1973–), *The American Recorder* (1960–), *The Consort* (1929–), *Journal of the Viola da Gamba Society of America* (1964–), *The Lute Society Journal* (1959–), *The Journal of the Lute Society of America* (1968–), *Continuo* (1977–), *Historical Performance* (1988–), published by Early Music America, and *Performance Practice Review* (1988–), published by the Music Department of the Claremont Graduate School in California. The more general scholarly music journals may occasionally contain articles on performance practice; these are best found by consulting the bibliographies listed at the end of this section.

References on Basic Style Problems

Given below is a selection of specialized studies in English that investigate in more detail some of the problematic aspects of Renaissance performance style. References on other topics such as Instrumentation, Tuning and Temperament, and Pronunciation, are given following the respective articles in this book. Not listed are the corresponding articles in standard works such as *The New Grove Dictionary of Music and Musicians* and the *New Harvard Dictionary of Music* (Cambridge, MA: Harvard University Press, 1986). Also not cited again are the pertinent sections in the McGee and the Phillips and Jackson books and *Performance Practice: Music before 1600*, ed. Brown and Sadie. Within each topic the studies of broadest coverage are listed first.

Tempo
Bank–*Tactus*; Planchart–Tempo; Mendel–Some; Houle–Origins; Berger–Relationship.

Articulation and Phrasing
Harrán–Directions; Lindley–Keyboard; Le Huray–English; Horsley–Wind.

Pitch
Mendel–Pitch; Bowers–Performing; Harwood–Case; Parrott–Transposition.

Musica Ficta
Berger–*Musica–Theories*; Berger–*Musica–Performance*; Routley–Practical; Lowinsky–Foreword; Bent–*Musica*.

Ornamentation
Ferand–*Improvisation*; Brown–*Embellishing*; Ferand–Didactic; Horsley–Improvised.

Text Underlay
Lowinsky–Problem; Harrán–Vincentino; Harrán–In Pursuit; Atlas–Paolo; Towne–Systematic 1–2.

Bibliographies of Performance Practice

(Most recent items are listed first)

Knighton/Fallows–*Companion*; Brown/Sadie–*Performance*; Jackson–*Bibliography*; Phillips/Jackson–*Performing*; McGee–*Medieval*; Brown/McKinnon–Performing; Donington–*Interpretation*; Sadie–*Grove–Instruments*; Vinquist/Zaslaw–*Performance*.

22

Tuning and Temperament

Ross W. Duffin

Sensitivity to tuning and awareness of historical tuning systems is a vitally important part of Renaissance performance style. Perhaps the single most important facet of the Renaissance approach to tuning over that of more recent eras is the primacy of the pure major third: the preference for a major third that is narrower than an equal-tempered major third by about 1/7 of a semitone. Such a major third is called "pure" because it produces no "beats" (audible pulsations produced when two slightly out-of-tune notes are sounded together). Unfortunately, modern musicians are generally so used to equal-tempered major thirds that they initially hear a pure major third as dolefully narrow or flat. This is something most listeners will quickly overcome once they have the purity of the interval pointed out to them and get used to hearing it. The really insurmountable problem related to tuning in the Renaissance, as should be evident from the discussion below, has to do with the basic incompatibility of the nature of sound with our instruments and our system of notes. But this is a problem that applies equally to music of any era, so don't be discouraged. There is still much that can be done with tuning to enhance the performance of Renaissance music, and it is not as difficult as it might seem at first.

Keyboard

We speak of the "circle of fifths," that procedure whereby, starting on any note and going up or down in series by the interval of a fifth, eventually we arrive at a note with the same name as the one we started on. The problem is that if we tune fifths that are acoustically pure, the note we arrive at after a circle of twelve fifths will be about one-quarter of a semitone sharp to the starting note. Similarly, we think of an octave as made up of a series of three major thirds, like C to E, E to G♯, and G♯ (or A♭) to C. But again, if we tune acoustically pure major thirds, we arrive at a note that is almost half a semi-tone flat to the starting note.

So, while acoustically pure fifths and acoustically pure major thirds would seem to be desirable sonorities to have in performance, there is no way that either one of them can be completely reconciled to the 12 available pitches of the keyboard octave. Either we tune 11 perfect fifths and leave the last one dissonant and unusable, or we compromise the perfection of the fifths and create what is known as a temperament.

Pythagorean Tuning

Until about the middle of the fifteenth century, practically the only system described or recommended by theorists was one involving the use of pure fifths. It had historical preeminence, since the mathematical ratio for pure fifths, 3:2, had first been expounded by the Greek philosopher Pythagoras and continued to be cited by theorists throughout the medieval period. It also made sense musically, since in so much of the music of the time, the interval of the open fifth was the predominant sonority. And few enough accidentals were used that it was usually possible to avoid the dissonant "fifth"—the "wolf fifth" as it was called—without too much difficulty. We know this system now as Pythagorean Tuning or Pythagorean Intonation.

Equal temperament is actually not a bad approximation of Pythagorean Intonation. The dissonance of the Pythagorean "wolf" is averaged out over the circle of twelve fifths, so that each interval is only slightly narrower than pure, a difference of only about 1/50 of a semitone.

The real shortcoming of Pythagorean Tuning (and of equal tempera-ment, for that matter) is the imperfection of the major thirds. Pythagorean thirds are very wide—not at all pleasant, so as composers began to use more thirds in their harmonic writing in the fifteenth century, performers must have found the system to be increasingly unsatisfactory. As we shall see, one solution was to "transpose" the system so that it had more usable major thirds.

The standard Pythagorean Tuning is represented in Table 22.1 using a system of "cents" in which 100 cents is equal to an equal tempered semi-tone. The tuning is created by tuning pure fifths (702c) down to E♭ and up to G♯, leaving the "wolf" between those two notes.

You will notice that there are two sizes of semitone, termed major (M) and minor (m). The major third which appears commonly in the system

TABLE 22.1 Pythagorean Tuning expressed in cents

C	C♯	D	E♭	E	F	F♯	G	G♯	A	B♭	B	C
0	114	204	294	408	498	612	702	816	906	996	1110	1200
M	m	m	M	m	M	m	M	m	m	M	m	

(C–E, D–F♯, etc.) is more properly known as the Pythagorean ditone and consists of two major and two minor semitones (2M + 2m). This is the interval that is extremely sharp, at 408c (the *pure* major third is only 386c). But it can also be seen that a *good* major third (384c) occurs in four places in this system as a diminished fourth (M + 3m): B–E♭ (D♯), F♯–B♭, C♯–F, G♯–C. Henri Arnaut (ca. 1440) introduced or, at least, transmitted a transposed Pythagorean system in which three of those good major thirds occurred in more useful places: B–D♯ (as in Pythagorean), D–F♯, E–G♯, A–C♯ (see Table 22.2). While these may not seem at first glance to be so useful, they occur often at approaches to cadences, whereas cadential resolutions are still, in the early to mid-fifteenth century, likely to be open fifths and therefore less in need of good major thirds. Arnaut's system is created by tuning perfect fifths down to G♭ (which Arnaut still calls F♯) and up to B. This leaves the wolf fifth at the interval B–F♯, which, of course, may need to be adjusted for a particular piece if it occurs prominently.

TABLE 22.2 Arnaut's transposed Pythagorean Tuning expressed in cents

C	G♯	D	E♭	E	F	F♯	G	G♯	A	B♭	B	C
0	90	204	294	408	498	588	702	792	906	996	1110	1200
	m	M	m	M	m	m	M	m	M	m	M	m

Meantone Temperaments

Pythagorean Tuning works fairly well into the second half of the fifteenth century, giving good realizations of many of the works in the *Buxheim Organ Book,* for example, particularly those based on early fifteenth-century chansons. But by the late fifteenth century, according to indications in *Musica practica* of Ramos de Pareja (1482), keyboard players seem to have arrived at a new solution—one that made extensive use of the ratio for the pure major third, 5:4, first formally revived from classical theory by Gafurius in 1518. In the classic temperament of this type, 1/4 comma meantone (among the many varieties of meantone temperaments—I once heard Bob Marvin refer to this one as "God's Meantone"), there are eight pure major thirds (2M + 2m), and four excruciating ones (3M + m). The real cost of the pure major thirds is not these four unusable ones, however, but rather that in order to achieve the pure major thirds, it is necessary to temper (narrow) the fifths more than 2–1/2 times the amount necessary for equal temperament, rendering them noticeably narrow and dissonant compared to those of the Pythagorean or even the equal tempered system. Most Renaissance music has lots of thirds, however, and the bitterness of the fifths tends to get lost in the overwhelming sweetness of the thirds. *It is impossible to overemphasize the positive and colorful effect of 1/4 comma meantone on keyboard music of the Renaissance.*

The name 1/4 comma meantone (Table 22.3) comes from two different characteristics of the temperament: If you were to tune four pure fifths up

TABLE 22.3 1/4 comma meantone: usual notes expressed in cents

C	C♯	D	E♭	E	F	F♯	G	G♯/A♭	A	B♭	B	C
0	75.5	193	310.5	386	503.5	579	696.5	772/814	889.5	1007	1082.5	1200
m	M	M	m	M	m	M	m/M	M/m	M	m	M

from C (C up to G, to D, to A, then to E), the note E that you arrive at would be sharper than a pure major third above C by 22c (about 1/5 of a semitone), an amount known as a *syntonic comma*. But if, in order to tune that E as a pure major third, you divide up the discrepancy among the four fifths, each interval of a fifth would be tempered (narrowed) by 1/4 of that amount, hence "quarter-comma." The term "meantone" comes from the fact that, in this system, the whole tone is exactly half of the pure major third. (Note that, as in Pythagorean Tuning, there are two different sizes of semitone; in meantone, however, the chromatic semitone is minor and the diatonic semitone is major.)

To set 1/4 comma meantone on the keyboard, tune C–E in the tenor octave as a pure major third then, using a flashing metronome, narrow the C–G fifth to beat at about 74 beats/minute at a′ = 440 (70/min. at a′ = 415); widen the D–G fourth to beat at 110 (104)/min.; narrow the D–A fifth to beat at 82 (77)/min.; check that the E–A fourth is beating about 123 (116)/min.; if it is not, check the above intervals again. (If you are using an A fork, tune A–D–G–C, then C–E pure, checking it with the A.) The rest of the temperament can be set entirely by tuning pure major thirds above and below those notes. The usual question is G♯/A♭, which can be set as a pure major third either to E or to C depending on which note is needed for the music.

In practice, 1/4 comma meantone works beautifully as long as a note is not used in more than one of its enharmonic forms throughout a piece of music. This can include some fairly chromatic works, such as Giles Farnaby's "His Humour" from the *Fitzwilliam Virginal Book* and Sweelinck's *Fantasia chromatica*. However, once a note is used in more than one enharmonic form, as happens more frequently in music after 1600 (e.g., Frescobaldi's *Cento Partite*), it is necessary either to have split keys on the keyboard, to tolerate one or more pungent surprises, to set the pitch of the note halfway between the two pure major third positions, or to choose a different temperament.

Other meantone systems advocated in the Renaissance include 2/7 comma (Zarlino, 1558) and 1/3 comma (Salinas, 1577)—temperaments in which the fifths and the major thirds are even smaller than in 1/4 comma meantone. (1/3 comma meantone was actually intended for an instrument with many split keys and, as such, results in a useful system of 19 equal notes to the octave, pure minor thirds, and no wolf fifth.) It is also possible that less extreme forms of meantone, such as 2/9, 1/5, and 1/6 comma as well as some irregular temperaments (having many different sizes of fifth and major third) might have evolved in practice in a search for better fifths than 1/4 comma's, even though the improving fifths result in worsening major thirds. These temperaments, especially the less extreme forms of regular meantone systems, may be useful as a compromise, if the keyboard instrument must play with fretted instruments.

Fretted Instruments

And more than once I have felt like laughing when I saw musicians struggling to put a lute or viol into proper tune with a keyboard instrument . . .

—Giovanni de' Bardi to Giulio Caccini (ca. 1580)
(quoted in Strunk, *Source Readings,* p. 297)

The nature of fretted instruments, with strings tuned in fourths and a major third, yet needing the frets to serve for all the strings and produce pure octaves and unisons across the compass, does not easily allow the use of unequal fretting. To cite some examples, if the one major third between open strings is tuned pure, it becomes more difficult to tune octaves from one side to the other of that interval. If the fourth fret of an A lute is tuned as a pure major third to the open string to accommodate all the sharp notes there, it ruins the tuning if the fourth fret E♭ is used extensively in a piece. So while adjustments in the fretting can be made (and were made during the Renaissance), and while good players can vary the pitch of a note against the frets by pulling and pushing the stopped string (*intensione* and *remissione* according to Aaron, 1545) to raise and lower, respectively, the pitch, fretted instruments like to play in equal temperament. After 1550, this was clearly a prevalent system, which is why the conflict with keyboard instruments arose. However, some writers were advocating Pythagorean Tuning into the middle of the sixteenth century(!), and there is some musical and theoretical evidence for the use of meantone temperaments right through the century. Thus, shadings one way or the other from equal temperament are possible and, indeed, when fretted instruments are played with keyboards, we assume that some sort of compromise was made which enabled them to sound in tune with each other.

Pythagorean Tuning

Pythagorean Tuning would not seem to be very appropriate for music as late as it was still recommended (Bermudo, 1555). Probably, the sixteenth-century theorists advocating it were not in close touch with the practical aspects of lute and viol playing. Still, instructions such as those provided for Pythagorean Tuning by Oronce Fine in 1530 result in a workable system for the fifteenth century at least, corresponding to Arnaut's transposed system for keyboard (see Table 22.5). Along a single string, the arrangement of major and minor semitones is the same as in Arnaut's scale with the exception of the last two intervals, which are reversed, since Fine tunes the eleventh fret as a pure fourth to the sixth fret rather than as a pure fifth to the fourth fret. (In cents, the value would be 1086 rather than 1110.)

Equal Temperament

A Pythagorean whole tone has the ratio 9:8. In attempting to divide that into semitones and still use simple ratios, some Renaissance writers advocated that 9:8 (18:16) be divided into 18:17 (minor semitone) and 17:16 (major semitone). Interestingly, in practice, musicians found only 18:17 to be useful in fretting. According to Martin Agricola in 1545, many lutenists and gambists made all their frets equal and used only the minor semitone. In fact, 18:17 as a ratio from one fret to the next results in a very satisfying equal temperament comparable to one using the more correct scientific method (see Table 22.5). It is possible that the discrepancies are made negligible by such variables as the increased tension of the string when it is depressed to the fingerboard. It is also likely that any temperament such as this was shaded by ear by a good player, with frets 1, 4 (especially), and 6 being the obvious candidates for slight adjustment toward a meantone scheme.

Meantone Temperaments

It seems clear that some music for fretted instruments, particularly before 1550, is better served by a meantone system than an equal-tempered one. Certain tablature choices of string and fret in situations where there is more than one possibility lead to that conclusion. Also, although no one has yet done a thorough study of them, surviving sixteenth-century instruments with fixed frets (including citterns, bandoras, and orpharions) show a tendency toward meantone schemes. In addition, some fretting instructions from the period speak of major and minor semitones in places that would correspond to meantone rather than to Pythagorean Tuning. Obviously, players could not have tuned their open fourths so wide and the major third so narrow, or adjusted their frets to the extent that they were unable to push or pull the unisons and octaves into tune. But they may have preferred the coloristic effect of a meantone approximation, and they must have done something to make it possible to play with keyboard instruments. In fact, it *is* possible to approximate meantone tuning on a fretted instrument, but it requires two things: the setting of the frets according to the interval ratios in meantone, and the tuning of the open strings to the intervals created by the fretting (this may be checked against a meantone-tuned keyboard). Table 22.4 is a reference chart showing the notes for open strings and frets of three common tunings for Renaissance lutes and viols. Table 22.5 gives

TABLE 22.4 Chart of notes for fretted instruments in G, A, and D

Fret							Fret							Fret						
	G	C	F	A	D	G		A	D	G	B	E	A		D	G	C	E	A	D
1.	G#	C#	F#	B♭	E♭	G#	1.	B♭	E♭	G#	C	F	B♭	1.	E♭	G#	C#	F	B♭	E♭
2.	A	D	G	B	E	A	2.	B	E	A	C#	F#	B	2.	E	A	D	F#	B	E
3.	B♭	E♭	G#	C	F	B♭	3.	C	F	B♭	D	G	C	3.	F	B♭	E♭	G	C	F
4.	B	E	A	C#	F#	B	4.	C#	F#	B	E♭	G#	C#	4.	F#	B	E	G#	C#	F#
5.	C	F	B♭	D	G	C	5.	D	G	C	E	A	D	5.	G	C	F	A	D	G
6.	C#	F#	B	E♭	G#	C#	6.	E♭	G#	C#	F	B♭	E♭	6.	G#	C#	F#	B♭	E♭	G#
7.	D	G	C	E	A	D	7.	E	A	D	F#	B	E	7.	A	D	G	B	E	A
8.	E♭	G#	C#	F	B♭	E♭	8.	F	B♭	E♭	G	C	F	8.	B♭	E♭	G#	C	F	B♭
9.	E	A	D	F#	B	E	9.	F#	B	E	G#	C#	F#	9.	B	E	A	C#	F#	B
10.	F	B♭	E♭	G	C	F	10.	G	C	F	A	D	G	10.	C	F	B♭	D	G	C
11.	F#	B	E	G#	C#	F#	11.	G#	C#	F#	B♭	E♭	G#	11.	C#	F#	B	E♭	G#	C#
12.	G	C	F	A	D	G	12.	A	D	G	B	E	A	12.	D	G	C	E	A	D

fretting ratios for Pythagorean Tuning, equal temperament, and 1/6, 1/5, and 1/4 comma meantone temperaments. In order to use the information in Table 22.5, measure the distance from the nut to the bridge on the instrument in question and multiply that amount by the ratios to give the correct theoretical placement of the frets in each system. It should be noted that while professional players may start with formulas for placing the frets, they always make minute adjustments based on checking octaves and unisons across the strings.

Finally, in attempting to achieve a flexible meantone system, some modern players have had success with "split frets" or taped-on partial frets to accommodate both *mi* and *fa* possibilities. For a bass viol of average string length, this would require separation of the strands of the fret by just over

TABLE 22.5 Fretting ratios for Pythagorean Tuning, equal temperament, 1/6 comma meantone, 1/5 comma meantone, and 1/4 comma meantone

	Pythagorean	Equal	1/6 Comma	1/5 Comma	1/4 Comma
Fret					
1.	.0508	.0561	.0499(.0605 Fa)	.0471(.0625 Fa)	.0429(.0654 Fa)
2.	.1112	.1091	.1074	.1067	.1056
3.	.1563	.1591	.1615	.1625	.1641
4.	.2100	.2063	.2033(.2133 Fa)	.2020(.2148 Fa)	.2000(.2183 Fa)
5.	.2500	.2508	.2515	.2518	.2523
6.	.2881	.2929	.2889(.2969 Fa)	.2871(.2986 Fa)	.2845(.3012 Fa)
7.	.3333	.3326	.3320	.3317	.3309
8.	.3672	.3700	.3724	.3735	.3750
9.	.4075	.4054	.4037	.4030	.4018
10.	.4375	.4388	.4398	.4403	.4410
11.	.4661	.4703	.4678	.4667	.4650
12.	.5000	.5000	.5000	.5000	.5000

half an inch for the first fret, proportionately less for the fourth and sixth frets. In practice, the first fret is the one most in need of "splitting" and the one where the separation is large enough to allow even lutenists to make the necessary distinction in difficult situations such as bar chords. This is a good compromise, but if you are using single frets, try working with *fa* on the first fret and *mi* on the fourth and sixth frets. There is also the possibility that the tied frets on lutes and viols were sometimes slanted. The first fret of a G lute, for example, might be slanted to give a longer string length in the bass in view of the sharped notes there, and a shorter string length in the treble in view of the flatted notes there, although the top string's first fret note would be unusable as a G♯ in such an arrangement.

Voices, Violins, and Other Musical Wind Instruments

Performance media such as these with greater "real-time" tuning flexibility than keyboard and fretted instruments may aspire to the perfection of Just Intonation, a system in which all fifths and major thirds are tuned pure. This is not to say that they cannot use other systems as well. Many woodwind makers, for example, use a 1/4 comma meantone basis for their instruments even though there may still be a tendency for players to want to play the fifths as pure as possible. On the other hand, I have found that singers will quite easily accommodate themselves to singing with an organ tuned in 1/4 comma meantone in spite of the discomfort of singing the narrow meantone fifths *a cappella*. Thus, it is clear that performers with tuning flexibility can and should adjust to instruments with fixed systems.

But what of Just Intonation? Is it a chimera? Performances by vocal groups like the Hilliard Ensemble, the Tallis Scholars, and Gothic Voices have made it apparent that approaching perfection in tuning is not an impossible dream. While a good part of their tuning precision is due to good ears, outstanding musicianship, and intuition, there are a few conscious adjustments that can be made that will begin to "justify" the tuning of any ensemble.

The Just scale contains some characteristics of both the Pythagorean and 1/4 comma meantone systems. However, many of the notes in the system must maintain the flexibility to adjust depending on the context. Some notes are fairly stable and others need only a couple of different positions. Of the notes in the C diatonic scale, A is the most likely to need adjustment; its sharper form makes a pure fifth with the regular D, and its flatter form makes a pure fifth with E and a pure major third with F. D itself may occasionally need adjustment if the A is already prevailing in its flatter form. Similarly, F or B♭ will need to be adjusted when those two notes sound together. The other accidentals are tuned as pure major thirds and fifths to the diatonic notes, the most common flip-flop being at the G♯/A♭ level. Table 22.6 gives a cents chart of the most commonly used pitch relationships in Just Intonation.

TABLE 22.6 Just Intonation: most common cents values and frequent alternates

C	C♯	D	E♭	E	F	F♯	G	G♯/A♭	A/A	B♭	B	C
0	70	204	316	386	498	590	702	772/814	884/906	1018	1088	1200
	(92)	(182)			(520)					(996)		

Bibliography

Original Sources

Agricola–*Musica*; Arnaut de Zwolle–Manuscript; Aaron–*Toscanello*; Aaron–*Lucidario*; Bermudo–*Declaración*; Fine–*Epithoma*; Gafurius–*Practica*; Gafurius–*De harmonia*; Ramos de Pareja–*Musica*; Salinas–*De musica*; Zarlino–*Istitutione*.

Secondary Sources

Perhaps the best introduction to the subject is Mark Lindley's "Temperaments" in *The New Grove*.

For keyboard tunings, the following may be useful: Barbour–*Tuning*; Jorgenson–*Tuning*; Leedy–Personal; Lindley–Early; Lindley–Instructions; Pepe–Pythagorean; Reply Marvin–*Courant*.

For fretted instrument tunings, the most thorough source is Lindley–*Lutes*.

For Just Intonation, a useful discussion with scrutiny of many tuning systems is found in Blackwood–*Structure*.

See also Knighton/Fallows (Covey-Crump)–*Companion*.

Suggested Listening

Keyboard
Pythagorean
Miri it is. Organ played by Alan Wilson. Plant Life PLR 043.

Meantone
Buxheimer Orgelbuch. Ton Koopman. Astrée AS 78.
William Byrd: Harpsichord Music. Colin Tilney. EMI-Reflexe 1C063–30 120.

Fretted
Seventeenth-Century English Music for Viols and Organ, Les Filles de Sainte-Colombe with Frances Fitch, Organ. Titanic Ti-95. (1/4 comma with split keys and split frets).
John Dowland: Musicke for the Lute, Paul O'Dette. Astrée AS 90 or CD E7715 (1/6 comma approximation with split first fret).
Luys Milan: El Maestro, Hopkinson Smith. Astrée AS 95 (1/4 comma approximation with split frets).

Voices
Pythagorean and Just Intonation
The Service of Venus and Mars, Gothic Voices. Hyperion CDA 66238.

Just Intonation
Thomas Tallis: Lamentations of Jeremiah, The Hilliard Ensemble. ECM 1341 833308–2.
Victoria: Requiem, Tallis Scholars. Gimell CDGIM-012.
(*N.B.* There are many other recordings by these three ensembles that would serve as admirable examples of fine tuning.)

Acknowledgements

I would like to thank three individuals for their assistance. A former student, Michael Schultz, has achieved formidable expertise in the area of historical tunings for keyboard and has made a number of useful suggestions. A current student, David Dolata, continues to pursue studies into tuning on fretted instruments, and his work has influenced that part of the chapter. Finally, Rogers Covey-Crump of the Hilliard Ensemble and Gothic Voices showed me a few years ago that it was, indeed, possible and useful for singers to take an analytical look at tuning in unaccompanied vocal ensembles.

23

Pitch and Transposition

Herbert Myers

Pitch

One well-known "fact" is that pitch in olden times was lower than our present international standard of a′ = 440. This "fact" (often repeated in the popular press, usually in connection with the danger it poses for our priceless heritage of Stradivarius violins, and invariably calling for an invidious comparison of our "high-strung" era with a supposedly more relaxed past) is, of course, only half correct, since the truth is that pitch in earlier times was also *higher* than modern pitch. In fact, recorded standards of pitch have varied over a range of at least a fifth, from about a major third below modern to about a minor third above. Attempts to achieve an international standard—only a fond hope for musicians writing in the eighteenth century— were first begun in earnest in the nineteenth century; they first became a reality in 1939. Although we are all aware that adherence to this modern standard varies and that it is thus absolute only on paper, we still depend on it as a fixed point of reference from which the departures tend to be (on a grand scale) rather minute. Its establishment strongly colors our perception of the meaning of musical notation from earlier times, when composers may have had a much different standard—or none at all—in mind.

The advantages of a universal pitch standard (particularly for the traveling musician—and who among us doesn't travel nowadays?) are obvious. Perhaps less obvious, however, are some of the advantages of having different standards for different media, for which the musicians of earlier eras seem to have had some appreciation. Various reasons for these differing standards are mentioned by Michael Praetorius in his chapter concerning pitch (*Syntagma musicum* II, 1619: 14–18). First, pitch affects timbre: "For the higher-pitched an instrument (within its class and type) is made, as with cornetts, shawms, and descant fiddles, the fresher they sound; conversely, the lower the trombones, curtals, bassanelli, bombards, and bass fiddles are

248

tuned, the more solemnly and majestically they present themselves." A second consideration is convenience: a low pitch is more comfortable for voices and stringed instruments, and a high one (although he does not mention this) may be better for certain wind instruments, since it eases finger stretches. A final consideration, implicit in his discussion of organ pitch, is economic: the smaller the instrument, the lower the cost (accounting, at least in part, for the trend in his day toward higher organ pitches).

These advantages pale, of course, in the face of the difficulties when instruments try to play together. As Praetorius explains, the mixing of all sorts of instruments together was a comparatively recent development, to which the disparity of instrumental pitch still represented a common and severe impediment. It is precisely because it was such a problem that he felt the need to explain this rather complex situation to his contemporaries. We are indebted to his explanation for much of what we know about pitch in the Renaissance and early Baroque.

Praetorius applauds the comparative standardization of organ pitch that has taken place in the princely chapels of (North) Germany. This pitch, known as *Chorton* (choir pitch), has risen over the years a whole step from its former level, and is now equivalent to those of Italy and England (although English pitch is just a fraction lower, as evidenced by the cornetts and shawms manufactured there). Some, he says, would like to raise the pitch yet another semitone; this is not a good idea, in his opinion, since the current pitch is already too high for voices and stringed instruments. Indeed, players commonly tune down a whole tone in order to avoid breaking strings, causing some inconvenience for other instrumentalists (who must then transpose) but making life easier for singers.

For this reason Praetorius likes the distinction, made in Prague and some other Catholic choirs, between *Chorton* and *Kammerton* (chamber pitch). These pitches are a whole tone apart; the higher one—*Kammerton*—is equivalent to his North German standard *Chorton* and is used only at table and for convivial and joyous occasions, being the most convenient for instruments; the lower one is called *Chorton* and is used only in churches, primarily for the sake of singers, who both strain less and sound better at the lower pitch. (Students of Baroque practice will notice that this usage of *Chorton* and *Kammerton* is the exact reverse of that of Bach's day, when the *higher* pitches of church organs were called *Chorton* and *lower* pitches were called *Kammerton;* see the study by Bruce Haynes, listed below, for a detailed examination of pitch in Bach's day.) It would be good, he says, if organs could be tuned to this low version of *Chorton,* but he considers this to be impractical now that the high version (which he evidently intends to call *Kammerton* and to use as his reference pitch throughout his book) has become so well established in his German lands.

One other pitch standard figures in Praetorius's discussion, one a minor third below his *Kammerton* (and thus a semitone below the Prague *Chorton*). This, he says, is the pitch used in England formerly and in the Netherlands

still for most wind instruments, and is the one used by the celebrated Antwerp maker Johannes Bossus for his harpsichords, spinets, and organs.
While there is no denying that this is an advantageous pitch for harpsichords, flutes, and other instruments due to the lovely timbre it imparts, he
says, it is nevertheless impractical to include instruments built at this pitch
in concerted music, and one must stick by the aforementioned pitches,
Chorton and *Kammerton*. However, the very low pitch (that is, the one a
minor third lower than *Kammerton*) is much in use in Italy and in various
Catholic choirs of Germany because of its suitability for voices. For this reason, music is often sung at this pitch through transposition down a minor
third, solely for the sake of the voices; to instrumentalists such a transposition may seem offensive at first but is worth the trouble to learn to make.

The foregoing discussion treats pitch standards in relative terms. However, Praetorius was not content to leave it at that, and he attempted to
specify pitch in absolute terms as well. Unfortunately, however, there is still
some disagreement among scholars as to its exact level. This essay is certainly not the proper forum for an extensive continuation of the debate.
Suffice it to say that there is a discrepancy of about a semitone between the
two methods Praetorius chose to communicate his pitch standard: reconstructions of a set of little organ pipes according to dimensions he provided
produce a pitch just a little below $a' = 440$, while the pitch of a typical sackbut of Nuremberg make (with the slide extended by the width of two fingers, as he suggests) is just below a modern B-flat, or about $a' = 460$. The
latter pitch, it should be mentioned, is in better accord with the dimensions
of most of the other wind instruments in his plates, which are carefully rendered to scale. (Adding to the confusion are his occasional lapses in consist-
ency; despite his best intentions he sometimes reverts to local usage in calling his reference pitch *Chorton*, and he sometimes reports the pitch-names
of instruments according to lower standards instead of their "actual" pitches
according to *Kammerton* as promised. One must sometimes take him for
what he means rather than what he says, but getting two people to agree on
the interpretation can be difficult. Still, however, the argument over a semitone represents real progress; forty years ago the interval at issue was a
major third!)

The broad outlines of Praetorius's assessment are confirmed by surviving
instruments, although various scholars have chosen to "connect the dots" in
different ways, arriving at somewhat differing pictures. Most German organs
from the period are from one to two semitones above modern pitch. From
later sources we know that Venetian pitch was high and Roman was low,
accounting for Praetorius's two somewhat conflicting references to Italian
pitch. Recorders of Venetian manufacture (of the sort he illustrates) are
generally compatible with a pitch of about $a' = 460$, but not always at the
intervals we have come to regard as standard. (A much smaller number are
compatible with $a' = 440$.) Curved ("ordinary") cornetts, many of which are
also from Venice, range in pitch from $a' = 440$ to a tone above (with a very

few even higher), with the majority again at about a′ = 460. Mute cornetts, on the other hand, are more often at lower pitches (from a′ = 440 downward). Flutes range in pitch from about a major third below modern pitch to about a semitone above, with strong representations at a′ = 410 and a′ = 435. Surviving shawms and curtals appear to be at pitches above a′ = 440 (although the reed and player can have a huge influence here, and determining the exact pitch often remains a matter of argument).

The question of English pitch is a little more complicated than Praetorius realized, since his source of information seems to have been limited to woodwind instruments imported from England. The choral pitch in England appears to have been something entirely different. There is strong evidence that in the Jacobean period it was about a minor third higher than modern, and that the English organ was often a transposing instrument (producing the choir's F by sounding what was to the organist a C!); there is some further evidence that this pitch standard and transposition practice were not new in the seventeenth century but were continuations of traditions established in the Tudor period. Praetorius also fails to mention French pitch standards; we can only surmise from extant organs that the choir pitch there was quite low (often a tone below modern; some later sources equate French pitch with Roman). French instrumental pitches may not have been so low, however, before it became the practice there to combine instruments with voices in church—a practice that came later to France than to Italy and Germany. Certainly Mersenne's dimensions for Renaissance-type woodwinds do not differ significantly from those of surviving examples from elsewhere.

Concerning pitches before Praetorius the information is much less certain. Arnolt Schlick (1511) discusses the pitch of organs used to accompany choirs; he provides a measurement (a line in the margin, to be multiplied by 16) for the length of the bottom pipe, which is to sound F. Calculations of the pitch of this pipe suggest a tuning standard a little more than a tone below a′ = 440—on the low end of later standards, as we have seen, but not impossible. However, the suitability of such a low pitch for voices has been challenged, and thus the accuracy of transmission of the pipe measurement has been called into question. To add to the complexity of the issue, Schlick mentions building organs a fifth lower, using his suggested measurement instead for c rather than F (although the resultant pitch would be less convenient for singers, in his opinion). In discussing the pitch of surviving old organs, Praetorius mentions ones that are commonly a minor third or more higher than his *Kammerton,* as well as a good many that were a fourth higher (or a fifth lower—the same thing to an organist) than that current standard. In the light of all this diversity, it would seem silly even to speak of standardization of sixteenth-century organ pitches.

Attempts have been made to divine pitch standards for the fifteenth century and earlier. These have relied almost wholly on examination of part ranges, comparing them with the ranges of voices of the type thought to have been singing a particular repertory. (See the Bibliography below for some specific examples.) Here, we are in the realm of pure speculation, of course, but in the absence of more objective data this is the best we can do.

Transposition

It should be clear by now that closely bound up with the question of pitch is that of transposition: transposition, of course, is what you do if you don't like the pitch! With unaccompanied vocal music there is obviously no problem; the pitch can be set at any convenient level to accommodate the ranges of the parts to the singers at hand. As it became more and more the practice to accompany voices, first with organ and then with other instruments, transposition became a problem for instrumentalists and thus a topic of discussion by theorists.

The great majority of vocal polyphony of the sixteenth and early seventeenth centuries was written using only two combinations of clefs, one the "high clefs" (treble, mezzo-soprano, alto, and baritone clefs—i.e., G2, C2, C3, and F3) and the other the "low clefs" (soprano, alto, tenor, and bass clefs—C1, C3, C4, and F4). (Since the bass part in each case can have a larger range than the other parts, it is sometimes represented by a higher clef: tenor clef—C4—in the high set, or baritone clef—F3—in the low one.) In the eighteenth century, long after the distinction had gone out of fashion, the high clefs were dubbed the *chiavette* (literally "little clefs" in Italian) by writers who correctly understood that earlier music written in these clefs needed to be transposed downward to fit vocal ranges; the low clefs were called the *chiavi naturali* ("natural clefs"). Theorists and composers from the period itself commonly call for transposition downward by either a fourth or a fifth, although other intervals are also mentioned. The exact interval might depend on various factors: the particular vocal ranges of the parts, the skill of instrumentalists in coping with additional sharps or flats occasioned by the transposition, and the temperament of keyboard instruments (which may demand retuning or leaving out certain notes in the more remote keys). Among the theorists the only holdout seems to be Thomas Morley, who recommends *against* transposing downward pieces in the "high keys" lest they lose the quality of liveliness that for him is their true nature.

There were conventions of transposition for instruments as well, which seem to have changed somewhat during the course of the sixteenth century as the families of instruments themselves grew and developed. A set of recorders from about 1500, for instance, would have been made up of three sizes, separated by fifths: *bass* in F, *tenor* (sometimes called *alt-tenor*) in c, and *discant* in g (sounding about an octave higher, of course). A *soprano* (in the modern sense) seems not to have appeared until about the middle of the century. Although much of the contemporary literature fits on the F-c-g set as written, a number of pieces (usually in high clefs, including several in the *Glogauer Liederbuch* and the *Odhecaton,* and some favorites by Isaac) need to be transposed downwards; down a fourth usually works best. By the time of Praetorius the family had expanded to eight sizes: F-B♭-f-c′-g′-c″-d″-g″ (sounding pitch); the f-c′-g′ instruments are the original set, the first and last now renamed *basset* and *alt* in order to allow for an expanded terminology. It will be noticed that most of the members of the set are still separated by fifths (except at the "outer edges" of the set). Praetorius mentions the advantage of this arrangement: a quartet may be made up of any three adjacent sizes; for example, using a *bass* in B♭, two *bassets* in f, and a *tenor* in c′, players could pretend they were using the original set discussed above but produce a completely different timbre at the lower pitch. When a fourth size is mixed in, however, he suggests transposing either up a tone or down a fourth, as appropriate, in order to accommodate the bias of the higher instruments toward sharps. The real disadvantage of the system, he points out, comes when one combines instruments of five sizes, since the tonalities of the outer instruments are then separated by a major third (B♭ *bass* and d″ *discant,* for instance), causing severe tuning difficulties. Thus, he suggests, makers should produce alternate versions of the upper members, built a tone lower. We see the beginnings of this practice in the *discant* in c″, which he lists as an alternative to the one in d″; it was later carried out in full in the "C and F" alignment of Baroque woodwind families.

This discussion of the Renaissance woodwind system is found, in fact, in Praetorius's chapter on shawms, which, like the recorders, had come to be built in a multitude of sizes. A century earlier the shawm family, too, consisted of but three members, but only the upper two were in common use (since the bass part was usually played on the sackbut). These are the sizes Praetorius calls the *discant Schalmey* and *Altpommer;* they had, however, served as treble and *tenor* to the shawm band throughout the fifteenth century and much of the sixteenth. Praetorius reports their pitches as d′ and g, respectively, reckoned according to *Kammerton;* formerly, however, the pitch-names assigned to these two instruments were a fifth lower: g and c (the same ones given for the early *discant* and *alt-tenor* recorders, as we have seen). This means, then, that the pitch standard for shawms had originally been a fifth *higher* than Praetorius's standard, and that shawms had in effect transposed the music up a fifth or more from what we might now consider its written pitch (much in the same way that recorders and flutes transpose it up an octave). It was only when shawms came to be combined with other instruments and with voices (as Praetorius explains how to do) that it became necessary to think in terms of their "real" pitch as defined by the organ. In the meantime, development of the larger members of the family had made it practical to play at that pitch.

If the pitch standard of the shawms in the sixteenth century was very high, that of the viols was very low. This is suggested by the physical size of surviving Renaissance viols, which are considerably bigger than those in common use today. In fact, they are almost a size larger than standard modern viols, the treble having the dimensions of a smallish modern tenor, and the bass representing a size intermediate between a modern bass and an orchestral contrabass. Iconography corroborates this view of Renaissance viols and the late appearance of the "true" treble (which was certainly not yet known to Praetorius); the one extant sixteenth-century example (in the Ashmolean Museum, Oxford) must have been a rarity in its day and was probably considered a "sopranino" or "kleiner discant"—a size mentioned in a few late-sixteenth-century sources (Woodfield–*Early*: 186, 193).

Written sources from the period offer a multiplicity of viol tunings, but these break down into two basic groups, "high" and "low." Besides the standard modern D-G-d consort alignment, the high group includes D-A-d, E-A-d, D-G-c, and other variants. The low tunings are a fourth or fifth lower; they include A_1-D-A, G_1-D-G, and G_1-D-A. Modern scholars have usually taken these pitches literally, assuming that there were viols available capable of actually playing at both tessituras. In light of the physical evidence, however, it seems more likely that the high and low tunings were merely different nominal pitches for instruments whose "actual" pitch (from the modern point of view) was closer to that represented by the lower pitch names; taken as alternatives, the high and low tunings thus constituted a system of transposition. Indeed, Ganassi—one of several authors who provided both high and low tuning as alternatives—explains (*Regola rubertina*, 1542) that his low (A_1-D-A) system does not really differ in tuning from his D-G-d high system, but merely in the placement of clefs. He recommends the use of the high system, although he says most players "play a fourth higher" using the low one (once again, by the seemingly perverse logic we have come to expect in dealing with transposition, conceiving a lower pitch for the instrument results in an upward shift in sounding pitch). The advantage in imagining the high tunings is that the written notes are then placed lower on the instrument and are less likely to demand playing above the frets, especially with pieces in high clefs. The advantage in using the low tunings, on the other hand, would have been that the notes would then have sounded at "normal" (or 8-foot) pitch, useful when viols were combined with voices and most other instruments.

The majority of later Italian and German sources (Zacconi, Virgiliano, Banchieri, Cerone, and Praetorius) give low tunings, once again reflecting the growing tendency to report tunings in terms of a common pitch standard. Nevertheless, transposition (particularly in a downward direction) was still a practical necessity. Virgiliano, for instance, provides a chart for his A_1-D-A set of viols that, like his chart for cornett and sackbuts (reproduced on p. 98 of this *Guide*), details transpositions over the range of an octave, from a second above written pitch to a seventh below. In both charts, playing a tone up, at pitch, a tone down and a third down is associated with music in the low clefs, while playing down a fourth, fifth, sixth, and seventh is associated with the high clefs. Praetorius, too, makes reference to downward transposition when he says (*Syntagma* II: 44) that the English, when playing viols alone, play down a fourth or fifth by imagining that their instruments are at higher pitches than the "actual" ones reckoned according to *Kammerton*.

In Volume III of the *Syntagma musicum* (pp. 152–68) Praetorius offers many suggestions for instrumentation of motets and other concerted pieces according to clef combinations. Several of his solutions involve transpositions of the kind we have met in Volume II (discussed above). A few new ones come to the surface here and there, however; for instance, he suggests that pieces in dorian, hypodorian, and hypoaeolian modes should be transposed down by a tone when played on flutes, for reasons of both range and tonality. (For earlier information regarding transposition on flutes see the chapter on the Renaissance flute, p. 56.) While many of his recommendations are quite practical, they can be applied only with caution to music of earlier generations, particularly when they involve types and sizes of instrument that had only recently become available. The development and use of such instruments reflect an extravagance of expression more appropriate to early Baroque than to Renaissance sensibilities.

We have seen in the foregoing discussion that there was a multitude of instrumental pitch standards in the Renaissance, as well as a number of ways to relate to those standards in practice—and these are only the ones we know about! Each standard had its advantages and disadvantages as perceived at the time. Replicating all of them in the name of authenticity, even to the extent that might be possible, would be an extremely expensive proposition. Still, a well-funded early-music ensemble starting from scratch might do well to acquire copies of recorders, curved cornetts, shawms, curtals, and crumhorns at a semitone above a' = 440, and flutes, mute cornetts, and perhaps some soft reeds at a semitone below a' = 440; although such a choice still represents an oversimplification of Renaissance practice, it does follow one defensible interpretation of Praetorius's *Chorton-Kammerton* plan and helps emphasize the difference in timbre between classes of instruments. (It has the further advantage of allowing the Renaissance winds to combine with Baroque strings, whose players often prefer to play at low pitch; copies of Renaissance strings are still very rare.) This being the real world, however, most of us will have to content ourselves with following the spirit rather than the letter of Renaissance practice, finding the best compromise using the equipment at hand (which will usually be at a' = 440). Flexibility and skill in transposing are required in any case, regardless of the instrumental pitch standard. Above all, performance pitch was not considered a moral issue in the Renaissance, and it should not become one now (as it has among some practitioners of Baroque music). There is no particular virtue in adherence to any one standard at the expense of other musical values.

For Further Reading

There are two major figures in the study of the history of pitch, Alexander J. Ellis and Arthur Mendel. Ellis–History led ultimately to the adoption of a′ = 440 as the international standard. In 1948 and 1955 Mendel–Pitch and Mendel–On challenged many of Ellis's conclusions; the articles were reprinted (with corrections) along with Ellis's as *Studies in the History of Musical Pitch* (Amsterdam, 1968). Mendel's conclusions, in turn, were challenged in Thomas/Rhodes-Schlick; these two scholars are also the principal authors of the article "Pitch" in *The New Grove*. A year before his death Mendel's final reconsideration appeared as Mendel–Western. More recent controversy regarding Praetorius's pitch has appeared in *Early Music*: see Myers–Observation and a rebuttal by Segerman. Haynes-Johann carries the question deeper into the Baroque period, arriving at conclusions that differ from Thomas and Rhodes as well as from Mendel.

Pitches of surviving recorders are reported by Marvin–Recorders; of flutes by Puglisi–*Survey*; of cornetts by Tarr–Katalog; of sackbuts by Fischer–*Renaissance*; of curtals by Stanley/Lyndon-Jones–Curtal.

Information concerning *chiavette* is discussed by Mendel–Pitch-III and by Hermelink–Chiavette (*New Grove*). This and related information as it concerns the performance of one particular work is presented by Parrott–Transposition. Transposition on viols is discussed by Brown–Notes and by Brown/Spencer–How. Information on English choir and organ pitch in the sixteenth and seventeenth centuries is given by Bray–More. The question of fifteenth-century vocal pitch is examined by Bowers–Performing with further discussion by Christopher Page, Andrew Parrott, and Bowers in *Early Music*, ix (1981), pp. 71–75, and by Fallows–Specific.

24

Pronunciation Guides

Ross W. Duffin

This is not the place to give more than the briefest recommendations on the historical pronunciation of languages commonly used in early music. Historical pronunciation is a gargantuan subject—witness the volume on the subject edited by Timothy McGee and co-authored by several scholars: *Singing Early Music: An Introductory Guide to the Pronunciation of European Languages in the Middle Ages and Renaissance,* forthcoming from Indiana University Press at the time of this writing. It is nonetheless an important subject and one demanding the attention of the early-music director in order to get the most natural sonorous effect out of each work. Composers set texts with the ambient pronunciation in mind and that includes Latin texts, too. Accentuation, rhyme, and the sheer tone color of a vocal work can be radically transformed by the use of historically appropriate pronunciations.

My own predilection to obsession in this area was tempered several years ago. I was coaching a student medieval ensemble in the performance of one of the two mid-fifteenth-century English songs discussed and edited by David Fallows in a then recent *Early Music Magazine* (1977, pp. 38–43, musical supplement *EM* 28). I had invited a specialist in late-medieval English to attend a rehearsal and coach the group on pronunciation. She listened to the work, asked the date (ca. 1450), gave a few pronunciations, frowned, and asked if the date was really accurate. I told her that the musical setting was from about 1450 but that the text was from John Lydgate's *Temple of Glas* (ca. 1420). "Well," she said, "which do you want, 1420 or 1450?"

Pronunciations change rapidly, as the PBS series *The Story of English* illustrated so well in the segment on "received" pronunciation at English public schools over the last generation. Furthermore, contemporary regional differences are often more striking than generational—one thinks of American accents like those of Maine, Brooklyn, Georgia. Do we really have much hope of nailing down exactly what Renaissance composers had in mind, removed as we are by several centuries and thousands of miles from the point of origin? The answer is, probably not, but we have to try. Even if this means that we approach some kind of standardization within a country and within, say, a century, it is better than not paying any attention to proper pronunciation at all.

Now that we have a central source on historical pronunciation for singers, it should no longer be necessary to search through tomes on history, pronunciation, and orthography of the language in question except to answer the most detailed questions. But for those without *Singing Early Music*, and for those who wish to pursue some questions in more detail, the information that follows may be useful.

First of all, it must be said that historical pronunciations cannot replace good diction as a way of putting texts across to an audience. And it is also true that many aspects of modern pronunciation and inflection for these languages carry over to their Renaissance forms as well. Still, the differences between the current and historical pronunciations are sometimes an important key to an overall change in sound or effect.

In **French**, for example, the vowel combination *oi* was pronounced [wɛ], as in the modern English *west; au* was [ɑo] up to the early sixteenth century and [o] thereafter; *r* was dental rather than uvular as it is in modern spoken French; *o* was frequently pronounced [u], especially in situations where the spelling eventually changed to that, as in *joissance* = *jouissance*; the final *s* was silent except at the end of a poetic line; and up to around 1500, nasalizing consonants were pronounced in addition to the nasalized vowels.

In **German**, one of the main differences was that *sp* and *st* were frequently pronounced as they are in English, not [ʃp] and [ʃt] as they are in modern German. This was especially true in the northwest part of Germany.

In **Italian**, many of the regional differences of today existed in the Renaissance as well. These include the soft *c*, which, besides its usual [tʃ], was also heard as [ts], [s], and [ʃ] in various regions. Soft *g* was frequently pronounced [dz] or even [z] in the north.

In **Spanish**, perhaps the most obvious differences are in the pronunciation of soft *c* or *ç*, which was either [ts] or [s], the *z*, which was probably [ds], and the *x*, the *j* and the soft *g*, all of which were [ʒ] like the modern French *j*, or a cross between that and [ʃ].

In **English**, the period of the Renaissance corresponds to what linguistic historians call the "Great Vowel Shift." The long *i*, for example, changed throughout this period from the diphthong [ɪi] to [əi] (eventually becoming the modern [ɑi] by the eighteenth century). The long *a* moved from [ɑ] to [æ] as in modern English *bad*, or [ɛ] as in *bed*, not [ei] as it is heard in modern English. The vowel combination *ea* in the sixteenth century was usually [ɛ], as preserved in the modern English pronunciation of *head* and *pleasure*. The pattern *ti* as occurring frequently in the ending *-tion* was probably [si] up to around 1600 when it began shifting to [ʃi] and [ʃ] as it is in modern English. Again, the regional variants were numerous, compounding the difficulty of dealing with the chronological changes.

After *Singing Early Music*, perhaps the most convenient source for pronunciation guides to English (1100–1450, Elizabethan), French (1100–

1600), and German (1050–1500) is Phillips/Jackson–*Performing*. The French language portion is taken from Alton/Jeffery–*Bele* (it also covers Provençal, Picard, and Norman). For even more detail on French texts, you might consult such texts as Bourciez–*Phonetique*; Brunot–*Histoire*; and Fouche–*Phonetique*.

A fourth linguistic text also containing information on Provençal, Spanish, Portuguese, Italian, and Romanian is Bourciez–*Elements*. Another source for Portuguese is Williams–*From Latin*.

A volume specializing in the Italian language is Grandgent–*From Latin*.

There are not many studies of historical German pronunciation. Two useful sources are Bithell–*German* and Penzl–*Vom Urgermanischen*.

Three linguistic texts on the English language, including information on the early Renaissance (omitted in Phillips/Jackson), are Dobson–*English*; Ellis–*On Early* (this is old but encyclopedic); and Pyles–*Origins*.

Since Latin was essentially pronounced like the vernacular languages during the period covered by this study, the pronunciation guides for those languages are fundamentally the same as for regional Latin pronunciations. There are some variants from vernacular practice, however, as well as specific information about Latin pronunciations, and these are discussed in the following: Copeman–*Singing* (Harold Copeman also collaborated with George Rigg on Latin Pronunciation in *Singing Early Music.*); Duffin–National; and Scherr–*Aufführungspraxis* (German Latin pronunciations only).

See also Knighton/Fallows (Wray, Hillier)–*Companion*.

VII

PRACTICAL
CONSIDERATIONS

25

Performance Editions

Frederick Gable

Commercial

The amount of Renaissance music published in commercial performing editions continues to increase steadily, so that only a small sample of the kinds of music available can be given here.

Vocal music of the Renaissance forms a significant part of standard choral repertory and is well represented in many commercial choral collections or single octavo editions. Keep in mind that the works will often be rather heavily edited, transposed, and translated. Both McGee and Phillips and Jackson discuss the problems of editions and offer guidelines for choosing good editions. The most reliable and accurate versions of vocal music are best found in the scholarly editions dealt with below, but *Das Chorwerk* (Moseler Verlag) is an authoritative large series devoted to a wide range of early choral music, as is Doblinger Verlag's *Thesauri Musici* series. The old *Antiqua Chorbuch* (Schott) is a gold mine of German secular and sacred music from the fifteenth through eighteenth centuries. The *Oxford Book of Tudor Anthems* contains many famous English sacred works in a high-quality paperback edition. Also highly recommended are *The Oxford Book of English Madrigals* and *The Oxford Book of Italian Madrigals,* which make a large number of these works available in convenient and authoritative paperback editions. A varied collection of vocal works from the New York Pro Musica repertory can be found in *An Anthology of Early Renaissance Music,* edited by Noah Greenberg and Paul Maynard. Galaxy Music's series of *Invitation to the Madrigal* collections offers a wide range of secular vocal music for various ensembles in a handy-size format.

For the Renaissance instrumental repertory the editions of one publisher will give you many years of music to perform: London Pro Musica Editions. LPM puts out many series, each devoted to a specific type of music: The Attaingnant Dance Prints, Early Dance Music, German Instrumental Music *ca.* 1600, Music for Crumhorns, Renaissance Chansons, Venetian Music *ca.* 1600, The Italian Madrigal, Keyboard Repertory, the miscellaneous series Thesaurus Musicus, Dolce Editions, and others. A complete catalog is probably available from your local music dealer or from Magnamusic in Sharon, Connecticut, Kelischek Workshop in Brasstown, North Carolina, and the Early Music Shop of New England, Brookline, Massachusetts. Most of the early-music specialty shops will have a good selection of LPM's music in stock. The editions normally include introductory notes and authoritative advice on performance, as well as separate parts in many cases. Editorial policies can be trusted to give you accurate music texts.

Schott (London) has long published a good series of English and Italian instrumental music, mainly edited for recorders. The age of the series may make copies hard to obtain, but many libraries will have some selections. Holborne dances, Byrd and Gibbons fantasias, Morley canzonets, some arrangements from English keyboard music, and anonymous Italian dances form some of the repertory in this series.

Two old but continuing series of chamber music contain some Renaissance music: *Hortus musicus* (Bärenreiter) and *Nagels Musik Archiv* (Nagel), although both emphasize Baroque instrumental music. Several other European publishers issue reputable series devoted largely to early instrumental music: Moeck in Germany issues the *Zeitschrift für Spielmusik* and the series *Der Bläserchor*; Musikhaus Pan in Zurich has recently begun a *Fontana di Musica* series of ensemble music from the late sixteenth and seventeenth centuries; *Die Tabulatur* (Hoffmeister) contains music for lute and other plucked string instruments; the *Consortium* series of Heinrichshofen in Wilhelmshaven offers music from the collections of Phalèse and Mainerio, and music by Brade, Gabrieli, Schultz, Simpson, Ferrabosco, and others.

Performing from original notation in a facsimile edition is an instructive challenge for any performer. *Ogni Sorte Editions* published Renaissance music in facsimile notation and modern score with instructions for performing from the original notation. One issue may contain various settings of the same chanson tune, or works by one composer. Many other facsimile editions of sixteenth-century music prints are becoming more easily obtainable. Minkoff Editions of Geneva, Switzerland, has an especially large catalog of music facsimiles, and Garland Publishing of New York has recently begun to issue *Renaissance Music in Facsimile,* a multivolume set of late fifteenth- and sixteenth-century music manuscripts. Other facsimile series are *English Lute Songs in Facsimile, Corpus of Early Music* (in facsimile), some volumes of *Monuments of Music and Music Literature in Facsimile,* and the extensive series of facsimile lute books, *Musical Sources.*

Scholarly

More unusual repertory, specific compositions, or less-often performed Renaissance music can be found in the scholarly editions or monuments of music literature. Sets devoted to the complete works of a composer are the most important of these editions. Complete editions exist for Dufay,

Josquin, Obrecht, Gombert, Byrd, Hassler, Gabrieli, Gesualdo, Goudimel, de Monte, Palestrina, Lassus, and many other Renaissance composers. The American Institute of Musicology dominates the publication of complete works of Renaissance composers via its elegant series *Corpus Mensurabilis Musicæ*.

In the extensive national sets may be found music associated with a single European country: Austria, Germany, England, Spain, France, Italy, Poland, Portugal, Sweden, and others. These and smaller national collections may be found listed by country in McGee's section on Repertory, pages 227–33. Individual volumes of a set may be devoted to Renaissance music, such as "Music of John Dunstable" or "Dowland Ayres" in *Musica Britannica*; the "Glogauer Liederbuch" and works of Senfl in *Das Erbe Deutscher Musik*; secular music of Heinrich Isaac and vocal works of Jacob Handl and Jacobus Vaet in *Denkmäler der Tonkunst in Österreich* (*DTÖ*); chansons of Claude le Jeune and others in *Les Maîtres Musiciens de la Renaissance Française*; motets of Morales and organ works by Cabezón in *Monumentos de la Musica Española*.

Many miscellaneous series provide a wealth of Renaissance music: *Recent Researches in the Music of the Renaissance, Early English Church Music, Corpus of Early Keyboard Music*, 4 vols. of *Smith College Music Archives, Anthology of Music (Das Musikwerk), The English Madrigal School*, and *Music of the Florentine Renaissance*. Garland's ambitious new Renaissance music series includes *The 16th-Century Chanson, Italian Instrumental Music of the 16th and early 17th Centuries, The 16th-Century Madrigal*, and *The 16th-Century Motet*.

The main problem with scholarly editions is gaining access to specific works within a set. This is best done by first consulting A. H. Heyer, *Historical Sets, Collected Editions, and Monuments of Music* (Chicago: American Library Association, 1980) via the composer index volume, or Sidney Charles, *A Handbook of Music and Music Literature in Sets and Series* (New York: Free Press, 1972). Even though these are a bit dated and do not often cite specific pieces but only types of pieces, they are a great aid in finding works of a specific composer in the maze of musical monuments. A handy (and free!) guide to scholarly editions is *Broude Brothers' Musicological Publications: a Reference Catalogue*. Although not indexed and primarily a retail dealer's catalog, its detailed, volume-by-volume listing of all the important collected editions and historical sets is a valuable quick reference source. The *New Grove* articles on individual composers contain works lists with citations leading to published scholarly editions. For the instrumental music repertory the most comprehensive guide to original prints and scholarly editions is Howard M. Brown's *Instrumental Music Printed Before 1600* (Cambridge, MA: Harvard University Press, 1965). An older, yet still valuable bibliographic source is Gustave Reese, *Music of the Renaissance*, revised edition (New York: Norton, 1958). A composer or title entry in the index can direct you to a footnote reference to works published in an older scholarly series, article, or monograph. Often, obscure settings of melodies can be tracked down in this way.

General anthologies of early music form an often overlooked source of music for concert performances and much of the music is not often heard in live or really excellent recorded performances. The most standard anthologies are Davidson and Apel, *Historical Anthology of Music*, Vol. 1 (Cambridge, MA: Harvard University Press, 1949); Schering, *Geschichte der Musik in Beispielen* (Leipzig: Breitkopf & Härtel, 1931); Parrish and Ohl, *Masterpieces of Music before 1750* (New York: Norton, 1951); Parrish, *A Treasury of Early Music* (New York, Norton, 1958); and Palisca, *The Norton Anthology of Western Music*, 2nd ed. (New York: Norton, 1988).

26

Copyright

Phillip Crabtree

Copyright protections are a matter of necessity to the writer and composer, the results of whose creative efforts may be enjoyed by society as a whole long after the works were created. In general, the matter of copyright is little understood by the musician and educator, a factor coupled with a recent law that could prove to be problematic and costly to both individuals and institutions, since the penalties for copyright infringement may be as high as $10,000 to $50,000 for a single violation. It is hoped that the following information will be helpful in gaining an understanding of the purpose, scope, and workings of the present copyright law.

Copyright: Definition and Intent

Copyright protection covers many things, including published books and articles, music, and sound recordings, to cite the most obvious materials affecting musicians. Copyright means literally the "right to copy." In the case of music this right extends both to the music itself and to recorded performances of music. The "exclusive" right to copy in unlimited quantity is reserved to copyright holders—composers and authors, or their agents (commonly, publishers acting on their behalf)—for a limited period of time. The intent of such a law is to protect the creative efforts of such individuals by reserving the rights to their artistic or literary creations for a limited period of time, thus enabling them to benefit monetarily from these creative efforts, while society as a whole enjoys the general enrichment such works provide.

U.S. Copyright Law

The Constitution "empowers Congress to promote the arts and sciences by granting to authors the exclusive rights in their writings for a limited time." The initial U.S. copyright law covering books, charts, and maps dates from

1710, and protection for music was added in 1831. The second major copyright law was enacted in 1909.

The present copyright law, identified as the Copyright Act of 1976, and by various other names, went into effect on January 1, 1978. It differs substantially from the Copyright Act of 1909, which it replaces. One major difference in the new law is the length of protection provided for copyrighted works. For works created after January 1, 1978, the new law provides protection for a period of fifty years beyond the death of the author or composer (or of the last to die, in the case of multiple authors or composers). Works published before this date are protected according to the same formula. This extended protection now more closely resembles the copyright protection provided in other Western countries. Since all countries do not have reciprocal copyright agreements with the United States, international copyright protection as such does not exist. However, the United States is a member of the Universal Copyright Convention (UCC). A list of those countries having copyright agreements with the United States can be secured by requesting *Circular 38a* from the Copyright Office.

Copyrights and Trademarks

To gain copyright a work must be original, and the matter of quantity is part of that consideration. Brief items, such as "names, titles, and other short phrases or expressions," are covered under the Federal Trademark Act. "In general, the Federal trademark statute covers trademarks, service marks, and words, names, or symbols that identify or are capable of distinguishing goods or services" (see *Circular R13 Trademarks*). Trademark protection, as opposed to copyright, is gained through the Commissioner of Patents and Trademarks, Washington, DC 20231.

Securing Copyright

The new copyright law essentially joins two forms of copyright protection under the old law—common law protection and public law—into a single statute. It provides for automatic protection when a work is created, but the work must ultimately be registered to secure a claim. Registration can be done at any time during the period of protection by obtaining the necessary registration forms and related information from the Copyright Office, Library of Congress, Washington, DC 20599.

Registration of a work is accomplished by depositing with the Register of Copyrights two copies of a published work, or one of an unpublished work, along with the completed registration form and designated fee. The following three items are essential components of a proper copyright notice to insure protection: the word Copyright, its abbreviation Copr., or the international symbol ©; the year of first publication of the work; and the name of the copyright owner of the work (an individual or publisher). These items appear together at the bottom of the initial page of a copyrighted work and bear witness to its protection under the copyright act.

For purposes of informing the public of copyrighted works, the U.S. Copyright Office published a *Catalog of Copyright Entries* from 1871 to 1979. Since the new law went into effect new registrations exist only on microfiche in the U.S. Copyright Office. When desirable, this office can be requested to do a copyright search for a nominal hourly search fee.

Fair Use

The copyright law provides for a limitation on the exclusive rights of the copyright owner by the "fair use" privilege, cited in section 107 of the Copyright Law, "for purposes such as criticism, comment, news reporting, teaching (including multiple copies for classroom use), scholarship, or research," but there are specific provisions for each of these. The four factors specified to determine fair use are the following:

1. the purpose and character of the use, including whether such use is of a commercial nature or is for nonprofit educational purposes;
2. the nature of the copyrighted work;
3. the amount and substantiality of the portion used in relation to the copyrighted work as a whole; and
4. the effect of the use upon the potential market for or value of the copyrighted work.

Rather specific guidelines are given for applying these principles, which can be summarized as follows:

1. a single copy may be made by the teacher or scholar for research or study purposes or to prepare for a class;
2. multiple copies for the class may be made if the rules of brevity are followed, i.e., less than a performable unit may be copied, and if each copy carries a copyright notice.

Prohibited Uses

The law specifies the following prohibitions to the fair use doctrine, which should be noted:

1. copying to create or replace or substitute for anthologies, compilations or collective works;

2. copying of or from works intended to be "consumable" in the course of study;
3. copying for the purpose of performance, except in emergency and provided replacement copies are substituted in due course;
4. copying for the purpose of substituting for the purchase of music, except as in 3 and exclusive of performable units; and
5. copying without inclusion of the copyright notice which appears on the printed copy.

Public Domain Works and the Ensemble Director

The director of the early-music ensemble is, for the most part, dealing with public domain works and therefore has special considerations. Works are considered to be in the public domain when one of the following circumstances exists: (1) the work was created prior to the existence of copyright protection, for instance, any of the works by such composers as Josquin des Pres, William Byrd, or J. S. Bach, for example; or (2) the original copyright protection has now expired, as in the case of more recent works. Once material is in the public domain it can never again gain copyright protection. In general, then, the ensemble director can safely draw on such music for study and performance under normal educational circumstances, but note the following.

Newly Copyrighted Editions of Public Domain Works

A potential problem exists in the area of newly copyrighted public domain works, including historical sets and monuments of music. New editions of public domain music should be examined for copyright notices. Where these exist, it should be understood that newly attained copyright protection is not for the music per se—since this has passed into the public domain—but rather for what is termed "editing." Editing can be any of a number of things, including but not limited to the following: reconstructed missing parts; *musica ficta*; phrasing, fingering, bowing, pedaling, and various performing suggestions; realization of a figured bass; and textual translations; as well as editorial or critical notes and prefaces.

Copyright can also cover (1) publishers' anthologies—including works in the public domain—specifically assembled for publication in a given collective format, and (2) editions of public domain works that are the creative result of scholarly collations of manuscripts or early printed sources. With regard to the first instance, one may have free use of the music contained in an anthology of public domain music—though not to the entire anthology as assembled—and not to the prefatorial or other new editorial material, except for a single copy for study purposes. In the second case, the matter is sometimes difficult to determine, but the editorial notes should clarify the scholarly and editorial process leading to the resulting edition. Mere transcriptions of public domain music are not covered by copyright. Thus, from the editor's preface the ensemble director can normally make a considered judgment about what is covered by copyright before providing multiple copies of a public domain work for study or performance in a class or ensemble situation. To summarize, one may have access to public domain music as such, without the newly copyrighted material that often accompanies it.

Certain publishers, such as A-R Editions, Inc., in their *Recent Researches in the Music of the Renaissance* and other series, have provided a creative innovation, for the benefit of their subscribers and patrons of subscribing institutions, known as their Copyright-Sharing Policy, "under which the contents of this volume [and others] may be reproduced free of charge for study or performance." Specific information may be obtained by writing to A-R Editions, Inc., 315 West Gorham Street, Madison, Wisconsin 53703. In the future perhaps other publishers will come up with such creative alternatives for educators and performers relying on the use of works in the public domain.

Recorded Music and Taping of Performances

Recordings, cassette tapes, and CDs are protected by the same copyright restrictions as are books, scores, and other materials. Therefore, they are subject to the same fair use and prohibition guidelines summarized above. For example, a single copy or excerpt of a copyrighted recorded work can reasonably be made under the uniform fair use guidelines that pertain to literary and musical materials. Librarians have special considerations when making recorded examples of music for class use, however. These are spelled out in *Circular R21*, published by the U.S. Copyright Office, and in some of the sources listed below in the Bibliography. The matter of making a single tape or recording of your own performance—whether of public domain or original copyrighted material—if the intent of the recording is for educational purposes, as for example to play back a concert performance for your students, is permissible under the fair use guidelines. But while you can, under the law, make a single tape recording of copyrighted material for your own study purposes or to play back for a student in a lesson, for example, making multiple copies for an entire ensemble or class of students, or for playback over the airwaves—whether by a university radio station, an NPR affiliate, or others—goes outside the stated fair use provisions of the law.

Most schools and universities, as well as radio stations, have special licensing arrangements to cover royalties for performances of copyrighted works, including operas and other dramatic works. These protections normally apply, however, only to composers/editors who are members of such licensing organizations as ASCAP and BMI. Since few scholarly editors are members of such organizations, this common arrangement for collecting royalty fees for certain published music is not in place. Thus, a gray area exists in the case of early-music performances when it comes to collecting royalties for the copyright holder, and litigation might be perceived as the only way to accomplish this. In view of the high penalties that could be levied for infringements of the law, one should be cautious in this area. In any case, when the intent of the performance of a copyrighted work or works (whether for concert or recording) is to generate money, an infraction of the law occurs.

Summary

The matter of copyright protection is a complicated one, and its purpose is to balance the protections of authors and composers of creative works with consumers of music and art in our society. Fair use guidelines are provided for in the new Copyright Act of 1976, but laws are ultimately interpreted in the courts. Care should be exercised not only for one's own protection but even more for that of our collective colleagues, including directors of early-music ensembles, who as composers and editors of early music stand to gain or lose in relation to the public's response to the copyright law.

The large body of public domain material existing in historical sets and monuments (e.g., *Musica Britannica* or *Corpus Mensurabilis Musicæ*) and in composers' complete sets on which early music ensembles heavily rely makes possible easy access to much musical literature for the typical ensemble performing early music. However, one cannot legally copy entire anthologies or newly published performing editions of public domain works containing prefatorial notes or critical commentary, textual translations, new editorial material, figured bass realizations, and the like, or published editions of specific works designated "as performed by" (i.e., any individual edition by a current or recent performing ensemble or conductor that contains their personal performing solutions), often published as so-called "performing editions." Remember, too, that the United States has long-standing reciprocal copyright agreements with many other countries. Thus, foreign editions are often subject to the same copyright restrictions as are works published in this country.

Furthermore, while certain freedom is permitted in the use of copyrighted materials in educational institutions, according to the fair use guidelines, many of these same privileges do not extend to private and professional groups. Even educational institutions should be warned that when any performance of copyrighted material becomes a performance-for-profit circumstance and admission is charged for the generation of profits beyond the normal covering of expenses of the performance, or when the performers are paid, the fair use privilege normally extended to educators is lost. In such instances permission of the copyright holder is required.

Selected Bibliography

Copyright Office Brochures
Circular 1: *Copyright Basics.*
Circular R21: *Reproduction of Copyrighted Works by Educators and Librarians.* (These and other
brochures are available by writing the U.S. Copyright Office, Library of Congress, Washington, DC 20599—or phone 202/707–9100.)

Books
Althouse–*Copyright*; Erickson–*Musician's*; United-National–*Final*; Reed–*Copyright*; Strong–
Copyright.

27

Publicity Guidelines for Early-music Concerts

Beverly Simmons

So much time and effort go into the rehearsal and performance of a concert by the early-music ensemble that publicity often gets forgotten. The result is a small (but undoubtedly appreciative) audience. If a little advance planning—and perhaps a little advance money—is also spent on publicity, that appreciative audience can be a big one.

What Kind of Publicity?

Depending on the time, staff, and budget available to you, you can choose how extensive a publicity campaign to wage. Studies have shown that it takes about seven times for a message to sink in (hence the endless repetition of TV commercials). In surveys of concert audiences, many organizations have found that *everything* contributes to getting people there: posters, mailings, newspaper, radio, magazines, word-of-mouth.

I advise you to try to do all of the above (i.e., everything you can think of and afford), but don't neglect word-of-mouth—that's the most powerful (and the least expensive) form of publicity. Tell everybody you know about the concert, and get your friends and students to tell everybody they know. Then, after somebody they know sees a poster, gets a flyer in the mail, reads it in the newspaper, and hears it on the radio, when a friend calls to ask if she wants to come along to the concert, she will!

In addition, you should:

1. distribute a press release to the local media;
2. send a direct mailing to a targeted audience; and
3. utilize the medium of radio as much as possible to convey the sounds of your instruments and music to your potential audience.

The Press Release

The press release is essential; it is free publicity. Through it your event will at least be listed in local events calendars, and at best be featured in an announcement or advance story (if an editor's interest is sufficiently piqued).

Even if your institution has an Office of University Communications (aka Public Relations), *you*, as director of the early music ensemble, are the best person to write the press release, because you know your artistic goals and can best translate them into words. If you do have a contact person in PR, then draft a press release and send it to her or him for a rewrite in the institution's standard form (you can ask to approve the revised copy, to ensure that only the format and not the meaning has been revised). Then it can be sent to the appropriate media contacts.

In the absence of a PR person, the task of sending out the press release falls to you. For this you need to develop a media list. Start with the listings in the yellow pages under "Newspapers," "Radio," "TV," and so forth. Then call each station and publication to ask for the name and title of the person who receives press releases and the deadline for their receipt.

Start early, because a press release may be required as much as two months in advance of the event, particularly for monthly publications. Newspapers usually require two or three weeks, and radio and television may require only a few days. Figure 27.1 is a Sample Press Release, and Figure 27.2 an outline of Press Release Etiquette.

A picture is worth a thousand words (or notes), and early instruments and musicians are so interesting looking! So by all means get some good photographs made of yourself, your students, the instrument collection, or whatever. Then submit the photo(s) to the major arts magazines and newspapers in your area, along with your concert announcement. Attach a label on the back identifying the people and/or instruments in the photo and crediting the photographer. Tape your press release to the back of the photo, or include both in a folder (aka Press Kit), so they remain together.

Don't forget to send all this information to the student newspaper on your campus, the faculty-staff weekly publication, the student radio station, and other outlets. These are excellent vehicles for publicity, since they are targeted to your audience and have a vested interest in promoting your work.

The Direct Mailing

The fact that every day we get unsolicited mail by the wastebasketful is a tribute to the effectiveness of this means of marketing. An attractive concert announcement that arrives at the home of a potential audience member just might find itself posted on the refrigerator or by the phone, thus serving as a continuous reminder of the upcoming event.

275

FOR IMMEDIATE RELEASE
February 15, 1988

Contact: Tony Holborne
215–555–1212

BIG RED COLLEGIUM MUSICUM IN CONCERT

On Saturday, April 1, 1988, at 8 PM, in the Fine Arts Center of Big Red University, the Collegium Musicum, directed by Dr. Henry Isaacs, will present a concert entitled "Last One In Is a Sackbut: Music for Renaissance Brass." The program features works by 16th- and early 17th-century composers from Italy and England, played on cornetts, sackbuts, and serpents.

The Collegium Musicum was founded in 1971 as an active ensemble in which students study and perform music of the Medieval and Renaissance eras. Because of its richly varied repertoire performed on instruments of great intrinsic appeal, the Collegium Musicum consistently draws enthusiastic audiences from throughout the community to its concerts. Critics have praised the performances as "brassy" and "ornamental," and of the director, it has been said that "nobody is better at blowing his own horn."

The instruments featured in the April 1st concert are modeled after Renaissance instruments extant in European museums. The Sackbut, despite its unusual name, is recognizable to modern audiences as the predecessor of the trombone. The Cornett is a hybrid instrument, made of wood with fingerholes like a recorder, but with a mouthpiece like a trumpet. The Serpent is a bass cornett, curved in a gentle "S" shape, thus resembling visually the animal after which it is named. Overall, the Ensemble's sound is similar to that of a modern brass choir, with a broad pallette of tone colors and expressive possibilities.

Tickets for the Big Red Collegium Musicum performance are $5 regular, $3 seniors and no charge for students; they may be obtained at the door or at the Big Red Department of Music. For more information, call 555–2323.

-30-

FIGURE 27.1 Sample Press Release

Format

At top: "For Immediate Release" & today's date

"Contact" name and phone number (not necessarily the same as "For Info")

At bottom: "-more-" if continued on next page; "-30-" or "###" if end of release

Inverted Pyramid Shape

Start with the most important material, tapering off to least important at end (except for ticket information)

Writing Style

Keep sentences simple (and preferably short)

Vary beginnings of sentences with introductory clauses, etc.

Repeat name of ensemble throughout

Be up-beat and enthusiastic

Twice Too Much Material

Include enough information that it can be cut in half, if necessary (from the bottom up)

First Paragraph: Who, what, where, when, why

Give Hall address, if necessary

Include sponsoring organization name, if appropriate

Debut or other noteworthy feature of performance

Next Paragraph(s): History, Explanation, Details (not necessarily in this order):

Use general terms, keep jargon to a minimum

History of organization gives credentials, e.g., founding date, where it has performed (geography & venue), critical response, impressive accomplishments

Other items of interest: descriptions of instruments, names of composers, unusual or favorite repertoire, etc.

Final Paragraph: Ticket costs and availability. "For Information, call"

Context

Send with cover letter to specific person (call to get correct name and title)

Check deadlines of media (6 weeks ahead, 15 days before beginning of month before ...)

Include photograph, brochure, tentative program, previous reviews, more detailed explanations, references, etc.

FIGURE 27.2 Press Release Etiquette

The printed piece that you send is limited only by your imagination. To get ideas, start collecting brochures and ads, decide what attracts you and what repels you, and trust your judgment. (After all, while your audience members are probably not graphic artists, they will respond positively or not to the flyer.) Early music lends itself to wonderful visual expression through calligraphy, Renaissance or medieval woodcuts or drawings, illustrations of instruments, or musical notation (the Dover publications listed below offer a number of possibilities). If neither you nor your students want to design the flyer, perhaps you can find a graphic-arts student at your institution who will design it for you. For the actual printing your institution's printing office or local "quick-copy" photo-offset printer or photocopy firm will suffice. (Be sure to take advantage of their automatic folding machines, too.)

The most economical way to reach a large number of people through the mail is with a bulk mailing (your institution probably has a bulk mailing permit). Check with the Post Office for their regulations regarding weight, size, and cost (as of this writing, third-class postage for a non-profit organization with a bulk-rate permit is $.081 to $.111 per piece, weighing less than 3.314 oz., and measuring less than 11 1/2″ x 13 1/2″). It is true that preparing hundreds or thousands of flyers for a bulk mailing—labeling, counting, sorting, and bundling according to the Post Office's meticulous rules—is very time consuming. But the labor can be shared in various ways, such as inviting all the musicians to a labeling party, where cameraderie can ameliorate the task's tedium.

Your mailing list should be as large as you can afford, advisably at least five times as big as your audience capacity, because the percentage response for bulk mail alone is not high (it improves when combined with all your other efforts, as discussed above). If you do not already have a mailing list, then start by asking everybody you know to write down the names and addresses of everybody they know; and/or borrow (or rent) a list from another local arts organization with a similar size and type audience as yours. An old mailing list can be updated by printing "Address Correction Requested" on your flyer; if an address is incorrect, the Post Office will return it to you at a charge of about $.29.

Keep the list up to date by having sign-up sheets at all your events. A tried-and-true method of finding out who is attending your concerts is to offer a drawing of some sort, the entry form for which, complete with blanks for names and addresses, is included with the concert program. Definitely use a computer to manage your mailing list.

Other Distribution

Post and distribute announcements of the concert on campus (possibly using the same printed piece that goes out in your mailing). Your institution may have a central service where you can send a pile of posters to be attached to kiosks and bulletin boards around campus. If not, ask a friend of the early-music ensemble to do so and thank him or her with an acknowl-edgment in the program.

Leave piles of flyers in high-traffic areas, such as the student union, local restaurant, bookstore, or record store. If you ask, other arts organizations in the community might be willing to let you stuff their programs or leave your flyers in the lobby for a performance they're giving, as long as you offer to reciprocate. You might be able to send flyers to all the dorms, or to every department in the university, through interdepartmental mail (which is usually free). Public library systems sometimes have such services, as well. Use your imagination and your knowledge of the community.

Radio

Radio can be a very effective means of drawing an audience, because it does not require translation of the aural into visual (as in the flyer) or verbal (as in the press release). It is in your best interest to develop a rapport with the staff of the radio station in your community broadcasting to your potential audience; get to know the music director, general manager, PR person; offer your services as a volunteer; be a contributor or supporter. This can pay off when a concert is impending, because of the many ways radio can serve you in promoting it.

Corresponding to the press release for print media is the public service announcement (PSA) for broadcast media. Radio and television stations used to be required to provide free PSAs every day for a certain percentage of their air time; since deregulation, that is no longer the case. Nevertheless, for good will, community relations, and the like, most stations still offer some PSAs for worthy causes (like early-music concerts). The form for a PSA is similar to that of a press release; however, since it is to be spoken rather than read, it is shorter and a bit more repetitive. PSAs usually run 15, 30, or 60 seconds (time them by reading aloud). Depending on the format of the radio station, you might be able to suggest or produce background music for the spoken announcement (an excerpt taped from an early-music en-semble concert, or a selection from a commercial recording). Accept the possibility that the PSA may be relegated to the 2–5 A.M. time slot; even at that hour, it is a useful tool. See Figure 27.3 for a sample Public Service Announcement.

Should you have a budget for advertising, spending it on radio spots can actually enhance your chances of receiving good PSA coverage. Some radio stations actually match PSAs to ads, essentially giving you more than you pay for. In addition, buying ads allows you to specify the time period (e.g. eve-ning drive-time or just after an early-music broadcast) during which your announcement will be aired. You are not limited to commercial radio sta-tions, because NPR stations, which do not normally carry advertisements, may sell ads to non-profit organizations.

If there is an admission charge for your concert, offer some free tickets

FOR IMMEDIATE RELEASE   Contact: Tony Holborne
February 15, 1988   215–555–1212

MUSIC Up and Under.

ANNOUNCER: Celebrate the season with the splendid sounds of
Renaissance brass. This Saturday at 8 in the University Fine Arts
Center, the Big Red Collegium Musicum presents its spring concert, entitled "Last One in is a Sackbut!" You'll hear dances and
canzonas by 16th- and 17th-century masters played on cornett,
sackbut, and serpent. Tickets are available at the Big Red Department of Music or at the door. For more information, call
555–2323. That's Saturday, April 1st, at 8 PM.

MUSIC Up and Out.

-30-

FIGURE 27.3   Public Service Announcement

through the radio. Arrange with the radio announcer to run ticket
giveaways during the week or two prior to your event, and be sure to supply
lots of attractive music recordings (by your ensemble or others that you ad-
mire) to be played during the contests. Also, by all means, make yourself
available for telephone or in-station interviews!

Despite the prohibitive expense of TV advertising, there's considerable
potential for free publicity on this medium. For example, television stations
also use PSAs. They can air the one that you have made for radio, perhaps
adding a color slide (that you provide) of your campus or your instruments.
They may simply include your event in a calendar of events read at some
point during the broadcast day. A local morning or afternoon program
might jump at the chance to feature a few minutes of live interview-plus-
performance by students in your early-music ensemble (after all, they are
always looking for something out of the ordinary). Or a TV station may send
a crew to film your rehearsal for its local news program. (These latter two
scenarios may require a little lobbying by you or your institution's PR person, not to mention a little extra rehearsing.)

A Word of Encouragement

"Whew!" you may say, "what a lot of work! And all in addition to the programming, rehearsing, and logistics of the concert." Yet, if you think of publicity as not only essential, but also creative, your time and effort spent in
getting the word out can be both satisfying and productive.

Remember that there is a symbiotic relationship between musicians and the public. Your audience, in return for attending the concert, is entertained and enlightened by your performance. Your ensemble, having worked together in rehearsals and concert preparations, gets the invaluable experience of communicating with an audience. And you, wearing your many hats as scholar, musical director, publicist, and more, can enjoy the fruits of these combined labors. It's a win-win-win situation!

Bibliography

Books about Publicity

Highstein–*Making* (see Chapter V, "The Press and Public Relations."); Newman–*Subscribe* (see Chapter 16, "The Development and Use of Mailing Lists," through Chapter 20, "The Boon of Radio and Television Public Service Time."); Papolos–*Performing* (see Chapter 9, "Spreading the News: You and Your Public."); Wolf–*Presenting* (see Chapter 3, "Filling the Auditorium.").

Sources for Illustrations

Appelbaum–*Triumph*; Fraenkel–*Pictorial*; Gillon–*Decorative*.

28

Thoughts on the Program and Its Notes

Dean Nuernberger

Puncti Contra Punctos—*Some Notes Contrary to Notes*

I greatly envy those who can approach the writing of program notes with some degree of pleasure and then can finish them with dispatch. For me at least, the task has remained an onerous one, usually to be undertaken at a most inopportune time, fraught with difficulties, demanding countless revisions, and finally yielding results that often have seemed quite nebulous and even disproportionate to the time and effort I expended.

To devise, research, and direct an early-music program is not unlike running a kind of super marathon race that extends over several months. One must be ever alert to pacing and how energy is to be distributed over the distance so that something is left for that final kick in the home stretch—the concert itself. Early on, the strategy entails a search for music of sufficient merit and stature to last the course. Then aid and support from appropriate historical, literary, and musical sources must be sought and somehow found. Subsequent rehearsals—or turns about the track if you will—determine just how practical and durable the initial choices were. Some works ultimately prove too burdensome and have to be jettisoned and replaced by less weighty counterparts. After an extended interval of considerable experimentation and effort, one finally gains that second wind where some form of unified plan for the entire program takes shape. Appropriate translations for the texts can then be undertaken, dates assigned for the composers chosen, and the nucleus formed for a program that can subsequently be printed. Ironically, just at this point, with the finish and concert now at least within sight, tradition intervenes with an insistence on program notes, which threatens to divert energy and attention desperately needed for the final sprint. For me, the same nagging questions then inevitably surface: Is there not sufficient information in the program already without adding notes? Are notes actually worth the additional effort and energy that will be required at this crucial time? Since notes garner only silence, not response, how can it be known if any bother to read them? Yet, tradition is a formidable adversary! I have always reluctantly surrendered to it, spurred on by a stubbornly recurring conviction that surely some will gain more understanding and enjoyment of the program and the music if commentary is included.

Scylla and Charybdis

My struggles with program notes over the years and my encounters with those written by others have engendered in me several strong prejudices. I have become increasingly intolerant of sprinklings of unproven superlatives such as "unparalleled mastery," "unsurpassed *tour-de-force*," "unique genius," "most outstanding example," which serve only as thinly disguised efforts to shape audience reaction. My aversion extends as well to those equally unproven personal insights that purport to uncover something like a composer's "affirmation of life" in certain of his harmonies; or possibly "a rustic humor" in his rapid scale passages; and perhaps "a defiant spirit," or even "a tragic love affair," in his approach to chromaticism. Effusive evaluations and fantasies can quite rightfully be assumed the prerogative of any individual listener, but not necessarily, I feel, of the writer of program notes.

Finally, I have become equally irritated by that particular academic approach that, determined to account for every facet of the total research undertaken, culminates in a voluminous biographical, historical, and political survey—usually resting on top of a thicket of corroborating footnotes. Obviously patterning the program notes after those commonly found in record albums, the writer fails to recognize the significant differences between a live performance and a recording. A recording, capable of infinite-replayings, becomes a multiple event in time over which the listener has complete control—any segment of a record or CD can be selected, repeated, or interrupted at whim with relevant portions of the accompanying notes then either consulted or ignored at the listener's pleasure. A live performance, in marked contrast, is a unique event in time over which the audience has no control—minimal pauses between works or dim lights in the recital hall may even make any sustained reading impossible. Furthermore, since there is but one opportunity to enjoy and attempt to follow the formidable mix of compositions peculiar to most early-music programs, few persons will be disposed to direct even more of their attention and concentration toward unraveling a complex written discourse. Overly comprehensive notes simply pose a labyrinthine maze that most listeners will be forced either to glance over quickly or, far more likely, to circumvent.

Effusion and excess are consequently, I submit, the Scylla and Charybdis for program notes. If the writer can thread his way carefully through the narrow strait that separates these two perils, he may possibly even guide his audience safely beyond to the glories of the music itself.

Verbal Program Notes—Time Instead of Space

There remains, of course, as a substitute for written program notes, the oral alternative. The Canadian Brass and King's Singers have perhaps most successfully explored and popularized this possibility. On review, however, I believe their successes stem far more from their comedic skill and timing than from any general appreciation and interest in the musicological information they might impart. Within the context of a program demanding primarily serious commentary, those in attendance are much more prone to become restless and, subsequently, bored. Whereas anyone may elect not to read written program notes, all are compelled to forfeit equal amounts of time whether they choose either to ignore or to heed spoken explanations. Speech can thus easily become merely a common barrier that indiscriminately prohibits an audience more immediate access to the music itself. Patience and curiosity are frequently not strong enough in many individuals to overcome such a challenge. As a consequence, oral commentary, unless done by exceptionally skilled and knowledgeable speakers, is often more likely to alienate a listener than to provoke his interest.

Some Remaining Options

If one then finally elects to write the explanations for the music to be performed and can successfully avoid effusive and excessive commentary, what acceptable possibilities remain? The options depend on the type of performing organization and the make-up of each individual program.

Traditional orchestral concerts that feature a guest vocalist or instrumentalist ordinarily comprise four or five works of moderate length. The music is most often relatively familiar, so few notes beyond obligatory translations and dates for composers are usually necessary. A brief biographical sketch of the visiting artist, coupled with a short summary of each work and its particular relationship to the life of the composer, normally suffices. An early-music program, in stark contrast, usually introduces about twenty-five short works that are virtually unknown to most of the audience. The effectiveness of the program notes will now depend primarily on how well and how concisely the program itself is organized.

Since most early-music ensembles are associated with educational institutions, their programs should endeavor not only to provide musical entertainment, but to educate as well. The most efficient means of accomplishing both aims, while avoiding a tangle of disjointed explanatory notes in the process, is to structure a program around a central topic or theme. Once a suitable focus is established, the commentary can then relate all of the works in some manner to the subject chosen. I personally prefer topics that are not specifically musical in nature. The music itself can then provide the subject matter with entirely new and unique perspectives.

One of our early-music programs, "The Composer as Geometer," divided a variety of canonic works into four different groups, each of which represented a type of geometric symmetry. Those canons exhibiting retrogrades and inversions illustrated bilateral symmetry; perpetual canons traversing through a cycle of keys, or canons employing a prime simultaneously with its retrograde inversion (i.e., the crossword diagram), represented aspects of rotational symmetry; strict canonic imitations at any of the various intervals demonstrated translatory symmetry; and canons with augmentation or diminution in various proportional relationships portrayed dynamic symmetry. Supported by appropriate diagrams and geometric figures, the program notes amounted simply to a composite of the explanatory sentences that prefaced each composition to associate the form and order of the canonic entries present with the corresponding type of symmetry.

Another of our programs, entitled "Prosody, Poetry, Melody," separated various madrigals, hymns, motets, and lute songs into categories corresponding to the specific types of meter found in the texts: classical prototypes, octosyllabics, decasyllabics, or fixed forms (*sonnet, terza rima, sestina,* etc.). This format produced interesting examples of poems that, although markedly dissimilar in content and mood, were constructed in similar meters and set to identical melodies. Explanatory notes, when supplemented under each of the headings within the program by appropriate letter diagrams for the rhyme schemes, seemed in this instance best assembled at the end of the program in short paragraphs that corresponded to each of the metrical types.

Positioning

If the works within each major division of the program share sufficient mutual characteristics, commentary can best be generalized into single paragraphs for each division and then assembled at the end of the program as a synopsis or a short general essay. Clearly, this procedure provides the best solution for meeting deadlines. The bulk of the program can then be submitted early to the printer, and the final page for notes can be retained to undergo further thought and revision. If each of the works, however, should differ sufficiently from the others within a section to require an individual explanation, the respective comments are then better broken up into short sentences and placed within the program itself before each of the compositions under discussion. The listener is thus spared numerous annoying page turns. Substantial amounts of writing will also be reduced, if both works and explanations are carefully organized into specific categories and placed under appropriate headings and subheadings within the program.

Pruning

One of the most difficult aspects of finalizing any program and the accompanying notes is summoning up the courage to abandon redundancies and, in a truly Darwinian sense, to select only the strongest of several like specimens. There is a curious human tendency to protect zealously every aspect of the total effort that has gone into both the rehearsals and the research for a performance. That effort seems somehow jeopardized if any work or concept is subsequently dropped, particularly at a late date, from the program. Of much more importance, however, is any action taken for the betterment of the entire concert. When material previously selected or undertaken proves inappropriate at any time, it must be discarded or replaced without remorse or regret. An entire program, or even section of a program, restricted to the same mood, tonality, tempo, or dynamic level can become oppressively dull. The most eloquent composition will suffer if it is surrounded by compositions of the same type or placed next to a work of equal eloquence. Even a composer of the stature of Josquin or Lassus becomes wearisome if he is represented solely by a cluster of his greatest motets—all of similar solemnity. Unity without any variety threatens to become tedious, just as variety without unity tends to become chaotic.

Summation

It was never the intent of this chapter to dismiss program notes as either unnecessary or irrelevant, or to denigrate the efforts of those who rise to the challenge and succeed in a variety of ways to master them. The ideal set of notes, like the ideal performance, is something for which one ever strives but never attains. My own reluctance to write them stems essentially from dread of the enormity of the difficulties and responsibilities with which I know I must inevitably contend each time. Program notes for any live performance, if read, regardless of how well written, will still remain a certain imposition on the time and patience of those for whom they are intended. To justify that imposition I believe the writer must constantly strive to present only the most significant and pertinent facts in the most succinct and lucid manner. Sentences and paragraphs must tend to be ever shorter, language ever less convoluted, and thoughts ever more cogent and readily understandable. Notes should provide a gateway, not an obstacle, to the music on the program. The listener deserves the quickest, simplest, and most pleasant route to that gate.

Bibliography

Knighton/Fallows (Pickett)–*Companion*.

VIII

ASPECTS OF
RENAISSANCE
THEORY

29

Renaissance Theory*

Sarah Mead

Despite the common division between the academic and applied aspects of music, most teachers of performance also find themselves teaching the structure and historical context of the music. While someone coaching a Haydn string quartet can rely on the students having a basic understanding of the language of tonal music, those who teach the music of other cultures or periods need to give their students more detailed guidance in understanding the music in its own context. Thus, the director of an early-music ensemble is called on to be familiar not only with several families of instruments, vocal production, repertory, and performance practice, but with the theory of the music as well, and effective and concise ways to teach its applications in a non-lecture setting.

Although this century has seen a growing interest in atonal music, people of Western cultures are most commonly exposed to tonal sounds in the media, and most would have no problem recognizing a tonal cadence. This inherent bias can make it difficult for us to hear pretonal music except in tonal terms. Yet, although we recognize the music of the European Renaissance as an ancestor of our modern tonality, those who lived in sixteenth-century Europe might have difficulty recognizing its distant progeny today. We can better understand Beethoven when we have studied Mozart, and Wagner when we have studied Beethoven, but if we tried to reverse this and understand Mozart in terms of nineteenth-century thinking, we would be missing much of the point. For the same reason, today's students of early music need some way to approach the music of the Renaissance from its own perspective and not through hindsight.

This chapter is not intended to be a complete or in-depth resource for pretonal theory, but a practical introduction for performers. Just as it is not necessary for a performer of contemporary music to understand all the complexities of set-theory to create a sensitive performance, so it is not a prerequisite for the intelligent and musical performance of sixteenth-

---

* This chapter draws on a series of articles originally published in *Boston Early Music News* (1984–1985), and subsequently reprinted as an instructional pamphlet entitled "Plain & Easy: A Practical Introduction to Renaissance Music."

century music for the performers to have pursued advanced studies in musicology. But there are aspects of Renaissance theory that are directly applicable to performance, and an understanding of their derivation and use will enhance the quality of any performing, reading, or listening experience. These condensed descriptions encapsulate the material that I have found useful to introduce into my own coaching and can serve either as a refresher to the ensemble director or as a direct resource for the students.

The Gamut, Hexachords, and Solmization

In the sixteenth century, children of the educated classes began their music instruction almost as early as they learned to read and write. Music, considered one of the seven basic subjects necessary to a well-rounded education, had its place in daily lessons along with such fields as philosophy, theology, and astronomy. Not only was an educated person expected to be able to sing and play an instrument, but also to understand the basic theoretical rules of notation and composition, to sight-sing, and to provide counterpoint *ex tempore.* Just as the alphabet is the cornerstone of reading and writing, the Gamut was taught to children as the cornerstone of music.

The Gamut, like the alphabet, is a system used to organize and define a series of sounds. The Gamut, however, is used to name the notes of the scale, rather than the sounds of speech. Like most aspects of Renaissance music theory, it was first developed in the Middle Ages; in this case, as an aid in teaching sight-singing to monks. Guido d'Arezzo, an eleventh-century Italian monk, apparently first introduced the six syllables used in the Gamut as a way of memorizing intervals in the note sequence C-D-E-F-G-A. He used a chant known to most novices, "*Ut queant laxis,*" as the source of his syllable names. As seen in Example 29.1, each phrase of this chant starts one step higher than the preceding one, starting with C at the beginning of the first phrase, and ending with A at the beginning of the last. The syllable that began each phrase of text in the original hymn was taken by Guido as the syllable to represent that pitch. Thus the six syllables *ut, re, mi, fa, sol, la* were assigned to the six ascending notes:

EX. 29.1 The hymn *"Ut queant laxis"*

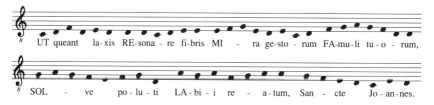

You will recognize these syllables as the basis of our modern solfège in which "ut" has been changed to a more singable "do" and "ti" or "si" has been added as the seventh note of the scale. (The syllable "si," first added in the seventeenth century, was probably derived from the initials of "Sancte Ioannes," found at the end of the chant.)

In the sequence of six notes from C to A, the only semitone occurs between E and F, the third and fourth notes, to which the syllables *mi* and *fa* are assigned. This same pattern of whole and half steps can be found by starting at G and ascending through E. Once again, the semitone appears between the third and fourth notes, this time B to C. This pattern of six notes, known as a "hexachord," can also be found by starting at F, if a B-flat is added. The medieval notation for a B-natural was ♮, a square or "hard" B, while the symbol for B-flat was ♭, known as the round or "soft" B. (These distinctions are still seen in the German expressions "*B dur*" and "*B moll*.") The hexachord on G thus became known as the "hard" hexachord, the one on F as the "soft" hexachord, while the original one, on C, was called the "natural" hexachord. You can see the origin of our modern accidental signs in these early symbols for natural and flat.

By overlapping a series of hexachords—natural, soft, and hard—a whole range of notes could be produced, each with a particular syllable or set of syllables attached to it. Medieval theorists combined seven hexachords to make up a range of twenty notes, from G an octave and a fourth below our modern middle C, to E an octave and a third above it. This range was adequate to accommodate the music of the Middle Ages, since the human voice (created by God) was considered to be the model for all the lesser instruments (created by man), and the twenty notes thus outlined covered the average range of an all-male choir. As Thomas Morley put it in his *A Plaine and Easie Introduction to Practicall Musicke* of 1597, "That compass was the reach of most voices, so that under *Gam ut* (the lowest note) the voice seemed as a kind of humming, and above E *la* (the highest) a kind of constrained shrieking." Even though by the fifteenth century both vocal and instrumental music had pushed beyond these bounds, these twenty notes continued to be the basic "alphabet" for music students through the sixteenth century. Example 29.2 shows how the seven hexachords are overlapped to create the full Gamut:

EX. 29.2 The full Gamut

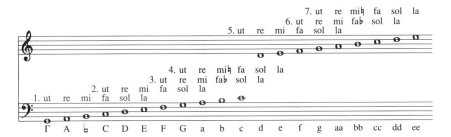

As you can see, most of the notes have more than one syllable associated with them. Thus, the entire name of a note, such as "C *sol fa ut*," could specify a particular pitch. In this case, we know that middle C has been named, not the octave below ("C *fa ut*"), or the octave above ("C *sol fa*"). Five notes have the same names in two different octaves starting with "E *la mi*." These could be differentiated by register as Morley does by calling the upper of the two Es "E *la mi in alt.*" Often the various syllables belonging to a note were combined to make up a single word, as in "*delasol.*" At least one Renaissance musician took such a word as his *nom de plume;* the early sixteenth-century music scribe Peter van der Hove went by the name of "Petrus Alamire," not only in his musical career, but also as a spy for Henry VIII.

Octaves were further differentiated in most treatises by using different alphabets or letter-types, as shown in the above example. The bottommost G was represented by the Greek G, "Γ" or *Gamma.* Its full name, "*Gamma ut*" or "*Gam ut*," came to represent not only the lowest note but the full range of notes. Our modern use of the word in such phrases as "it ran the full gamut of emotions" derives from its Renaissance meaning of the complete scale or range.

By the thirteenth century the mnemonic aid known as the "Guidonian Hand" was being used to train students in the notes of the Gamut. Named for the monk Guido d'Arezzo, it assigned each of the twenty notes to a different joint of the left hand (Fig. 29.1). The teacher could then hold up his open left hand and point to the various joints with his right index finger, while the students sang the notes indicated. Nowadays we have hand signals representing the solfège syllables, and a teacher can similarly lead a class through sight-singing exercises by hand. Pictures of the Guidonian Hand continue to be found in music textbooks throughout the sixteenth century, and the Hand was used by more conservative theorists as a ground for protesting against the avant-garde use of chromaticism. Chromatic notes, such as E♭, were considered "outside the hand" (*extra manum*) and thus not justifiable.

Although most notes on the Guidonian Hand are identified by more than one syllable, only one is actually used in singing, depending on the context in which the note appears. Within this system, most notes can take on several functions. In the natural hexachord, for example, D is called *re* and is the first whole step above *ut.* In the hard hexachord, the same note is called *sol* and functions as the fifth above *ut.* Since in modal as well as tonal music the fifth is a very strong interval, and the fifth note of a scale is second in importance only to the first note, D-*sol* functions differently, both musically and psychologically, from D-*re.* In the soft hexachord D is called *la,* and serves as the topmost note of the hexachord, a sixth above *ut,* yet another very different function. In the same way the note E can have two different functions, depending on which hexachord is considered. In the natural hexachord it is called *mi* and is the lower member of the *mi-fa* semitone. In

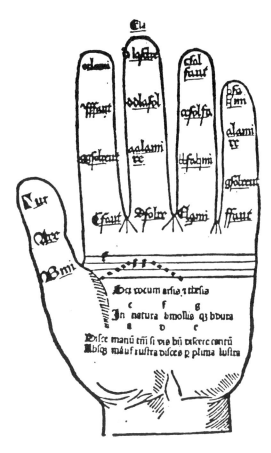

FIGURE 29.1 The Guidonian Hand

the hard hexachord it is *la* and, as the top of the hexachord, has no relationship with the F above it.

Of all the notes only B and its flat have a single function. B is not found at all in the natural or soft hexachords, while in the hard hexachord it is a *mi*, related to the C above it as a half of the *mi-fa* semitone. Similarly B-flat is only found once, in the soft hexachord, where it is called *fa*, and functions as the upper member of the *mi-fa* semitone. Because of these two very different rôles for the two types of B, the term B-flat was not really necessary. In the Renaissance it was known instead as *befa*, while the natural B was called *bemi*, thus distinguishing the two Bs by their functions in the hexachord system.

With all the notes of the diatonic scale, as well as B-flat, thus covered, it was possible for students to solmize most melodies. The term "solmization" means the assigning of syllables to individual notes as an aid to remembering pitch relationships. Such aids are found throughout music history, both in Western music and in the Orient. Many systems of syllables have been tried in the past 300 years, but the one that came from *ut-re-mi-fa-sol-la* has remained the most popular as our modern solfège.

The three hexachords appear to serve very nicely as solmization tools so long as a melody is confined to one of these sets of six notes. But what happens if a line of music goes beyond the boundaries of a given hexachord? Since the hexachords overlap, and most notes have more than one possible function, it is possible to move or "mutate" from one hexachord to another in order to encompass a larger range of notes. This idea seems simple enough in theory, but can at first seem confusing to apply in practice. How do we know with which hexachord to begin? When is it best to mutate?

In many instances each phrase of a melody will fall within the compass of one hexachord, particularly in music from the early part of the sixteenth century. In this case it is relatively easy to choose which hexachord will accommodate the phrase and mutate as necessary to fit the next one. In pieces with less simple melodic structures, more thought is necessary. It can help to consider first the mode of the melody and its range. If there is a B-flat in the key signature, then probably the soft and natural hexachords will be most often used, the hard hexachord only coming into use if a B-natural is introduced. The lowest and highest notes of the phrase will dictate in part which hexachords will be needed to encompass them.

Although many sixteenth-century theorists give examples of mutation, it becomes clear from the rules and examples that the choice of where to mutate was quite subjective. Still, it makes sense to base the solmization of a line on musical factors, and thus to use syllables that not only help in reading the intervals but also illustrate the shape of the line. In Example 29.3, all but the last three notes fall within the compass of the natural hexachord.

EX. 29.3   Sample melody for solmization

Mutation could then take place after A-*la* (which can also function as *re*), so that the last five notes could be solmized *sol-la-mi-mi-fa*. However, with this interpretation the last three notes appear simply to have been tacked on, not acting as part of the whole phrase. If you sing or play the melody, you may notice that the last five notes have the same configuration as the first five, and if considered in the hard hexachord, they can be sung to the same syllables, *ut-re-mi-mi-fa*. Using the same syllables for the beginning and end of the phrase illustrates its symmetry and helps the singer to hear it. Some theorists state that *ut* can only be used on the lowest note of any given phrase, however. Since G functions in this phrase as both *sol* and *ut* (as the note on which the mutation occurs), purists would say that it should be sung as *sol,* C having already been defined as *ut.* The whole phrase would then be solmized thus: *ut-re-mi-mi-fa-re-mi-mi-sol-re-mi-mi-fa.* The repeated *re-mi-mi,* sung three times, also gives shape to the phrase.

It might appear that such a system requires so much intellectualization that it would be impossible to use it to sight-read without first working out and writing down the syllables. However, the system grew out of and, in turn, was the basis for, the music of the time. You will find that when the hexachord system of solmization is put into practice, it very quickly becomes second nature, since it fits the patterns of the music so well. Example 29.4 shows how a longer phrase of music might be solmized (from Thomas Morley's "La Caccia"):

EX. 29.4 Opening of Morley's "La Caccia" solmized

This system continued to be useful in sight-singing until the introduction of real chromaticism. Individual sharps or flats, added at cadences or as word-painting, could be seen in their context, related in function to the notes around them. Thus, most sharpened notes served as the lower half of a semitone and could be called *mi,* while flattened notes, whether or not they were Bs, were sung as *fa.* These *mis* and *fas* were therefore borrowed from fictitious hexachords. This system was particularly necessary in transposed modes, which will be discussed in the next section.

The term "hexachord" is actually a modern invention. Throughout the Middle Ages and Renaissance the six notes of the hexachord were known as the *sex voces* or *voces musicales,* the word *vox* in this case meaning "note" or "pitch." The term *voces musicales* can be found in the titles of many compositions. In Josquin's *Missa L'Homme Armé super voces musicales* the melody used as the *cantus firmus* is repeated at successively higher pitches, starting at C and going through A. In Ludwig Senfl's beautiful *Fortuna ad voces musicales,* there are two *cantus firmi,* the *Fortuna* melody and the hexachord, which is played in the way it was often taught to beginners, as a succession of building blocks, "*ut, ut-re, ut-re-mi, ut-re-mi-fa. . . .*"

Many works of the sixteenth and seventeenth centuries were based on the hexachord itself. Ferrabosco wrote at least three complex chromatic fantasies for viols in which one part plays eight successive descending hexachords as a *cantus firmus,* each starting a semitone below the previous one. Often the syllables of the hexachord were used in the title of a piece to illustrate its opening motive, as in Isaac's *La mi la sol,* which begins A-E-A-G, or Ockeghem's Missa *Mi-Mi,* which used the interval A–E throughout its movements. Syllables were also used as puns in Josquin's *Vive le Roy*; the vowels u-i-u-e-e-o-i found in the title (the letters v and u, as well as i and y, were interchangeable in the Renaissance) were translated by Josquin into the hexachord syllables with those same vowels, and "*ut-mi-ut-re-re-sol-mi*" became the *cantus firmus*.

Composers often could not resist the temptation in texted music to set the syllables of text that sounded like hexachord syllables to their appropriate pitches. The Italian words "*Mi fa . . .*" ("it makes me . . .") appear in a number of madrigal texts, and, as might be expected, are usually set to a rising semitone. Josquin's *Missa La Sol Fa Re Mi*, it is said, got its *cantus firmus* from a clerical in-joke: apparently a powerful man of the church habitually put off his responsibilities with the phrase "Lascia fare mi" ("leave it to me"). His catchphrase became the basis of more than one musical pun.

Students in the Renaissance learned the names and sounds of the pitches of the hexachord first and then the intervallic relationships between them. Their sung exercises would have been familiar to all educated people. As noted above, several composers used these familiar exercises as thematic material or as the *cantus firmus* of a new composition. Singing these lines with their syllables can help a modern student to become familiar with the syllables and to get a sense of some of the teaching devices of the sixteenth century. I have found it useful to have students practice the hexachord and the basic intervals by singing the second *cantus firmus* of Senfl's setting of *Fortuna* described above, first alone and then in the context of the piece. A useful example for practicing solmization and mutation is Ferrabosco I's *Ut re mi fa sol la* (*Musica Britannica* XLIV, *Elizabethan Consort Music*, p. 2), which uses the six notes of the natural and soft hexachord as the basis of all three parts. Knowledge of the Gamut helps students to develop their skills in sight-reading through solmization and to hear more clearly the relationships between the voices. Familiarity with the Gamut also helps us to break away from our own tonal concepts of the scale and allows us to accept more easily the idea of the modes. An understanding of the hexachord can further help in making decisions about the use of *musica ficta*, which will be discussed in a later section.

The Modes and Modality in Polyphonic Music

Since the mid-seventeenth century the majority of Western music has been written in one of two modes: major or minor. Although in the past century many composers abandoned tonality altogether, our popular music continues to be based on these two modes. We associate particular moods with the two modes; American children will be quick to tell you that a minor piece is sad or frightening, no matter what the text, while the major mode connotes contentment, joy, or celebration.

Actually, despite the strong associations, the difference between any of the modes is quite small when analyzed. A mode is defined by the pattern of whole steps and half steps that makes up the scale whose notes are used in a given composition. In the major mode the half steps occur between the 3rd and 4th and the 7th and 8th degrees of the scale, while in the minor they are found between the 2nd and 3rd and the 5th and 6th degrees. We thus distinguish the two modes by the inflection of the third and sixth above the tonic.

Prior to the late seventeenth century, many more modes were recognized by theorists and used in composition. The characteristics of eight modes had been set down in the Middle Ages to help codify chant melodies. Theorists found that the existing melodies could be categorized by the "final," or last note of the chant, by the "species" of fifth and fourth used in the melody (that is, the sequence of tones and semitones making up those intervals), the "ambitus," or range of the chant, and the types of leaps commonly used. Each of these modes was also associated with a particular repercussion or psalm-tone tenor, the pitch at which the psalm would be intoned.

The modes could be divided into four "authentic" and four related "plagal" modes (Example 29.5). Each of the four authentic modes was built from one of the four species of fifth, to which an ascending fourth (one of three species) was added to create the full octave. The bottom of the fifth served as the final. Their associated plagal modes were built by causing the same fourth to descend from the bottom of the fifth, thus making an ambitus one-fourth lower. The lowest note of the fifth remained the final. The plagal thus shared with its authentic the species of fourth and fifth, as well as the final, but had a different range and repercussion. The repercussion or reciting tone for the authentic falls one fifth above the final, except when this would be a B in which case it is raised to a C. The repercussion for the plagal falls one third below that of its related authentic, with the same exception. Thus, although we tend to view the eight modes today as scale patterns, they were seen at the time to be made up of smaller building blocks.

EX. 29.5 Modes, Species, Repercussions

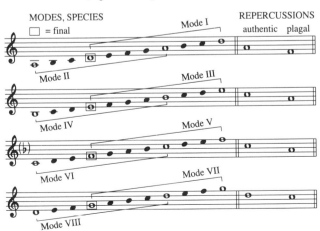

Still, a keyboard can help us in visualizing these modes. The authentic modes can be found by playing a scale of all white notes starting, respectively, on D (I), E (III), F (V), and G (VII). In these four modes the final is the note on which the scale begins. The four plagal modes are derived from the other four, each having a range one fourth below that of its related authentic, but sharing its final. For example, Mode I begins with the fifth from D to A, with the pattern TSTT (T = tone, S = semitone), and is completed by the fourth from A to D with the pattern TST. Mode II, its associated plagal, is based on the same species of fifth, but descends below it from D down to A in the same pattern of tones and semitones. The final in both cases is D. If you continue this pattern, you will find that when you get to the eighth mode you are repeating the scale you had played for the first mode. What, then, is the difference? Actually, it is quite great, if viewed not as a scale but as a combination of smaller units. The species of fifth on which this mode is based can be heard in the interval from G to D with the pattern TTST. When the fourth from D to G (TST) is added below, you do get the same pitches as in Mode I, but with a different final (G), and a different species of fifth. In the first mode the principal degrees will be D and A. In the eighth they will be G and D (as well as C, its repercussion). As a result the compositions based on these two modes will be quite different.

With the advent of polyphony this form of analysis became more difficult. The types of intervallic leaps became determined by the simultaneities of multiple parts, and could no longer be seen as characteristics of a mode. The ranges of the individual voices differed and so could not easily help to identify the mode of the piece. Theorists struggled to adapt their analysis to the new challenges and developed ways of describing polyphony in modal terms. Since compositions were usually based on the tenor or tenor-soprano pair, with other parts added subsequently, the mode of the piece could usually be defined by those primary voices, their ranges, species of fifth and fourth, and the pitches used for points of imitation and cadences. The secondary voices (alto and bass) will usually fall in the associated plagal mode with its lower ambitus.

Renaissance scholars looked back to the writings of antiquity for models to support their theories. Although the music of ancient Greece must have differed enormously from their own, elaborate reconstructions of archaic theory were undertaken in order to create the sense of an unbroken tie to the past. Thus, the eight church modes became associated with Greek modes and were often referred to, respectively, as Dorian, Phrygian, Lydian, and Mixolydian for the four authentics and Hypodorian, Hypophrygian, and so forth for their plagals.

The Greeks wrote of their modes as having emotional associations, sometimes so strong as to elicit changes in the behavior of the listener. Although Renaissance theorists supported this idea in their descriptions of the modes, they did not always agree on the affects of the modes. They also allowed for the fact that both the composer and the performer could have an effect on how the mood of the piece is perceived. Our current two-mode system does not allow for the subtleties of affect associated with a wider range of modes, and we are sometimes surprised today to find that those modes most closely related to our own major and minor did not always carry the same significance in the sixteenth century. For example, Mode VI, despite its similarities to our C Major, was categorized as "mournful," "pious," and "lachrymose," while Mode VIII, with a melodic minor third in the lower tetrachord, was "gladdening," "agreeable," and "sweet" to the late medieval theorists who served as sources for Renaissance writers.

Since the modes were characterized by their species of fifth and fourth, they could be transposed with the aid of signature flats. Thus, a melody starting and ending on G, with a B-flat in the key signature, would still be called Mode I, rather than Mode VII. The final would now be G and the repercussion D, just as they are in the seventh mode, but the sound of the first mode would be unchanged, since the species of intervals had been retained.

Except when the modes were transposed, however, only one accidental was allowed by theorists into this system: B-flat. You will notice that if B-flat is added to the Dorian mode, the resultant scale sounds identical to the minor scale defined earlier. If the B in the Lydian mode is flatted, the result is a major scale. Thus, already in the Middle Ages, both major and minor were possible modes. By the mid-sixteenth century, these modifications were so common that some theorists decided to define two more modes, one starting on C and one on A so that it would no longer be necessary to modify Lydian and Dorian to get those scalar configurations. The two new modes were called by some Ionian (on C) and Aeolian (on A). With their accompanying plagals they brought the total number of modes to twelve. Some confusion arises nowadays from the fact that theorists differed on the naming and numbering of the twelve modes, but the structure of the modes was consistent. It is interesting to note that although the possibility of a mode on B was sometimes discussed, its sound was so disturbing (since it is built from a diminished fifth and an augmented fourth) that it was never seriously considered beyond a theoretical standpoint.

The twelve modes continued to figure in theoretical treatises for another hundred years and were part of an educated child's basic foundation in music. Many composers wrote collections of pieces ordered according to the twelve modes in the sixteenth century, and a few such cycles are found as late as the nineteenth century, but as the years progressed, such works were increasingly regarded as curiosities or intellectual exercises.

In instructing my students I have found it helpful for them to experience the different sounds of the modes by having them sing or play the Kyrie from Ockeghem's *Missa cuiusvis toni* in all four authentic modes. A very useful edition of this piece, edited by George Houle, with notes, examples, and modern and original notation, is now available from Indiana University Press. Because this piece was written to work in all four modes, however, it necessarily lacks some of the characteristics of modal writing that can be seen more clearly in other works, most specifically the use of the repercussion as a primary degree in cadences and imitations, since the relationship of the repercussion to the final differs between mode III and the other authentics. Also, since the text is the same in all four versions, it is more difficult to discuss the differences in affect.

Mid-sixteenth-century French chansons can be excellent examples for modal analysis, being quite short and free of chromaticism. The tenor usually serves as the primary voice, paired with the soprano, with which most cadences are made, and these two voices will generally share the same range, separated by an octave. Imitative opening motives will tend to outline the species of fifth and fourth, and cadences will take place on the primary degrees of the mode (the final, fifth, repercussion, and sometimes the third), going further afield into "irregular" cadences (outside the mode) toward the middle of the piece, and returning to the final at the end. The bass and alto with their lower ranges, added after the first two parts were written, usually fall within the range of the related plagal.

Such examples must be carefully chosen, since the application of modal theory is very complex and subject to discussion and disagreement among both modern theorists and their Renaissance counterparts. A form of analysis developed for chant falls short in describing polyphony, and it is clear from the range of solutions proposed by sixteenth-century theorists that modal theory was largely inadequate to describe the works of their contemporaries. Our students do not need to be able to carry out an in-depth analysis of the music they play, but they do need to understand that it was in these fundamentals that Renaissance musicians, both professional and amateur, were trained, and that the language of modality was the foundation for their music. It is all too easy for the modern performer to assume that major and minor tonality are natural phenomena that the Renaissance composer had failed to discover, and not simply the chosen modes of one recent culture.

Musica ficta and Cadences

Students are often confused by the phenomenon of accidentals placed above the staff. Some have heard these accidentals called *musica ficta,* and will know that these can be a source of discussion and disagreement in rehearsals. But what are those accidentals doing there? Should they be played? How do they differ from accidentals written on the staff? And what governs where they appear?

One reason that the rules for *musica ficta* are not always clear to us as modern players is that it takes some familiarity with solmization as well as modal theory to understand their application. The term *musica ficta* (or *musica falsa*) originated in the Middle Ages and referred to those notes falling outside the Guidonian Hand, the range of notes encompassed by the

Gamut (or *musica recta*). Since they were not part of this system, such notes were considered false, or imaginary. Thus, soprano F, one step above E-*la*, the top of the Gamut, was called *fa ficta*. It was even sometimes notated with a flat before it, not to lower it, but to indicate that it was outside the system.

All accidentals, except for B-*fa*, were outside the Hand; however, they were sometimes necessary in order to avoid a dissonance or to reinforce a cadence. Instead of notating these changes in the music, composers assumed that performers would know where such accidentals would be called for, and that they would automatically raise or lower the appropriate notes as common usage dictated. We know relatively little about the common usage of the Middle Ages; it probably varied from region to region. But by the end of the fifteenth century certain rules had become generally accepted and were expounded in a number of treatises.

By the sixteenth century some sharps and flats were notated, not only in the form of signature flats (for transposition of modes) but in the music itself, although those governed by rules of *musica ficta* continued to be left to the performer's discretion. Toward the end of the century, as composers began to experiment with increased chromaticism, they began to find it necessary to notate more accidentals in order to clarify their intentions. By the beginning of the Baroque era, almost all accidentals were being notated.

When musicologists began to revive an interest in early music in the early 1900s, some editors went overboard in the use of *musica ficta*. In an attempt to make Renaissance music more accessible to modern ears, editors often used their license to obscure the original modality of a piece, rendering it either major or minor by the addition of accidentals. Since nothing was done to indicate which accidentals were original and which were editorial, this "modernization" was not readily detectable. Nowadays editors try not to impose their subjective opinion on music that they publish. Anything not found in the original notation of a piece is marked, either with footnotes or parentheses, and it has become accepted custom to notate *ficta* accidentals above the staff in order to differentiate them from those given by the composer. Editors provide these notations on the assumption that not all players will know the rules of *ficta*. But the application of these rules is somewhat subjective, so it helps if you can familiarize yourself with them in order to make your own informed decisions about the use of *ficta*.

The most common rules for applying *ficta* accidentals are summed up in two Latin phrases: *mi contra fa, diabolus in musica* and *una nota supra la semper est canendum fa*. Both of these rules require a knowledge of the hexachord.

The first phrase can be translated "*mi* against *fa* is the devil in music." At first reading, this appears to indicate that the intervals of the semitone and diminished octave are to be avoided, and it is true that these intervals were considered dissonant. But the semitone is not the demonic interval referred to in this axiom. The real problem arises when *mi* and *fa* from two different hexachords come together to create a tritone (so called because it is made up of three whole steps). You can hear why this interval was considered so unpleasant by playing together an F-natural (*fa* in the natural hexachord) and a B-natural (*mi* in the hard hexachord), or an E-natural (*mi*, natural hexachord) against a B-flat (*fa*, soft hexachord). This interval, either occurring vertically between two parts or melodically within one, was to be avoided whenever possible. Thomas Morley says, "It is against nature"; indeed, it is a naturally disturbing sound, as the two notes in a tritone share no basic harmonics. The interval is used today for sirens because it is so jarring. Tritones were almost always eliminated by flatting the *mi* rather than sharping the *fa*. Despite the seeming gravity of this rule, not all tritones need be omitted when conflicts arise; early theorists espoused a set of prioritized rules to deal with them. Because of the recent research in this area, the performer today often has to second-guess the editorial solutions offered in the music.

In solmization a flatted note is called *fa* and a sharped note *mi*, whenever they occur. The syllables serve as symbols of intervallic relationships. Since *mi-fa* is the only half step interval in the hexachord, these syllables can represent the lower and upper members of any half step. Thus, the *diabolus in musica* can be exorcised by changing a *mi contra fa* to *mi-mi* (for example, B-natural and F-sharp) or *fa-fa* (B♭ and E♭). However, there are occasions when a tritone clearly cannot be avoided. Correcting one dissonance may cause other dissonances. Sometimes an unavoidable tritone seems to have been intentional, expressive writing on the part of the composer; sometimes it is just poor counterpoint. (Some modern theorists have proposed that such writing is evidence of a hidden chromaticism, created by a chain of *ficta* notes set off by a tritone, the accidentals kept secret because of a religious establishment that disapproved of modernism! This idea of a secret chromatic art may have finally been laid to rest by Berger; see the Bibliography.)

The second Latin phrase translates thus: "One note above *la* is always sung as *fa*." As we have already seen, there are only six notes in each hexachord. A melody covering a greater span than this can be accommodated by mutating from one hexachord to another. But if the melody falls primarily within the compass of one hexachord, traveling beyond it by just one step, (for example, D-A-B-A), the uppermost note is sung as *fa*. In other words, the note should be flatted, making an interval of a semitone with its neighbor below. This example would then become D-A-B♭-A, solmized thus: *re-la-fa-la*. This rule helps to avoid a melodic tritone, if there is a *fa* in the phrase (D-F-A-B-A). But in many cases there is no tritone to be avoided; the rule simply reflects common usage.

Various treatises give other rules for the use of *ficta*, but those rules are either variations on those already mentioned, are particular to cadential formulæ (which will be dealt with below), or come under the elusive heading of *per causa pulchritudinis* ("for the sake of beauty"). Interpretation of this phrase varied among theorists, and we can be sure that it was widely interpreted by performers. We can get some sense of what was considered appropriate from string and keyboard tablatures of the time. Since tablature indicates the position of the fingers rather than the pitches themselves, any accidentals intended by the composer are incorporated in the notation. Thus, intabulations can provide us with a picture of the performance practice of the time. However, we cannot assume that an intabulated German work can tell us anything about French vocal practices, or that late sixteenth-century lute tablature can tell us how *ficta* were applied to the same songs a generation earlier. The best we can do is to apply the rules of which we are sure, avoiding tritones wherever possible, and then letting our experience of Renaissance music and aesthetics help to dictate what we ourselves might consider the most beautiful.

Sometimes *ficta* accidentals are added to avoid unpleasant dissonances, as in the case of *mi contra fa*, while at other times they reflect aesthetic conventions. The following two rules apply in particular to cadences, or closes.

In brief, the first says that an imperfect consonance expanding to a perfect consonance should be major, and the same interval contracting to a perfect consonance should be minor. Second, we are told that the third in a final chord should be major (as Morley puts it, "No close may be flat"). These rules are better understood once we have considered the concept of the cadence in the sixteenth century.

Our instruction in tonal music has accustomed us to thinking that a cadence is a harmonic event. However, the Renaissance composer approached music linearly, not as a sequence of vertical events. A tonal cadence is a harmonic phenomenon, described at its simplest by the formula V-I, or dominant-tonic; the motion of the individual parts, though dictated by voice leading, is less important than the function of the chord as a whole. The Renaissance cadence, like the modern one, was likened to the period in a sentence, but unlike the tonal cadence, it achieves this effect from the interaction of melodic lines, rather than by harmonic means.

In the Renaissance, music students learned to compose by improvising counterpoint to a melody according to rules governing the intervals allowable between two parts. Additional voices could be added following those guidelines. The distance or interval between two notes could be either consonant or dissonant. Dissonances are those intervals that are considered disturbing to the ear, heard as incomplete and in need of resolution. In the Renaissance the dissonant intervals were the major and minor second, the perfect fourth, the major and minor seventh, and, worst of all, the tritone, or augmented fourth (Ex. 29.6a). The consonant intervals were the perfect unison, fifth, and octave, and the major and minor third and sixth (Ex. 29.6b). The first three of these were called "perfect" consonances, because they conveyed a sense of completion or rest; the relationship of their frequencies makes these intervals the easiest to tune perfectly. The third or sixth consonances, which could be either major or minor, were known as the "imperfect" consonances. The cadence, or "close" as it was more commonly called, was arrived at by the motion of an imperfect consonance to the nearest perfect consonance (Ex. 29.7):

EX. 29.6 The dissonant (a) and consonant (b) intervals

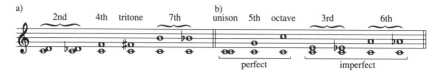

EX. 29.7 Motion of imperfect to perfect consonances

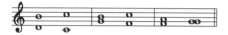

The rules of *musica ficta* indicate that when an imperfect interval expands to a perfect interval (Ex. 29.8a), the imperfect interval should be major. When, instead, it contracts to the perfect interval, it should be minor (Ex. 29.8b). As you can see in these examples, this means that in a close, one of the parts moves by the interval of a semitone, while the other moves by a tone. In most modes the voice which is ascending is given the half step motion, and for this reason it is sometimes necessary to add a *ficta* sharp to the penultimate note in the rising voice. However, in the Phrygian mode (either on E or in one of its transpositions) the half step naturally occurs in the descending voice (Ex. 29.8c), between the second degree and the final.

EX 29.8 Expanding to a close (a); contracting to a close (b); cadential motion in the phrygian mode (c)

As you can see, the cadence is defined by the interaction of just two parts. The disposition of the other parts in a larger composition changed over the course of the fifteenth and sixteenth centuries. By the fifteenth century the fifth, though a perfect interval, was no longer considered sufficiently final to make a full close, and cadences occurred only at the unison or octave. A third voice might be added between or below the two cadencing voices, and this resulted in different types of cadences. If the added voice was below the tenor, there was a difficulty in where it could move at the cadence and still form a perfect interval with the tenor (the third was not usually included in the final cadence until the following century). This problem was solved by having the added voice leap an octave to make a fifth with the tenor (Ex. 29.9a. NOTE: In the following three examples the open notes represent the two cadencing voices, the black notes showing the added part). Another form of fifteenth-century close was the Burgundian, or double leading-tone cadence, in which the third voice occurred as an inner part, and rose by a half step to the fifth above the tenor, thus moving in parallel fourths with the altus (Ex. 29.9b). Often in cadences of this time the upper voice moves down a step before rising to the cadence, a characteristic sound of the early Renaissance, a form of cadential embellishment that died out toward the beginning of the next century (Ex. 29.9c).

EX. 29.9 Cadences with three voices: octave leap (a); double leading tone (b); under third (c)

In the sixteenth century the bass at final cadences took on the function we recognize as cadential in later music, leaping down a fifth to an octave with the tenor, or up a fourth to a unison (Ex. 29.10a). Since this meant that three parts all had the same note, the fourth voice in a four-part composition supplied the fifth of the chord. If the composer wished to add a third (always major at final cadences) either this fifth would have to be sacrificed or it would have to come from one of the two cadencing voices (Ex. 29.10b). In this case the original two-voice form of the close becomes obscured.

This was not the only motion possible for the bass at closes, but was considered the most effective at important cadences, since it reiterated the cadential notes. At times the bass could be one of the two voices carrying the close (Ex. 29.10c) or could move to an imperfect rather than a perfect consonance with the close, thus making what we now call a deceptive cadence (Ex. 29.10d). Morley terms these "false closes, being devised to shun a final end and go on with some other purpose." It is important to note that it is the motion of the two cadencing voices that defines the close, not what the other parts are doing. Certain types of motion in the other voices can make a close more or less final, but it is still considered to be a close so long as two voices are moving from an imperfect interval to a perfect one.

EX. 29.10 Construction of four-voice cadences

Sixteenth-century closes commonly employ a suspension, or what Morley confusingly calls a "cadence," defining it thus: "A cadence we call that when, coming to a close, two notes are bound together and the following note descendeth thus" (Ex. 29.11).

EX. 29.11   Morley's "cadence" (suspension)

This suspension creates a dissonance before the close, and contributes to a greater sense of finality. Example 29.12 shows the use of a suspension in closes of two, three, and four parts.

EX. 29.12   2-, 3-, and 4-part cadences with suspensions

It is useful to be able to recognize cadences for several reasons. First of all, it helps in making decisions about the use of *ficta.* In 1517 the theorist Ornithoparcus said that the greater the number of closes a piece had, the greater was its beauty. This implies that whenever we find two voices moving from an imperfect to a perfect interval we should treat it as a close, and add *ficta* to raise the leading tone, if necessary. But sources disagree on this, and tablatures of the time cast some light on the subject. It appears that the love of closes increased as the century went on, and by the late 1500s it was probably common practice to raise the leading tone whenever two voices would make a cadence. But taste was and is still the final arbiter, and players must judge whether a final cadence is weakened by too many closes preceding it, or whether a phrase seems broken up by internal cadences.

When students can recognize and identify cadencing parts, it increases their understanding of how their lines interrelate. An awareness of cadencing lines helps students to tune their perfect intervals, as well as to recognize appropriate places to breathe or articulate. Another reason to identify cadences is to identify where ornamentation should be used. The majority of treatises on divisions concentrate on cadential formulae, and recognizing where closes occur makes it possible for the player to apply these appropriately.

Notation, Signs, and Symbols

In order to understand the music of the sixteenth century it is helpful to have some familiarity with the notation of the time, not necessarily in order to sight-read it, but because it can give insight into the performance practice of the period. Seeing how the notation of early music differs from our own notation also serves as a reminder of how different the music of an earlier age is from the music of today, how it needs to be approached on its own terms, not ours.

Our musical notation originated in the Middle Ages as a form of short-hand used by monks to help them remember the many chants they were called upon to sing during the course of the liturgical year. These notations were often no more than scribbles, called "neumes," above the chant text to remind a singer already quite familiar with the music where the line rose or fell. As the chant melodies proliferated, a more specific notation became necessary, and a couple of staff lines were added above the text to help no-tate exact intervals instead of simply the general outline of the tune. Simi-larly, distinctions began to be made between note lengths, although at first there was only a differentiation between long and short notes, with no fixed durations.

The development of polyphony required a further development in nota-tion. In order to sing two or more different lines simultaneously, it was nec-essary to know the relative lengths of notes—particularly when the individ-ual parts began to be written on different parts of the page rather than one above the other. Rhythm began to be notated with a complex system of interdependent note values, some distinguished by the use of colored ink. The idea of musical notation was soon adopted in secular music as well, and by the late fourteenth century the possible permutations of notated music had become so complex that musicians sometimes challenged each other to play their convoluted writings.

But by the sixteenth century the style of composition had changed and, with it, notation. We find music of this period fairly easy to read from our modern perspective. Still, aspects of the notation harking back to its more obscure origins remain unfamiliar to us. The first difference that we can see between the notation of the sixteenth century and our own is the shape of the notes themselves. Since musical notation developed at a time when broad pens were in common use, noteheads reflected the shapes most easily drawn with that instrument. Rather than being round like today's notes, they were square or diamond-shaped. Even after the introduction of the hollow noteheads of "white" notation, the rounded notes (which must have been easier to execute quickly than a hollow diamond) found in musicians' sketchbooks were recopied with corners in the final draft of a piece. This shape continued to be used after the introduction of music printing, and only died out as engraving and crow quills replaced movable type and broad pens in the seventeenth century.

Despite the angular shapes, we can recognize the whole note, half note, quarter, and eighth, but there are also some Renaissance note shapes that are not so familiar: one shaped like a box, and one like a box with a tail. Occasionally the first of these appears in a modern score, where it is called a double whole note. In the Renaissance, it was known as a *breve;* with the addition of a tail it became a *long.*

307

The names and shapes of the breve and long originated centuries before, when chant notation differentiated only between short and long notes. For many generations these represented the commonest note values, and their durations were relatively quick—perhaps comparable with today's quarter and half notes. As music became more complex, and intricate rhythms began to be notated, these original note values became subdivided into smaller values, and the duration of the breve and long increased. The shapes and names of the various note values in use in the Renaissance are shown in Figure 29.2, starting with the *maxima*, even greater than the long, and decreasing in length to the *fusa*, our modern eighth note. With the greater note values each note can equal either two or three of the next smallest notes, dictated by the time signature, while the smallest note values always have a duple subdivision.

FIGURE 29.2 Renaissance note shapes and names

The shapes of rests in the Renaissance are easily recognized as forebears of our modern ones. They are shown in Figure 29.3, paired with notes of comparable lengths. The difference in their shape from those we use today can be explained, as were the note shapes, by the style of pen used when they were developed. These shapes were adapted for printing at the beginning of the sixteenth century, and it was not until the seventeenth century, when engraving replaced movable-type printing, that more flowing shapes appeared.

A Renaissance piece transcribed literally from sixteenth-century notation to the notation of today can look very odd to us, as the note values appear to be so slow, due to the preponderance of whole notes and double whole notes. Nowadays such notes are performed very slowly, but in the Renaissance they moved more quickly. We know something about the relative durations of notes because of the phenomenon of *tactus*.

In 1490 Adam von Fulda gave the first detailed discussion of *tactus*. Musicians kept time together by having someone beat the *tactus*, either by lowering and raising his hand at a regular tempo, or, when the hands were occupied by instruments, with the foot. One downstroke plus one upstroke made one complete *tactus*. Contemporary accounts state that the speed of the *tactus* should be equal to the pulse of a man breathing normally—in other words, between sixty and eight beats per minute (although some annotations indicate that late sixteenth-century composers expected a measure of flexibility and even rubato, at least in certain styles of music). The

FIGURE 29.3 Note shapes related to their rests

length of the *tactus* was one semibreve in normal time, one breve in diminution, or one minim in augmentation. The time signature indicated which note value was to receive the pulse, and how that beat was to be subdivided. Thus the signature was an indication of both meter and tempo, and because it related specific note values to the *tactus*, it could also serve within the piece to show proportional relationships between sections. For a discussion of proportions consult the sections on tempo and proportion in the chapter On Singing and the Vocal Ensemble.

As was noted earlier, the larger note values could be subdivided either by two or by three, the duple division being called imperfect and the triple perfect (the mystic number "3" symbolized the Trinity, the ultimate perfection). The subdivision of breves into semibreves was called *tempus*, and the subdivision of semibreves into minims was called *prolation*. The perfect subdivision of the long occurred only rarely in the sixteenth century, most often in instructional manuals. (The long and maxima by this time were almost entirely confined to use at the end of pieces, where they signified a note to be held until all other parts were finished, akin to a *fermata*). Tempus was indicated in the signature by a circle: a full circle represented perfection, or three subdivisions; an incomplete or half circle, in appearance like the letter C, represented imperfection, or a subdivision of two. Prolation was noted by the presence or absence of a dot in that circle, the dot signifying a triple subdivision. The combinations of perfection and imperfection give us the metrical equivalents of the modern signatures shown in Figure 29.4 (assuming a reduction of note values, as discussed below):

FIGURE 29.4 Mensuration signs with their modern equivalents

A slash through a whole or half circle means that the breve receives the *tactus*; otherwise the semibreve receives the *tactus*. A slash through a half circle gives us our modern symbol for cut-time, also known to this day as *alla breve*.

If each breve was the length of one *tactus* in cut-time, then each semi-breve equalled one downstroke or upstroke of the arm. Experiment with this by moving your hand down and back up at the rate of your pulse and you will get an idea of the speed at which the breve could move in this meter. As you can see, in cut-time the whole note (semibreve) of the Renaissance moved at about the speed we usually equate with the quarter note today, while in normal time it was twice as slow. For this reason many editors, fearing that modern players will be discouraged by the slow appearance of Renaissance music, halve or even quarter the note values when making modern editions.

This is just one example of the kind of changes modern editors sometimes make in an attempt to make early music more accessible to the modern player. But in actual fact these changes can obscure the way the original music was perceived. When note values are reduced, we get a preponderance of eighth and sixteenth notes. Since it is modern practice to beam tailed notes together into rhythmic groups, these notes, heretofore separate, are beamed. This beaming can bias the player's perception of the music so that groups of notes are seen as rhythmic units and thus played with an emphasis not implied in the original. Modernization of the notation can thus change how the music is played.

In the same way, when scores are made from music that, out of custom as well as financial necessity, was originally published in parts, we are likely to perceive it differently when we play it than we would if we were reading from individual parts. Modern scoring generally necessitates the insertion of bar lines in order to line up the parts. In music that was originally published in parts, bar lines were not necessary and rarely occurred except on occasion to mark where all the parts cadenced together. Renaissance rhythms did not always fall into the regular patterns dictated by modern bar lines, and the *tactus* was an unstressed beat indicating relative speed but not accent. Insertion of bar lines into sixteenth-century music thus adds a metric bias that did not exist in the original, giving modern players the impression that certain beats should receive a greater stress than others and creating syncopations where such accents were not originally intended. A section from the altus part of Josquin's *Bergerette Savoyenne,* reproduced in both its sixteenth-century and twentieth-century forms (Fig. 29.5, Ex. 29.13), illustrates this problem.

FIGURE 29.5 Josquin's *Bergerette Savoyenne* (altus): original (without bar lines)

EX. 29.13 Josquin's *Bergerette Savoyenne* (altus): transcription (with bar lines)

Although modern editors have produced various kinds of barless scores, the notes still have to be spaced at regular intervals across the page to allow the parts to coincide, which can obscure the shape of the line.

In looking at a piece of sixteenth-century music we see that each piece begins with a clef and key signature, if any, as well as a time signature, much as they do today, but the appearance of the clefs can differ from ours. A key signature was first used, like other notational conventions, as a space-saver so that a frequent accidental did not have to be written repeatedly. It is an indication of a transposed mode (except in the Lydian mode, where a B-flat was common). The phrase "key signature" is a modern one and obviously was not used before the concept of keys themselves was developed.

The common clefs were the C-clef, F-clef, and G-clef, although this last occurs less often than the others. F-clefs were mostly used for bass- and baritone-range parts. All of these clefs could appear on any line of the staff in order to avoid the use of ledger lines, which were more difficult to write or print; for this reason the clef sometimes changes within a piece. The forms of the clefs may be unfamiliar and can be mistaken for notes, bar lines, or rests on first encounter (Fig. 29.6).

FIGURE 29.6 Common clef forms

A number of less familiar symbols also appear in Renaissance music. These include the sign of congruence, the *custos*, and the ligature, none of which has an exact equivalent in modern notation. The sign of congruence (*signum congruentiæ*) takes on several forms in printed or manuscript sources, but is generally a decorative and symmetrical symbol, often looking like a backwards question mark surrounded by four dots. The purpose of this sign is to indicate a place where all the parts come together. Often, it marks a principal cadence. It is also one of the ways to indicate a repeat, or the point at which parts in a canon should enter.

The usefulness of such a sign becomes clear when reading from original parts. If the ensemble falls apart, it becomes necessary to return to the beginning, since without a score there is no easy way to find a place to start together. Modern parts avoid this problem by using rehearsal letters. The sign of congruence serves a similar function. Not only does it serve as a helpful place within a piece to start, but it can confirm that you are actually in the right place after negotiating a particularly difficult section.

A repeat can be indicated in a number of ways: one is with a repeat sign similar to our modern one; in another the opening notes of the section to be repeated are given, and the player looks back in the music for that pattern of notes (this can only work when the repeat comes at the end of the piece); or in yet another way, with a sign of congruence, which usually appears twice—at the end of the piece, to show that the repeat is to take place, and during the piece, to mark the place to which the repeat returns. Once again this symbol is only effective when used at the end of a piece; otherwise there would be no way to distinguish it from its other function.

The *custos* is another unfamiliar symbol in early notation that is often mistaken for a note. Its name means "guardian" and is the root of our English word "custodian." The sign looks like a check mark with an extra turn, and it occurs at the end of the stave. Its purpose is to mark where the first note on the next stave will occur. It is an effective aid in sight-reading, since it prepares the eye for the next line, and is especially useful when reading in unfamiliar clefs, or in pieces where the clef changes frequently. This symbol can be a helpful addition to modern editions as well and has often been adopted by my own students to prepare them for unexpected leaps that occur between staves.

The ligature was a holdover into the Renaissance from the notation of much earlier music. As its name implies, the ligature ties several notes together in one symbol. Its use arose many centuries earlier in the notation of chant, for which the first symbols had been flowing squiggles representing several pitches with one gesture. As notation developed, groups of notes continued to be written as units; how these units were written and juxtaposed defined the "rhythmic mode" of the music. However, this "modal" notation was limited in the variety of rhythmic subdivisions it could express. It was eventually replaced by "mensural" notation in which the meter was designated by a sign at the beginning of the piece. Although it was no longer necessary to group several notes within one symbol, ligatures continued to be used as a convenience, since they took up less room—hence wasting less paper—than separate notes. They are still found in the sixteenth century, side-by-side with more modern notation in passages of longer note values.

Since ligatures developed out of a very different form of notation, they may not seem logical to us. Although people have come up with a variety of mnemonic devices to aid in deciphering ligatures, there is no easy way to remember what note values each type of ligature represents. It is probably easiest just to keep a chart of them in a drawer somewhere and refer to it as needed, until you are familiar with the most common forms. Figure 29.7 is a diagram of ligatures and the note values they represent (L = long, B = breve, S = semibreve).

FIGURE 29.7 Basic ligature formations

You will see that there is one type of ligature used for semibreves, while many forms are used for longs and breves. A ligature of two notes with a tail going up from the left represents two semibreves. The diagram shows only two-note ligatures, but they can also encompass many more pitches. Fortunately, any notes between the first and last in a long ligature are always breves (unless one is stemmed). If a longer ligature has a tail going up at the beginning, the first two notes are semibreves, and the remaining notes follow the regular rules: all the notes in the middle are breves, and the value of the final note is decided by its shape, its tail (if any), and whether it is ascending or descending, as shown in the diagram above.

Some people find it difficult to figure out just what pitches are represented in a ligature. The square type of note is fairly easy to read, since it sits on a space or line just like a breve. The oblique ones are harder to interpret, since they look as though they cover a whole swathe of pitches. In reality, they actually represent only two notes, the one where the diagonal begins, and the one where it ends. Looked at in this way it is usually fairly easy to figure out the pitches.

But why is it necessary to know any of this? If there is no occasion to read from original notation, it is certainly pointless to memorize the types of ligatures. But it is useful to know that they existed, because they can tell us something about the performance of the music. First of all, we can see that musicians and amateurs of the sixteenth century were sophisticated readers who felt comfortable with a complex system of notation. Second, we know that a line that contains ligatures must come from a partbook, because a single symbol representing many notes would not work in score-writing—it could not be lined up with other parts. Finally, we know from treatises of the time that in vocal music the syllable cannot change during a ligature. This makes good sense, since there would be no clear way to underlay the text. In modern editions any pitches that originally appeared as a ligature are marked by a bracket above the staff. For singers this indicates that the underlay should not be altered. For wind players it suggests that taking a breath within this group of notes is inappropriate.

As for the other signs and symbols that may be encountered in original notation, they are mostly what might be expected. In the sixteenth century, dots had the same significance as they do now: they lengthen the note by half again its value. Sharps and flats have a recognizable form (the sharp may appear as a single or double "X"), but are used slightly differently. An accidental applies only to the note it precedes, although it can modify several repeated notes if no other note intervenes. When you consider that there were usually no bar lines, this usage is obvious. Also, the sharp and flat signs can serve the same function as our modern natural, by temporarily canceling out an earlier accidental or one in the key signature.

The appearance of early notation can vary widely, depending on the method of printing or the manuscript style, but all the same elements can be found in any example. With frequent use it becomes easier to recognize these elements. Figure 29.8 shows excerpts from three different pieces: the first in manuscript, the second printed with movable type, and the third using two impressions—one for staves and one for notes. These illustrate some of the many differences in appearance to be found in music of this period.

Tablature is an alternate form of notation that unlike regular staff notation, does not indicate actual pitches. It was the usual form of notation for lute music in the Renaissance, and its symbols represented where the fingers should be placed on the fingerboard. It was also used for the viola da gamba played "lyra way"—that is, in chords. A form of tablature is used today to indicate guitar chords in popular songs' sheet music. Lute and viol tablatures take the form of a large staff of six lines in which each line represents a string. Letters or numbers representing the frets ("a" or "0" for open string, "b" or "1" for first fret, and so on) are placed on the line standing for the appropriate string. Rhythm is indicated by note stems, without the

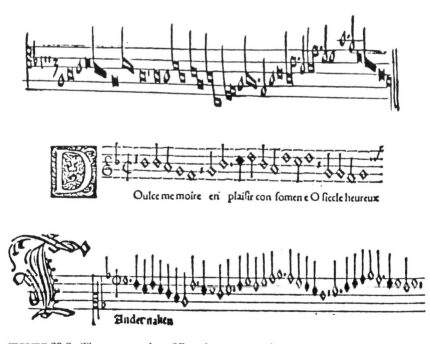

Oulce memoire en plaifir con fomen e O fiecle heureux

Andernaken

FIGURE 29.8 Three examples of Renaissance notation

heads, placed above the staff. There were also keyboard tablatures, particularly in Germany, and wind tablatures as well.

The advantage of tablature is that it can be applied to any size of a family of instruments, without the necessity of transposition. Since the actual pitches are not given, but simply directions for how to produce them, the notation applies equally well to any instrument. Tablature also allows the player to use unusual tunings without having to learn a new technique. Some lyra-viol music is written for an instrument specially tuned to create a particular resonance (for example, all octaves and fifths). If the music for these strange tunings was written in regular notation, the player would have to relearn how to play the instrument. But with tablature, the player can follow the notations as though in a normal tuning.

In addition to the symbols of music notation, some instructions are occasionally given in the form of text. Verbal instructions for tempo or for instrumentation can occur in the sixteenth century, although they became far more common in the late Renaissance. One verbal instruction, however, was commonly used throughout the period, and that was the canon.

Nowadays we use "canon" interchangeably with "round." However, while a round is a kind of canon, a canon is not always a round. Canon means "rule," actually referring to the text at the beginning of the music that tells you how to derive the parts, but has also come to mean a piece using this compositional device. The canon, or rule, of a simple round is that each voice enters after a set interval of time, at the same pitch, using the same notes. But much more complex canons have been written, deriving many parts from one, or even one from nothing! There are canons that give not only the interval of time between entrances, but an interval of pitch. Some canons call for an inversion or reversal of the notes. Others are simply verbal puns from which a scholarly musician could discover his part from clues alone.

Many facsimile editions of Renaissance music are now available. Most university libraries will have the larger collections, such as Petrucci's *Odhecaton, Canti B,* and *Canti C,* which are very clear prints with few errors. Working through a short chanson from the original, and then comparing it to a modern edition of the same piece, can point out to the student how the notation of the period reflected its music. A piece that takes up several pages of modern score can occupy a single page in parts. The close-set notation, uninterrupted by bar lines, makes imitations between the parts more apparent, as do the clefs, which often allow imitating parts to appear similar on the page. The unbeamed notes allow the player or singer to detect melodic patterns more easily, and the lack of bar lines helps to promote a rhythmic flow unimpeded by the perception of syncopation. Although most directors of early-music ensembles cannot afford the time to teach all their music from original notation, experiencing one piece from a particular period as it was seen at the time will have an effect on the students' perception of other pieces in that genre.

Further Study

The articles on modes, solmization, *ficta*, and notation in the *New Grove Dictionary of Music and Musicians* continue to be some of the most comprehensive on the subjects treated here and afford a wealth of additional information. The bibliography below contains original sources (in translation) and textbooks and articles (secondary sources). These will provide a greater sense of the issues of analysis as they were perceived by the theorists of the day. The textbooks are seminal works in the areas touched on in this chapter: the history of theory, the modes, *musica ficta*, and notation. The articles provide concrete examples of the application of these ideas to specific pieces. The article by Pat Carpenter, a lucid and engaging application of the writings of Tinctoris to Dufay's *Nuper rosarum flores,* is a particularly good introduction to this approach.

Bibliography

Original Sources

Aaron–*Toscanello*; Gaffurio–*Practica*; Glareanus–*Dodecachordon*; Morley–*Plaine*; Tinctoris–*De natura*; Tinctoris–*Liber*; Tinctoris–*Expositio*; Zarlino–*Art*; Zarlino–*On the modes.*

Secondary Sources

Apel–*Notation*; Bank–*Tactus*; Berger–*Musica–Theories*; Caldwell–*Editing*; Carpenter–Tonal; Crocker–Discant; Dahlhaus–*Studies*; Godt–Reading; Knighton/Fallows (Curtis, Wegman, Segerman)–*Companion*; Meier–*Modes*; Perkins–Mode; Rastall–*Notation*; Riemann–*History*; Treitler–Tone.

IX

INTRODUCTION TO RENAISSANCE DANCE

30

Renaissance Dance

Ingrid Brainard

In recent years directors of early-music groups have been programming Renaissance and Baroque dance music on concerts that include reconstructions of the actual dances from the period by a small group of dancers. This makes good sense for a number of reasons. In general, the addition of dancing in period costume adds an extra dimension to any concert program; it provides a refreshing alternation between pure music and the combination of music and motion, and it offers relief to the ear when the attention span has reached its limit, by permitting the eye to enjoy the visual aspect of choreography. In particular, instrumentalists will profit from playing for dancers by actually having to familiarize themselves with the basic step-sequences of the fashionable dances of the past. This will result in an increased awareness of the subtleties of tempo, phrasing, and articulation, and it will challenge their improvisational skills to the limit.

For the dance-minded director, the expansion of the ensemble's activities brings with it the additional responsibility of forming a dance ensemble, ideally under the direction of, or with the assistance of, an experienced historical dance teacher. Here it should be pointed out that teachers of ballet or modern dance are *not* automatically qualified to instruct students in the dance techniques and styles of early dance. There is, however, a growing number of early dance specialists in this country who will be happy to assist in getting a new dance group started or will answer questions over the telephone (see Checklist #1, p. 323). With the notable exceptions of the University of California (Los Angeles and Riverside campuses) and York University in Toronto, few university dance departments include Early Dance in their curriculum.

With regard to recruiting, professional dance students are the least likely candidates for membership in an early dance ensemble. Folk dancers, on the other hand, and members of the English or Scottish Country Dance Societies have on occasion joined in a historical venture with enthusiasm. Theatre departments are a possible source of personnel, as is the community at large. Beginners as well as experienced early-dance people, including directors of early-music ensembles, will find participation in an early-dance workshop or a summer program devoted to early dance informative and helpful (see Checklist #2, p. 324).

Once an ensemble has been formed it must be trained. This is a slow and exacting process of fundamental importance, because without impeccable technique, stamina, poise, and demeanor proper to the chosen period, there can be no dancing worthy of the name. At least one ninety-minute rehearsal per week is necessary; two would be better. The lesson plan of a ballet or modern dance class can serve as a model, but must be modified in accordance with the historical focus. There are three distinct dance idioms between about 1450 and 1700, each with its own characteristics. The director of the early-music ensemble is advised to consult a specialist concerning the best way to develop the manner of dancing to be used on the next early-music program.

As the newly formed dance ensemble trains, a repertory of choreographies naturally develops. A wealth of primary dance sources, manuscripts as well as printed books, is at one's disposal. Some of these are collections of choreographies only, while others are instruction books with detailed step descriptions, rules concerning manners and deportment, and advice to the musicians. These sources begin in the middle of the fifteenth century; for the fourteenth century and earlier no choreographic sources exist, and therefore no dances can be reconstructed.

For a fledgling historical dance ensemble, the best source to begin with is Thoinot Arbeau's *Orchésographie* (1588/89, 1596). Arbeau's treatise contains directions and music for *Pavane, Gaillarde, Branles, Pavane d'Espagne* and some others, besides a fine sword dance for four men: *Les Bouffons*, which is not recommended for beginners. Even when working with a manual as relatively simple as Arbeau's, the person responsible for dance reconstruction should always have a copy of the original French text alongside the translation.

Since we know that exemplars of Arbeau's book were in the hands of English dance aficionados (Dr. John Bull, for instance, owned a copy of the 1596 edition), the dances described in this French source can be used in the context of a concert dealing with music of the Elizabethan age. The Commonplace Books from the London Inns of Court (cf. Cunningham–*Dancing* and Wilson–*Dancing*) give, side by side with English *Measures* (*Almaines*) and Italian dances, directions for "The French Brawles" (*Branles*) and thus justify the use of these agreeable ballroom dances in an English setting.

The English *Measures* themselves are well suited for beginners. They are pleasant, easygoing dances, mostly in processional formation with slightly figured floor patterns. A nice selection, in reliable reconstructions and with music in four- to five-part settings, has been published by Puglicse/Casazza *Practise*.

Technically more demanding and much harder to reconstruct are the Italian dances of the late sixteenth century: Caroso–*Il Ballarino*, Caroso–*Della*, and Negri–*Le Gratie*. The advantage of the latter source is that it contains the original text as well, enabling one to cross-check as one goes along, for the fact remains that no translation is ever entirely satisfactory. It is always better to reconstruct dances directly from the original source and to use the translation, if one exists, as a crutch. For other topics, such as the wearing and handling of garments and accessories (Caroso–*Nobiltà*, for instance, abounds in this information), a translation will serve very well.

The music of most of the late sixteenth-century Italian choreographies is transmitted in lute tablature, sometimes with the addition of a melody line. Although these lute tablatures represent rehearsal scores only, the music will sound very nice when played on that instrument alone. Ideally, though, in performance they should be played by an ensemble of viols or recorders, assisted by lute or harpsichord, if available.

The Caroso/Negri repertory consists of *balli* and *balletti* of various kinds, many designed as compact suites in three or four movements. There are *Cascarde* and *Canarios, Pavaniglias, Spagnolettas* and *Brandos*; some are for solo couples, others for three, four, and six or more performers.

Present in all sixteenth-century dance instruction books are *Galliard* sequences in large numbers, over and beyond the *gagliarda* passages in the Italian *balli* and *balletti*. Some, like the "Kick to the tassel" *Gagliarda* in Negri, are extremely difficult, while others, like the ones in Arbeau, are well within a beginner's reach. With the exception of the fully choreographed *Galliards* in the manuals of Caroso and Negri, these vigorous jumping dances have to be put together by the ensemble's dance-master/mistress. The method is that of the period itself: first the various five-, eleven-, seventeen-step sequences must be learned individually, then they can be combined into dance phrases that fit the chosen musical accompaniment. In order to create a *Galliard* that resembles a genuine Renaissance dance, one must be careful to avoid an overindulgence in technical feats. The style of late sixteenth- and early seventeenth-century choreography demands that there should be a balance between passages of technical brilliance and sections of calm and poise. Furthermore, a clear distinction has to be made between men's and women's *Galliard* steps. Those for men can be as vigorous and difficult as the dancer can manage; those for women should be graceful, controlled, and light. The many *Gagliarda* sections in the *balletti* of Caroso and Negri can serve as models for the construction of *Galliards;* they also give the prospective choreographer ideas regarding floor patterns. It takes a great deal of study and a profound understanding of the principles at work in Renaissance choreography to create a truly convincing *Galliard*, but it can be done.

Music for such dances as *Pavanes, Branles,* and *Galliards*, among others, is contained in the many collections of dance pieces published by Attaingnant, Gervaise, Susato, d'Estrée, Phalèse, and others in virginal and lute books, volumes of consort music, and the like. One of the best reference books for musical purposes is Brown–*Instrumental*, which lists sources as well as modern editions. Since then, a great deal of dance music has been published (see listing below). Music librarians and owners of stores specializing in early music are usually willing to assist in the search for the proper music. If you cannot find help locally, you may write to The Provincetown Bookshop, 246 Commercial Street, Provincetown, MA 02657.

I have left the discussion of fifteenth-century dance materials to the last because the problems of reconstruction are so great that they can hardly be overcome without the assistance of a specialist in early Renaissance dance. Information on how to do the steps is scattered all over the twelve extant manuals; the choreographic descriptions must be read in their original Italian or French because up to the present time no reliable English translations exist (Inglehearn's translation of the Cornazano–*Libro* creates more problems than it solves). Microfilm copies of practically all fifteenth-century manuscripts can be obtained from the New York Public Library, Dance Collection, Lincoln Center. The known sources are listed in Brainard–*Art.* This study provides the reader with practical solutions to the execution of fifteenth-century dance steps and concludes with nine reconstructions of Burgundian and Italian dances and their melodies. No one should be discouraged from tackling this very beautiful and exciting repertory; one must simply be aware that only a big investment of time and effort can bring results. There is nothing instant about historical dance. From the musician's point of view, fifteenth-century dances are particularly challenging. The sixty-odd *basse danse* tenors from Burgundy and France are notated in blackened breves only and must be filled in and ornamented in the style of the period. In the best of all possible situations two of the three players in a *cappella alta* should provide genuine improvisations around the notated tenor; it takes musical experience and specialized musicological knowledge to do this correctly, but it is worth the effort. The melodies for Italian *balli* and *balletti* require a similar improvisational treatment. They can work, however, when played as unaccompanied tunes, without ensemble cushioning. The Italian melodies have been transcribed into modern notation by Kinkeldey–*Dance* and by Marrocco–*Inventory*, which list the sources as well as the individual dances. Unfortunately, Marrocco's transcriptions are full of errors; Kinkeldey's versions are more reliable. For descriptions of fifteenth-century dance sources and some interesting historical commentaries, see Gallo-Il 'Ballare.

Costumes

Early in the rehearsal process, the matter of costuming has to be dealt with. Don't wait until the last minute for this! It takes time to make historically accurate garments, and accuracy is essential if the dances are to look right for the period and the region to which they belong (e.g., fifteenth-century Burgundy, sixteenth-century France, etc.). Correct attire includes accessories and underwear (corsets *must* be worn from the mid-sixteenth century on!), shoes, hats, cloaks, gloves, swords, and the like. The weight of the fabric matters, as do colors and trims. Discount fabric stores can be found practically everywhere; drapery departments generally have fabrics with Renaissance and Baroque patterns, heavy enough for historical garments. Decisions on cut and construction can often be ascertained from the many existing costume books; museum collections and galleries have precious holdings of paintings that show details, jewelry, collars, fans, and the like, as well as seaming.

With regard to shoes there are theatrical shoe companies, especially in England and Germany, that carry lines of historical footwear. However, such lines are often incomplete and the merchandise is very expensive. Here and there a creative shoemaker will make desired items to order, but at a price. Normally one has to compromise: ballet slippers (preferably with a full sole) will have to do for the period from about 1450 to about 1560; the so-called "Greek sandals" for women and tie shoes (jazz oxfords) for men, both with a small heel, will work for dances from about 1575 to about 1675. For dances from the next period one has to increase the height of the heel to make the proper Baroque alignment of the body possible. Unless the ensemble director is especially well informed in matters of dress, he or she would be wise to place a knowledgeable individual in charge of costuming and wardrobe.

Checklist 1: Resource Persons, United States

This is a random list only. Specialists are also listed in the *Dance Magazine Annual,* in the directory of the Early Music Association, in local artists directories, and in similar publications.

Elizabeth Aldrich (English masque)
  31 Union Square West, Suite 15D
  New York, NY 10003
  (212) 255–5545
Ingrid Brainard (15th- and late 16th/17th-century dance)
  37 Princess Road
  West Newton, MA 02165
  (617) 332–4064
Angene Feves (late 16th-century and Baroque dance)
  70 Karol Lane
  Pleasant Hill, CA 94523
  (415) 943–1356
Charles Garth (late 16th/17th-century dance)
  31 Union Square West, Suite 15D
  New York, NY 10003
  (212) 255–5545

Kate van Winkle Keller (English and American country dance)
  13125 Scarlet Oak Drive
  Darnestown, MD 20878
Dorothy Olsson (late 16th/17th-century dance)
  160 Claremont Avenue, Apt. 41
  New York, NY 10027
  (212) 865–7797
Patri J. Pugliese (English country dance)
  39 Capen Street
  Medford, MA 02155
  (617) 396–2870
Julia Sutton (late 16th-century dance)
  24 Graymore Road
  Waltham, MA 02154
  (617) 893–0856
Emma Lewis Thomas (15th- and 16th-century dance)
  c/o Dance Department, W.G. 205
  University of California, Los Angeles
  405 Hilgard Avenue
  Los Angeles, CA 90024

All persons listed here are scholars as well as practitioners in early dance and their competence extends well beyond their principal specialty.

Checklist 2: Summer Schools

The International Early Dance Institute. This Institute takes place annually in early June and usually lasts for two weeks. Currently it is held at Goucher College in Towson, Maryland.

Offerings for the first week (suitable for beginners and advanced students) include

15th-century dance
16th-century dance
Baroque dance
19th- and early 20th-century ballroom dance
Early 19th-century ballet
Feuillet notation
Seminar in the methodology of dance reconstruction

Offerings for the second week include intensive studies of selected topics, which change from year to year. Regular instructors are

Elizabeth Aldrich (19th and early 20th century)
Ingrid Brainard (15th century and reconstruction seminar)
Charles Garth (late 16th century)

Sandra Hammond (early 19th-century ballet)
Wendy Hilton (Baroque and Feuillet notation)

For information contact the director:

Charles Garth
The Historical Dance Foundation
31 Union Square West, Suite 15D
New York, NY 10003
Phone: (212) 255–5545

Smaller workshops are given periodically by many of the resource persons listed previously and can be arranged by special request. Keep an eye open for these, or get in touch directly with the individual you would like to have.

Checklist 3: Dance Organizations

For the English Country Dance Society, the Scottish Country Dance Society, and the American Recorder Society, look for your local chapters in the telephone directory.

The Society for Creative Anachronism is a nationwide student organization, which in certain regions of the United States (east coast, west coast, Iowa) cultivates early dance seriously and has reference personnel available. Check with your local college or university.

The Society of Dance History Scholars (SDHS)
c/o Program in Dance
University of California
Riverside, CA 92521

The Congress on Research in Dance (CORD)
Dance and Dance Education Dept.
New York University
35 West Fourth Street, RM. 675
New York, NY 10003
(212) 998–5410

Both SDHS and CORD run annual conferences and publish proceedings, newsletters, and research journals.

In England the Dolmetsch Early Dance Society and the Early Dance Circle do the same.

Checklist 4: Bibliography

Fifteenth-Century: Brainard–*Art*; Dixon–*Nonsuch*; Inglehearn–*15th Century*. Sixteenth and seventeenth centuries: Dixon–*Nonsuch*; Feves–*Dances*; Feves–*Homage*; Francalanci–*Balli*; Inglehearn–*Ten*; Pugliese/Casazza–*Practise*; Sharp–*Country*; Thomas/Gingell–*Renaissance*.

In addition to the above-mentioned recordings there are quite a number of records with music for early dance, too many to be listed individually. Consult the *Schwann Catalogue.*

Concerning the available reconstructions: there is a distinct difference in the approach to the primary sources by American dance historians and those active in England. Because of the confusion this diversity can cause in the mind of the new early-music director, my advice would be to start with the American readings first and leave Dixon and Inglehearn for later—for a time, that is, when a basis for sound judgment has been formed through firsthand experience in dealing with the material.

Reconstructions are also contained in the books by Mabel Dolmetsch and Melusine Wood, published in the 1940s and 1950s and reprinted by Da Capo Press in 1975. The two English authors will forever be esteemed as pioneers in the field of early dance; but while their historical comments are useful even now, their method of reconstruction leaves much to be desired by modern standards, and the resulting choreographies can no longer be considered acceptable.

X

FOR THE EARLY-MUSIC DIRECTOR

31

Starting from Scratch

Jeffery Kite-Powell

Course Description/Justification

So you have the bright idea you want to start an early-music ensemble (also known as Collegium Musicum, although the sole use of this name today for "college" early-music groups somewhat misrepresents the original, broader application) at your school, but you don't know how to go about it. Well, the first thing you have to do is write a course description, and then you have to come up with a justification for wanting to offer the course, as no administrator can approve a new course offering without these two items. It goes without saying, of course, that there is sufficient "room" in your teaching load to allow for this additional course, or that others are available to take up the slack without undue burden—another point of considerable interest to your administrator. Two other possibilities present themselves in case the boss balks at having to shuffle teaching loads and assignments: (1) you can offer to volunteer your services for the first semester or two, until the group has established a "track record," or (2) you can offer the course through Continuing Education or some other area of your institution that is not directly related to credit offerings. But let us assume you have the administration's blessing to start an early-music ensemble.

Depending on the school, the course description will have to contain much of the following information:

> Course name, number of credits, meeting time and place, professor's name, room number and office hours, method of evaluation and testing, grading procedure, attendance requirements and penalties, and a general description of the course, outlining what will be required of the student and how he or she will benefit from having taken the course. If texts or supplemental readings are involved, they should also be listed here.

Each student should receive a copy of this syllabus on the first day of class, so that it is clear from the outset what is expected. This also provides you with a certain amount of protection when a student complains about a grade at the end of the semester.

The justification is only for the administrators and need not be more than one or two paragraphs. It should contain a strong statement of need and a clear rationale for offering the course. Build your case around the students and how unfortunate it is for them to be getting an education at your institution without any "hands-on" experience with early instruments and early music. You might also refer to the increasing emphasis being placed on historically informed performances of music written prior to 1800 by professional and collegiate musicians and by recording artists and critics all across Europe and North America today. Examples of a course description (syllabus) and a Justification (in this case, one supporting the need for applied instruction in early instruments) are located at the end of this chapter in Figures 31.1 and 31.2.

Recruiting

Once you have the authorization to start an early-music ensemble you can begin recruiting for it. It is, of course, difficult to entice students into something that has not existed previously, as they simply don't know what to expect. Many of them will harbor the notion that they would not be permitted to join in the first place, as they neither own nor have proficiency on any of the instruments involved. So you have to wage a recruitment campaign in which you try to convince a few courageous souls that they should sign up for the new ensemble. Ideally, you should have a trio or quartet of fairly competent recorder players (faculty and/or student players) who could visit various classes and demonstrate the instruments and the consort. This group could also play in the student lounge or cafeteria, or anywhere that students congregate. Selecting upbeat, catchy Renaissance tunes (dances in particular) would be most appropriate; of course, they need to be played well. One or two selections played on a set of crumhorns (if available) would surely be the highlight of the show.

If need be, though, you can do it all yourself, demonstrating how easy it is to learn to play the recorder. At each performance/demonstration you should announce the formation of the new, credit-generating ensemble, its meeting days, times, and place, and that a group for beginning recorder players is the first order of business. Parenthetically, this approach might be quite attractive to schools that offer teacher-training classes, as better than adequate recorder playing should be a must for elementary school teachers. Placing well-designed flyers and posters (see Fig. 31.3 at the end of the chapter) strategically around the music department will also help stimulate interest in the ensemble.

Another gimmick that often works well is to offer extra credit to anyone taking Music Literature or Music History (or any other course you choose) who enrolls in the ensemble. You obviously have to obtain the professors' permission before you can offer the extra credit, but my experience has been that they are always willing to help out. It is also a good idea to contact the various applied-music teachers (flute, clarinet, oboe, bassoon, trumpet, trombone, etc.) and ask them to recommend your ensemble to their students, or have them give you the names of a few students you could get in touch with.

A further area of likely support is the choral department—specifically the director of the madrigal singers. On most campuses this group is generally required to stage a madrigal dinner (banquet, feast, or party) in early December. You might suggest to the director that you would be happy to involve a few of your early-instrument consorts, which would in turn provide a great deal more variety visually as well as aurally to the event, if he or she would support your endeavors with the administration and the students. There might well be several more opportunities for you to team up with this group on future concerts (Masses, motets, etc.), so it is always prudent to have a good rapport with these folks. You may also want to entice some of the singers from the choral department actually to join the early-music ensemble so that you have your own vocal consort; the idea of one singer on a part is often most appealing to singers who all too frequently become lost in the sea of voices in the choral ensembles. Be on the lookout for ruffled feathers when rubbing elbows with choral directors—they may feel threatened by your ensemble.

One of the best recruitment maneuvers is to invite an early-music ensemble from a nearby college or university, or a good amateur group (if there is one in your community), to come and play for your student body. This may cost you a small honorarium and a few lunches or dinners, but it would be well worth it. If you can get your hands on some *real* money, you can contract a professional group to present a concert for your students and the community at large.

These recruiting measures may be used until you have more students than you can handle. As your group becomes larger, you can be more selective by holding auditions and limiting the number of students allowed in the group. If everything continues to go well, you will eventually have an early music ensemble that is divided into several subensembles, which may also be divided into subensembles as follows:

The Early-Music Ensemble

Recorders I
  Recorders II
  Recorders III
Crumhorns I
  Crumhorns II
Loud Band (Shawms & Sackbuts)
Cornett & Sackbut Ensemble
Viols I
  Viols II
  Viols III

Singers
Mixed Consort
(Consorts of curtals, Schreierpfeifen, cornamuses, rackets, lutes, and a violin band are additional possibilities for groups of players.)

There will be some occasions on which you will need to use all but your very beginning players together, and there will be times when you will want to present the various consorts of your ensemble separately. But if you are planning for the future (when your best players have graduated), you will always have a few beginner and even intermediate ensembles (recorders and viols in particular) working in the wings. This kind of depth allows you to field your up-and-coming players in emergencies, and it also keeps the top players on their toes, as they know that there are those who would love to replace them. It must be stressed at this point, however, that *big in no way means better*. Schools with small music departments and modest budgets can and do produce outstanding early-music concerts. The directors of these programs may never have multiple ensembles with which to work, but that does not diminish the quality of their work in any way.

Leadership

But who is supposed to direct all of these ensembles? you ask. That is a tricky question, as each subensemble should meet twice a week, and you cannot be expected to be at every rehearsal. The best solution, if graduate assistants are not an option, is to let (encourage or assign) the best player in each ensemble lead the group. You should decide what repertory each group is to work on, and you should drop by the rehearsals periodically to make sure they are working seriously at mastering their instruments and the music. You may even be able to prevail on the lead viol and recorder students to take on the beginning groups. It may be necessary for you to attend one of the rehearsals per week, while the designated student takes the other—it all depends on how much you want to be, need to be, and are able to be involved.

Scheduling

This can be a nightmare for an early-music ensemble that has multiple subensembles. Initially, however, you should tell the administration that you want to meet your ensemble two (or three) days a week at a given time for between one and one and a half hours each day. These will be your *official* meeting times, and you should plan it so that these times have the least important things going on with regard to other classes and ensembles. It would not be advisable, for example, to schedule your group during the time the band, orchestra, or chorus meets, as you automatically preclude those students from participation in your group. It is also good to avoid scheduling against theory, sight-singing/ear training, history, and large literature classes. You may even have to meet in the early evening in order to have access to the most students. Whatever you do, try not to change the rehearsal schedule every semester. Once the students know that the early-music ensemble always meets at such-and-such a time, they will arrange their schedules so they will be free at that time. The larger the group becomes, the more difficult it is to have them all rehearsing at the same time in the same room. Realistically, not many pieces work well with multiple players and timbres on a part. There will be times when you will want to rehearse the entire ensemble together (see "Large Ensemble" in the chapter on Practical Instrumentation), but generally speaking, you are going to want to meet each subensemble (consort) by itself. In order to do this you will need additional rehearsal rooms or different meeting times.

Ensembles consisting of several consorts may find the following suggestions helpful in solving scheduling problems. During the first official class meeting, pass out a blank schedule sheet (see Fig. 31.4 at the end of the chapter) and ask the students to fill in their current class *and* work schedules; all times when they *cannot* meet should be entered on the schedule sheet. Make sure they answer the questions at the top of the sheet and on the back (Fig. 31.5 at the end of the chapter) so that you know a little bit about them and their preferences. When this is completed announce that you will post the individual consort rehearsal times on the door the following day, so they should check to see when their consort will meet.

After the students have been dismissed, separate the schedule sheets into groups based on the students' entries under item #1 (instruments they want to play or learn this semester). Go through each pile and separate each group into level of playing ability (beginner, intermediate, advanced). Next, take a blank schedule sheet and label it "Recorder I" or "Shawm Band" or whatever each stack represents. Go through each student's schedule and copy every entry onto the master schedule for that group (you don't actually have to enter each student's specific activity for each hour, just block that hour out on the master schedule). The remaining blocks of time are potential rehearsal times for that particular consort. Repeat this procedure for each stack of schedules so that when you are finished you have master schedules with available rehearsal times for all of the consorts. Now take one more blank schedule sheet (which will soon become the ensemble's overall master schedule) and enter two rehearsal times a week for each consort, based on the available times from each consort's master schedule. You should attempt, if at all possible, to keep the rehearsals at the same time of day on alternate days of the week (e.g., Recorders I: M/W 10:00, Crumhorns: T/Th 11:00, Viols II W/F 2:30, etc.). Keeping the same time of day will not always work out, as someone will invariably have a conflict with everyone else in the group, but it is easier for the students to remember when their rehearsal is if the same time of day for each rehearsal can be arranged. Keep in mind that the ensemble's regularly scheduled rehearsal time can be used for one of the consorts if you are not going to need that block of time for massed rehearsals of several groups.

When this is completed post the final master schedule on the door and hope the students don't have a lot of last-minute schedule changes. I have found it useful to make a list (in alphabetical and numerical order) of all the students enrolled in the ensemble along with their instrument(s) and phone numbers, which I then put on the back of the master schedule for distribution to the students and other interested parties.

Rehearsal Planning

In ensembles with enrollments of twenty or more students, any system or device that facilitates the planning and running of rehearsals is welcomed, and the following procedure is presented with this in mind. Once you have determined which compositions you are going to work on during the semester and who is going to play which part in each piece, you should assign each work in the entire repertory a Roman numeral. You should then prepare a listing of the semester's repertory, which should contain the following information: Roman numeral, title of work, composer of work, and the numbers (from the roster) of the students who are playing in each work (see Fig. 31.6 at the end of the chapter). This saves time and space by not having to list students' names and prevents any confusion that might arise when there are three Johns or two Sallys. This list of works should be posted on the door of the room along with the schedule and the ensemble roster, and a copy should be given to each student.

When planning your rehearsals you can easily notify your students which pieces will be practiced during the week (or month) simply by posting their Roman numerals in a specially designated place on the door. In this way, the students will be able to check quickly to see if they are playing in those particular pieces, and when they will be rehearsed. As you can see, the door becomes the primary mode of communication between you and your students, and with all the proper information on it, there is little room for error. Passing by the door on a regular basis should become a habit of all enrolled students!

Financial Support

The question you are surely asking at this point is: "How do you get enough money for all the instruments that are needed for such a huge ensemble?" The answer lies to a certain extent on your salesmanship abilities. If you were able to sell the administration on the idea of creating an early-music ensemble in the first place, then they surely must have known that it would not be long before you would be coming to them for financial support for instruments, music, equipment (reeds, strings, etc.), and publicity (flyers, programs, ads, etc.). You need to get a long-term commitment from them that they will provide you, as the new kid on the block, with sufficient money to build a well-rounded program, and you had better be prepared to show them your five-year plan, or where you want the ensemble to be at a certain time and how much it's going to cost. If you are starting from scratch, you are going to need a minimum of $2,000 for each of the five years. This is a drop in the bucket, though, when compared to the amount of money it takes to maintain a full-sized band or orchestra, and many smaller schools would be far better served by investing their limited resources in a first-rate early-music program than spending thousands of dollars on instruments and in scholarship money each year for string, horn, oboe, and bassoon players for a medium-sized, less-than-stunning orchestra.

Some states have Fine Arts Councils that provide grant money for such capital outlay expenditures, especially if you can convince them that their money will enable you to present concerts on an ongoing basis to the general public on instruments heretofore never seen in your community.

I have had a great deal of success over the years (a violone, regal, Baroque bassoon and oboe, and an entire curtal and shawm family, for instance) by tapping into our student government activities account. In the spring of each year the student senate accepts proposals for financial assistance for specific items, personnel, and/or projects being requested by groups and organizations from all across the university. Find out if your music department has a student representative in the senate and go to this person for advice on how to submit your grant request. When writing your proposal be sure to make the point that current as well as future students will benefit from this grant allocation—not just those actively playing the requested instrument(s), but those in the audience as well! (See Fig. 31.7 at the end of the chapter.) One other note of advice: when requesting more than one instrument, place them in priority order and be prepared to have the last one or two items left unfunded. It gives the student representatives the feeling of being fair, yet fiscally sound. I have found, however, that asking for just one instrument, even if it is a substantial purchase, is a highly successful tactic, as you don't appear greedy to the committee, and because they often don't have the heart to reject your one-item request altogether.

Another way to obtain funding is to approach the various music and civic clubs in town and ask them if your early-music ensemble could present a half-hour lecture-demonstration of Renaissance instruments and music for their noontime luncheon meeting for a donation to your instrument fund. Many times state, county, or local governmental agencies need entertainment for events they are sponsoring, and the same is true for large malls, particularly at Christmas. Weddings, parties, and Renaissance fairs are all potential money-makers and are often quite a lot of fun, too. You will have to be the judge on how much of a donation or fee to ask, but I would recommend starting at around $250–$300, and then coming down a bit if necessary. It takes a lot of time and energy to attain this level of performance, and you shouldn't give it away!

The School Board is another source for funding, if you can convince them of the need to expose third and fourth graders to the joys and benefits of playing the recorder, preparatory to learning a much more complicated band or orchestral instrument. Explain to them that by the time the children switch to modern instruments, they will already know how to read the notes on the staff and rhythmic notation, and that they will have made great progress in controlling their breath, coordinating their fingers, and playing in an ensemble. It helps, of course, if local music teachers use the recorder in their classes, but this might just be the way to introduce them to it if they don't. Design a thirty-minute lecture-demonstration by your best quartet of recorder players for eight-to-ten-year-olds, and make sure that the show is highly entertaining, educational, and transportable. Even schools using the Orff instruments and method can benefit from such a program.

Charging admission to concerts on campus is generally frowned on, but if you can present a full-length concert in a public hall or church there is no reason why you cannot sell tickets or at least ask for a donation at the door—either to defray expenses or for the instrument fund, whichever tack you wish to take.

A final suggestion regarding money matters concerns the identification of a wealthy patron (or patroness) in your community whom you might approach with the proposal that you will name an entire set of instruments in his or her name if he or she agrees to purchase the instruments. Part of the agreement can be your promise that the name of the collection will appear in each concert program for the next two (four, six, etc.) years. A university fund-raising specialist would be helpful in this endeavor.

Community Support

It is important to have the backing of the community (both the university community and the township) in which your ensemble is active. This can be achieved by your support of their activities and events to the extent you think is feasible. Volunteering a group of players for a worthy cause puts you in a good light, and the community sponsors and participants are not soon likely to forget your contribution. Sending a group of players to old folks' homes, retirement centers, and homes for the mentally ill, retarded, or otherwise impaired individuals, as well as certain wards in hospitals, is a laudable endeavor any time of year and as often as time allows.

If your city has a large ethnic group with a European heritage you could plan a concert around a theme or a group of composers representing this group. Many communities, for example, have a large Spanish- (or German-, Italian-, Polish-, French-, etc.) speaking population, who undoubtedly would be appreciative of a concert that not only focused on their background but performed in their community center as well.

Performances for the kinds of audiences mentioned above are not only important for humanitarian reasons, but they will eventually help increase the size of your audience at your regularly scheduled concerts. Be sure to submit script and advertising copy in plenty of time to be included in the public service announcements on your local television and radio stations and in the newspapers. It also helps to have your students post flyers of upcoming concerts in the major supermarkets and other prominent locations in town and around campus. (See the chapter entitled Publicity, p. 274. It contains all the information you need on how to advertise your concerts.)

The whole idea of these pages has been to convey to you the idea that establishing an early-music ensemble on your campus or in your town is not an insurmountable task. There will surely be obstacles along the way, but they can generally be removed when approached with sufficient conviction and determination. If you are in dire straits, call a colleague or contact Early Music America for a reference person. Good luck!

Bibliography

The following items offer a wealth of information to the early-music ensemble director, beginner, and old-timer alike. It is recommended that these sources become a part of your personal library.

Kottick–*Collegium*; McGee–*Medieval*; Petersen–*Guide*; Phillips/ Jackson–*Performing*.

FIGURE 31.1   Course Syllabus—Early-Music Ensemble

Course Numbers: MUN 2470, 4470, 5475 | Number of Credits: 1

Meeting Times: Tues/Thurs 4:00–5:15 | Rehearsal Room: HMU 229

Instructor: J. Kite-Powell | Rm Nr: 227 | Office Hours: Posted

Objectives: The purpose of the early-music ensemble is to study and perform original literature for various consorts and combinations of instruments on replicas of instruments that were used prior to 1700. Emphasis will be placed on the musical styles and forms of the Middle Ages, Renaissance, and early Baroque. The students will develop their ability to perform in small ensembles and improve such aspects of playing as intonation, articulation, phrasing, balance, and interpretation. In addition, they will gain proficiency on the instruments of these periods. Further, the students will:

1. constructively evaluate and criticize their personal level of performance and the performance of others
2. master terminology involved with tempo markings, performance instructions, and interpretations
3. prepare music outside of class (practice)
4. exhibit leadership and fellowship in the group effort
5. maintain a cooperative attitude and show mutual respect
6. learn and demonstrate professional stage presence
7. show responsibility for music and school-owned instruments and equipment
8. attempt to conform to group-designated standards—memorization (when applicable), dress, and attendance
9. demonstrate pride in membership in the group by recruiting for the organization and representing the organization willingly.

Attendance: Students are required to attend all classes (rehearsals) and performances. The final grade will be lowered for unexcused absences as follows:

Grade

One unexcused absence	B+
Two unexcused absences	B
Three unexcused absences	C+
Four unexcused absences	C
Five unexcused absences (withdrawal recommended)	F
Three unexcused tardinesses = one unexcused absence	

FIGURE 31.1 (*continued*)

Grading: Grades will be assigned on the following basis:

Level of Ability	Level of Accuracy	Grade
High	90–100	A
High-medium	80–89	B
Medium	70–79	C
Medium-low	60–69	D
Low	Below 59	F

Graduate students may be asked to compile concert program notes.

Because of the increased interest in historically informed performances of early music in general and the expanded growth of early-music activities at Florida State University in particular, a real need to be in a position to offer private instruction in historical instruments has presented itself. A school of music with such comprehensive offerings as FSU should provide its students with the opportunity to study early instruments at the applied level when the appropriate instruments and expertise to teach them are available. Students seeking the Certificate in early music, the BM in music history and literature, the BA in music, an MM or Ph.D. in musicology with an emphasis in early music, or a graduate degree with an early instrument as a secondary instrument, should be extended the option of selecting an early instrument as their primary (or secondary, as the case may be) instrument.

The School of Music already has in its possession a large assortment of replicas of historical instruments, and the collection increases annually.

The early-music ensemble consists of several small consorts as well as larger groups in which interested students may participate; the Baroque Ensemble offers a variety of performance possibilities as well. Both groups perform several concerts per year on the University campus and in and around Tallahassee.

FIGURE 31.2 Justification for Applied Music in Historical Instruments

"*Pastime with good company*"

Mediæval and
  Renaissance Music
Multi-Choir Ensembles
Mixed Consorts
Song and Dance
Vocal Ensemble
  (Cantores Musicæ Antiquæ)
Instrumental Ensembles
  Recorder / Crumhorn
  Shawm-Curtal-Racket
  Cornett & Sackbut
  Viola da Gamba
Other Instruments
  Lute, Theorbo, Harp
  Psaltery, Hurdy Gurdy
  Portative Organ, Regal
  Harpsichord, Violone
  Rebec, Vielle, Kortholt
  Percussion, Bag Pipe
  Schreyerpfeif, Flute

Perform Early Music at
Florida State University
Join the Early Music Ensemble

Tuesdays & Thursdays - 4:00-5:15 - Room 229

FIGURE 31.3 Sample Flyer

EARLY-MUSIC SCHEDULE SHEET
  FOR FALL/SPRING/SUMMER SEMESTER; 19__

NAME _____ MAJOR COURSE OF STUDY _____

ADDRESS _____ YEAR OF STUDY: Fr / So / Jr / Sr / Gr

PHONE(S) ___(home) ___(work) MAJOR INSTRUMENT_____

EARLY INSTRUMENTS YOU ALREADY PLAY _____

LIST THE INSTRUMENT(S) YOU WOULD LIKE TO PLAY THIS
SEMESTER (each instrument selected requires two (2) hours of
ensemble rehearsal per week) (see reverse side).

1. _____   2. _____

3. _____   4. _____

HOUR	MON.	TUES.	WED.	THUR.	FRI.
8:00– –8:50					
9:05– –9:55					
10:10– –11:00					
11:15– –12:05					
12:20– –1:10					
1:25– –2:15					
2:30– –3:45					
4:00– –5:15		EARLY MUSIC ENSEMBLE		EARLY MUSIC ENSEMBLE	
5:30– –6:45					
EVENING (specify time)					

FIGURE 31.4 Blank Rehearsal Schedule

Strings

Cittern
Harp
Hurdy Gurdy
Lute
Psaltery

Rebec
Theorbo
Vielle
Viol (Tr T B)
Violone

Woodwinds

Bagpipe
Crumhorn (S A T Bx)
Curtal (S A T B)
Flute (Renaissance tenor)
Korholt (S B)
Pipe (& Tabor)

Renaissance Racket
  (T T B Gb Cb)
Recorder
  (Renaissance: Ss S A T B Gb)
Schreyerpfeif (S A T)
Shawm/Pommer (S A T Tx B)

Brass

Cornettino (mute, straight, curved) Lysarden (cornetto basso)
Cornetto (mute, curved)   Sackbut (A T B)

Keyboard

Chamber Organ
Clavichord
Harpsichord

Portative Organ
Regal

Voice

Please give your range on the reverse side under 1, 2, or 3 if you intend to sing this semester. (Soprano (type), Alto, Countertenor, Tenor, Baritone, Bass)

Please Answer the Following Questions

Do you read early notation? yes / no: Black Mensural / White Mensural / Tablature (type?) _____

Would you like to learn to play from early notation? yes / no

Would you like to learn Renaissance dances? yes / no

Would you register for lessons on an early instrument if a teacher were available? yes / no Which instrument(s)? _____

Would you participate in weekend or week-long early music workshops in other cities? yes / no

FIGURE 31.5 Instruments of the Early-Music Ensemble

Nr	Group	Title	Composer	Instr (top-to-bottom)	
I	Mixed ens.	Quodlibet à 7	Maistre	1-Vo/6-ARec,12-Vo/17-trV1/16-Vo,24-Skb/13-BV1/29-BCur,/28-BV1,5-Vo	
II	Mixed ens.	Benedicta Es Coelorum à 6	Josquin	23-Cor,1-Vo,12-Vo/13-TCur/24-Skb/11-Skb,5-Vo/28-BV/29-BCur	
III	Mixed ens.	Tandernack Quinque à 5	Senfl	6-TRec/17-trV1/13-ACur/11-Skb/28-BV1	
IV	Mixed ens.	Nato Canunt Omnia à 5	Brumel	6-TRec/17-trV1/13-ACur, all singers/24-Skb/28-BV1	
V	Mixed ens.	Forti animo esto à 8	J. Praetorius	Ch.I:17-TRec,1-Vo/23-Cor 12-Vo/24-Skb/11-Skb Ch.II:28-SSha/6-SCur, 16/13-ACur,5/29-BCur	
VI	Mixed ens.	Ave Maria à 6	Senfl	6-TRec,1-Vo/17-TRec, 12-Vo/24-BRec,16-Vo/11-Skb/13-BV1,5-Vo/28-BV1	
VII	Brass	Verbum caro	Hassler		à 6
VIII	Brass	Maria Stabat	A. Gabrieli		à 6
IX	Viols	Fantasia	Ferrabosco		à 4
X	Viols	In Gottes Namen	Heinrich Finck		à 4
XI	Racket	Es ist ein Ros	M. Praetorius		à 4
XII	Shawm	Heth sold ein meisken	Anonymous		à 4
XIII	Curtal	The Servant of his	Benet		à 4
XIV	Rec	Fairie-round	Holborne		à 6
XV	Rec	Mach mir ein lustiges	Haiden		à 4
XVI	Crum	Chi Chilichi	Lasso		à 6
XVII	Crum	Mein Lieb wil mit mir	Hassler		à 8

FIGURE 31.6 Concert Repertory

The Florida State University
Tallahassee, Florida 32306–2098
School of Music

M E M O R A N D U M

To: The Student Government Budget Committee

From: Jeffery Kite-Powell, Director
  FSU Early-music Ensemble

Date: January 25, 1993

The FSU Early Music Ensemble (EME) specializes in music written between the years 1200–1650. The average enrollment is over 30 students per semester, divided equally between graduates and undergraduates. Every semester the ensemble performs two to three full-length public concerts at the School of Music, and we frequently perform off campus (in and around Tallahassee and south Georgia). During spring break each year a small component of the EME visits all of the elementary schools in Leon county as part of the Arts in the Public Schools program to demonstrate early instruments (the recorder in particular) to the students, and, for the last few years, the ensemble has rented the student government van to participate in weekend early-music workshops at Tulane University, Louisiana State University, and the University of Alabama at Birmingham. We have also performed for the regional meeting of the Southern Chapter of the American Musicological Society in Lafayette, La. and at FSU's Appleton Museum of Art in Ocala, Fl. As you can see, the EME is a highly visible group.

The EME is also an especially unique group, as the instruments the students learn to play are replicas of instruments used in the Renaissance. While performing on these instruments certainly broadens the students' understanding of earlier instrumental music, the instruments are such specialty items—mostly **still handcrafted** and **prohibitively expensive**—that the students are **unable to purchase their own.**

The School of Music is simply unable to meet all of the budgetary needs of its many ensembles. The EME is able to purchase one or two instruments annually from funds provided by the school and with funds raised by the ensemble itself, but we are still in need of several very crucial instruments in order to reproduce the music of the Renaissance authentically. The instrument I am requesting this year will complete the basic family of shawms, the preeminent outdoor double reed instrument of the period. The Student Government has already helped us with two other instruments from this family, and the students of the EME would greatly appreciate the addition of the bass (lowest) instrument. You can be assured that it will be played by a large number of students and appreciated by many audiences in the years ahead.

On behalf of the students of the EME I would like to thank you for your careful review and consideration of this proposal.

FIGURE 31.7 Student Government Memorandum

Bibliography

AARON, PIETRO. *Toscanello in musica.* Venice, 1523. Trans. Peter Bergquist. Colorado College Music Press Translations no. 4. Colorado Springs: Colorado College Music Press, 1970.

———. *Lucidario in musica.* Venice, 1545.

ABBOTT, DJILDA, and EPHRAIM SEGERMAN. "Gut Strings." *Early Music* 4/4 (1976): 430–437.

ADRIAENSEN, EMMANUEL. *Novum Pratum Musicum,* Antwerp: Phalese, 1584. Facs. ed. Geneva: Minkoff, 1977.

AGAZZARI, AGOSTINO. *Del sonare sopra il basso.* Siena, 1607. English translation in Oliver Strunk, *Source Readings in Music History.* New York: Norton, 1950.

AGRICOLA, MARTIN. *Musica instrumentalis deudsch.* Wittenberg, 1529, rev. 1545. English translation by William W. Hollaway of the 1529 ed. of *Musica instrumentalis deudsch,* as edited by Robert Eitner and published in 1896; Ph.D. diss., North Texas State University, 1972.

ALTHOUSE, JAY. *Copyright: The Complete Guide for Music Educators.* East Stroudsburg, PA: Music in Action, 1984.

ALTON, JEANNINE, and BRIAN JEFFERY. *Bele Buche e Bele Parleure: A Guide to the Pronunciation of Medieval and Renaissance French for Singers and Others.* London: Tecla Editions, 1976.

APEL, WILLI. *The Notation of Polyphonic Music: 900–1600.* Cambridge: The Medieval Academy of America, 1953.

APPLEBAUM, SAMUEL. *The art and science of string performance.* Sherman Oaks, CA: Alfred Publishing Company, 1986.

APPELBAUM, STANLEY, trans. and ed. *The Triumph of Maximilian I: 137 Woodcuts by Hans Burgkmair and Others.* New York: Dover, 1964.

ARBAN, J. B. *Complete Conservatory Method for the Cornet.* New York: Carl Fischer.

ARBEAU, THOINOT (JEAN TABOUROT). *Orchésography, a treatise in the form of a dialogue whereby all manner of person may easily acquire and practice the honourable exercise of dancing.* Trans. Cyril W. Beaumont with a preface by Peter Warlock. London: Baumont, 1925.

———. *Orchésographie. Méthode et téorie en forme de discours et tablature.* Lengres, 1589. Facs. ed. Geneva: Minkoff, 1972. Trans. M. S. Evans. Republished with new introduction and notes by Julia Sutton, New York: Dover, 1967.

ARNAUT DE ZWOLLE, HENRI. *Manuscript treatise* (ca. 1440).

ARNOLD, DENIS. *Giovanni Gabrieli and the Music of the Venetian High Renaissance.* London: Oxford University Press, 1979.

ARNOLD, FRANCK T. *The Art of Accompaniment from a Thorough-Bass.* London: Oxford University Press, 1931. Rep. in 2 vols. with an introduction by Denis Stevens. New York: Dover, 1965.

ATLAS, ALLAN. "Paolo Luchini's *Della Musica*: A Little-Known Source for Text Underlay from the Late Sixteenth Century," *Journal of Musicology* 2 (1982): 62–80.

BAINES, ANTHONY. "Fifteenth-century Instruments in Tinctoris's *De Inventione et Usu Musicæ*," *Galpin Society Journal* III (1950): 24.

———. *Woodwind Instruments and their History.* Rev. ed. New York: Norton, 1963.

———. *Brass Instruments: Their History and Development.* London: Faber & Faber, 1976.

———. *The Oxford Companion to Musical Instruments.* Oxford: Oxford University Press, 1992.

BANK, J. A. *Tactus, Tempo and Notation in Mensural Music from the 13th to the 17th Century.* Amsterdam: Annie Bank, Anna Vond-Straat 13, 1972.

BARBOUR, JAMES MURRAY. *Tuning and Temperament. A Historical Survey.* East Lansing: Michigan State College Press, 1953. Rep. New York: Da Capo Press, 1972.

BARCLAY, ROBERT. *The Art of the Trumpet-Maker: The Materials, Tools, and Techniques of the 17th and 18th Centuries in Nuremberg.* Early Music Series 14. Oxford: Clarendon Press, 1992.

BARTLETT, CLIFFORD, and PETER HOLMAN. "Giovanni Gabrieli: A Guide to the Performance of his Instrumental Music." *Early Music* 3/1 (1975): 25–32.

BASSANO, GIOVANNI. *Ricercate, Passaggi et Cadentie.* Venice 1585. Modern edition ed. R. Erig. Zurich: Pelikan Edition no. 975, 1976.

BECK, SYDNEY, ed. *The First Book of Consort Lessons.* New York: Peters, 1959.

BEIER, PAUL. "Right Hand Position in Renaissance Lute Technique." *Journal of the Lute Society of America* 12 (1979): 5–24.

BENT, MARGARET. "*Musica Recta* and *musica ficta*." *Musica disciplina* 26 (1972): 73–100.

———. "*Resfacta* and *Cantare Super Librum.*" *Journal of the American Musicological Society* 36 (1983): 372–391.

BERGER, ANNA MARIA BUSSE. "The Relationship of Perfect and Imperfect Time in Italian Theory of the Renaissance." *Early Music History* 5. Ed. I. Fenlon. London: Cambridge University Press (1985): 1–28.

BERGER, KAROL. *Musica ficta: Theories of Accidental Inflections in Vocal Polyphony from Marchetto da Padova to Gioseffo Zarlino.* Cambridge: Cambridge University Press, 1987.

———. "*Musica ficta.*" See Brown/Sadie–*Performance*: 107–125.

BERMUDO, JUAN. *Declaración de instrumentos musicales.* Ossuna, 1555. Facs. ed. by M. S. Kastner (in *Documenta musicologica*). Kassel: Bärenreiter, 1957.

BESSELER, HEINRICH. "Die Entstehung der Posaune." *Acta Musicologica* 22 (1950): 8–35.

———. *Bourdon und Fauxbourdon: Studien zum Ursprung der niederländischen Musik.* 2d rev. ed. Ed. Peter Gülke. Leipzig: 1974.

BILLINGE, MICHAEL, and BONNIE SHALJEAN. "The Dalway or Fitzgerald Harp (1621)." *Early Music* 15/2 (1987): 175–187.

BISHOP, MARTHA. *Method for Classroom or Private Study.* Atlanta: Emory University, 1990.

BITHELL, J. *German Pronunciation and Phonology.* London: Methuen, 1952.

BLACKWOOD, EASLEY. *The Structure of Recognizable Diatonic Tunings.* Princeton: Princeton University Press, 1985.

BLADES, JAMES. "Percussion Instruments of the Middle Ages and Renaissance: Their History in Literature and Painting." *Early Music* 1/1 (1973): 11–18.

———. *Percussion Instruments and their History.* Leeds: Faber & Faber, 1975.

———. *Early Percussion Instruments from the Middle Ages to the Baroque.* Oxford: Oxford University Press, 1970.

BLADES, JAMES, and JEREMY MONTAGU. "Capriol's Revenge." *Early Music* 1/2 (1973): 84–92.

BORDAS, CRISTINA. "The Double Harp in Spain from the 16th to the 18th Centuries." *Early Music* 15/2 (1987): 148–163.

BORGIR, THARALD. *The Performance of the basso continuo in Italian Baroque Music.* Ann Arbor, MI: UMI Research Press, 1987.

BOSSINENSIS, FRANCISCUS. *Tenori e contrabassi intabulati col sopran in canto figurato . . . Libro primo.* Venice, 1509. *Libro secundo.* Venice, 1511. Ed. B. Disertori as *Le frottole per canto e liuto intabulate de Franciscus Bossinensis.* Milan: Istituzioni e monumenti dell'arte musicale italiana, Nuova Serie III, 1964.

BOTTEGARI, COSIMO. *The Bottegari Lutebook.* Ed. Carol MacClintock. Wellesley edition Nr. 8. Wellesley, MA: 1965.

BOTTRIGARI, ERCOLE. *Il Desiderio overo, De' concerti di varii strumenti musicali.* Venice, 1594. *Concerning the playing together of various musical instruments.* Trans. Carol Mac-Clintock in *Musicological Studies and Documents* 9. American Institute of Musicology, n.p., 1962.

BOULEZ, PIERRE. "The Vestal Virgin and the Fire-stealer: Memory, Creation, and Authenticity." *Early Music* 18/3 (1990): 355–358.

BOURCIEZ, EDOUARD. *Éléments de Linguistique Romane.* 4th ed. Paris: C. Klincksieck, 1946.

_____. *Phonétique Française: Etude historique.* Paris: C. Klincksieck, 1967.

BOWERS, JANE. "New Light on the Development of the Transverse Flute between about 1650 and about 1770." *Journal of the American Musical Instrument Society* 3 (1977): 5–56.

BOWERS, ROGER. "The Performing Pitch of English Fifteenth-Century Church Polyphony." *Early Music* 8/1 (1980): 21–28.

BOWLES, EDMUND. "Iconography as a Tool for Examining the Loud Consort in the Fifteenth Century." *Journal of the American Music Instrument Society* 3 (1977): 100–121.

_____. *Musikleben im 15. Jahrhundert.* Bd. III, Vol. 8 in the series: *Musikgeschichte in Bildern.* Ed. Werner Bachmann. Kassel: Bärenreiter-Verlag, 1987.

_____. *Musical Ensembles in Festival Books 1500–1800: An Iconographical & Documentary Survey.* Ann Arbor, MI: UMI Research Press, 1989.

BOXALL, MARIA. "English keyboard technique up to the death of Henry Purcell." Thesis, Trinity College, London, 1970.

_____. "Girolamo Diruta's *Il Transilvano* and the early Italian keyboard tradition." *English Harpsichord Magazine* 1/8 (1976): 168.

_____. *Harpsichord Method Based on 16th- to 18th-Century Sources.* 2 vols. London: Schott, 1977.

_____. "New light on the early Italian keyboard tradition." *English Harpsichord Magazine* 2/3, (1978): 71–72.

_____. *Harpsichord Studies.* New York: Schott, 1980.

BOYDELL, BARRA. *The Crumhorn and Other Renaissance Windcap Instruments.* Buren: Frits Knuf, 1982.

BOYDEN, DAVID. *The History of Violin Playing from its Origins to 1761 and Its Relationship to the Violin and Violin Music.* Oxford: Oxford University Press, 1965.

_____. *The New Grove Violin Family.* London: Macmillan, 1989.

BRAINARD, INGRID. *The Art of Courtly Dancing in the Early Renaissance.* West Newton, MA: 1981. (Available from the author at 37 Princess Road, West Newton, MA 02165 for $12 plus $1.50 shipping & handling.)

BRAY, ROGER. "The Interpretation of *musica ficta* in English Music *c.*1490–*c.*1580." *Proceedings of the Royal Musical Association* 97 (1970–71): 29–45.

_____. "More Light on Early Tudor Pitch." *Early Music* 8/1 (1980): 35–42.

BIBLIOGRAPHY

Brett, Phillip. "Text, Context, and the Early Music Editor." See Kenyon: 83–114.

Brown, Adrian. *The Recorder: A Basic Workshop Manual.* Brighton: Dolce Edition, 1989.

Brown, Howard M. *Instrumental Music Printed before 1600: A Bibliography.* Cambridge, MA: Harvard University Press, 1965.

———. "Psyche's Lament." *Words and Music: The Scholar's View. Festschrift for A. Tillman Merritt.* Ed. Laurence Berman. Cambridge, MA: Department of Music, Harvard University, 1972, 1–27.

———. *Sixteenth-Century Instrumentation: The Music for the Florentine Intermedii.* Rome: American Institute of Musicology, 1973.

———. "A Cook's Tour of Ferrara in 1529." *Rivista italiana di musicologia* X (1975): 216–241

———. *Embellishing Sixteenth-Century Music.* Early Music Series 1. Oxford: Clarendon Press, 1976.

———. "Instruments and Voice in the Fifteenth-Century Chanson." In *Current Thought in Musicology.* Ed. J. W. Grubbs et al. Austin: University of Texas Press, 1976, 89–137.

———. "Choral Music in the Renaissance." *Early Music* 6 (1978): 164–169.

———. "Lira da braccio." In *New Grove Dictionary of Music and Musicians.* 20 volumes. Ed. Stanley Sadie. London: Macmillan, 1980.

———. "Notes (and Transposing Notes) on the Viol in the Early Sixteenth Century." In *Music in Medieval and Early Modern Europe.* Ed. Iain Fenlon. Cambridge: Cambridge University Press, 1981, 61–78.

———. "Notes (and Transposing Notes) on the Transverse Flute in the Early Sixteenth Century." *Journal of the American Musical Instrument Society* 12 (1986): 5–39.

———. "Pedantry or Liberation? A Sketch of the Historical Performance Movement." See Kenyon: 27–56.

———. "Petrarch in Naples: Notes on the Formation of Giaches de Wert's Style." In *Essays on Italian Music in the Cinquecento* in the series: *Altro polo.* Ed. Richard Charteris. Sydney: F. May Foundation for Italian Studies, Italian Institute for Culture, and the University of Sydney, 1990, 16–50.

Brown, Howard M., and Stanley Sadie. *Performance Practice: Music before 1600.* New York: Norton, 1989. Articles by Brown: "Introduction," 147–166 and "Instruments," 167–184.

Brunot, Ferdinand. *Histoire de la langue française des origines à nos jours.* Vols. 1–2 (of 13). Paris: Armand Colin, 1966.

Caldwell, John. *Editing Early Music.* Early Music Series 5. Oxford: Clarendon Press, 1985.

Cardan, Jerome. *De musica* (ca. 1546). In *Hieronymus Cardanus: Writings on Music.* Trans. and ed. Clement A. Miller in *Musicological Studies and Documents* 32. American Institute of Musicology, n.p., 1973.

Caroso, Fabritio. *Il Ballarino.* Venice, 1581.

———. *Della Noblitá di Dame.* Venice, 1600. Facs. rpt. New York: Broude Brothers. Trans. Julia Sutton. London: Oxford University Press, 1986.

Carpenter, Pat. "Tonal coherence in a motet of Dufay." *Journal of Music Theory* 17 (1973): 2–65.

Carver, Anthony. *Cori spezzati.* Vols. 1 & 2: *An Anthology of Sacred Polychoral Music.* Cambridge: Cambridge University Press, 1988.

Charles, Sidney. *A Handbook of Music and Music Literature in Sets and Series.* New York: Free Press, 1972.

COLLVER, MICHAEL. *215 Chop-Busters for the Cornetto.* Available from the compiler at 14 King Street, Lexington, MA 02173 ($10).

COLLVER, MICHAEL, and BRUCE DICKEY. "Musik für Zink—Ein Quellenkatalog." *Basler Jahrbuch für historische Musikpraxis* V (1981): 263–314.

CONRAD VON ZABERN. *De modo bene cantandi choralem cantum.* Mainz, 1474. "Singing with Proper Refinement." Intro. & trans. Joseph Dyer. *Early Music* 6/2 (1978): 207–238. Excerpt in MacClintock–*Readings*: 12–16.

COPEMAN, HAROLD. *Singing in Latin.* 1990. Available from the author at 22 Tawney Street, Oxford OX3 1JN, England. Also available, *The Pocket Singing in Latin.*

CORNAZANO, ANTONIO. *Libro dell'arte del danzare.* 1455/65. Trans. Madeleine Inglehearn. London: Dance Books, 1981.

CROCKER, RICHARD. "Discant, counterpoint and harmony." *Journal of the American Musicological Society* 15 (1962): 1–21.

CRUM, ALISON. *Play the Viol: the complete guide to playing the treble, tenor, and bass viol.* Oxford: Oxford University Press, 1989.

CRUTCHFIELD, WILL. "A Report from the Battlefield." *The New York Times* (Sunday, 28 July 1985). Sec. 2, p. 1.

———. "Fashion, Conviction, and Performance Style in an Age of Revivals." See Kenyon: 19–26.

CUNNINGHAM, JAMES. *Dancing in the Inns of Court.* London: Jordan and Sons, 1965.

DAHLHAUS, CARL. "Zur Theorie des Tactus im 16. Jahrhundert." *Archiv für Musikwissenschaft* 28 (1961): 223.

———. *Studies on the Origin of Harmonic Tonality.* Trans. Robert O. Gjerdingen. Princeton: Princeton University Press, 1991.

DANNER, PETER. "Before Petrucci: The Lute in the Fifteenth Century." *Journal of the Lute Society of America* 5 (1972): 4–17.

DART, THURSTON. "How they sang in Jena in 1598." *Musical Times* (April 1967): 316–317.

———. *The Interpretation of Music.* London: Hutchinson & Co. LTD, 1954. Rep. New York: Harper & Row, 1967.

DICKEY, BRUCE. "The Decline of the Cornett." *Musick* (Journal of the Vancouver Society for Early Music) (March 1983): 26.

DI PASQUALE, MARCO. "Gli strumenti musicali dell'Accademia filarmonica di Verona: un approccio documentario." *Il Flauto Dolce* 17–18 (1987–88): 3–17.

DIXON, PEGGY. *Nonsuch Early Dance.* Vol. I: *Mediaeval to French Basse danse.* 1985, copyright Peggy Dixon. Dance reconstruction and practice tape.

———. *Nonsuch Early Dance.* Vol. II: *Quattrocento Italian and Caroso & Negri Dances.* 1985, copyright Peggy Dixon. Dance reconstruction and practice tape.

DOBBINS, FRANK. *Music in Renaissance Lyons.* Oxford: Clarendon Press, 1992.

DOBSON, E. J. *English Pronunciation, Fifteen Hundred to Seventeen Hundred.* 2 vols. London: Oxford University Press, 1975.

DODD, GORDON. *Thematic Index of Music for Viols.* London: Viola da Gamba Society, 1980.

DOE, PAUL, "Another View of *musica ficta* in Tudor Music." *Proceedings of the Royal Musical Association* 98 (1971–72): 113–122.

DONINGTON, ROBERT. *The Interpretation of Early Music.* New Version. New York: St. Martin's, 1974.

———. "The Present Position of Authenticity." *Performance Review* 2 (1989): 117.

DOWNIE, MARGARET. "Rebecs in French Literary Sources from 1379–1780." *Journal of the Viola da Gamba Society of America* 19 (1982): 71–98.

DREYFUS, LAURENCE. "Early Music Defended Against its Devotees: A Theory of Historical Performance in the Twentieth Century." *Musical Quarterly* 69 (1983): 297–322.

DUFFIN, ROSS W. "National Pronunciations of Latin ca. 1490–1600." *Journal of Musicology* 4 (1985–86): 217–226.

EDWARDS, HARWICK (ed.). *Music for Mixed Consort.* Musica Britannica 40. London: Stainer & Bell, 1977.

EDWARDS, JEAN. "The Experience of Early Music Singing." *Continuo* 8/3 (1985): 2–5.

EINSTEIN, ALFRED. *The Italian Madrigal.* Trans. Alexander H. Krappe, Roger H. Sessions, and Oliver Strunk. 3 vols. Princeton: Princeton University Press, 1949.

ELLIS, ALEXANDER. "On the History of Musical Pitch." *Journal of the Society of Arts* 27 (1880): 293–336, 400–403; 29 (1881): 109–112. Reprinted in *Studies in the History of Musical Pitch.* Amsterdam: Frits Knuf 1968.

––––––. *On Early English Pronunciation, with Especial Reference to Shakespeare and Chaucer.* 5 vols. London: Asher & Co., 1869–89.

ELSNER, EMILIE. *Untersuchung Instrumentalen Besetzungspraxis der weltlichen Musik im 16. Jahrhundert in Italien.* Ph.D. diss., Friedrich-Wilhelms-Universität, Berlin, 1933.

ERICKSON, J. GUNNAR, et al. *Musicians's Guide to Copyright.* Rev. ed. New York: Scribner's, 1983.

ERIG, RICHARD, with VERONIKA GUTMANN. *Italian Diminutions from 1553–1638.* Zürich: Amadeus Press, 1979.

FALLOWS, DAVID. "Specific Information on the Ensembles for Composed Polyphony, 1400–1474." *Studies in the Performance of Late Mediæval Music.* Ed. Stanley Boorman. Cambridge: Cambridge University Press, 1983.

––––––. "Secular Polyphony in the 15th Century." See Brown/Sadie–*Performance*: 201–221.

FERAND, ERNST. *Improvisation in Nine Centuries of Western Music. Anthology of Music,* Vol. 12. Cologne: Arno Volk Verlag, 1961.

––––––. "Didactic Embellishment Literature in the Late Renaissance: A Survey of Sources." *Aspects of Medieval and Renaissance Music.* New York: Norton, 1966, 154–172.

FERGUSON, HOWARD. *Keyboard Interpretation from the 14th to the 19th Century: An Introduction.* New York and London: Oxford University Press, 1975.

FEVES, ANGENE. *Dances of a Noble Gathering. 16th-Century Italian Court Dances from Il Ballarino by Fabritio Caroso (1581).* Consortium Antiquum, Inc., Pleasant Hill, CA, 1985. Dance reconstruction booklet plus cassette tape.

––––––. *Homage to Amor. Sixteenth Century Dances of Love from Fabritio Caroso's Il Ballarino (1581) and Nobiltà di Dame (1600).* Played by Les Verres Cassés. Copyright Angene Feves, 1987. Cassette tape only; booklet in preparation.

Final Report of the National Commission on New Technological Uses of Copyrighted Works, July 31, 1978. Washington, DC: Library of Congress, 1979.

FINCK, HERMANN. *Practica Musica.* Wittenberg: Erben Rhau, 1556. Book V: "On the Art of Singing Elegantly and Sweetly." Trans. in MacClintock–*Readings*: 61–67.

FINE, ORONCE. *Epithoma musice instrumentalis.* Paris, 1530. Facs. in D. Heartz, ed. *Preludes, Chansons and Dances for Lute.* Neuilly-sur-Seine: Société de Musique d'Autrefois, 1964.

FINK, REGINALD H. *The Trombonist's Handbook.* Athens, OH: Accura Music, 1977.

FISCHER, HENRY GEORGE. *The Renaissance Sackbut and Its Use Today.* New York: Metropolitan Museum of Art, 1984.

FITZPATRICK, HORACE. "The Medieval Recorder." *Early Music* 3/4 (1975): 361–364.

FOUCHÉ, PIERRE. *Phonétique historique du français.* 2nd ed. Paris: C. Klincksieck, 1966.

FRAENKEL, GOTTFRIED S., comp. *Pictorial and Decorative Title Pages from Music Sources: 201 Examples from 1500 to 1800.* New York: Dover, 1968.

FRANCALANCI, ANDREA. *Balli e Balletti da Ballare. Danses de la Renaissance Italienne.* Cassette tape, 1987. ADDA distribution AD 14.

FRAUNCE, ABRAHAM. *The Arcadian Rhetorique* (1588). Ed. Ethel Seaton. Oxford: Blackwell, 1950.

GABLE, FREDERICK. "Some Observations concerning Baroque and Modern Vibrato." *Performance Practice Review* (April 1992): 90–102.

GAFFURIUS, FRANCHINUS. *Practica musicæ.* Milan, 1496. Trans. Clement A. Miller in *Musicological Studies and Documents* 20. American Institute of Musicology, n.p., 1968.

_____. *De Harmonia Musicorum Instrumentorum Opus.* Milan, 1518.

GALLO, ALBERTO. "Il 'Ballare Lombardo' (*circa* 1435–1475)." *Studi Musicali* 7 (1979): 61–84.

GAMMIE, IAN. *A Book of Bowings.* Hertfordshire: Golden Phoenix Publications, 1986.

GANASSI, SYLVESTRO DI. *Opera intitulata Fontegara.* Venice, 1535. Facs. rpt. 1934/1970. German trans. H. Peter. Berlin-Lichterfelde: Robert Lienau, 1956. Eng. trans. H. Peter and Dorothy Swainson. Berlin Lichterfelde: Robert Lienau, 1959.

_____. *Regola Rubertina.* Venice, 1542. Facs. rpt. 1924/1970. Teil 1 und Teil 2. Ed. Hildemarie Peter. Berlin: Robert Lienau, 1972. English trans. Richard Bodig in *Journal of the Viola da Gamba Society of America* 18 (1981).

_____. *Lettione seconda.* Venice, 1543. English trans. Richard Bodig in *Journal of the Viola da Gamba Society of America* 19 (1982).

GERLE, HANS. *Musica teusch, auf die Instrument der grossen unnd kleinen Geygen, auch Lautten,* Nuremberg, 1532. Typescript of English translation and transcription of examples by Gordon J. Kinney. Lexington: M. I. King Library, University of Kentucky, 1977.

GILLON, EDMUND V., JR., comp. *Decorative Frames and Borders: 396 Examples from the Renaissance to the Present Day.* New York: Dover, 1973.

GLAREANUS, HENRICUS. *Dodecachordon.* Trans. Clement A. Miller in *Musicological Studies and Documents,* No. 6. American Musicological Society, n.p., 1965.

GODT, IRVING. "Reading Ligatures from their Ground State." *Early Music* 4/1 (1976): 44–45.

GODWIN, JOSCELYN. "The Renaissance Flute." *The Consort* 28 (1972): 70–81.

_____. "Playing from Original Notation." *Early Music* 1/2 (1974): 15–19.

GOUSE, CHARLES. *The Cornett: Its History, Literature, and Performance Praxis.* D.M.A. thesis, Boston University, 1974

GRANDGENT, C. H. *From Latin to Italian: An Historical Outline of the Phonology and Morphology of the Italian Language.* Cambridge, MA: Harvard University Press, 1927.

GRIFFIOEN, RUTH VAN BAAK. *Jacob van Eyck's Der Fluyten-Lusthof.* Utrecht: Vereniging voor Nederlandse Muziekgechiedenis, 1991.

GUTMAN, VERONIKA. "Viola bastarda—Instrument oder Diminutionspraxis?" *Archiv für Musikwissenschaft* 35 (1978): 178–209.

HAAR, JAMES. "Monophony and the Unwritten Traditions." See Brown/Sadie–*Performance*: 240–266.

HADAWAY, ROBERT. "The Re-creation of an Italian Renaissance Harp." *Early Music* 8/1 (1980): 59–62.

_____. "A Knot of Harp Strings." *Early Music* 11/1 (1983): 63–68.

HANTELMANN, GEORG. *How to Play the Crumhorn, Cornamusa and Curtall* [*Kortholt*]. Celle: Moeck Verlag, Nr. 2077, 1975.

HARRÁN, DON. "Vincentino and his Rules of Text Underlay." *Musical Quarterly* 59 (1973): 620–632.

_____. "New Light on the Question of Text Underlay Prior to Zarlino." *Acta musicologica* 45 (1973): 24–56.

_____. "In Pursuit of Origins: the Earliest Writing on Text Underlay (ca. 1440)." *Acta musicologica* 50 (1978): 217–240.

_____. "Directions to Singers in Writings of the Early Renaissance." *Revue belge de musicologie* 41 (1987): 45–61.

HARWOOD, IAN. "A Case of Double Standards? Instrumental Pitch in England ca. 1600." *Early Music* 9/4 (1981): 470–481.

HAYNES, BRUCE. "Johann Sebastian Bach's Pitch Standards: The Woodwind Perspective." *Journal of the American Musical Instrument Society* 11 (1985): 55–114.

HEARTZ, DANIEL, ed. *Preludes, Chansons and Dances for Lute.* Neuilly-sur-Seine: Société de musique d'autre fois, 1964.

HENAHAN, DORAL. "When vibrato is on shaky ground." *American Choral Review* 29 (1987): 10–12, n. 2.

HERLINGER, JAN, review of Karol Berger, *Musica ficta: Theories of Accidental Inflection in Vocal Polyphony from Marchetto da Padova to Gioseffo Zarlino. Journal of the American Musicological Society* 42 (1989): 640–647.

HERMELINK, SIEGFRIED. "Chiavette." In *New Grove Dictionary of Music and Musicians*, ed. Stanley Sadie in 20 vols. London: Macmillan, 1980, 4/321–23.

HETTRICK, WILLIAM. "Sebastian Virdung's method for recorders of 1511: a translation with commentary." *The American Recorder* 20/3 (1979): 99–105.

_____. "Martin Agricola's Poetic Discussion of Recorder and Other Woodwind Instruments." *The American Recorder* 21/3 (1980): 103–113; 23 (1982): 139–146; and 24/2 (1983): 51–60.

HEYDE, HERBERT. *Hörner und Zinken.* Leipzig: VEB Deutscher Verlag, 1982.

HEYER, A. H. *Historical Sets, Collected Editions, and Monuments of Music.* Chicago: American Library Association, 1980.

HIGHSTEIN, ELLEN. *Making Music in Looking Glass Land: A Guide to Survival and Business Skills for the Classical Performer.* New York: Concert Artists Guild (850 Seventh Avenue, New York, NY 10019), 1991.

HOLLAND, JON B. "Francisco Correa de Arauxo's *Faculdad organica:* a translation and study of its theoretical and pedagogical aspects." Thesis, University of Oregon, 1985.

HOLMAN, PETER. "The Harp in Stuart England: New Light on William Lawes's Harp Consorts." *Early Music* 15/2 (1987): 188–203.

_____. *Four and Twenty Fiddlers (the Violin at the English Court 1540–1690).* Oxford: Clarendon Press, 1993.

HOPPIN, RICHARD, "Partial Signatures and *musica ficta* in Some Early 15th-Century Sources." *Journal of the American Musicological Society* 6 (1953): 197–215.

HORSLEY, IMOGENE. "Improvised Embellishment in the Performance of Renaissance Polyphonic Music." *Journal of the American Musicological Society* 4 (1951): 3–19

_____. "Wind Techniques in the Sixteenth and Early Seventeenth Centuries." *Brass Quarterly* 4 (1960): 49–63.

_____. "The Early Music Performer in the University." *College Music Symposium* 12 (1972): 11–13.

_____. "Full and Short Scores in the Early Baroque." *Journal of the American Musicological Society* 30 (1977): 466–99.

HOULE, GEORGE. "Origins of the Measure in the Seventeenth Century." *Meter in Music, 1600–1800.* Bloomington: Indiana University Press, 1987, 1–34.

HUBBARD, FRANK. *Three Centuries of Harpsichord Building.* Cambridge, MA: Harvard University Press, 1965.

HUGHES, ANDREW. *Manuscript Accidentals: ficta in Focus, 1350–1450. Musicological Studies & Documents* 27. American Institute of Musicology, n.p., 1972.

HUNT, EDGAR. *The Crumhorn.* Edition 11239. New York: Schott, 1975.

INGLEHEARN, MADELEINE. *15th Century Dances from Burgundy and Italy.* Witham, Essex, England: The Companie of Dansers, 1981. Booklet with instructions, music for the dances, plus cassette tape.

_____. *Ten Dances from Sixteenth Century Italy.* Witham, Essex, England: The Companie of Dansers, 1983. Instruction booklet plus cassette tape.

JACKSON, ROLAND. *A Bibliography of Performance Practice.* New York: Garland, 1988. Annual supplements in *Performance Practice Review.*

JAMBE DE FER, PHILIBERT. *Epitome musical.* Lyon, 1556. *The Epitome Musical.* Eng. trans. with notes by Gordon J. Kinney. Microfilm of transcript. Lexington: M.I. King Library, University of Kentucky, 1977. Facs. ed. François Lesure, "*Epitome musical* de Philibert Jambe de Fer (1556)." *Annales Musicologiques* 6 (1958–63): 341–86.

JORGENSEN, OWEN. *Tuning the Historical Temperaments by Ear.* Marquette: Northern Michigan University Press, 1977.

_____. *The Equal-Beating Temperaments.* Raleigh, NC: Sunbury Press, 1981.

KÄRSTADT, GEORG. "Zur Geschichte des Zinken und seiner Verwendung in der Musik des 16.-18. Jahrhunderts." *Archiv für Musikforschung* 2/4 (1937): 385–432.

KAYE, MARTIN. "Cornett on the Margins." *Continuo* (December 1986): 7–10; "The Cornett in Context" (January 1987): 2–6; "Future Cornett: A Personal Exploration" (Summer 1987): 2–5; "Future Cornett: Conclusion" (February 1988): 14–17.

KENYON, NICHOLAS. "Authenticity and Early Music: Some Issues and Questions." *Authenticity and Early Music.* Ed. Nicholas Kenyon. Oxford: Oxford University Press, 1988, 1–18.

KERMAN, JOSEPH. "The Historical Performance Movement." Chap. 6 in *Contemplating Music: Challenges to Musicology.* Cambridge, MA: Harvard University Press. 1985.

KEYL, STEPHEN. *Arnolt Schlick and Instrumental Music circa 1500.* Ph.D. diss., Duke University, 1989.

_____. "Tenorlied, Discantlied, Polyphonic Lied: Voices and Instruments in German Secular Polyphony of the Renaissance." *Early Music* 20/3 (1992): 434–445.

KINKELDEY, OTTO. "Dance Tunes of the Fifteenth Century." In *Instrumental Music: A Conference at Isham Memorial Library.* Ed. David G. Hughes. Cambridge, MA: Harvard University Press, 1959. Rpt. New York: Da Capo, 1972, 89–152.

KIRK, DOUGLAS. "Cornetti and Renaissance Pitch Standards in Italy and Germany." *Journal de Musique Ancienne* 10.4 (Juin 1989). Available from the Studio de Musique Ancienne, 3894 St. Hubert, Montreal, Quebec, CN H2L 4A5.

KLOP, G. C. *Harpsichord Tuning: Course Outline.* Gerderen, Holland: Werk plaats voor clavecimbelbouw, 1974. Trans. Glen Wilson. Raleigh, NC: Sunbury Press, 1974.

KNIGHTON, TESS, and DAVID FALLOWS. *Companion to Medieval & Renaissance Music.* New York: Schirmer Books, 1992.

KOOPMAN, TON. "My Ladye Nevell's Booke and old fingering." *English Harpsichord Magazine* 2/1 (1977): 5–10.

KOTTICK, EDWARD L. T*he Collegium: A Handbook*. Stonington, CT: October House, 1977.
———. *The Harpsichord Owner's Guide*. Chapel Hill: University of North Carolina Press, 1987.

KREITNER, KENNETH. "Minstrels in Spanish churches, 1400–1600." *Early Music* 20/4 (1992): 533–546.

LAMBRECHTS-DOUILLEZ, JEANNINE. "Een contrabas blokfuit in het Museum Vleeshuis te Antwerpen: curiosum en wereldunicum." *Miscellanea Josef Duverger*. Ghent: 1968, 907–919.

LANFRANCO, GIOVANNI. *Scintille di musica*. Brescia, 1533.

LANGWIL, LINDSAY. *The Bassoon and Contrabassoon*. New York: Norton, 1965.

LANHAM, RICHARD. *A Handlist of Rhetorical Terms*. 2 ed. Berkeley: University of California Press, 1991.

LASOCKI, DAVID. "The Recorder Consort at the English Court 1540–1673." Part I, *The American Recorder* 25/3 (1984): 91–100; Part II, *The American Recorder* 25/4 (1984): 131–135.

LEECH-WILKINSON, DANIEL. "The Limits of Authenticity: A Discussion." *Early Music* 12/1 (1984): 13–16.

LEEDY, DOUGLAS. "A Personal View of Meantone Temperament." *The Courant* 5/3 (1983): 3–19.

LE HURAY, PETER. *The Fingering of English Virginal Music*. London: Stainer & Bell, 1981.
———. "English Keyboard Fingering in the 16th and early 17th Centuries." In *Source Materials and the Interpretation of Music: A Memorial Volume for Thurston Dart*. Ed. Ian Bent. London: Stainer & Bell, 1981, 225–257.

LEONARDS, PETRA. "Historische Quellen zur Spielweise des Zinken." *Basler Jahrbuch für historische Musikpraxis* 5, 1981: 315–346.

LE ROY, ADRIAN. *A Brief and Plaine Instruction to Set All Musicke . . . in Tableture for the Lute*. London, 1574. *Les Instructions pour le Luth*. J. Jacquet, P.-Y Sourdes, and J.-M. Vaccaro, eds. Paris: Ballard, 1977.

LINDLEY, MARK. "Early 16th-Century Keyboard Temperaments." *Musica Disciplina* 28 (1974): 129–151.
———. Instructions for the Clavier Diversely Tempered." *Early Music* 5/1 (1977): 13–23.
———. "Ammerbach's 1583 exercises." *English Harpsichord Magazine* 3/8 (1983): 59; *The Courant* ii (1984).
———. "Early keyboard fingerings: a selected bibliography." *English Harpsichord Magazine* 3/8 (1983): 155–161.
———. *Lutes, Viols and Temperaments*. Cambridge: Cambridge University Press, 1984.
———. "Early English Keyboard Fingerings." *Basler Jahrbuch für historische Musikpraxis* 12 (1988): 9.
———. "Early Keyboard Fingerings: Some Editing Problems and Some New Readings for John Bull and J.S. Bach." *Early Music* 17/1 (1989): 60.
———. *Ars ludendi. Early German Keyboard Fingerings*. Neuhof: Tre Fontane, 1992.
———. *Early German Keyboard Fingerings*. Neuhof: Tre Fontane, 1993.
———, and MARIA BOXALL. *Early keyboard fingerings, a comprehensive guide*. Mainz: Schott, 1992.

LITTLE, MEREDITH. "Recent Research in European Dance, 1400–1800." *Early Music* 14/1 (1986): 4–14.

LOCKWOOD, LEWIS. *Music in Renaissance Ferrara 1400–1505*. Cambridge, MA: Harvard University Press, 1984.

LORETTO, ALEC. "When Is a Ganassi Recorder Not a Ganassi Recorder?" *The American Recorder* 27/2 (1986): 64–66.

LORRAINE, KEITH. *A Handbook on Making Double Reeds for Early Winds.* Musica Sacra et Profana. Available from the author: 787 Liberty Road, Petaluma, CA 94952.

LOWINSKY, EDWARD. "The Problem of Text Underlay." In *The Medici Codex of 1518.* Chicago: University of Chicago Press, 1968, 90–107.

LOWINSKY, EDWARD. "A Treatise on Text Underlay by a German Disciple of Francisco de Salinas." In *Festschrift Heinrich Besseler.* Leipzig: 1961, 231–251.

_____. "Foreword." *Musica nova. Monuments of Renaissance Music.* Ed. H. Colin Slim. Chicago: University of Chicago Press, 1964, v–xxi.

_____. "Music of the Renaissance as Viewed by Renaissance Musicians." In *The Renaissance Image of Man and the World.* Ed. Bernard O'Kelly. Columbus: Conference on the Humanities, Ohio State University Press, 1966.

MAFFEI, GIOVANNI CAMILO. *Delle lettere . . . Libri Due.* Naples, 1562. "Letter on Singing." trans. in MacClintock–*Readings:* 37–61.

MacCLINTOCK, CAROL. *Readings in the History of Music in Performance.* Bloomington: Indiana University Press, 1979.

MacMILLAN, DOUGLAS. "The Crumhorn—A Historical Survey." *The Consort,* no. 30 (1974): 63–66.

MARIX, JEANNE. *Histoire de la musique et des musiciens de la cour de Bourgogne sous le règne de Philippe le Bon (1420–1467).* Strasbourg: Heitz et Co., 1939, 105–106.

MARROCCO, W. THOMAS. *Inventory of 15th Century Bassedanze, Balli & Balletti.* CORD (Congress on Research in Dance), New York: Dance Research Annual XIII, 1981. New York University.

MARVIN, BOB. "Recorders & English Flutes in European Collections." *Galpin Society Journal* 25 (July 1972): 30–57.

_____. "Making Renaissance Recorders." *Continuo* (January 1985): 2–7.

MASON, KEVIN. *The Chitarrone and its Repertory in Early Seventeenth-Century Italy.* Leeds: Boethius Press, 1989.

_____. "Per Cantare e sonare: Lute Tablature Accompaniments of Italian Vocal Polyphony at the End of the Renaissance." *Playing the Lute, Vihuela and Guitar: Historical Practice and Modern Interpretation.* Cambridge Studies in Performance Practice, ed. Victor Coelho. Cambridge: Cambridge University Press, 1994.

McGEE, TIMOTHY. *Singing Early Music: An Introductory Guide to the Pronunciation of European Languages in the Middle Ages and Renaissance.* Bloomington: Indiana University Press. (Forthcoming)

_____. *Medieval and Renaissance Music: A Performer's Guide.* Toronto: University of Toronto Press, 1985.

MEIER, BERNHARD. *The Modes of Classical Polyphony described according to the sources.* Trans. Ellen S. Beebe. New York: Broude Brothers, 1988.

MELII, PIETRO PAOLO. *Intavolaturea di Liuto Attiorbato. Libro Quarto,* 1616. Facs. ed. Florence: SPES, 1979.

MENDEL, ARTHUR. "Pitch in the 16th and Early 17th Centuries." *Musical Quarterly* 34 (1948): 28–45, 199–221, 336–57, 575–93. Reprinted in *Studies in the History of Musical Pitch,* Amsterdam: Frits Knuf 1968.

_____. "On the Pitches in Use in Bach's Time." *Musical Quarterly* 41 (1955): 332–354, 466–480.

_____. "Some Ambiguities of the Mensural System." In *Studies in Music History: Essays for Oliver Strunk*. Ed. Harold Powers. Princeton: Princeton University Press, 1968, 137–160.

———. "Pitch in Western Music since 1500—a Re-Examination." *Acta musicologica* 50 (1978): 1–93.

MERLIN, FRANÇOIS, and JACQUES CELLIER. *Recherche de Plusieurs Singularités*. Bibliothèque Nationale, Paris, ms français 9152.

MERSENNE, MARIN. *Harmonie universelle: contenant la theorie et la pratique de la musique.* Paris, 1636. Facs. ed. with introduction by François Lesure. Paris: Centre national de la recherche scientifique, 1965. *Harmonie universelle: the books on instruments.* Trans. Roger E. Chapman. The Hague: M. Nijhoff, 1957.

MERTIN, JOSEF. *Early Music: Approaches to Performance Practice.* Trans. Siegmund Levarie. New York: Da Capo Press, 1986.

MEYER, KENTON. *The Crumhorn: Its History, Design, Repertory, and Technique.* Ann Arbor, MI: UMI Research Press, 1983.

MINOR, ANDREW, and BONNER MITCHELL. *A Renaissance Entertainment.* Columbia: University of Missouri Press, 1968.

MOECK, HERMANN. *Typen europäischer Blockflöten in Vorzeit, Geschichte und Volksüberlieferung.* Celle: Moeck Verlag, 1967.

MONTAGU, JEREMY. "Early Percussion Techniques." *Early Music* 2/1 (1974): 20–24.

———. *Making Early Percussion Instruments.* Oxford: Oxford University Press, 1976.

———. *The World of Medieval and Renaissance Musical Instruments.* New York: Overlook Press, 1976.

MORGAN, FRED. "Making recorders based on historical models." *Early Music* 10/1 (1982): 14–21.

MORGAN, ROBERT. "Tradition, Anxiety, and the Current Musical Scene." See Kenyon: 57–82.

MORLEY, THOMAS. *A Plaine and Easie Introduction to Practicall Musicke.* Ed. R. Alec Harman. New York: Norton, 1973.

MORROW, MICHAEL. "Musical Performance and Authenticity." *Early Music* 6/2 (1978): 233–246.

———. "16th-Century Ensemble Viol Music." *Early Music* 2/3 (1974): 160–163.

———. "The Renaissance Harp: the Instrument and its Music." *Early Music* 7/4 (1979): 499–510.

MOUNTNEY, HUGH. "The Regal." *Galpin Society Journal* 22 (1969): 3–22.

MUNROW, DAVID. *Instruments of the Middle Ages and Renaissance.* London: Oxford University Press, 1976.

MYERS, HERBERT. "The Musical Resources of the Fifteenth-Century Shawm Band." DMA Term Project, Stanford University, 1980. Available from the author: 2180 Monterey Avenue, Menlo Park, CA 94025.

———. "The Practical Acoustics of Early Woodwinds." DMA Final Project, Stanford University, 1980. UM 81–09,026.

———. "Observations: Praetorius's Pitch." *Early Music* 12/3 (1984): 369–371. Reply by Ephraim Segerman. *Early Music* 13/2 (1985): 261–263.

MYERS, JOAN. "Vihuela Technique." *Journal of the Lute Society of America* 1 (1968): 15–18.

NEGRI, CESARE. *Le Gratie d'Amore.* Milan, 1602. Facs. rpt. by Forni, Bologna. Trans. Gustavia Y. Kendall, 1985. Available from UMI, Ann Arbor, MI.

NEUMANN, BERTOLD. " . . . kompt pfeift und trombt . . . On the Use of Percussion Instruments in the Dance Music of the Renaissance." Trans. Herbert Myers. *Histori-*

cal Performance 4/2 (1991): 88–93. Reply by Ben Harms, "To the Editor." *Historical Performance* 5/1 (1992): 32–33.

NEUPERT, HANNS. *The Clavichord.* 1956. Trans. from the 2d German ed. Ann Feldberg. Kassel: Bärenreiter, 1965.

NEVEN, ARMAND. "L'Arpicordo." *Acta Musicologica* 42 (1970): 230–235.

NEWCOMB, ANTHONY. "Secular Polyphony in the 16th Century." See Brown/Sadie–*Performance*: 222–239.

——. *The Madrigal at Ferrara* 1579–1597. Princeton: Princeton University Press, 1980.

NEWMAN, DANNY. *Subscribe Now!* New York: Theatre Communications Group (935 Lexington Avenue, New York, NY 10017), 1977.

NORDSTROM, LYLE. "The Cambridge Consort Books." *Journal of the Lute Society of America* 5 (1972): 70–103.

——. "The English Lute Duet and Consort Lesson." *Lute Society Journal* 16 (1976): 5–22.

——. "The Lute Duets of John Johnson." *Journal of the Lute Society of America* 9 (1976): 33.

——. "The Lute in Settings for Consort." *Proceedings of the International Lute Symposium, Utrecht 1986.* Utrecht: Stimu, 1988, 50–63.

——. *The Bandora: Its Music and Sources.* In *Detroit Studies in Music Bibliography,* no. 66. Warren, MI: Harmonie Park Press, 1992.

NORTH, NIGEL. *Continuo Playing on the Lute, Archlute and Theorbo.* London: Faber & Faber, 1987.

NURSE, RAY. "Vibrato in Renaissance Music." *Musick* (Journal of the Vancouver Society for Early Music) 8/2 (1986): 2–8.

——. "On the Development of Renaissance Lute Construction." *Proceedings of the International Lute Symposium, Utrecht 1986.* Utrecht: Stimu, 1988, 101–112.

O'BRIEN, GRANT. *Ruckers: A Harpsichord and Virginal Building Tradition.* Cambridge: Cambridge University Press, 1990.

O'DETTE, PAUL. "Some Observations About the Tone of Early Lutenists." *Proceedings of the International Lute Symposium, Utrecht 1986.* Utrecht: Stimu, 1988, 86–91.

ORTIZ, DIEGO. *Tratado de glosas sobre clausulas y otros generos de puntos en la musica de violones.* Rome, 1553. Facs. ed. Florence: Studio per edizioni scelte, 1984. English trans. Peter Farrell in *Journal of the Viola da Gamba Society* 4 (1967).

OWEN, BARBARA, and PETER WILLIAMS. *The Organ. The New Grove Musical Instrument Series* 2: 838–916. New York and London: Norton, 1988.

PACOLONI, GIOVANNI. *Longe Elegantissima . . .* 1546. Facs. ed. Geneva: Minkoff.

PAGE, CHRISTOPHER. "Going Beyond the Limits: Experiments with Vocalization in the French Chanson, 1340–1440." *Early Music* 20/3 (1992): 446–459.

PALISCA, CLAUDE. "Vincenzo Galilei and some links between pseudo-monody and monody." *Musical Quarterly* 46 (1960): 344–360.

PANOFSKY, MARGARET. *Bass Viol Technique.* Albany, CA: PRB Publications, 1991.

PAPOLOS, JANICE. *The Performing Artist's Handbook.* Cincinnati: Writer's Digest Books (9933 Alliance Road, Cincinnati, OH 45242), 1984.

PARAS, JASON. *The Music for Viola Bastarda.* Bloomington: Indiana University Press, 1986.

PARKINS, ROBERT. "Keyboard Fingering in Early Spanish Sources." *Early Music* 11/3 (1983): 323–331.

PARROTT, ANDREW. "Transposition in Monteverdi's Vespers of 1610: An 'Aberration' Defended." *Early Music* 12/4 (1984): 490–516.

PENZL, HERBERT. *Vom Urgermanischen zum Neuhochdeutschen: eine historische Phonologie.* Berlin: Erich Schmidt Verlag, 1975.

PEPE, EDWARD. "Pythagorean Tuning and its Implications for the Music of the Middle Ages." *Courant* 1/2 (1983): 3–16. Reply by Bob Marvin. *Courant* 1/3 (1983): 28–29.

PERKINS, LEEMAN L. "Mode and Structure in the Masses of Josquin." *Journal of the American Musicological Society* 26 (1973): 189–239.

PETERSEN, ALICE. *A Guide to the Development and Direction of an Early Music Performance Program.* DA diss., Ball State University, 1980. UM 81–20735.

PHILLIPS, ELIZABETH, and JOHN-PAUL JACKSON. *Performing Medieval and Renaissance Music: An Introductory Guide.* New York: Schirmer Books, 1986.

PHILLIPS, PETER. "Performance Practice in 16th-Century English Choral Music." *Early Music* 6/2 (1978): 195–199.

PIRROTTA, NINO. "Music and Cultural Tendencies in 15th-Century Italy." *Journal of the American Musicological Society* 19 (1966): 127–161.

PLANCHART, ALEJANDRO. "Tempo and Proportions." See Brown/Sadie *Performance:* 126–144.

PLAYFORD, JOHN. *Musick's Recreation on the Lyra Viol.* London, 1652. Facsimile of *Musick's recreation on the viol, lyra-way,* 1682. London: Hinrichsen Edition, 1965.

POLK, KEITH. "Flemish Wind Bands in the Late Middle Ages, A Study in Improvisatory Performance Practices." Ph.D. diss., University of California at Berkeley, 1968. UM 69–03,674.

_____. "The Trombone in Archival Documents—1350–1500." *International Trombone Association Journal* 15/3 (1987): 24–31.

_____. "Augustein Schubinger and the Zinck: Innovation in Performance Practice." *Historic Brass Society Journal* 1 (1989): 83–92.

_____. "Vedel and Geige—Fiddle and Viol: German String Traditions in the Fifteenth Century." *Journal of the American Musicological Society* 42 (1989): 504–545.

_____. "Voices and Instruments: Soloists and Ensembles in the 15th Century." *Early Music* 18/2 (1990): 179–198.

_____. *German Instrumental Music of the Late Middle Age: Players, Patrons, and Performance Practice.* Cambridge: Cambridge University Press, 1992.

POULTON, DIANA. *Lute Playing Technique.* The Lute Society of the United Kingdom, London. 1981.

PRAETORIUS, MICHAEL. *Syntagma musicum* II. Wolfenbüttel, 1618, with *Theatrum instrumentorum,* Wolfenbüttel, 1620. Facs. Ed. Wilibald Gurlitt. Kassel: Bärenreiter, 1958. *Syntagma musicum* II. *De organographia:* parts I and II. Trans. and ed. David Z. Crookes. Oxford: Clarendon Press, 1986. *The Syntagma Musicum* vol. 2. *De Organographia,* parts I and II, of Michael Praetorius. English trans. Harold Blumenfeld, plus all 42 original woodcut illustrations from *Theatrum instrumentorum.* New York: Da Capo Press, 1980.

_____. *Syntagma Musicum* III. *Termini musici.* Wolfenbüttel, 1619. Trans. Hans Lampl, unpublished DMA diss., University of Southern California, 1957. "Instruction for Singers." *Syntagma Musicum* III. Trans. in MacClintock–*Readings:* 162–170. [Editor's translation in progress.]

PUGLIESE, PATRI, and JOSEPH CASAZZA. *Practise for Dauncinge, Some Almans and a Pavan, England 1570–1650.* Cambridge, MA, 1980. (Book, dance reconstructions, and practice tape can be ordered from the author at 39 Capen Street, Medford, MA 02155 for $5 plus $1.50 postage.)

PUGLISI, FILADELFIO. "A Survey of Renaissance Flutes." *Galpin Society Journal* 41 (1988): 67–82.

Pyles, Thomas. *The Origins and Development of the English Language.* New York: Harcourt, Brace, 1964.

Radke, Hans. "Beiträge zur Erforschung der Lauten-Tabulaturen des 16.-18. Jahrhunderts." *Die Musikforschung* 26 (1963): 34–51.

Ramm, Andrea von. "Singing Early Music." *Early Music* 4/1 (1976): 12–15.

Ramos de Pareja, Bartolomeo. *Musica Practica.* Bologna, 1482.

Rastall, Richard. *The Notation of Western Music: An Introduction.* New York: St. Martin's, 1983.

Reed, Mary Hutchings. *The Copyright Primer for Librarians and Educators.* Chicago: American Library Association; Washington, DC: National Education Association, 1987.

Remnant, Mary. *Musical Instruments of the West.* New York: St. Martin's, 1978.

———. *English Bowed Instruments from Anglo-Saxon to Tudor Times.* Oxford: Clarendon Press, 1986.

———. *Musical Instruments: An Illustrated History from Antiquity to the Present.* London: B. T. Batsford Ltd., 1989.

Rensch, Roslyn. *Harps and Harpists.* (Revision and update of *The Harp.*) Bloomington: Indiana University Press, 1989.

Reynolds, Christopher. "Sacred Polyphony." See Brown/Sadie–*Performance*: 185–200.

Riemann, Hugo. *History of Music Theory.* Vols. 1 & 2: *Polyphonic theory to the sixteenth century.* Trans. Raymond H. Haggh. Lincoln: University of Nebraska Press, 1962.

Riley, Maurice. *The Teaching of Bowed Instruments from 1511 to 1756.* Ph.D. diss., The University of Michigan, 1954. UMI no. 8236.

Ripin, Edwin. "A Reevaluation of Virdung's *Musica getutscht.*" *Journal of the American Musicological Society* 29/2 (1976): 189–223.

Robertson, Daniel. "Anyone for the Galliard?" *Early Music* 2/2 (1974): 83–84.

Rodgers, Julane. "Early keyboard fingering, ca. 1520–1620." Thesis, University of Oregon, 1971.

Rognoni, Richardo. *Passaggi per la semplice voce humana.* Venice, 1592.

———. *Passaggi per potersi essercitare nel diminuire terminatemente con ogni sorte d'instromente.* Venice, 1592.

Rooley, Anthony. "Dance and Dance Music of the 16th Century." *Early Music* 2/2 (1974): 79–83.

———, and James Tyler. "The Lute Consort." *The Lute Society Journal* 14 (1972): 13–24.

Routley, Nicholas. "A Practical Guide to *musica ficta.*" *Early Music* 13/1 (1985): 59–71.

Russell, Raymond. *The Harpsichord and Clavichord.* 2nd ed. Rev. and ed. Howard Schott. New York: Norton, 1973.

Sachs, Barbara, and Barry Ife. *Anthology of Early Keyboard Methods.* Cambridge: Gamut, 1982.

Sachs, Curt. *Musik und Oper am kurbrandenburgischen Hof.* Berlin: Julius Bard, 1910. Rep. Hildesheim & New York: Georg Olms Verlag, 1977.

Sadie, Stanley, ed. *The New Grove Dictionary of Music and Musicians.* London: Macmillan, 1980.

———. *The New Grove Dictionary of Musical Instruments.* London: Macmillan, 1984.

———. *Early Keyboard Instruments. The New Grove Musical Instrument Series.* New York and London: Norton, 1989.

Salinas, Francisco. *De Musica Libri Septem.* Salamanca, 1577.

Salmen, Walter. *Musikleben im 16. Jahrhundert,* III/9 in the series: *Musikgeschichte in Bildern.* Ed. Werner Bachmann. Kassel: Bärenreiter, 1983.

SANDYS, WILLIAM (1792–1874). *The History of the Violin and Other Instruments Played with the Bow from the Remotest Time to the Present.* London, 1864.

SCHERR, VERA. *Aufführungspraxis Vokalmusik: Handbuch der lateinische Aussprache.* Kassel: Bärenreiter, 1991.

SCHOTT, HOWARD. *Playing the Harpsichord.* London: Faber & Faber, 1971.

SCHLOSSER, JULIUS. *Die Sammlung alter Musikinstrumente.* Vienna: Kunstverlag Anton Schroll & Co., 1920.

SELFRIDGE-FIELD, ELEANOR. *Venetian Instrumental Music from Gabrieli to Vivaldi.* Oxford: Blackford, 1975.

_____. "Bassano and the Orchestra of St. Mark's." *Early Music* 4/2 (1976): 153–158.

SHANN, F. T. "Flemish Transposing Harpsichords—An Explanation." *Galpin Society Journal* 37 (March 1984): 62–71.

SHARP, CECIL. *The Country Dance Book.* 6 vols. London, Novello, 1909–1922. Rep. with some revisions by Maud Karpeles. Wakefield, West Yorkshire, England: EP Publishing Ltd., 1975–77. Contains dance reconstructions only; music is in separate volumes.

SIMPSON, CHRISTOPHER. *The Division-violist, or, An introduction to the Playing upon a Ground.* London, 1659. Chelys, minuritionum artificio exornata. *The division-viol; or, The art of playing ex tempore upon a ground.* Brome at the Gun in Ivy-Lane, 1665. Fasc. ed. New York: G. Schirmer, New York: 1955.

SMITH, ANNE. "Die Renaissancequerflöte und ihre Musik: Ein Beitrag zur Interpretation der Quellen." *Basler Jahrbuch für historische Musikpraxis* 2, (1978): 9–76.

_____. "The Renaissance Flute." in *The Early Flute* by John Solum. Early Music Series 15. Oxford: Clarendon Press, 1992: 11–33.

SMITH, DAVID HOGAN. *Trombone Technique in the Renaissance.* San Francisco: The King's Trumpetts and Shalmes, 1989. Available from the author at 1720 19th Ave., San Francisco, CA 94122.

_____. *Reed Design for Early Woodwinds.* Bloomington: Indiana University Press, 1992.

SMITH, JUDY, and IAN GATES. "What did Prince Henry do with his Feet on Sunday 19 August 1604?" *Early Music* 14/2 (1986): 199–208.

SODERLUND, SANDRA. *Organ Technique: An Historical Approach.* 2nd ed. Chapel Hill, NC: Hinshaw Music, 1986.

SPARLI, BARBARA. "The 15th-Century balli Tunes: A New Look." *Early Music* 14/3 (1986): 346–357.

SPENCER, KATHLEEN MORETTO, and HOWARD M. BROWN. "How Alfonso della Viola tuned his viols, and how he transposed." *Early Music* 14/4 (1986): 520–533.

SPENCER, ROBERT. "Chitarrone, Theorbo and Archlute." *Early Music* 4/4 (1976): 407–423.

_____. "Performance Style of the English Lute Ayre *c.* 1600." *The Lute Society Journal* 24, pt. 2 (1984): 55–68.

SPINACINO, FRANCESCO. *Intabulatura de Lauto. Libro Primo & Libro Secondo,* 1507. Facs. ed. Geneva: Minkoff, 1978.

STANLEY, BARBARA. "Reed Making for Capped Reed Instruments" (pamphlet available from the author, see next entry)

_____, and GRAHAM LYNDON-JONES. *The Curtal* (1983). Available from the authors at 20 Queen Street, St. Albans, Hertfordshire AL3 4PJ, England.

STEINKOPF, OTTO, and VOLKER KERNBACH. *Directions for Playing the Shawm, Dulcian, and Rackett.* Celle: Moeck Ed. no. 2079.

STEVENS, DENIS. *Musicology: A Practical Guide.* New York: Schirmer Books, 1980. (See especially Part Three: "Applied Musicology": 91–216.)

STRONG, WILLIAM S. *The Copyright Book: A Practical Guide.* 3rd ed. Cambridge, MA: MIT Press, 1990.

Studies in the History of Musical Pitch: Monographs by Alexander Ellis and Arthur Mendel (no ed.). Amsterdam: Frits Knuf, 1969.

SUTTON, JULIA. "Triple Pavans: Clues to Some Mysteries in 16th-Century Dance." *Early Music* 14/2 (1986): 175–181.

TARR, EDWARD. "Ein Katalog erhaltener Zinken." *Basler Jahrbuch für historische Musikpraxis* 5 (1981): 11–262.

TARUSKIN, RICHARD. "The Pastness of the Present and the Presence of the Past." See Kenyon: 136–207.

——. "The Musicologist and the Performer." In *Musicology in the 1980s: Methods, Goals, Opportunities.* Eds. D. Kern Holoman and Claude Palisca. New York: Da Capo Press, 1982, 101–117.

——. "On Letting the Music Speak for Itself: Some Reflections on Musicology and Performance." *Journal of Musicology* 1 (1982): 338–349.

——. "The Limits of Authenticity: A Discussion." *Early Music* 12/1 (1984): 3–12.

——. "The Spin Doctors of Early Music." *The New York Times* (Sunday, 29 July 1990), Arts & Leisure: 1, 21.

——. "Tradition and Authority." *Early Music* 20/2 (1992): 311–325.

TEMPERLEY, NICHOLAS. "The Limits of Authenticity: A Discussion." *Early Music* 12/1 (1984): 16–20.

TERZI, GIOVANNI ANTONIO. *Intavolatura di Liutto . . . Libro Primo,* 1593, and *Libro Secondo,* 1599. Facs. ed. Florence: Studio per edizioni scelte, 1981.

THOMAS, BERNARD. "An Introduction to the Crumhorn Repertoire." *Early Music* 1/3 (1973): 142–146.

——. "Playing the Crumhorn: First Steps." *Early Music* 2/3 (1974): 151–156.

——. "The Renaissance Flute." *Early Music* 3/1 (1975): 2–10.

——. "Renaissance Music in Modern Notation." *Early Music* 5/1 (1977): 4–11.

——, and JANE GINGELL. *The Renaissance Dance Book: Dances from the Sixteenth and Early Seventeenth Centuries.* London Pro Musica edition, 1987. Dance reconstructions, music, and cassette tape.

THOMAS, W. R., and J. J. K. RHODES. "Schlick, Praetorius, and the History of Organ Pitch." *Organ Yearbook* 2 (1971): 58–76.

TINCTORIS, JOHANNES. *De inventione et usu musicæ.* Naples, ca. 1487.

——. *Liber de arte contrapuncti.* Naples, ca. 1477. (Art of counterpoint). Trans. Albert Seay in *Musicological Studies and Documents* 5. Rome: American Institute of Musicology, 1961.

——. *Expositio manus.* Naples, after 1477. (The Expositio Manus of Johannes Tinctoris). Trans. Albert Seay in *Journal of Music Theory* 9 (1965): 194–232.

——. *De natura et proprietate tonorum.* Naples, 1476. (Concerning the nature and propriety of tones). Trans. Albert Seay. *Colorado College Music Press Translations* No. 2. Colorado Springs: Colorado College Music Press, 1970.

TOMLINSON, GARY. "The Historian, the Performer, and Authentic Meaning in Music." See Kenyon: 115–136.

TOWNE, GARY. "A Systematic Formulation of Sixteenth-Century Text Underlay Rules." Part I, *Musica Disciplina* 44 (1990): 255–287. Part II, *Musica Disciplina* 45 (1991).

TREITLER, LEO. "Tone system in the secular works of Guillaume Dufay." *Journal of the American Musicological Society* 18 (1965): 131–169.

TROEGER, RICHARD. *Technique and Interpretation on the Harpsichord and Clavichord.* Bloomington and Indianapolis: Indiana University Press, 1987.

TYLER, JAMES. *The Early Guitar: A History and Handbook.* London: Oxford University Press, 1980.

———. "The Mandore in the Sixteenth and Seventeenth Centuries." *Early Music* 9/1 (1981): 22–31.

———. "Checklist of music for the cittern." *Early Music* 2/1 (1974): 25–29.

———, and PAUL SPARKS. *The Early Mandolin.* London: Oxford University Press, 1989.

UBERTI, MAURO. "Vocal techniques in Italy in the 2nd half of the 16th Century." *Early Music* 9/4 (1981): 486–495.

ULRICH, BERNHARD. *Concerning the Principles of Voice Training During the A Capella Period and Until the Beginning of Opera (1474–1640).* Ph.D. diss., Leipzig, 1910; Eng. trans. John W. Seale. Minneapolis: Pro Musica Press, 1973.

VAN DER STRAETEN, EDMUND (1855–1934). *The History of the Violin, its Ancestors and Collateral Instruments from Earliest Times to the Present Day.* London: Cassell and Co. Ltd., 1933.

VIAERA, FREDERICUS. *Nora et Elegantissima in Lythara Lidenda Carmina.* Louvain, 1564.

VINQUIST, MARY, and NEAL ZASLAW, eds. *Performance Practice: A Bibliography.* New York: Norton, 1971. Supplements in Current Musicology, nos. 12 & 15.

VIRDUNG, SEBASTIAN. *Musica getutscht und Ausgezogen,* Basle, 1511. Facs. ed. Kassel: Bärenreiter, 1970. *Musica getutscht: A Treatise on Musical Instruments by Sebastian Virdung.* English trans. & ed. Beth Bullard in Cambridge Musical Texts and Monographs. Cambridge: Cambridge University Press, 1993.

VIRGILIANO, AURELIO. *Il Dolcimelo.* Bologna? ca. 1600. Rep. Florence: Studio per Edizioni Scelte, 1979.

WALKER, D. P., et al. *Musique des intermèdes de "La Pellegrina." Les fêtes du mariage de Ferdinand de Médicis et de Christine de Lorraine.* Florence, 1589. Paris: Editions du Centre National de la recherche scientifique, 1963.

WALLS, PETER. "Common 16th-Century Dance Forms: Some Further Notes." *Early Music* 2/2 (1974): 164–165.

WARD, JOHN. "The Maner of Dauncying." *Early Music* 4/2 (1976): 127–142.

———. "Changing the Instrument for the Music." *Journal of the Lute Society of America* 15 (1982): 27–39.

WEAVER, ROBERT. "Sixteenth-Century Instrumentation." *Musical Quarterly* 47 (1961): 363–378.

WEBER, RAINER. "Recorder Finds from the Middle Ages, and Results of their Reconstruction." *Galpin Society Journal* 29 (May 1976): 35–41.

WEGMAN, ROB C. "What is *Acceleratio mensuræ?*" *Music & Letters* 73 (1992): 515–524.

WEIDLICH, JOSEPH. "*Battuto* Performance Practice in Early Italian Guitar Music (1606–1637)." *Journal of the Lute Society of America* 11 (1978): 63–86.

WELLS, MARCUS. "The Crumhorn, Historical Sources." *Early Music* 1/3 (1973): 139–141.

WILLAERT, ADRIAN. *Intavolatura di li Madrigali di Verdellotto.* Venice, 1536. Facs. ed. Florence: 1980.

WILLIAMS, EDWARD BUCHER. *From Latin to Portuguese: Historical Phonology and Morphology.* Philadelphia: University of Pennsylvania Press, 1938.

WILLIAMS, PETER. *The European Organ 1450–1850.* 2nd ed. London: Batsford, 1968.

———. *Figured Bass Accompaniment.* 2 vols. Edinburgh: University of Edinburgh Press, 1970.

———. *A New History of the Organ.* Bloomington and London: Indiana University Press, 1980.

WILSON, D. R. "Dancing in the Inns of Court." *Historical Dance: Journal of the Dolmetsch Historical Dance Society* 2/5 (1986–87): 3–16.

WOLF, THOMAS. *Presenting Performances: A Handbook for Sponsors.* New York: American Council for the Arts (570 Seventh Avenue, New York, NY 10018), 1983.

WOODFIELD, IAN. *The Early History of the Viol.* Cambridge: Cambridge University Press, 1984. AIGHT, DENZIL. "Vincentius and the Earliest Harpsichords," *Early Music* 14/4 (1986): 534–38.

WRAIGHT, DENZIL. "Vincentius and the Earliest Harpsichords." *Early Music* 14/4 (1986): 534–538.

WRIGHT, CRAIG. "Performance Practice at the Cathedral of Cambrai 1475–1550." *Musical Quarterly* 64/3 (1978): 295–328.

WRIGHT, LAURENCE. "The Medieval Gittern and Citole: A Case of mistaken identity." *Galpin Society Journal* 30 (1977): 8–42.

ZACCONI, LUDOVICO. *Prattica di musica.* Venice, 1592. Rep. Hildesheim: Georg Olms, 1982. Trans. of section entitled "The Manner to be Observed in Making Diminutions and the Use of Modern Passages" in MacClintock–*Readings*: 68–75.

ZANNETTI, GASPARO. *Il Scolaro di Gasparo Zannetti per imparare a suonare di violin et ultra stromenti.* Milan, 1645.

ZANIOL, ANGELO. "The Recorders of the Middle Ages and Renaissance: Dordrecht to van Eyck in three parts." *Continuo* 8/1 (1984): 2–7; 8/2 (1984): 12–15; 8/3 (1985): 6–9.

ZARLINO, GIOSEFFO. *Le istitutioni harmoniche.* Venice, 1588. Rep. New York: Broude Brothers, 1965. Modern facs. of part III, trans. as *The Art of Counterpoint.* Part 4 trans. Vered Cohen, ed. with introduction by Claude V. Palisca. New Haven: Yale University Press, 1983.

———. *Art of counterpoint,* Part 3 of *Le istitutioni harmoniche.* Trans. Guy A. Marco and Claude Palisca. *Music Theory Translations Series* No. 2. New Haven: Yale University Press, 1968.

———. *On the modes,* Part 4 of *Le istitutioni harmoniche.* Trans. Vered Cohen and Claude Palisca. *Music Theory Translations Series* No. 7. New Haven: Yale University Press, 1968.

Index

A

Aaron, Pietro, 242, 246, 316
a cappella, 21, 33, 170, 245
Accademia Filarmonica of Verona, 54, 80, 144
accompaniment
 plucked insts., 144–45, 148–50, 203–13, 224
 organ, 180, 252
Adriaensen, Emanuel, 144–45, 152
Adson, John, 107
Agazzari, Agostino, 145, 203, 205, 207, 209–12, 213
Agricola, Martin, 41, 45, 50, 51, 56–58, 61, 114, 115, 123, 137, 161, 164, 171, 218, 220, 222–23, 243, 246
air de cour, 11, 145
A la Bataglia (Isaac), 230
Alamire, Pierre, 122, 292
Aldrich, Elizabeth, 323–24
alla bastarda, 116, 209
almain, 226, 320
Alma redemptores mater (Ockeghem), 21, 33
alta cappella. See loud ensemble/consort
Althouse, Jay, 273
Alton, Jeannine, 259
Amati, Andrea, 125
American Recorder, The, 236
American Recorder Society, xix, 325
Ammerbach, Elias, 193–95
Ancor che col partire, 9
andante, 22
Andrea, M., 80
angel consort, 156
Anthology of Music, 265
Anthology of Renaissance Music, An, 263
antico, 117
Antiqua Chorbuch, 263
Apel, Willi, 177, 266, 316
Apollo, 113, 204
Applebaum, Samuel, 110, 123, 281
Arban, Jean-Baptiste, 89, 96

Arbeau, Thoinot, 52, 55, 132, 161, 163, 167, 171, 320–21
archcittern, 148
archlute, 149, 151–52
Arnaut de Zwolle, Henri, 182, 240, 242–43, 246
Arnold, Denis, 231
Arnold, F. T., 273
aria, 27, 31
articulation, 9, 18, 41, 50, 65, 74, 88, 89, 105, 110, 111, 128–30, 132, 135, 142, 180, 210, 228, 235, 237, 338
ASCAP, 271
Ashworth, Jack, xix, 175, 203
Atlas, Allan, 24, 237
Attaingnant, Pierre, 56, 61, 144, 168, 181, 204, 206, 221, 321
Azzaiolo, Filippo, 204

B

Bach, Johann Sebastian, 83, 249, 270
bagpipe, 63, 70, 164, 219
Baines, Anthony, 55, 68, 71, 74, 95, 98, 107, 152
Bakfark, Valentin, 140
balance, 27, 28, 30, 180, 219, 221–22, 224–26, 231, 338
ballad, 11
ballet de cour, 212
balletto, 321–22
ballo, 321–22
Banchieri, Adriano, 190, 195, 220, 254
bandora, 122, 145–49, 152, 208, 213, 226, 228, 243
Bank, J. A., 237, 316
Banquet of the Vow, 44
Barbour, James, 246
Barclay, Robert, 107
Bardi, Count Giovanni de', 242
Bartlett, Clifford, 68, 231
bassanello, 218, 248
Bassano, Giovanni, 7, 9, 52, 80–82, 89, 96, 137
basse danse, 69, 219, 322

Hughes, Andrew, 25
Hunt, Edgar, 68
hurdy-gurdy, 219
Hutchison, Frank, xix

I

iconography, 43, 45, 70, 87, 103,
    113–14, 132, 140, 144, 146, 150,
    154–55, 158, 161, 163, 184, 208,
    217, 219–20, 222, 225, 230, 253,
    292
Ife, Barry, 199
Il Dolcimelo (Virgiliano, 1600), 58, 98
Il Transilvano (Diruta, 1593), 194
Il Vero modo di diminuir (Dalla Casa,
    1584), 7
imperfect intervals, 20
improvising/improvisation, 7, 69, 72,
    113, 117, 128, 130, 132, 204, 208–
    09, 219, 226, 230, 235, 289, 303,
    322
In feuers hitze, 9
Inglehearn, Madeleine, 322, 325–26
In Nomine, 117, 143
Instrumental Music Printed before 1600,
    265
intabulation, 52, 117, 140, 143–45,
    152, 158, 203–05, 209, 220, 303
integer valor, 34
intermedi(o), 81, 95, 100, 107, 113,
    118, 150, 152, 206–07, 212, 217
International Society for Early Music
    Singers, xix
interpretation, 18, 21, 23
intonation, 3–4, 10, 15, 17, 23–24, 27,
    30, 35, 41, 43–44, 48–49, 54–55,
    59, 60, 65, 67, 127, 210, 338
Invitation to the Madrigal, 263
Isaac, Heinrich, 21, 34, 37, 230, 253,
    265, 295
Istitutione harmoniche (Zarlino, 1558),
    23
*Italian Instrumental Music of the 16th
    and 17th Centuries,* 265

J

Jackson, John-Paul Christopher, 235–
    37, 259, 263, 337
Jambe de Fer, Philibert, 41, 45, 47,
    54, 57–59, 61, 126, 137, 218, 220
jazz, 131
Jeffery, Brian, 259

jew's harp, 219
Johnson, John, 140
Jones, Lewis, 231
Jorgensen, Owen, 188, 246
Josquin des Prez, 15, 21, 23, 33, 37,
    265, 270, 286, 295–96, 310–11
Journal of the Lute Society of America, 236
*Journal of the Viola da Gamba Society of
    America,* 236
Just Intonation, 23, 30, 34–35, 85,
    245–46

K

Kammerton, 249–51, 253, 255
Kapsberger, Johannes, 150
Kärstadt, Georg, 95
Kaye, Martin, 95
Kees Boeke Consort, 232
Keller, Kate van Winkle, 324
Kelly, Frances, 159
Kenyon, Nicholas, xix
Kerman, Joseph, xix
Kernbach, Volker, 78
kettledrum, 161–62, 165–66, 229
keyboard fingering, 175–76, 181, 187,
    189–99, 270
Keyl, Stephen, 11, 231
key signature, 24, 294, 311, 314
Kimbal, Joan, 232
King's Noyse, The, 137
King's Singers, The, 284
Kinkeldey, Otto, 322
Kirk, Douglas, 79, 95
Kirnberger, Philip, 175
kit, 114, 121
Kite-Powell, Jeffery, 63, 76, 122, 228,
    329, 338, 344
Kleber, Leonhard, 181
Klop, G. C., 188
Knighton, Tess, xix, 4, 11, 25, 123,
    153, 181, 231, 235, 246, 259, 286,
    316
Koopman, Ton, 199, 246
kortholt, 66–67, 77, 229
Kotter, Hans, 181
Kottick, Edward, xix, 175, 187, 337
Kreitner, Kenneth, 70

L

Lambrechts-Douillez, Jeannine, 54
lament, 16
Lanfranco, Giovanni Maria, 220